I0120813

Loss and Discovery

A Lost Friend, A Lost Manuscript, and A Lost Culture

Loss and Discovery

A Lost Friend,
A Lost Manuscript,
and A Lost Culture

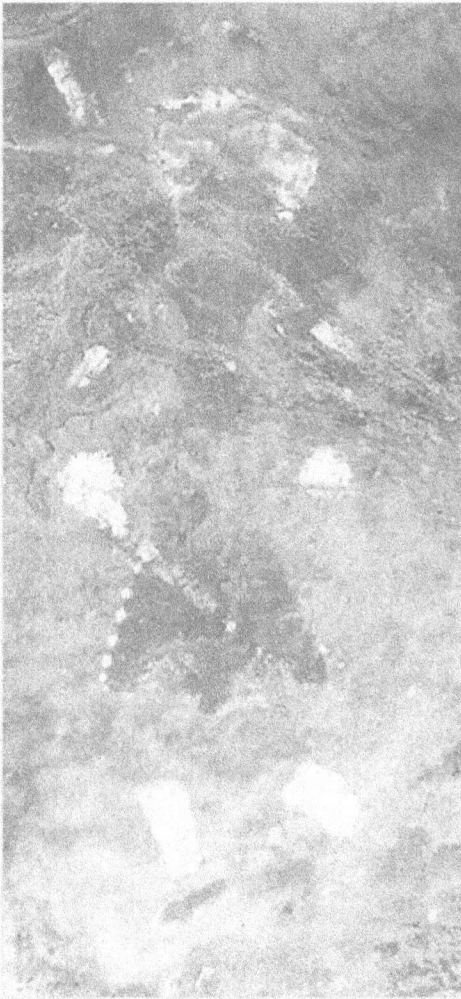

Stuart J. Baldwin, PhD
and the Piro-Tompiro Pueblo
Culture of Abo Pass Salinas
Region of Central New Mexico

Volume I
Ethnohistory
by
Stuart J. Baldwin, PhD

Compiled and Edited
by
Paul R. Secord

SUNSTONE
PRESS
SANTA FE

© 2018 by Paul R. Secord
All Rights Reserved
No part of this book may be reproduced in any form or by any electronic
or mechanical means including information storage and retrieval systems
without permission in writing from the publisher,
except by a reviewer who may quote brief passages in a review.

Sunstone books may be purchased for educational, business, or sales promotional use.
For information please write: Special Markets Department, Sunstone Press,
P.O. Box 2321, Santa Fe, New Mexico 87504-2321.

Star Kachina: carving recreation by Greg Lasiloo, 2017
Pictograph photograph near Tenabo by Paul R. Secord, 1982
Book and cover design › Vicki Ahl
Body typeface › Minion Pro
Printed on acid-free paper
∞

Library of Congress Cataloging-in-Publication Data

Names: Baldwin, Stuart J., author. | Secord, Paul R., compiler, editor.
Title: Loss and discovery : a lost friend, a lost manuscript, and a lost
    culture : Stuart J. Baldwin, PhD and the Piro-Tompiro Pueblo Culture of
    Abo Pass Salinas Region of Central New Mexico / Stuart J. Baldwin, Paul R.
    Secord.
Other titles: Lost friend, a lost manuscript, and a lost culture |
    Piro-Tompiro Pueblo Culture of Abo Pass Salinas Region of Central New
    Mexico
Description: Santa Fe, New Mexico : Sunstone Press, [2018]- | "The story of
    the discovery of an unpublished 1988 manuscript by Stuart J. Baldwin, PhD,
    and is a comprehensive overview of the archaeological remains of the
    Tompiro Pueblo Indian Culture of Central New Mexico, plus the complete
    site reports of Dr. Baldwin's excavations at Tenabo and Abo
    Pueblos."--Provided by publisher. | Includes bibliographical references.
    Contents: volume 1. Ethnohistory ~ volume 2. Archaeology.
Identifiers: LCCN 2018041557 | ISBN 9781632932419 (v. 1 : pbk. : alk. paper)
    | ISBN 9781632932426 (v. 2 : pbk. : alk. paper)
Subjects: LCSH: Piro Pueblo Indians--Antiquities. | Piro Pueblo
    Indians--History. | Excavations (Archaeology)--New Mexico--Salinas Pueblo
    Missions National Monument. | Salinas Pueblo Missions National Monument
    (N.M.)--Antiquities.
Classification: LCC E99.P63 B35 2018 | DDC 978.9/6301--dc23
LC record available at https://lccn.loc.gov/2018041557

WWW.SUNSTONEPRESS.COM
SUNSTONE PRESS / POST OFFICE BOX 2321 / SANTA FE, NM 87504-2321 /USA
(505) 988-4418 / ORDERS ONLY (800) 243-5644 / FAX (505) 988-1025

Dedication

To the Piro-speaking peoples
of central New Mexico.

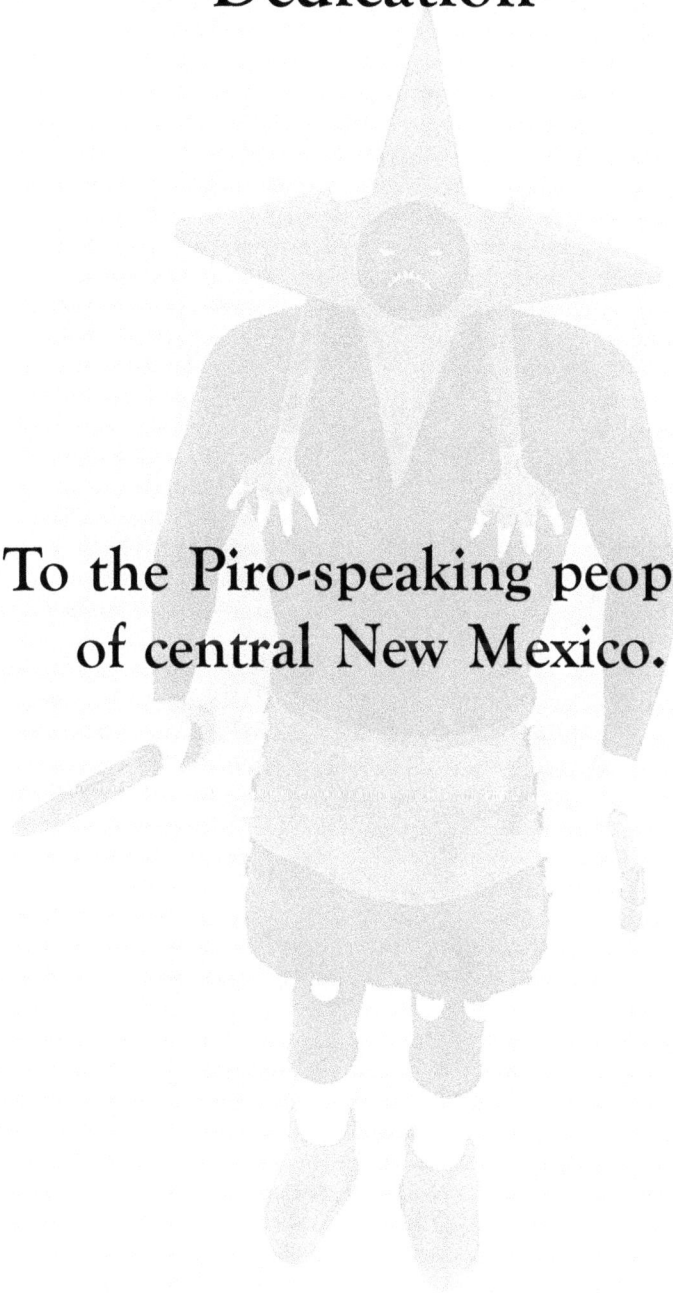

Contents

List of Figures

List of Tables

Foreword

The Lost People of Central New Mexico, Stuart James Baldwin, PhD (1946–1999) and the Tompiro

This work, in two volumes, comprises the complete unpublished (for the most part; some chapters were originally published in local/regional archaeological journals) manuscript on the Tompiro prepared solely by Stuart J. Baldwin, PhD and finished in 1989. It is the culmination of over ten years of his study of Native American culture in the Abo Pass area of central New Mexico.

The original manuscript of 1,361 pages and 16 chapters with references and appendices was formatted as a doctoral dissertation, i.e. single sided, double spaced, printed as 8.5" x 11" pages on a dot matrix printer, and inserted into a three ring binder. Only one incomplete copy of the original manuscript appears to have survived.

The compiler of these two volumes was able to reconstruct missing pages and the entire text was retyped and formatted. The manuscript's original organization has been retained. However, figures, tables, references and appendices were digitized and incorporated into the text as they had been in the original.

The manuscript is composed of three sections: the first is an introduction and background discussion, the second is a comprehensive overview of the ethnographic and historic record of Abo Pass, and last a broad survey of regional archaeology and site reports for excavations carried out by Baldwin in the 1980s at Tenabo and Abo Pueblo ruins. Due to size limitations and the distinct differentiation of topics covered, the manuscript has been split into two parts, Volume I is the first two sections addressing "ethnohistory" and includes all of the original references, while Volume II covers archaeology and includes all the appendices.

Each volume includes the same introduction with an overview of Baldwin's life and describes the discovery of the original manuscript and the process leading to the realization of these publications.

Acknowledgements to the Original Manuscript
by Stuart J. Baldwin

Any effort on the scale of the Piro-Tompiro Ethnohistory and Archaeology Project can be brought to fruition only through the encouragement, help and cooperation of numerous individuals and institutions. To begin, I wish to acknowledge the main sources of inspiration that led to my work on the Piros and Tompiros and which guided my research approach over the years taken up by this project.

Firstly, I acknowledge Dr Florence Hawley Ellis, in whose classes at the University of New Mexico I first learned of the Piros and Tompiros and the great need there was for archaeological work on these people. Also Dr Donald Cutter, whose classes on New Mexican and Southwestern history helped inspire my continuing commitment to the integration of historical, ethnographic and archaeological data on the Pueblo Indians.

The conjunctive approach to archaeology proposed by Dr Walter W. Taylor and practiced so brilliantly by Dr Charles Di Peso and his colleagues of the Amerind Foundation served as a guiding light in my own fieldwork. Further, the previous establishment of local research institutions by Harold S. Gladwin and Harold Colton served as inspirational models for myself and my associates when we established the short-lived Central New Mexico Research Association (CNMRA) in 1982.

Basic to the success of the excavations at Tenabo was the support by the landowners, R. L. and Norabelle Chilton, who gave permission for the work at Tenabo and for the travel about the Chilton Ranch for purposes of archaeological survey. They also helped materially during the 1981 and 1982 field seasons in permitting usage of ranch buildings. Their son Lynn Chilton and his wife Carol also assisted us in many ways, great and small.

Financial support for the Tenabo excavations was provided by the University of Calgary, the Wenner-Grey Foundation, the Sigma Xi Society, and CNMRA. The Laboratory of Tree-ring Research Contributed the analysis of the tree-ring samples from Tenabo. The Socorro office of the U.S. Bureau of Land Management contributed use of an alidade for site mapping purposes.

The U.S. National Park Service, through Salinas National Monument and the Southeastern Region Office greatly assisted the project by permitting and partially funding the excavations at Abo. Superintendent Thomas Carroll and Archeologist Jim Trott at the monument and Dave Brugge at Southwestern Region are specially thanked for their support. Salinas National Monument also supported the project through provision of quarters and workspace in 1982–1983 at Abo. Tom Carroll was always very helpful and enthusiastic about the project. Many of the monument's employees assisted us in a great many ways over the years, including Glen Fulfer and Sammy Chavez.

Archaeological survey work in the Chupadera Basin was done under the auspices of the Socorro office of the U.S. Bureau of Land Management (BLM) which provided a vehicle, fuel, film, and permission to survey on lands in Socorro County administered by the BLM. Bill Knight, Mark Henderson, Joel Farrell, and other BLM personnel expedited this and other aspects of our research. CNMRA personnel were directly engaged in this survey work.

All persons who made contributions to the CNMRA thereby directly helped to fund excavation and survey work. Paul R. Secord and Marcia Secord of Pasadena, California, contributed both financial aid and personal labor to excavations at Abo and Tenabo and to survey work. Kenneth M. Hewett and K. P. Medlin, of CNMRA, put in innumerable hours in all capacities, as well as contributing to transportation, feeding, and the general well-being of other crew members.

Students from the University of Calgary who contributed to excavation and survey include Vern Albush, Colleen Barry, Deborah Ferguson, Karen McInnis, Susan Marshall, Maureen Reeves, Allen Stevenson, and Donna Unruh. John

Preface to the Original Manuscript by Stuart J. Baldwin

The studies presented in this work represent a personal commitment to elucidating the history and prehistory of the Piro speaking peoples of central New Mexico. This is a broad subject, hence not easily reduced to a single scholastic "theme" or line of study. Certainly, the academic committee that rejected this work as a suitable doctoral dissertation could not discern any such linking thread.

However, I believe that any attempt to pull together and present available information on an aboriginal New World people whose cultural identity has been extinguished by the European invaders has its own logical coherence, even if it is "only" the morality of saving a people from historical obscurity.

Wilson of the University of New Mexico spent two month excavating at Abo. Other individuals who contributed varying amounts of time to the excavations include Kathy and Tim Carlson, Jan Chen, Alison Freese, Dudley and Mari King, John Murphy, Jane Plosz, Jay Schaffer, Glenn Stuart, Lorna Way, and Chuck Wiggins.

Many members of the archaeological community in New Mexico gave encouragement and/or assistance to the project, including Pat Beckett, Bertha Dutton, Hayward Franklin, Marsha Jackson, Mike Marshall, Stewart Peckhan, Curt and Polly Schaafsma, Joseph Tainter, Rosemary Talley, and Regge Wiseman. Others who have assisted in various ways include Wesley Hurt, Ted Frisbie, Marc Simmons, and John Kessell.

Finally, I wish to thank the faculty members of the departments of Archaeology and History at the University of Calgary who read and commented upon portions of this work: Jane Kelley, Scott Raymond, Christon Archer, and Richard Forbis.

Loss and Discovery

A Lost Friend, a Lost Manuscript and a Lost Culture

These two volumes are the culmination of over 25 years of wondering and conjecture. Why didn't archaeologist Stuart Baldwin write a site report on his excavations at Tenabo Pueblo in Central New Mexico? Why didn't he return to the Southwest after 1987? Why did he produce a doctoral dissertation that, frankly, wasn't up to his intellectual standards? As Stuart's good friend, perhaps his best friend during the 1970s and 80s, was there more that I could have done for him? And in the end, why did his early passion for the Tompiro and the archaeology of the Abo Pass region seem to end once he received his doctorate?

My initial plan, even before Stuart's untimely death in 1999, was to ensure, at the least, a proper site report prepared for the years of work he had put into site survey in Abo Pass and excavations at Abo and Tenabo Pueblos. Baldwin's death rekindled my interest in the New Mexico work of the 1980s. However, my ability to revisit that place and time was hindered by my physical distance from New Mexico and, more significantly, by my intellectual distance from Southwestern archaeology. Years passed, but thoughts of Stuart and what happened continued to bubble to the surface. Then, in 2010, I retired and moved to Albuquerque. In that year, I made a trip to Mountainair and talked to Park Service personnel at the Salinas Pueblo Missions National Monument. Those talks led nowhere; I had more of Stuart's papers in my possession than they did. I tried to find Pat Medlin and Ken Hewitt, the two locals who had worked with Stuart at the time. No one seemed to know what had happened to Pat Medlin. (It was only this year, 2016, that I learned of his death.) Ken Hewitt was in very poor physical health and died within months of my visit with him in Mountainair, New Mexico.

Thoughts of the Tompiro people and Tenabo Pueblo languished until January, 2016, when I heard Michael Bletzer, PhD, speak to the Albuquerque Archaeological Society about his work on Piro sites in the Rio Grande Valley.

I immediately contacted him, and he responded; "I always wondered what happened to that guy. He is about the only one who has done any meaningful work in the Tompiro culture area." He in turn introduced me to Hayward Franklin, PhD, an expert in prehistoric Pueblo ceramics, who had been a Park Ranger with Stuart at Mesa Verde National Park in 1967. And both of these individuals were neighbors!

At about the same time, I discovered the location of all the materials excavated by Baldwin's University of Calgary field school during the early 1980s. I knew that material from the Abo excavations had been retained by the Park Service and was at their storage facility in Tucson. However, what had happened to the material from Tenabo was a mystery. Fortunately, it turned out that they had recently been beautifully curated, at the Museum of New Mexico, Laboratory of Anthropology's (LOA) new state of the art storage facility and laboratory in Santa Fe, New Mexico. I had heard several years before that Glen Fulfer, past Superintendent of the Salinas National Monument, had rescued the excavation material, related to Tenabo, from a room at the Shaffer Hotel in Mountainair after the National Park Service moved its headquarters from the Shaffer Hotel to a new building after the sale of the hotel. He told me that he had scooped it all up, put it in the back of his pickup, and had taken the boxes to Santa Fe, just before they were destined for the dump. But what had happened after that, I had not been able to determine.

The time was right to begin a reevaluation of the 1980s excavations. I gathered together all of the Stuart Baldwin papers in my possession, which comprised a comprehensive overview of the ethnohistory of the region, but lacked specific analysis of site excavation and survey data. Nonetheless, they were a place to begin. It was then that I discovered that there may have been a site report that was never published; a "lost" manuscript.

Before getting into a discussion of the manuscript, this is a good place to take a look at Stuart Baldwin's all to short life. He was an excellent archaeologist, and is remembered by former colleague Scott Hamilton as "...a good man. A gentle soul, whose career did not achieve his potential. Having his work live on would be a wonderful legacy."

I first met Stuart in the fall of 1968 when we were both undergraduates in Anthropology at the University of New Mexico, Albuquerque. We had been introduced by a mutual friend and, although he was several years old than I was, he immediately showed an interest in my love of Southwestern archaeology and history. He took me under his wing and by the time I began taking senior level courses on the Southwest, I already had a strong understanding of the material.

Stuart James Baldwin was born in Amarillo, Texas, on April 2, 1946 to Helen Louise Montgomery and James Baldwin. He had no bothers or sisters, and his father abandoned the family when Stuart was an infant. No subsequent record of James Baldwin could be found. His mother had a varied career, operating her own bookstore in Amarillo, Texas, serving as the society editor of the Carlsbad, New Mexico, *Current-Argus* newspaper, and teaching English at Peñasco Junior High School near Taos, New Mexico. In the early 1960s, Stuart and his mother moved to Alaska, where he remembered getting a haircut on the main street in Anchorage when the 1964 earthquake hit. Following the earthquake, they moved to Canada. When it was time for college, Stuart was anxious to return to the Southwest and he enrolled in anthropology at the University of New Mexico, a fascination with Native American culture having been a long-time passion.

Stuart excelled in college and worked in the late 1960s as a seasonal Park Ranger at Mesa Verde National Park. His friend Hayward Frankin remembers him from this time as a shy but always cheerful man who always asked impertinent questions about archaeology.

In 1970, Stuart was drafted to serve in the Vietnam War. He initially seemed, if not enthusiastic about the prospect of serving, at least resigned to making the best of it. That resignation lasted until completion of basic training at Fort Leonard Wood, Missouri by which time his opposition to the war, and an anti-military perspective in general, led him to go AWOL to Canada.

In the early 1970s, Baldwin enrolled in the Masters in Anthropology program at the University of Alberta, Edmonton, Canada. He received his M.A. in anthropology from the University of Alberta in 1980 with a thesis titled "*Chiapas and Guatemala: Contrasting Systems of Contemporary Indian Trade.*" The necessary fieldwork in Mexico and Central America put his New Mexico projects on hold.

Fortunately, on September 16, 1974, President Gerald R. Ford issued amnesty to those who had evaded the draft, as well as those who had deserted their duty while serving during the Vietnam War. His return to the southwestern US was no longer a problem.

The 1980s were the most productive period of his life. He moved to Calgary and began work on his doctorate. Clearly the topic area could only be the Southwest. His specific focus was chosen in 1980. In the summer of 1980, I flew in from Los Angeles and met Stuart at the bus station in Albuquerque in a 1967 Chevy Impala convertible from Rent-A-Wreck. It was the perfect rough terrain touring vehicle and over a period of two weeks we visited as many Piro and Tompiro sites as we could find. The details of what was to follow for the next ten years is covered in the 1988 manuscript reproduced here.

After such an auspicious start, his work and his life began to fall apart. In 1988 he submitted to the University of Calgary his dissertation: "*Studies in Piro-Tompiro Ethnohistory and Western Tompiro Archaeology*" a 1,361 page magnum opus on all that was known of the Tompiro in Abo Pass. His committee rejected it. Knowing him as I did, I can only conjecture that at some level, he must have felt failure and shame, this was to be a life's work. Fortunately, by October 1988, using data derived almost entirely from the May 1988 manuscript, Baldwin completed a more narrowly defined dissertation titled "*Tompiro Culture, Subsistence and Trade,*" and received his PhD degree from the University of Calgary in the Spring of 1989.)

Efforts to obtain contracts with the Park Service for further work in the Salinas were continually rejected. In addition, the "Central New Mexico Research Association, Inc.", that Stuart, Pat Medlin, Ken Hewett and I founded as a research nonprofit organization incorporated in 1982, ceased to be a functioning entity after 1987, for reasons that were never clear to me. The dissertation debacle must have taken a heavy toll on him, and the unexpected death of his local compatriot Pat Medlin in 1992 seems to finish off any more intense activity in the Salinas. To the best of my knowledge, Stuart never returned to the Southwest, although he did occasionally write on Southwestern topics, most notably a paper titled: *Apacheans Bearing Gifts: Prehistoric Influences on the Pueblo Indians*" which was published in the Arizona Archaeologist No. 29, Arizona Archaeological Society, February 1997.

My contact with Stuart diminished after he received his PhD in 1989. I had no idea that the 1988 manuscript was in fact a rejected dissertation. While we exchanged Christmas cards and the occasional letter, there was little discussion of New Mexico, for by then he was a professor of Anthropology at Lakehead University in Thunder Bay, Ontario, Canada on the north shore of Lake Superior and I was pursuing a career in Los Angeles.

And then, in 1999 I received word from the Anthropology Department at Lakehead University that Stuart had died unexpectedly. I was asked by them to appraise his small collection of Zuni Kachinas, textiles and a few other Native American items and was sent my correspondence to him from his files.

Faculty at Lakehead University recently informed me that his body had been found in his apartment by colleagues who paid for his burial and disposed of his property; some books and papers were sold, some were retained by the University, and materials pertaining to the Southwest were sent to "suitable institutions in the Southwest" (presumably the Salinas National Monument in Mountainair, New Mexico and the LOA in Santa Fe.) The proceeds of the sale of Baldwin's estate were used to establish a scholarship fund described on the University's 2016 website as follows: "*Stuart Baldwin Memorial Bursary* $100 (SBMBI). Created by friends and colleagues of Dr S. Baldwin, Professor of Anthropology, who passed away in 1999. Awarded to an in-course student majoring in Anthropology, on the basis of financial need and satisfactory academic standing."

When I began this project in February, 2016, I made every effort to assemble all the Baldwin materials in my personal files, including copies of what I thought were all of Baldwin's manuscripts and published reports concerning his studies of the Salinas Province, along with both sides of our correspondence. I only gave the letters a quick perusal. Later, I realized I should have paid more attention to them as they provided valuable insights concerning the 1988 manuscript and spurred my memory of some vaguely remembered computer disks. But more on that later.

Why the original manuscript was rejected by his committee in favor of a much abbreviated dissertation, is open to conjecture, although it does include the theme of an unproven Tompiro tri-part trading network. In discussing this issue with the few persons still alive who remember Baldwin, it appears that there may have been a conflict within his committee. The original Baldwin manuscript is modeled after the dissertation of his committee chair, Jane Kelley, PhD. in that it is a comprehensive overview, supplemented by archaeological excavation, of a specific culture area. Even in the late 1980s this was considered an "old school" approach, with modern dissertations being more narrowly designed to elucidate a specific intellectual theme.

While the approved dissertation is easily obtainable, the longer manuscript from which it was derived has been essentially hidden until now. Knowledge that such a document existed came to my attention in February 2016 during a careful reading of the dissertation that was ultimately accepted. In the dissertation, Baldwin constantly makes references to chapters of a 1988 "...report on file at Salinas National Monument, Mountainair, New Mexico."

Finding the 1988 report proved difficult. No copy of the document was found at the University of Calgary, Alberta, Canada where it was written, nor was it found in Baldwin's remaining papers at Lakehead University, Ontario, Canada where he was a professor of Anthropology from the mid-1990s until his death.

The document also could not be located in the archives of the Salinas Pueblo Missions National Monument (SPMNM) or at the National Park Service warehouse in Tucson, Arizona where much SPMNM archival material was stored following water damage and subsequent asbestos removal, from the Park's Mountainair headquarters in the 1990s.

At the same time that I was searching for the elusive 1988 report, I was also compiling a comprehensive bibliography of everything published concerning the Abo region. This included reviewing the bibliographic sources of a number of books, reports and documents cross referenced with their location in regional libraries. Helen Denise Smith's 1998 art history dissertation "*The Rock Art of Abo Pueblo: Analyzing a Cultural Palimpsest*", University of New Mexico, 1998, contained a reference to "*Studies in Piro-Tompiro Ethnohistory and Western Tompiro Archaeology*. Santa Fe: Museum of New Mexico, Laboratory of Anthropology (LOA), Manuscript on file, 1990. This seemed likely to refer to the May 1988 report.

A trip to the LOA Library verified this speculation. In the Library's collection was a massive unpublished manuscript dated May 1988 which contained finished versions of all of the reports and papers Baldwin had written on the Tompiros during the 1980s, along with comprehensive archaeological reports of site surveys and excavations at both Abo and Tenabo Pueblos. To help control access and address concerns over the protection of archaeological site location data, the original three hole punched looseleaf dot matrix printout was bound by the LOA into three volumes. Unfortunately, there were no acquisition records associated with the manuscript, although subsequent discussions with persons at the LOA indicate that it was most likely sent there, along with copies of Baldwin papers, by his colleagues at Lakehead University in about 2001. The LOA manuscript was almost certainly Baldwin's personal copy as it contains several spelling corrections in his handwriting.

Now that all of Baldwin's work on the Tompiros had at last been documented, attention focused on how to make this important record more readily available. Several problems were immediately encountered. The LOA Library is tasked both with the dissemination of information for scholarly and public purposes, along with the preservation not only of material in its collection, and also with guarding sensitive information pertaining to archaeological/historical site locations where dissemination of location information could lead to looting of those sites. The LOA Library instituted stringent rules on access to its collection in recent years to address problems of stolen library materials and compromised site location information. In addition, concerns over intellectual property rights, i.e. copyright restrictions, have also put the library on notice to exercise extreme caution with materials in its collection.

While more than justified, limitations on access that the LOA Library applied to the Baldwin 1988 manuscript since it had initially been acquired greatly minimized its distribution to a wider audience. The culmination of ten years of scholarship, in fact the life's work of a gifted archaeologist who had actually recorded his field work, seemed destined to remain hidden in plain sight, relegated to a single copy in a limited access library. The Baldwin manuscript contains nothing of aesthetic merit, i.e. there are no photographs, the drawings are of descriptive nature only, actual site location data is extremely limited and easily redacted, it is an unpublished manuscript, and copyright restrictions are cloudy at best.

How could Baldwin's important work come to the attention of a wider audience? Certainly there was no problem with using the work in the library. Those of us working on this project have the requisite credentials to access sensitive site information and have a demonstrated respect for the LOA Library collection. We could use this document like any other library holding, as a research aid to be used strictly within the Library building. Disseminating the information to a wider audience seemed to require rewriting and publishing under our own name(s) all of the material contained in nearly 1,400 pages, a herculean task.

I had no desire to rewrite a finished work so the next logical step seemed to be a clarification of copyright issues. The manuscript was composed over a period of about two years while Baldwin was a doctoral student at the University of Calgary, Alberta. Comments in the manuscript, and correspondence I had with Baldwin at the time, make it clear that the University of Calgary provided no monetary support for the document, and as the finished product was rejected as a suitable doctoral dissertation, it was never submitted, nor catalogued, in the University of Calgary library system. In addition, it was never published. However, there is a © symbol on the manuscript's title page.

The question became who holds the copyright and what does that actually mean? The LOA Library indicated that the copyright was held by Baldwin's estate and that Canadian copyright restrictions would only allow for copying no more then 10% of the total document and that strictly for research purposes.

Perhaps if the LOA held the copyright, it would allow the manuscript to be published. Thus began an investigation of the convoluted world of copyright law. In Canada, the controlling body for copyright ownership questions is the Copyright Board of Canada (CBoC), a federal governmental agency located in Ottawa that addresses copyright concerns and issues copyright licenses on a case by case basis. Fortunately, the CBoC has clear guidelines for the information they require to make a determination. Following their guidelines, a letter was sent to the Secretary General of the CBoC on April 15, 2016, documenting that Stuart Baldwin was a Canadian citizen, that he had no heirs, that the died in Canada in 1999, that if the copyright were to be reassigned it should most appropriately beheld by the LOA Library in Santa Fe, New Mexico, and that there were no past royalties involved in such a transfer.

Ten days after receiving our letter, the CBoC responded that they were not a in position to make a finding in this matter as: (1) the manuscript was never published, (2) a license would only apply in Canada (although the US and Canada have reciprocity agreements pertaining to copyrights), and (3) as there was no money involved, there were no issues to adjudicate. They suggested that contact be made with the Ontario Public Guardian and Trustee's Office (OPGTO) to see who might have been responsible for administering Baldwin's estate following his death.

On April 25, 2016 the OPGTO was contacted and it verified that there was no estate for a Stuart James Baldwin probated in Ontario Canada, as his entire estate was more than likely valued at less then $10,000 and would therefore have been handled locally. A subsequent call to the Thunder Bay, Ontario, Archives and Records office found no record of Baldwin's death beyond a death certificate.

With the copyright in limbo, and a single copy tightly controlled by the LOA, which was showing no independent interest in its publication, the Baldwin project had hit a serious roadblock. Where to go next? Perhaps there were some clues in the Baldwin correspondence files. Sure enough, there were.

In a letter dated November 11, 1989 I thanked Stuart for the arrival of an unbound printout copy of his dissertation and asked him to send me a disk(s) of the dissertation and the 1988 "*Studies on Piro-Tompiro Ethnohistory...*". I also told him that I would reimburse him for any costs, that format didn't matter as I could figure out a conversion, and that the hope was to eventually see this material put into a format for eventual publication. Here the subject ended as there was nothing else in the correspondence pertaining to the 1988 report.

This sent me to my garage, and an exploration of several boxes of files that had remained unopened since my move to New Mexico in 2010. There in a box marked "old computer backup" were half a dozen 5.25" floppy disks, labeled in Baldwin's hand, "1988 Tompiro." Unfortunately, these now archaic computer disks had been damaged in transit, as well as suffering water damage from sloppy storage. Efforts to recover the data on them proved potentially costly and, more than likely, futile. But at least Baldwin had independently sent me the dissertation and manuscript with the tacit understanding of some future publication.

And then on May 3, 2016 I gave a presentation about the Baldwin project to the Torrance County, Archaeological Society in Estancia, New Mexico. To my surprise and delight over forty-five persons attended, including several professional archaeologists who had always wondered what had happened to Baldwin, and a number of persons who had never heard of him or his work. After the presentation a former employee of the LOA came up to me and said, "I have a copy of that 1988 report, in fact there are two other copies of it, one in my personal library and one at the New Mexico State Office of Archaeological Studies." I was stunned. Perhaps this would all come together after all.

A week later, I found myself driving back to Albuquerque from Santa Fe with a complete copy of the 1988 Baldwin manuscript in a looseleaf binder. I immediately sent out notices of my find to key persons involved in the project, including the LOA Library. The responses were mostly positive with the exception of the response from the Library: "As xx's copy came from the LOA Library, it does not afford you the right to reproduce or distribute in hard copy or otherwise Paul! The LOA Library owns the Baldwin

'bible' as you call it, which affords it rights under the law. Please consult the Photo reproduction Policy I provided you. Xx may have a copy, that doesn't give him rights to reproduction or distribution either."

This was a most disheartening turn of events. My first reaction was to see if I could reconstruct the document from the various draft papers and reports in my position, which indeed proved to be the case for Sections I and II, but not Section III, the archaeological writeup. I then went back to the ancient disks and found that I would be able to resurrect most of Section III for an acceptable cost.

However, I was still concerned with any legal consequences of proceeding with a wider presentation of the Baldwin material. To this end, I consulted with Jeffrey D. Myers, Registered Patent Attorney, Peacock Myers, P.C., Intellectual Property Law Services in Albuquerque, which fortunately also has an office in Ottawa, Canada. Mr. Myers confirmed that the copyright was clouded and that there seemed little else I could do. He stated clearly that, as there was no money involved, nor was there any potential for any meaningful revenue, even if the work were to be published, neither the Canadian government, nor the LOA, seemed interested in pursuing the matter. Certainly, the LOA Library had no copyright authority over the document in question. I would be reconstructing the document from material that had been sent to me in the 1980s by the author with the understanding that it would be prepared by me for eventual publication. In addition, using parts of another copy of the 1988 manuscript, regardless of its origin, should not be an issue as that subsequent copy, even if it in fact proved to be a copy of the copy now in the possession of the LOA, was made at a time long before the current photo reproduction policies were put in place and had always been retained in private hands, i.e. not in the ownership or possession of the LOA.

Now, at long last, the legacy of Stuart J. Baldwin, PhD will be recognized as an important contribution to the history and prehistory of New Mexico. Not only had the site of Tenabo been documented and analyzed, but also there was a comprehensive overview of everything that Stuart could find on the Tompiro, from rock art to language to social structure. The manuscript presented here will finally become available to a wide audience of scholars and non-scholars alike. and help bring back to life a nearly forgotten people. Surely, this is what Stuart would have wished, even if it did take almost 30 years.

An effort has been make to present the document in a form that is as complete and as true to Dr Baldwin's vision as possible, while at the same time producing books that are up to current standards of printing and production. Pages that are missing in the LOA copy have been reconstructed from prior reports, so that the material presented here is 100% complete. However, information that could lead to the location of specific archaeological sites has been redacted, although this proved to be much less of an issue then initially anticipated, and is limited to the removal of topographic lines and locational references from several maps. The complete maps maybe viewed by any qualified scholar in the LOA copy in Santa Fe, New Mexico.

What was lost has now been found: a lost friend, a lost record of a life's work, and most importantly a comprehensive overview of a lost culture. Now the real work can begin.

—Paul R. Secord
Albuquerque, New Mexico

Section I

Background

1

Introduction

The genesis of the project reported herein is to be found in my undergraduate days at the University of New Mexico, when I can remember Florence Ellis, PhD, regretfully informing her Southwestern Archaeology class that she could not tell us much about the Piros because the necessary research had not been carried out. Occasionally, in the following years my thoughts would return to this gap in our knowledge of the Pueblo Indians, accompanied by the wish that I could do something about it. Finally, when considering the possibilities for a doctoral field project, the time seemed ripe to attempt to realize that wish.

From the beginning this project has had two goals: (1) to provide an ethnohistorical study of the Piro speaking peoples during the 16th and 17 centuries, and (2) to collect archaeological data, particularly on the Pueblo IV period, to help fill in the gap in our knowledge mentioned above. The first goal is realized within the second section of this study, while the second goal is addressed in the third section. The present (first) section provides explanatory and background information, while the fourth section provides discussion of various points and summarizes the conclusions reached by this project.

The history of the project (the Piro Tompiro Ethnohistory and Archaeology Project) began with my acceptance into the doctoral program at the Department of Archaeology, University of Calgary, in the spring of 1930. I began the ethnohistorical research that spring, and it has been ongoing ever since, concurrently with the archaeological aspect of the project. Minor results of this research have been published in Baldwin (1984c, 1986).

The archaeological aspect of the project began with a trip to New Mexico in July 1980 to visit and select a site or sites for excavation. This trip resulted in the choice of Tenabo (LA 200) as the focus of my field investigations. A first season of excavation at Tenabo and archaeological survey around it was conducted in June through August 1981. This was followed in the summer of 1982 by two months' excavation at Tenabo, two months' excavation at Abo, and further archaeological survey work. From October 1982 through August 1983, I lived and worked in the U.S. Park Service facility at the Abo Unit of Salinas National Monument, during which time the laboratory analysis of artifacts from Abo was conducted, along with additional archaeological survey around Abo and elsewhere in Abo Pass and supplementary excavation at Tenabo.

Meanwhile, in the spring of 1982, the Central New Mexico Research Association (CNMRA) was founded and was from that point on involved in this project. CNMRA was a non profit organization intended to promote and conduct scientific study in the Salinas Province, and was intended to survive and go beyond the limited objectives of the project reported herein. Unfortunately, internal weaknesses within CNMRA have led to its untimely demise and at the time of this writing (1987) it is a part of the past.

However, during its brief existence CNMRA rendered invaluable assistance to the conduct of this project. It was instrumental in securing and carrying out the excavation project at Abo in 1982, and in 1983 CNMRA conducted the Chupadera West survey in the Chupadera Basin. (See Chapter 9 in Volume II.) CNMRA also maintained a small storage and laboratory facility in Mountainair which most of the analysis of materials from materials from Tenabo was done.

The summer and early autumn of 1984 were utilized in artifact and faunal analysis, and in supplementary excavation at Tenabo. And the spring of 1985 saw the completion of artifact analysis of the materials reported herein. Most of the subsequent time has been spent on manuscript preparation. While a few preliminary statements on the archaeology have been published or otherwise made available (Baldwin 1983a, 1983b, and 1986), the main results are reported here for the first time.

Theory

Science with a human face; is such a thing possible anymore?

—Edward Abbey (1979: 123)

From its inception, this project has been oriented towards exploring the archaeological unknown, hence, my efforts have been directed primarily towards data collection and interpretation rather than matters of scientific philosophy and archaeological theory. However, I definitely have given these matters some thought since, as is now generally acknowledged, a researcher's assumptions, both explicit and implicit, have a definite effect upon data collection and interpretation.

My position in theoretical matters is an idiosyncratic one, although with roots in one of the "paradigms" of the past. In order to outline my position, it will be necessary to comment upon some aspects of the theoretical ferment of the past quarter century, and even earlier, within archaeology. For practical reasons this discussion cannot include a review of the whole history of Americanist archaeological thought and endeavor, for which see Willey and Sabloff (1974), but will necessarily briefly examine some of the issues raised and claims made by the movement calling itself the "New Archaeology."

During most of the 1960s "New Archaeology consisted chiefly of Lewis Binford and his students; however, by the late 1960s and early 1970s it had attracted interested, but critical outsiders, such as David Clarke and Kent Flannery. This resulted, during the 1970s, in an accelerating critical examination of the tenets and results of the "New Archaeologists" and the exposure of logical faults in their program for salvation of archaeology. As a part of this critical process, "New Archaeology" lost its cohesion as a movement and splintered. A hard core of original practitioners and their adherents, who would probably answer to the label "processualists," still exists and carries on a running battle with their chief competitors, the "behavioral archaeologists." In addition to these two groups, there is a numerous but amorphous group who consider themselves to be, more or less, "anthropological archaeologists." This latter group contains many persons who never considered themselves to be "New Archaeologists," per se but who agree with many of the original aims and interests of "New Archaeology." I would more or less fit last rather nebulous grouping.[1]

But what of the "Old Archaeology," that bogey man from whom the white knights "New Archaeology" were to save us? Well, it never really existed as an entity, as Dunnell (1978: 193-195) has pointed out. Binford and his followers were mainly reacting against what Dunnell calls the Culture History paradigm, with its dry "trait list" approach to defining and ordering archaeological remains (an excellent example of this is the McKern taxonomic system that was used so widely in the eastern half of North America. (See McKern 1939.) Interpretation within the Culture History paradigm was implicitly based upon a Euro American worldview and Victorian concepts of techno sociological "progress," hence, "can be viewed in the main as ethnocentric and producing understandings that are intrinsic to western culture." (Dunnell 1978: 195) It is basically this paradigm that Binford was reacting against in his "opening gun" of the New Archaeology crusade. (Binford 1962: 217)

A second paradigm, what Dunnell labels Cultural Reconstructionism, pre existed New Archaeology as a reaction to the Culture History paradigm. As Dunnell notes, it came into prominence during the 1930s and 1940s, and it is out of this intellectual tradition within archaeology and from one of its major practitioners in the Southwest, Florence Hawley Ellis, that I draw my fundamental inspiration. Cultural Reconstructionists practiced "anthropological archaeology" decades before Binford began to advocate it. A major tool of this approach was ethnographic analogy, which can be and all too frequently is abused through uncritical use. The same, however, can be said for any intellectual tool, for example statistics. (Thomas 1978) Another important element of Cultural Reconstructionism was its incorporation of a cultural relativist viewpoint that forced its practitioners to at least attempt to step outside the ethnocentric confines of archaeological remains. This infused the whole approach with a humanist orientation, where we were encouraged to try to see the people behind the potsherds. While such an orientation was sometimes taken to an extreme of romantic sentimentalism, I still much prefer it to the cold mechanistic determinism pervading much of the "processualist" thinking.

"New Archaeology" sought to replace the previous paradigms with an "explicitly scientific" approach to archaeology. This new approach, as a self conscious movement or "paradigm," developed a program for revolutionizing archaeology that can be roughly divided into two parts: theoretical and methodological. The theoretical part of the program included:

1) A characterization of archaeology as "anthropological," therefore as properly more concerned with

"cultural processes" (questions of "how" and "why") than with "cultural history" (questions of "what," "when," and "who"); and

2) An explicit search for deterministic "cultural laws" equivalent in kind to the classic laws of Newtonian physics. The methodology to accomplish these ends included:

    a) An attempt to make explicit all assumptions;

    b) The statement of research problems in terms of formal hypotheses as the means to be used to test the hypotheses;

    c) An emphasis on "quantification" of results, especially through the use of statistical methods.[2]

While the methodological portion of the New Archaeology's program is basically reasonable, and indeed represents needed reforms that have generally been adopted throughout the subdiscipline, the theoretical portion of its program has undergone intense criticism and has not survived intact. (See discussion of individual points below.) For myself, I have always been repelled by its determinism and implicit anti humanism. (Sometimes explicit anti humanism, see Zubrow 1975: xii) Hence, I have long sought to formulate an alternative approach that is both scientific and humanistic in nature. On the basis of some recent articles in the literature (Hodder 1985, Aberle 1987), it appears that I am not completely alone in this search.

The Nature of Archaeology

For me, archaeology is by definition "anthropological." I have always adhered to a definition of anthropology as being "the Study of Man," with archaeology, physical anthropology, social anthropology (ethnology), and linguistics as four subdisciplines within it. I believe that a well rounded anthropologist, although he/she may specialize in one of the subdisciplines, should have at least a basic knowledge of the others. Further, I see the traditional strained, artificial separation peculiar to the Euro American culture and having no scientific or rational basis. Therefore, I am personally inclined to include history under the anthropology umbrella.[3]

History and archaeology are alike in that they provide the rest of anthropology with a diachronic perspective: history through the study of written records, archaeology through the study of archaeological deposits (material culture and its contexts). The two subdisciplines often have worked hand in hand, as in Mesopotamia where archaeologists unearthed written records that were translated by linguists and then interpreted by historians.

Both social anthropology and history provide the rest of anthropology with information as to how human societies actually function. Ethnographic analogy and historical records provide the archaeologist with information for identifying material culture and archaeological contexts, and models of cultural behavior to guide interpretation. Please note that I have not said "to guide" interpretation, not to control or limit it.

Archaeology and social anthropology provide the rest of anthropology with information about non-literal human societies and about unrecorded aspects of literate societies.

I could go on expounding how linguists and physical anthropology are related to other subdisciplines of anthropology and how they contribute to our overall knowledge, but I believe my general message is clear: all subdisciplines are interdependent and interactive with the others (or potentially so). None should attempt to stand alone, nor should one attempt to dominate another or subordinate itself to another. Archaeology is not the handmaiden of social anthropology, nor is history, nor linguists, nor physical anthropology, its social anthropology subordinate to any of the others. Each has its own subject matter and therefore its own appropriate methodology. Given, then, the appropriateness of separate methodologies, are there subdisciplines united at the level of theory?

However, before tackling that sticky subject, more needs to be said about the nature of archaeology and of anthropology as a whole. For the most part, anthropology is an observational science. Observational sciences deal with phenomena that are either too large and complex, too distant in time and space, or that take place over periods of time too long for manipulation by man. In the case of anthropology, moral restrictions on an experimentation with human beings preclude most experimental possibilities.[4]

Dunnell very well describes differences between archaeology and the "hard sciences." Chemistry and physics, as examples of the latter, have basic units that are discrete, distinctly bounded, and universal in time and space, for example the elements of the periodic table or subatomic particles such as electrons. Archaeology, on the other hand, has basic units (such as cultural systems on pottery types) that are not only non universal in time and space, but are dynamic (changeable) over both time and space, hence lack discreteness and distinct boundaries. (Dunnell 1982: 8 9) As he puts it: "Relations between observations are constrained by both time and space. Relations cannot be rendered as timeless, universally true statements among entities because there is no constant set of entities." (Dunnell 1982: 89)

Dunnell's basic argument is that attempts to build an archaeological theory modeled after "hard science" examples run afoul of this fundamental difference in subject matter. Dunnell does not deny the possibility that cultural "laws" may exist, but points out that they must be different in character from "classical laws (that) require units that are independent of time and space." (1982: 9)

Similarly, Aberle, in describing anthropology as a whole as a "historical science," states: "The historical sciences are historical because they deal with entities and groups of entities that have traceable continuity over time, but that also change" (Aberle 1987: 556), and diachronic approaches in anthropology deal with irreversible, probabilistic, stochastic sequences. So, it is hopeless for anthropologists to pursue deterministic laws of the Newtonian type, which Deal with reversible phenomena. (Aberle 1987: 551)

I also would not deny the possibility that some sort of cultural laws may exist, but it disturbs me that many archaeological theorists assume they exist without being able to demonstrate an empirical basis for them. After all, physics built up its body of laws on the basis of empirical observations. Are archaeologists intrinsically superior, so that they can skip up to the top and build deductively downwards from a set of unproven assumptions? Was not that the approach taken by astrologers, who imposed a set of assumptions on the heavens, and then deduced a logical system at interpretations? Are archaeologists in danger of being remembered as the astrologers of modern science?[5]

Binford (1962) would have archaeologists turn to social anthropology both for a set of goals and for theoretical guidance. The problem here is that the contemporary social anthropology had long modeled itself after the "hard sciences" (see Aberle 1987: 551 552), thereby conceiving of cultural systems as discrete, bounded units that were viewed synchronically (i.e., as being present in a narrow span of time, the "ethnographic present" of the ethnographer). As such, cultural systems were treated as closed systems where the only kinds of change were cyclic changes (seasons cycles, social cycles, life cycles) that followed known, repeated patterns, or disruptive changes caused by contact with "more advanced" societies, such as Euro American culture, resulting in acculturation towards the more advanced society or complete destruction. In this structural functionalist view of human societies there was no allowance for dynamic system change: neither internal causes for change nor systemic

integration with the external world was recognized. For an extended critique of structural functionalism by a social anthropologist see Murphy (1971).

Thus, social anthropology long resisted concepts of cultural evolution, and when they were finally accepted they were phrased in terms of discrete technological/social steps ("stages"). This retained the closed system conception of culture by visualizing the changes between steps as rapid technological revolutions that transformed cultures from one step to the next in a short period of time, followed by long periods of systemic equilibrium. The technological revolutions were seen to be caused by some "prime mover" (mysterious irresistible forces such as "population pressure"). In keeping with persisting Victorian notions of "progress," the "stages" were progressive from "primitive" towards "advanced," with only one ultimate end: the modern industrial state. See Dunnell's exhaustive review of evolutionary concepts (Dunnell 1980, particularly his critique of the "Spencerian" conceptions underlying cultural evolution in social anthropology).

Thus, when Binford and his followers turned to social anthropology, particularly to Leslie White, for a theoretical underpinning for archaeology, they received a closed system conception of culture and a stage system of evolutionary concepts that are ill suited to the needs of archaeology.[6] Clearly then, uncritical borrowing of theory from social anthropology has not been the answer for archaeology.

The Interactive Model

If the structural functionalism of social anthropology is an inadequate basis for archaeological theory, then what might be? Murphy, after his critique of structural functionalism, would urge upon anthropology as a whole what he calls "dialectics." (Murphy 1971) Unfortunately, this is simply a retread of the conflict dialectic that is one of the basic assumptions underlying the Euro American worldview. To view the world solely as a series of dyadic conflicts seems to me a narrow view that fails to encompass the complex scope of human interactions, much less the interactions of humans and their cultural systems with the natural environment.[7]

Over the years, I have gradually built up a rough model of the functioning of the world around me that I currently term "the Interactive Model." Space and time considerations preclude exhaustive discussion of it here, and, anyway, this conception is still in the process of "becoming" and will probably remain that way for a long time. One reason for this is that I distrust rigid, absolutist theoretical positions, believing instead that flexibility and willingness to change one's opinions in the face of new evidence are prerequisites for the conduct of good science.

In keeping with this, I assert the primacy of evidence over opinion, of empirical fact over theoretical expectation.

A "Fact," of course, is the product of an observation and an interpretation, and if either of these is faulty then the "fact" is wrong. The history of science is one long demonstration of this. Thus, the current "facts" are approximations to the truth, and are potentially subject to revision. Thus, while I am an "empiricist," it is a relativistic empiricism that I avow.

My theoretical position, the Interactive Modle, is accompanied by a methodological approach that I term the "Heuristic Method"; this latter is discussed below under "Methodology." The basis of the Interactive Model is an acceptance of an open system viewpoint. (Salmon 1980) Based on Salmon's discussion (1978: 176 177), I offer the following thumbnail definition of a "system": a system is a set of elements and dynamic relationships between those elements. The key word is "dynamic," which serves to distinguish "systemic" relationships from "static" relationships. An example of a "static" relationship is the linear distance between two objects; the objects are in a systemic relationship only if they interact in some fashion. The word "dynamic" is defined as the transfer of energy and/or matter and/or information. Frequency of transfer is not at issue; hence, "unique" events can be as much a part of a system repetitive or cyclic events.[8]

I define the interactive model as having three components: the natural environment, the cultural environment, and the individual human being. These are all systemically related and interactive, each component itself being an open system. Changes that occur within the Interactive Model include cyclic changes, unique events, and evolutionary changes. I will not enter into a detailed discussion of evolutionary change (for which see Dunnell 1980), but I will note that I see at least three kinds of evolution: mechanical evolution (such as the trajectory of changes controlled by geological processes within the non living world), biological evolution, and cultural evolution.

As indicated above, I agree with Dunnell's (1980) critique of the "Spencerian" cultural evolutionism of Leslie White and other social anthropologists. On the other hand, I am wary of attempts to closely model cultural evolution after biological evolution, as some mechanisms of cultural change, such as diffusion, do not have true analogues in biology. My conception of cultural evolution is non deterministic, therefore, necessarily "multilineal" in the sense I

see no a priori series of steos ("stages") that cultural systems must follow during their historical existence. This allows for the existence of archaeological cultures that were not just replicas of ethnographically known cultural systems. (See discussion of evolution in Aberle 1987: 552 556.) This conception has clear implications for the use of ethnographic analogy, but that is a methodological matter. (See below.)

Cultural systems ("culture") have both ideational and material aspects. The ideational aspect includes knowledge, worldview, emotions (those not originating biologically), and the semantic component of language. The material aspect includes the phonetic aspects of language, material culture (including somatic modifications), and cultural behavior.[9]

To bring the individual human being into the picture, I would point out that each person is not a carbon copy of an ideal cultural persona. Each individual person is born with mental free will and is more or less enculturated towards the ideal cultural persona, but due to the capacity for individual judgment, circumstances of personal history, and a complex of other factors, each individual, willy-nilly, turns out to be unique to a greater or lesser degree. This is the "active" conception of the human individual discussed by Ian Hodder (1985: 1 3) which sees the individual human being as actively creating cultural behavior, rather than being only a puppet reacting to deterministic cultural laws. Hodder (1985) provides an important discussion of the interaction of the human individual and his/her cultural environment, which I urge the reader to examine carefully.

Of course, the biological make up of the human organism imposes a certain range of biological behaviors upon each individual (the need to eat, shit, sleep, etc.) that must be accommodated by both the individual and the cultural system. And there is mounting evidence that both humans and animals are genetically "primed" for learned behavior. (See Gould and Marler 1987.) This implies that cultural behavior may be more closely tied to human genetics than previously accepted in anthropology. I can certainly see that a genetically programmed urge to explore and learn one's environment (i.e. "curiosity") would be a positive survival trait in an arboreal animal, such as a primate or a feline. In the near future, we may have to completely rethink our past assumptions upon the separation of cultural and biological behavior.

Implicit in the above discussion is my view that the universe is causally complex. This is why an open system model of culture is perhaps the best way of attempting to represent human culture.

Methodology

We have to learn what we can, but remain mindful that our knowledge not close the circle, closing out the void, so that we forget that what we do not know remains boundless, without limit or bottom....
—*Stone Telling*, as quoted by LeGuin (1986: 31)

My "Heuristic Method" stresses the fine tuning of data collection, analysis, and integration of the results. Interpretation is made as objective as possible through careful consideration of alternative explanations or combinations of explanations. This is clearly a version of Walter Taylor's conjunctive approach (Taylor 1967: 150 200), as I feel that all available lines of evidence should be brought to bear on a particular problem, specifically including evidence from all the subdisciplines of anthropology. My explicit combination of ethnographic, historical, and archaeological evidence in this study is symptomatic of my methodology.

One of Taylor's injunctions is that "it is incumbent upon the archeologist to publish the empirical bases of all his inferences in order that the reader may judge for himself their acceptability" (Taylor 1967: 154), and this present study, being basically descriptive in nature, makes every effort towards full presentation of the data. This explains the massive descriptive sections contained within it.

As its name suggests, the Heuristic Method stresses "discovery," both at the level of description and that of interpretation/explanation. It is oriented toward the expansion of knowledge, therefore, deemphasizes a priori explanatory models that would bias data collection and interpretation. This does not mean that data collection is unfocused or without a purpose in mind, but it does mean that that all available data should be collected insofar as possible in order that the unexpected not be overlooked.[10]

While "problem oriented research" is subsumed within and is not contradictory to the Heuristic Method, the single working hypothesis orientation is discouraged and the multiple working hypothesis orientation is supported. (See Chamberlin 1931.) As I see causal complexity behind the workings of cultural and natural systems, monocausal explanations of cultural phenomena are immediately suspect. Except for large scale unique events, generally the larger the phenomenon, the more complex I would expect is causal explanation to be. It is because of this that I distrust simple explanatory concepts, such as the concept of "prime movers." Archaeology is not alone in suffering from simplistic interpretations; late in the last century, Leo Tolstoy castigated contemporary historians for this in his novel "War and Peace," as in this passage:

"The human intellect, without investigating the multiplicity and complexity of the conditions of phenomena, any one of which taken separately may seem to be the cause, snatches at the first, the most intelligible approximation to a cause, and says: "This is the cause!" (Tolstoy 1968: 1178)

As part of the Heuristic Method, quantitative description is seen to necessarily include both definition of a mean (a normative generalization of average) and a description of the range of variation. The concept of "range of variation" comes out of biology through the medium of physical anthropology, but is a necessary component of quantitative description. Typology must include range of variation as an essential property of each unit created. Comparison, then, must use range of variation, as well as generalized ideations (or perhaps in preference to any idealization).

In interpretation/explanation an interplay of induction and deduction is used. The naïve insistence upon deduction only by the New Archaeology has been soundly criticized. (See Salmon 1976: Sullivan 1978: 185 1987; Dunnell 1982: 67.) Even Binford has acknowledged the unsoundness of his original position: "Initially, new archaeologists argued that the solution to this problem was to adopt another form of reasoning, deductive argument, where the premises were stated, consequences deduced, and these deductively reasoned explanations taken to...what? The past, or the archaeological record? Clearly, archaeologists in the late 1960s and early 1970s who argued for the potential of deductive procedures had not fully though through the problem of the dependent status of their ideas regarding the past. Archaeological knowledge of the past is totally dependent upon the meanings which archaeologists give to observations on the archaeological record." (Binford and Sabloff 1982: 149)

As to such "meanings," I prefer to attempt as objective an appraisal of observations as possible. First by interpreting in terms of the context and characteristics of the observation itself, and only secondarily resorting to analogy, either archaeological or ethnographic. This is the direct application of my insistence upon the primacy of the evidence itself, rather than the immediate imposition of a priori interpretations. This involves a constant process of self questioning as to the evidential basis for each identification and interpretation.

I must stress this last point: I have made every attempt herein to clearly and reasonably base identifications and interpretations directly upon the evidence at hand. The careful reader, the reader who accepts the scholarly responsibility of sincerely attempting to understand an author's statements and their bases before critiquing them, should have no difficulty distinguishing my identifications and interpretations from the occasional speculation. Of course, some interpretations will have a firmer evidential base than others, especially in under researched subject areas, such as Piro and Tompiro ethnohistory and archaeology, and inevitably I shall be proved wrong on various points. However, I long ago decided that I prefer to risk the occasional mistake rather than "play it safe" by ignoring or suppressing evidence leading to interpretations that are not currently "trendy" or "acceptable." Still, especially in a work of this size, there will be the occasional lapse of interpretive logic for which I must take full responsibility, with apologies to the reader.

To return to the analytical methodology: I approach typology cautiously, as a necessarily evil. Typology in archaeology frequently requires the arbitrary subdivision of continua (pottery typology, especially), thus should not be overly rigid. On the other hand, the very need to create useable units for comparison and contrast require as much logical consistency as possible within a typology. Referring again to ceramics, I am neither a "lumper" nor a "splitter," as I consider either position to be too rigid or inflexible to be serviceable in our relativistic universe. Ideally, then, any typology should be based upon a complex of features, rather than just one or two.

Special field and analytical methodologies are described in the appropriate places within the later chapters. I will only note here that for excavation all fill was screened using 1/8 inch screens and almost all fill was excavated by trowel, dustpan, and brush methods. In the screening process an attempt to was made to save anything of potential cultural significance, with the exception of very small bits of wood charcoal. In the analysis, I attempted to do a 100% sample analysis of the materials recovered; the few exceptions are specifically noted.

Ethnohistory

I will only note here that excavation lies at intersection of history and social anthropology, and of archaeology as well. Howard (1976:1) States:

"There are two operational definitions of the term ethnohistory, both valid. One embraces the study and explication of 'western' historical materials relating to non western societies using the techniques of Anthropology and History in such a way as to minimize the cultural distortion which results when explorers, travelers, government officials, missionaries, etc., from one culture attempt to describe another culture with which they are only superficially acquainted. The other involves the study and explication of historical materials developed by various non western societies by themselves and for their own purposes in such a way as to make these materials fully comprehensible to western readers."

In the present cases, the non literate Piro and Tompiro cultural systems where we do not even have records of oral traditions but must rely completely on Euro American records, the kind of ethnohistory practiced is clearly that of the first definition.

With regard to the application of ethnohistorical data to archaeological materials, I have generally followed the direct historical approach (Steward 1942), particularly the principle of working form the known to the unknown which clearly underlies my methodology in Chapter 5. It is also clear in my concentration on the Pueblo IV period, which contains within it the transition from prehistory to history for the Piro and Tompiro.

In the use of published historical documents, I always checked Spanish texts (if available against the English translations for any data of critical import. I have not hesitated to disagree with previous interpretations if I think their rendition is faulty or questionable in some way, and have attempted to specify my basis for doing so. In general, I have attempted to apply professional methods of textual criticism insofar as possible.

The specific research questions guided the ethnohistorical and archaeological work arc formulated at the end of Chapter 3, as they are dependent upon the review of our previous knowledge of the Salinas Province and the Southwest.

Notes:

1. It should be realized that the current labels ("processualists," "behavioral archaeologists," "anthropological archaeologist") are imprecise and sometimes overlapping in their application and that there are probably few archaeologists who would entirely agree on either the terms or their application.
2. For more discussion of the relationship between history and anthropology, see Carmack (1972: 227 230).
3. For more complete statements of the "New Archaeology" paradigm, see Binford (1962, 1965, 1968) and Watson, LeBlanc and Redman (1971).
4. An experimental science is one where new knowledge is acquired through experimentation under controlled conditions; examples are physics and chemistry. An observational science is one where new knowledge is acquired through observation under semi controlled or uncontrolled conditions; examples are anthropology, astronomy and geology. Experimental and observational sciences

are "reality" based. Sciences may be based on abstracts, such as logical sciences where new knowledge is acquired through logical permutations of symbolic systems; examples being mathematics and philosophy.

In a different, but complementary, view of anthropology, Aberle (1987: 551 552) characterizes it as a "historical science."

5. Any reader who strenuously objects to my comparison of (some) archeological theoreticians with astrologers is referred to Stephen Lekson's comment after being confronted with one of Binford's more irrational statements about Southwestern archaeology: "We should debunk ourselves last we be debunked by others" (Lekson 1982: 21)

6. Kehoe (1981) has critiqued the imposition of assumptions from the Euro American worldview upon North American Indian cultures. I suspect that the tendency is more pervasive and more deeply rooted than she indicates.

7. While Binford does sometimes talk about "structural modifications of systems" (e.g., Binford 1962: 217), I have not found anywhere in his writings any clear indication that he is aware of the critical difference between open and closed systems. Some of his followers, however, did become aware of this distinction (e.g., Watson, LeBlanc, and Redman 1971: 71 73).

8. It can be seen that the Culture History paradigm's trait list descriptions of cultural entities only described static relationships: merely telling one that the listed items were known to appear together in the same archaeological contexts.

9. The term "material" in material aspects necessarily means "matter, energy, and their interaction." Therefore, cultural behavior is material since it is meaningful interaction of matter and energy controlled by a human being.

10. Sullivan has described the problem of a priori interpretations being imposed on archaeological remains as follows: The view that material remains are data (rather than a source of data) is phenomenological... To overcome the inadequacies of the phenomenological concept of data and evidence, it has been suggested that archaeologists select specified sets of material remains that bear on a particular problem... Accordingly, certain aspects of material remains become data when there is a match between expectations (test implications) and observations. The major difficulties with this view are that strong assumptions are being made about the process responsible for producing the sample examined by the archaeologist to generate the requisite data. The assumptions are that the patterning of variability in the archaeological record reflects past behavioral patterning...; that there has been little significant post depositional modification of material remains...; and that all deposits of material remains will yield data about most aspects of past phenomena if the archaeologist is clever enough to discover them... These assumptions are questionable, since archaeological patterning need have no past behavioral referent... A wide variety of processes... affect the structure of material remains and, therefore, the nature of the sample the archaeologist manipulates to generate data... And, finally, "All sites are not amenable to the solution of all problems "...given the diverse nature of the processes responsible for their production. (Sullivan 1978: 189 190)

2

Environment

Somewhere it is raining down.
Look to the north:
Up in the north they come, the black and white and blue.
The finest clouds I ever saw, like snow or cotton.
They are heavy down below,
Full of rainwater, heavy with rainwater.
Right down in the east, and from the east to the south.
That is the way the rain is going,
That is as the shiwanna said.
> —Corn grinding song from Santo Domingo
> (Densmore 1938: 115)

Variety is the keynote for understanding the environment in the Southwest. Unlike some other culture areas, such as the Great Plains, the Southwest culture area is not even relatively uniform in physiography, climate, or vegetation; instead great environmental diversity is the rule, frequently within very short geographical distances. Consequently, the boundaries of this culture area do not coincide with environmental boundaries and vary through time as prehistoric and historic cultural entities expand or contract. For the better-known portion of the Southwest, that north of the United States-Mexico border, the states of Arizona and New Mexico may be considered the geographical core of the culture area, although the eastern third of New Mexico consists of frontier region between the Southwest and the Great Plains.

Physiography, Geology and Soils

These elements of the environment are relatively staple and slow to change, hence may be considered as background to the more ephemeral elements, i.e., climate, flora and fauna, at the time scale employed in this study.

Physiography

The major physiographic provinces found within the Southwest culture area are delineated in Figure 2-1.

(See also Mallory 1972: 29-31 or Gerlach 1970: 60-61.) They consist of (1) The Southern Rocky Mountains: 5,000 to over 14,000 feet above sea level, composed of abrupt and rugged fold mountain ranges, deeply incised canyons, a few parks (intra-montane basins filled with lacustrine and alluvial sediments of Pleistocene and Holocene age), a few glaciers and permanent snow fields on the highest ranges, and narrow and swift freshwater streams and rivers. (2) The Colorado Plateau: a broad sedimentary platform dominated by sandstones, but with intrusive mountain ranges, some laccolithic in nature, and some volcanic features, ranging from ca. 4,500 to over 11,000 feet above sea level and characterized by mesas, canyons, and badlands. (3) The Basin and Range Province: from sea level to over 13,000 feet above sea level, it consists of an endless series of fault block mountain ranges with sedimentary basins between and occasional volcanic features. (4) The Southern Great Plains: a division of the Great Plains physiographic province, ranging from ca. 1,500 to 6,000 feet above sea level and consisting of broad, shallow river basins and extensive plateaus.

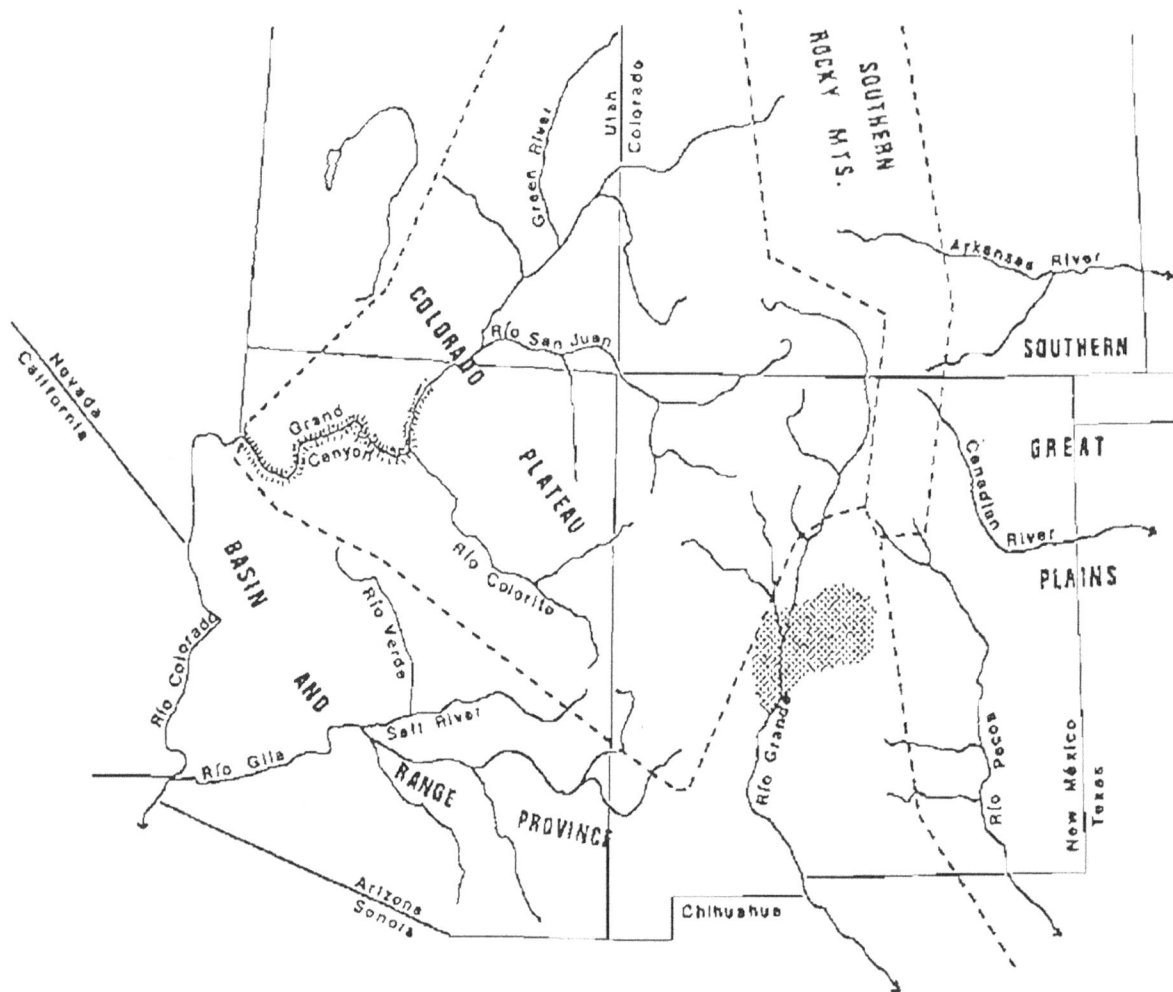

Figure 2-1

The shaded area in Figure 2-1 shows the area of concern in this study: a portion of the Rio Grande Valley and the highlands east of it within the tongue of the Basin and Range Province that projects north into the center of New Mexico. Figure 2-2 shows the major physiographic features of this study area, plus some of the modern cities and towns. Outlined in the center of Figure 2-2 are the two basins in which most of the archaeological portion of this study was conduct: The Abo Pass and the Chupadera Basin.

The Abo Pass is that area drained by Abo Arroyo and its tributaries east of the Los Pinos and Manzano Mountains. Abo Arroyo cuts westwards between these two range as Abo Canyon, issuing forth at the Bocas de Abo to flow westwards across the pediment deposits to the Rio Grande. To the northeast, the town of Mountainair sits on the drainage divide between Abo Pass and the Estancia Basin. The Estancia Basin has no external drainage and contains many salt lakes.

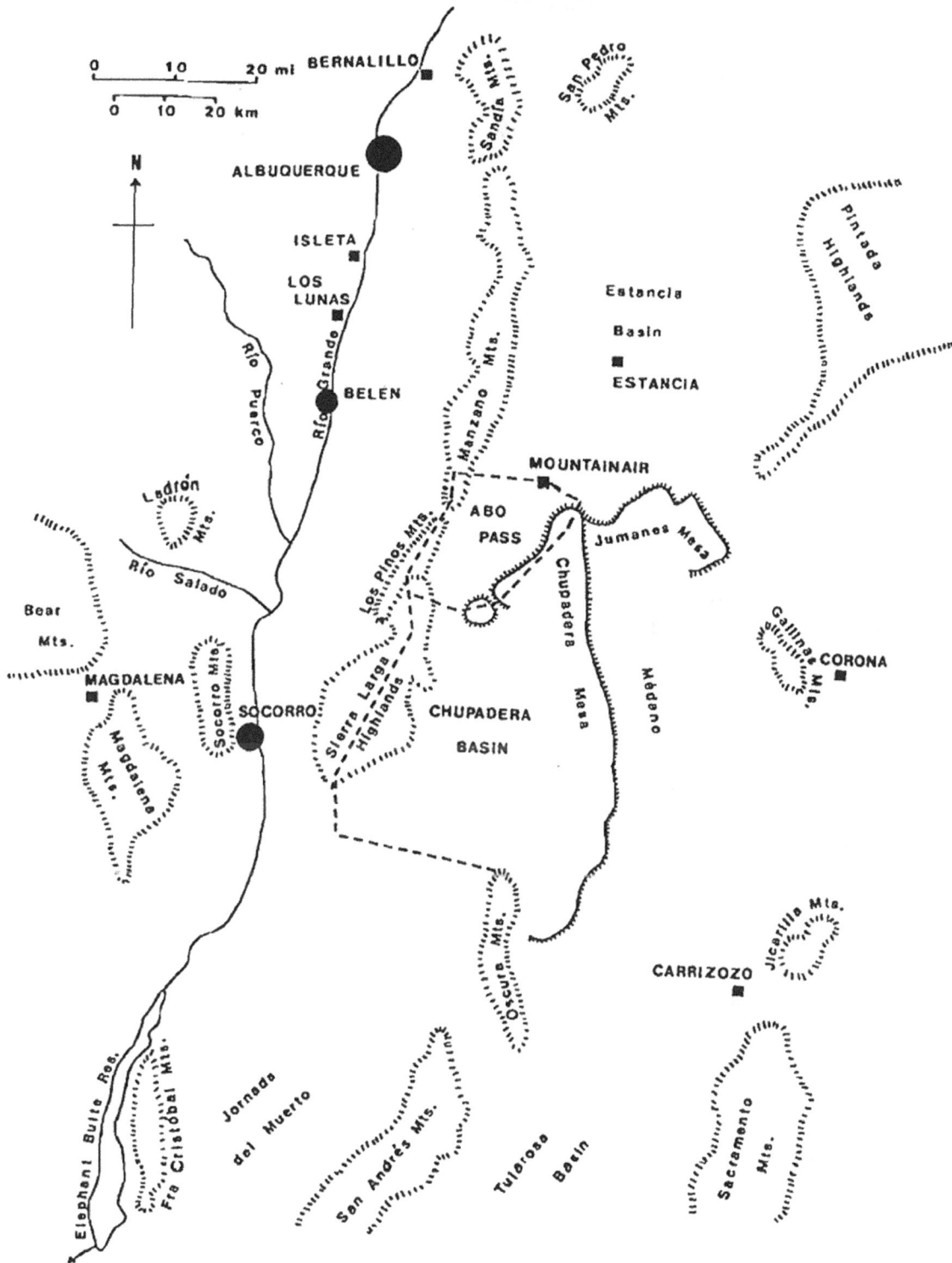

CENTRAL NEW MEXICO: MAJOR
GEOGRAPHIC FEATURES

Figure
2-2

Figure 2-2

South of Mountainair is a geologic feature known as the Chupadera Platform, a limestone massif bordered by escarpments on the north and dipping towards the south and east. The Platform is divided by another escarpment into Jumanes Mesa to the east and Chupadera Mesa to the west. The interior drainage of Chupadera Mesa and Sierra Larga Highlands (broken up and isolated by portions of the Chupadera Platform) is what is called the Chupadera Basin. The Medano is that area of the Chupadera Platform characterized by stabilized sand dunes. The Medano (and the Platform) mergers to the south and the northern end of the Tularosa Basin. Likewise, the Chupadera Basin merges with wastelands known as the Jornada del Muerto.

The various mountain ranges are fault block structures and the Rio Grande flows through the sunken graben between the ranges. While those structures are traditionally included within the Basin and the Range Province, it has been argued that the series of basins through which the Rio Grande runs in New Mexico are better interpreted as a rift valley complex. (V. C. Kelly 1952: 102) Basic sources on the structures of central New Mexico can be found in Johnson and Read (1952) and Kuellmer (1963).

Geology

Since the majority of this study took place the archaeological work reported in this study took place within the Abo Pass, this description will concentrate upon that drainage basin. Two geological profiles of the Abo Pass are presented in Figures 2-3 and 2-4 (also Table 2-1), the first showing a lengthwise cross-section through Abo Pass and the second an oblique line from the junction of Abo Canyon and Montosa Draw to the top of Chupadera Mesa. Each profile is drawn so as to pass through the location of one of the two largest archaeological sites in Abo Pass. Basic sources on the formations and geological features of Abo Pass are Bates, Wilpolt, MacAlpin and Vorbe (1947), Johnson and Read (1952), Kuellmer (1963), Myers (1977), Needham and Bates (1943), Spiegel (1955), and Stark (1956), Stark and Dapples (1946), and Wilpolt, MacAlpin, Bates, and Vorbe (1946).

The geology of the Chupadera Basin is similar to that of Abo Pass, with the exceptions that several large Quaternary and Tertiary volcanic features are present (Weber 1963), and large portions of the basin are covered with sand dunes, both stabilized and unstabilized, Jumanes Mesa.

Geology is described in Bates, Wilpolt, MacAlpin, and Vorbe (1947).

Basic description of the fault block mountains and the grabens filled with Tertiary and Quaternary sediments of the Rio Grande Valley can be found in Johnson and Read (1952) and Kuellmer (1963).

The Estancia Basin northeast of Abo Pass is the site of Pleistocene Lake Estancia and is filled with a complex of lacustrine sediments, see Bourlier, Neher, Creezee, Bowman and Meister (1970), Bachhuber (1971) and Titus (1969).

Further discussion of local geology is reserved to appropriate archaeological chapters.

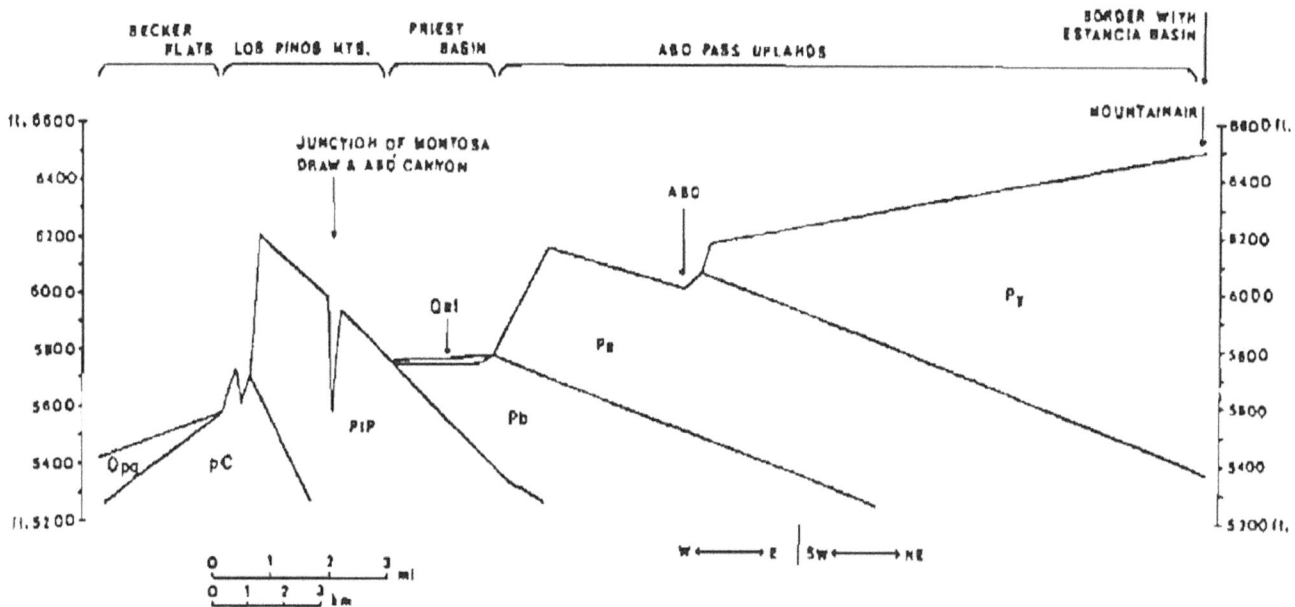

Qal   Quaternary Alluvium
Qpg   Quaternary Pediment Gravels
Py   Yeso Formation (undifferentiated)
      (Permian)
Pa   Abó Formation (Lower Permian)
Pb   Bursum Formation (Lower Permian)
PIP   Wild Cow Formation (Lower Permian
      & Upper Pennsylvanian)
pC   Pre-Cambrian Basement Rocks

Based on Myers (1977) and Maps 2-4
and 2-5 in Johnson and Read (1952:
47-48, 52).

ABO PASS GEOLOGIC STRATA

Figure

2-3

Figure 2-3

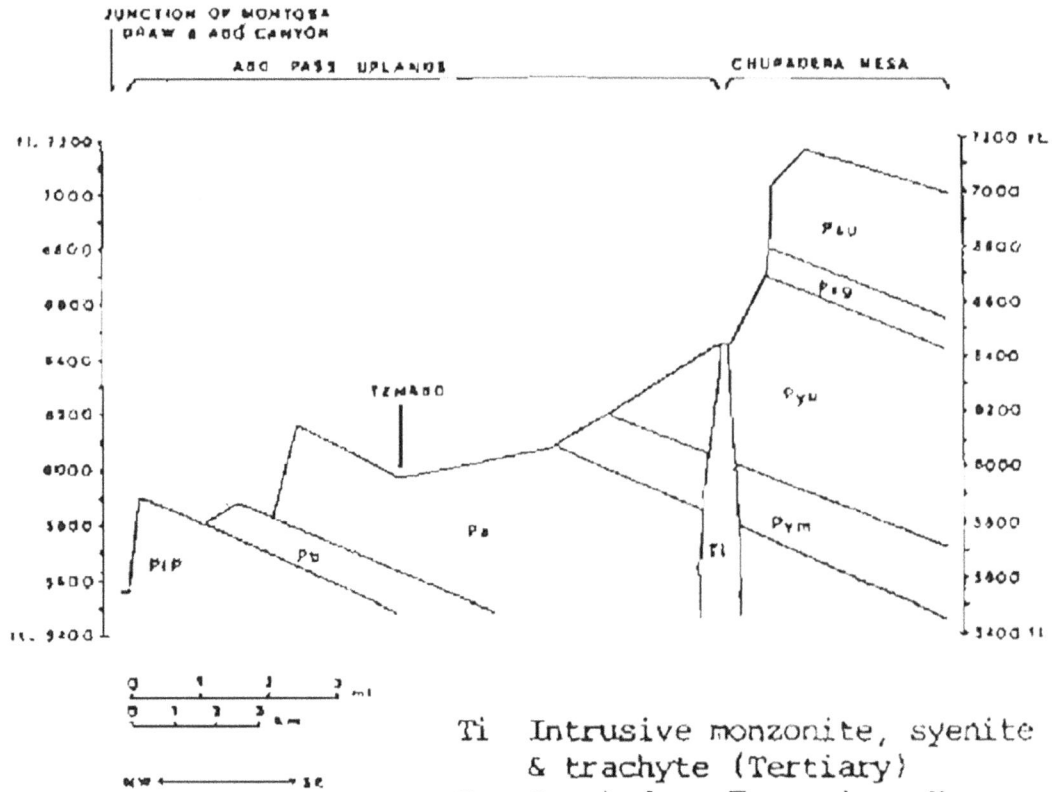

JUNCTION OF MONTOSA
DRAW & ABO CANYON

ABO PASS UPLANDS   CHUPADERA MESA

Based on Myers (1977)
and Map 2-4 in Johnson
and Read (1952: 47-48)

ABO PASS GEOLOGIC
STRATA

Ti   Intrusive monzonite, syenite
     & trachyte (Tertiary)
Psu San Andres Formation: Upper
     Members (Permian)
Psg San Andres Formation: Glorieta
     Member (Permian)
Pyu Yeso Formation: Upper Members
     (Lower Permian)
Pym Yeso Formation: Meseta Blanca
     Member (Lower Permian)
Pa   Abo Formation (Lower Permian)
Pb   Bursum Formation (Lower Permian)
PIP Wild Cow Formation (Lower Permian
     & Upper Pennsylvanian)

Figure 2-4

Figure

2-4

36

Table 2-1: EXPOSED GEOLOGICAL STATA IN ABO PASS

(includes south end of Manzano Mts. and Los Pinos Mts.)

Sources: Johnson and Read (1952: 47-48, 52), Myers (1977),
    Needham and Bates (1943), Stark and Dapoles (1946),
    Stark (1956).

Qal   Alluvium (Quaternary).

Qoa   Arkosic Pediment Deposits (Quaternery): decomposed
      and transported Priest Granite.

Qpg   Pediment Gravels (Quaternary): sand and gravel
      derived from limestone and metamorphic nodes.

Qf   Alluvial Fans (Quaternary).

Qls   Landslide debris (Quaternary).

Ti   Intrusive monzonite, syenite and trachyte (Tertiary).

Ps   San Andres Formation (Permian).

Psu   San Andres Formation: Upper Members (Permian): grey
      limestones (some fossiliferous); dark grey-to-black
      limestones (some fossiliferous); light coloured to
      grey sandstones.

Psg   San Andres Formation: Glorieta Member (Permian):
      cream-to-pale yellow sandstone.

Py   Yeso Formation (Lower Permian).

Pyu   Yeso Formation: Upper Members (Lower Permian): pink,
      red, white, grey sandstones; gypsum; grey limestone,
      siltstone, slate and shale.

Pym   Yeso Formation: Meseta Blanca Member (Lower Permian):
      pink, red, brown, grey sandstones and siltstone.

Pa   Abo Formation (Lower Permian): light-to-dark red
      sandstone and shale; copper minerals.

Pb   Bursum Formation (Lower Permian): red-brown
      sandstone and shale; grey-green limestone.

PIP   Wild Cow Formation (lower Permian-Upper
      Pennsylvanian): grey calcarenite; chert;
      some sandstone, shale, siltstone.

IPs   Sandia Formation (Middle Pennsylvanian): green,
      grey, yellow, brown sandstone and conglomerate.

pЄgp Priest Granite (Pre-Cambrian): grey granite.

pЄs   Sevilleta Metarhyolite (Pre-Cambrian): pink-to-grey
      rhyolite.

pЄwr White Ridge Quartzite (Pre-Cambrian): pink-grey,
      blue-white quartzite.

pЄbs Blue Springs Schist (Pre-Cambrian): bluish
      grey-to-greenish grey schist.

pЄsq Sais Quartzite (Pre-Cambrian): bluish-grey quartzite.

Table 2-1

Soils

The majority of the soils within Abo Pass have been mapped and published (see Bourlier, Neher, Cree, Bowman, and Meister 1970 and Pease 1975), but, unfortunately, the soil survey for Socorro County, which covers the location Tenabo, is not yet published. Consideration of the significance of the local soils is discussed in the archaeological survey chapter.

Flora Fauna, And Climate

Ocho meses de inverno y quarto de infierno.[1]
—The Spaniards' characterization of the climate of New Mexico in early AD 1600s. (Hammond and Rey 1953: 656)

These relatively ephemeral elements of the environment not only change cyclically (yearly weather and plant cycles, plant and animal life cycles, plant and animal community succession cycles, etc.), but it is known from both historical records and scientific studies that significant differences in climate, flora and fauna have existed in the past. Therefore, the conditions of the present will be described first, and then those of the past insofar as they are known.

Present Flora and Fauna

All of the Southwest culture area falls within the North Temperate Climatic Zone, consequently most vegetational differences are determined by altitudinal and topographic differences. Table 2-2 presents a summary of life zones and vegetation types for New Mexico. At present Abo Pass, the Chupadera Basin, the Estancia Basin, and Jumanes Mesa are characterized by pinon-juniper woodland and short grass. The Manzano Mountains are characterized by pinon-juniper woodland up through spruce-fir forest; and the Rio Grande Valley by desert and desert grass, except for this special riverine community of cottonwoods, salt cedar, willows and marsh plants along the river itself.

Present Climate

Central New Mexico lies right on the dividing lines between Dorroh's eastern and western zones (the dashed line on Figure 2-5). The eastern zone is primarily influenced by moist air masses originating over the Gulf of Mexico and moving northwestwards across the Southern Plains directly into eastern New Mexico. The majority of summer rain storms in central New Mexico result from the movement of this air mass; winter precipitation in this area is also primarily derived from the southeast, although the cold Polar Air Mass frequently intrudes from the north. Western New Mexico receives precipitation from both the Gulf of Mexico and from air masses originating over the Pacific Ocean to the west and southwest. (See Dorroh 1946: 1-4 for further discussions.)

While winter storms tend to cover large areas, summer storms are typically small in areal coverage and of short duration. Consequently, growing season precipitation in the Southwest is notoriously scattered and unpredictable. Annual precipitation is shown in Figure 2-6 and length of growing season (average number of days between frosts) is shown in Figure 2-7. The significance of these factors will be discussed along with agriculture in Chapter 9 in Volume II. Due to the relative dryness of the atmosphere over the Southwest, cloud masses tend to scatter and break up as they progress further from their points of origin. Hence, continuous cloud cover is relatively rare in central New Mexico, permitting near-maximum insolation during each day and near-maximum heat-radiation into space during each night. The next result is great daily temperature fluctuation. (See Figure 2-8 for two years' temperature records from Mountainair.)

Table 2-3 lists plants seen and recognized by the author within Abo Pass from 1980 through 1984, while Table 2-4 lists animals. (2) Appendix 1 gives a list of mammals for the central New Mexico area. One factor complicating faunal distribution in this area is that it is a zone of overlap between Great Plains, Rocky Mountain, and desert fauna, hence two or more species of a single genus may be present (e.g., the wood rats: *Neotoma* ssp.).

Table 2-2: VEGETATION TYPES IN NEW MEXICO

(Based on Table 1 in Little 1950)

Merriam's Life Zones	Vegetation Types & Characteristic Plants	Average Annual Rainfall	Location in New Mexico
Artic-Alpine ca. 11,500 ft. and above	Alpine Tundra: mountain areas, alpine grasses.	30-35" (762-889mm)	Summits of Sangre de Cristo and Jemez Mountains above timber line.
Hudsonian Zone ca. 9,500 - 11,500 ft.	Spruce-fir Forest: Engelmann spruce, alpine fir, corkbark fir: 8,500-12,000 ft.	30-35" (762-869mm)	High Mountains, e.g., Sangre de Cristo, Jemez, Sacramento, Mogollon Mts.
Canadian zone, ca. 8,000 - 9,500 ft	Douglas Fir: Forest: Douglas fir, white fir, quaking aspen, Limber pine: 8,000 - 9,500 ft	25-30" (635-762mm)	High Mountains in western 2/3 of state.
Transitional zone, ca. 6,500 - 8,000 ft.	Ponderosa Pine Forest: Ponderosa pine, Arizona pine 5,500-8,500 ft.	19-25" (483-635mm)	Mountains in western 2/3 and NE of state.
Upper Sonoran ca. 4,500- 6,500 ft.	Pinon-juniper Woodland: Pinon, Utah juniper, one-seed juniper, alligator juniper, Rocky Mountain juniper: 4,500 - 7,500 ft.	12-20 " (305-508mm)	Plateaus, foothills & mountains except in eastern quarter.
	Oak Woodland: Emory Oak, gray oak, Mexican blue oak, Arizona white oak: 4,500 - 6,000 ft.	12-20" (305-508mm)	foothills & mountains in southern quarter.
	Short Grass: Blue grama, hairy grama, galleta, buffalo grass: 4,500-6,500 ft.	9-20" (227-508mm)	Plains: mainly eastern central, & northern portions of state.
Lower Sonoran ca. 2,500 - 4,500 ft.	Oak Brush: Harvard oak: 3,600 - 4,800 ft.	13-18" (330-457mm)	SE corner of state.
	Desert Grass: Black grama, tobosa, dropseeds: 3,000 - 5,000 ft.	9-18" (227-457mm)	Plains in SE half of state.
	Desert: Creosote bush, mesquite, tarbush, catclaw, paloverdes, bur-sages, cacti, desert saltbush.	3-15" (76-381mn)	Plains & valleys of S third of state.

Table 2-2

Table 2-3: PLANTS RECOGNIZED IN ABO PASS, 1980-1984

TREES: (scientific names from Little 1950)

Pinon, *Pinus edulis.*

Ponderosa, *P. ponderosa.*

Juniper, *Juniperus monosperma,* commonly called
    "cedar".

Alligator Juniper, *J. deppeana.*

Salt Cedar (Tamarisk), *Tamarix pentandra,* restricted
    to entrenched sections of Abo Arroyo (see
    Robinson 1965: A4).

Cottonwood, *Populus* sp., restricted to Abo Arroyo and
    a few tributaries.

GRASSES:

Sacaton, restricted to alluvial bottoms.

Unidentified short grasses.

CACTUS: (scientific names from Earle 1963).

Cholla, *Cylindropuntia imbricata.*

Prickly pear, nopal, *Opuntia* cf. *compressa.*

Claret Cup Hedgehog, *Echinocereus trialochidiatus.*

Whitespined Claret Cup, *E. melanacanthus.*

OTHER: (scientific names from N.N. Dodge 1967, Dodge and
    Janish 1964, Patraw and Janish 1953).

Cattails.

Ground Cherry, *Physalis* cf. *fendleri.*

Wild Gourd, *Cucurbita* cf. *foetidissima.*

Goatsbeard, *Tragopogon dubius.*

Four O'Clock, *Mirabilis* cf. *multiflora.*

Broad-Leaf Yucca, *Yucca baccata.*

Narrow-Leaf Yucca, *Y.* cf. *elata.*

Beargrass, *Nolina* sp.

Fourwing Saltbush, *Atriplex canescens.*

Mormon Tea, *Ephedra* sp.

Juniper Mistletoe, *Phoradendron juniperinum.*

Sagebrush, *Artemisia* cf. *tridentata.*

Hollygrape, *Berberis fremontii.*

Table 2-3   Dock, *Rumex* sp.

Table 2-4: ANIMALS SEEN BY AUTHOR IN ABO PASS, 1980-1985

* = domesticated animal

MAMMALS: (scientific names from Hall and Kelson 1959).
    Horse, Equus caballus.*
    Cattle, Bos taurus.*
    Sheep, Ovis aries.*
    Goats, Capra sp.*
    Pronghorn, Antilocapra americana, also in Chupadera
        Basin.
    White-tailed Deer, Odocoileus (Dama) virginianus, only
        in Chupadera Basin.
    Dog, Canis familiaris.*
    Coyote, C. latrans.
    Domestic Cat, Felis domesticus.*
    Bobcat, Lynx rufus, tracks only.
    Kangaroo Rats and/or Jumping Mice, Dipodomys sp.
        and/or Zapus sp.
    Mice, Perognathus sp. and/or Reithrodontomys sp.
        and/or Onychomys sp.
    Mice, Peromyscus sp.
    Packrats, Neotoma sp., nests very common.
    Porcupine, Erethizon dorsatum.
    Ground Squirrels, Spermophilus sp.
    Cottontails, Sylvilagus sp.
    Jackrabbits, Lepus californicus, very common.
    Bats.
REPTILES: (scientific names from Stebbins 1954).
    Diamond-back Rattlesnake, Crotalus atrox.
    Prairie Rattlesnake, C. viridis.
    Bullsnake, Pituophis catenifer.
    Garter Snake, Thamnophis sp.
    Collared Lizard, Crotaphytus collaris.
    Whiptail Lizard, Cnemidophorus sp.
    Swift (Lizard), Sceloporus sp.
    Sonoran Skink, Eumeces obsoletus.
    Horned Toad, Phrynosoma sp.
    Ornate Box Turtle, Terrapene ornata, only in Chupadera
        Basin.
AMPHIBIANS: (scientific names from Stebbins 1954).
    Toads, Bufo sp.
FISH: (scientific names from Koster 1957).
    Goldfish, Carassius auratus, only in stock tanks.*
BIRDS: (scientific names from Hubbard 1978).
    Domestic Chicken, Gallus gallus.*
    Canada Goose, Branta canadensis.
    Mourning Dove, Zenaida macroura.
    Roadrunner, Geococcyx californianus.
    Raven, Corvus corax.
    Mockingbird, Mimus polyglottos.
    Pinon Jay, Gymnorhinus cyanocephalus.
    Nighthawk, Chordeiles minor.
    Kildeer, Charadrius vociferus, migratory.
    Barn Swallow, Hirundo rustica, nested at Harbert House
        in 1982.
    Turkey Vulture, Cathartes aura, nested near Tenabo
        in 1981.
    Redtailed Hawk, Buteo jamaicensis.
    Long-eared Owl, Asio otus, nested at Abo in 1983.
    Humming birds.
INSECTS AND SPIDERS:

Red and Black Ants	Centipedes
Bumblebee	Red (Fire) Ants
Praying Mantis	Gnats, near water
Small Black Ants	Mosquitos (rare)
Stink Beetle	Scorpions
Yellowjacket Wasps	Wolf Spider
Grasshoppers	House Flies
Antlion	Velvet Ants
Horse Flies	Daddy-Longlegs Spider
Tarantula	June Bugs
Millipedes	Cicadas.

Table 2-4

41

Recent Ecological Changes

Before discussing paleoenvironments it is necessary to point out that significant changes in the environment have occurred since AD 1850, which changes must be recognized so that it is clearly understood that the present is but a cracked and pitted mirror of the past.

One of the salient features of the present Southwestern landscape is the entrenched arroyo. However, this ubiquitous feature has become common only since about AD 1880, as has been well documented (see Bryan 1925, 1928a), and has been generally blamed on over-grazing by livestock and other land abuses associated with accelerated settlement of the Southwest after the American Conquest of 1846. (See R.W. Bailey 1935, Antevs 1952.) Once started, arroyo trenching of an alluvial deposit lowers the watertable, leading to desiccation of the soil and elimination of plant species that are sensitive to water-stress. (Bryan 1928b). As only aggradation (filling of the arroyos with new alluvium) can restore a higher watertable, the ecological change is not one that can be reversed simply by reduction or cessation of grazing. (Leopold 1951: 295)

In Abo Pass the main drainage channel, Abo Arroyo, is entrenched throughout its whole length. However, the largest tributary, Canon Saladito, which drains a large portion of the south side of Abo Pass, has been protected from total entrenchment by a concrete spillway constructed by the Santa Fe Railway just north of their trestle across the arroyo of Canon Saladito. Thus protected, Canon Saladito shows an interesting series of alternating entrenched and aggraded areas. Other tributaries that are not protected, such as Canon Espinosa, are entrenched like the main Abo arroyo. Neither Abert in 1846 (1848L77), nor Carleton in 1853 (1855: 299-300), nor yet Bandelier in 1883 (Lange and Riley 1970: 16-18) mention any entrenching of Abo Arroyo during their journeys through Abo Pass, suggesting that entrenchment may post-date 1883.

The fifteen-year drought of 1942–1956 (Thomas et alia 1963) has been blamed for the die-off of pinon pine (*Pinus edulis*) from the immediate vicinity of Tenabo (LA 200) in the early 1950s, leaving only the more drought-resistant junipers (*Juniperus monosperma*). Evidence of the recent present of the pinon at Tenabo is found archaeologically in the nutshells located in rodent burrows in the roomblocks. Pinon seedlings in the vicinity of the ruin suggest that this tree is in the process of natural reintroduction. An Old World tree, the salt cedar (*Tamarix pentandra*) has spread itself throughout western North America since about 1890

(see Robinson 1965) and is found in Abo Pass along Abo Arroyo.

Two major animals, the bison (*Bison bison*) and Merriam's elk (*Cervus merriama*) have become extinct in central New Mexico since 1850. First domestic sheep (*Ovis aries*) and then domestic cattle (*Bos Taurus*) have been introduced during the past century. A definite effect of grazing is the denuding of the pinon-juniper woodland of Abo Pass of its natural shrub understory. The forest itself has been destroyed in some areas through chaining and other "land management" practices which in theory should increase grass yield, but frequently merely accelerate erosion of the soil.

The overall effect of arroyo entrenchment, recent natural drought, heavy grazing use, and dubious land management practices is the impoverishment of the floral and faunal community to a low state probably never witnessed by the American Indians in the past.

Historical Descriptions of the Climate

Spanish descriptions of the climate of New Mexico during the Sixteenth and Seventeenth centuries uniformly complain of great seasonal temperature variations: bitter cold in winter and extreme heat in summer. These records begin with the Vazquez de Coronado Expedition of 1540–1542:

1) Referring to the Tiguex area (between modern Albuquerque and Bernalillo), Pedro de Castaneda comments in the Spring of 1541: "the ice in the river (Rio Grande) was thawing, after being frozen for almost four months, during which it was possible to cross over the ice on horseback." (Hammond and Rey 1940: 234)

2) The Relacion Postrera de Cibola states: "The land is extremely cold, and the river (Rio Grande) freezes so hard that laden animals cross over it, and carts could cross also." (Hammond and Rey 1940: 309) The Espejo Expedition of 1582–1583 also reported cold winter conditions.

3) On January 23, 1583, at a locality about 14 leagues (36.4 miles) north of the modern city of El Paso, was "a place we named La Cienega Helada (The Frozen Marsh), a marsh formed by the river. It was frozen so hard that it was necessary to break the ice with bars and picks in order to get drinking water." (Hammond and Rey 1966: 170) The colonists of the Onate expedition were particularly unhappy with the local climatic conditions.

4) Captain Luis de Velasco, in a letter to the viceroy of New Spain dated March 22, 1601, complained thus: "The cold is so intense that the rivers freeze over, and it snows most of the time during the winter, which lasts eight long months. After this there follows heat so oppressive that it rivals burning fire. It has driven us from our houses and forced us to sleep outdoors." (Hammond and Rey 1953: 610)

5) On July 30, 1601, in Mexico City, Gines de Herrera Horta testified: "he also saw snowfalls, for during the winter that he spent there (New Mexico) it snowed heavily. The cold is intense that drinking water must be heated over the fire, as this witness often found it frozen. He has seen the Rio del Norte (Rio Grande) and two arroyos near the camp of San Gabriel frozen over for most of their width." Several persons told him that they had crossed the river on horseback when it was completely frozen. (Hammond and Rey 1953: 645)

6) On July 31, 1601, in Mexico City, Captain Juan De Ortega testified that "the land is short of water, even in summer, as it rains but little. The greatest relief from the lack of moisture comes from the snow, of which there is a great deal. It moistens the soil." At the time that this witness was there, which was before and during Christmas, he saw the snow, as he has stated. The cold was so severe that the river (Rio Grande) froze and they crossed it on horseback in one place. (Hammond and Rey 1953: 661)

7) Nearly thirty years later Fray Alonso de Benavides, who had been custodian in New Mexico from 1626 to 1629, gave the following description: "The temperature is by extremes; for the winter is very rigorous and of so many snows, frosts…and old… that all the rivers, sloughs, and even the Rio del Norte freeze in (such) manner that (people) pass over them with loaded wagons, and very large bands of cattle at full speed, as if it were over very firm ground…everything is so frozen that to make a grave in the church, a fire is first built on top (of the earthen floor) that it may thaw it…and so every winter many Indians are frozen in the country and man Spaniards have their ears, feet, and hands frozen. And on the contrary, in summer the heat is more intolerable than the cold in winter." (Ayer 1916: 38-39)

8) In 1692, during his return journey from the successful reconquest of New Mexico, Don Diego de Vargas records the following: "Today, Tuesday, the ninth of the present month of December…I set out in a snowstorm from the said place (at the foot of the Sierra de Socorro) to look for the pueblo of Socorro, which was close at hand…Today, Wednesday, the tenth of the present month of December…I arrived at this place, on this side (west side) of the Rio del Norte, which, due to the severe cold, was found partially frozen over today. And in view of and a short distance from, the pueblo of Senecu, I made camp…" (J. M. Espinosa 1940: 246, 247)

9) And so on into the 18th century when Bishop Tamaron wrote the following description during the 1750s: "This river (Rio Grande) freezes in many years…in New Mexico, and (the inhabitants) pass over the ice on horseback and with carts." (Tamaron y Romeral 1937: 328)[3]

The above statements concerning the freezing of the Rio Grande and its adjacent marshes would startle present-day inhabitants of the Rio Grande Valley who are used to considerably milder winters and take them for granted as part of the natural order of things in their part of the world. Clearly, the above historical testimony indicates a significantly different climatic regime during the Spanish Colonial Period than at present.

Climatic Differences as Indicated by Scientific Studies

Recognition of the present cycle of arroyo cutting (see above) soon led to identification of earlier periods of entrenchment as recorded in the sediments of Southwestern valleys and canyons. (R.W. Bailey 1935, Hack 1942: 45-59, Bryan 1941: 226-231) Bryan (1941) demonstrated that these periods of entrenchment were synchronous throughout the Southwest (Table 2-5). His sequence of erosional and depositional events has been validated by more recent studies, with some elaboration. (See Miller and Wendorf 1958, Martin 1963: 61-68, S.A. Hall 1977: 1593–1598.) As to causes of the erosional and depositional events, there has been no consensus (see discussion in Bryan 1941: 232-237), with recent scholars reading contradictory erosion-triggering mechanisms from the same paleoenvironmental data. (See Martin 1963: 61-68 and Antevs 1962 for opposing views.)

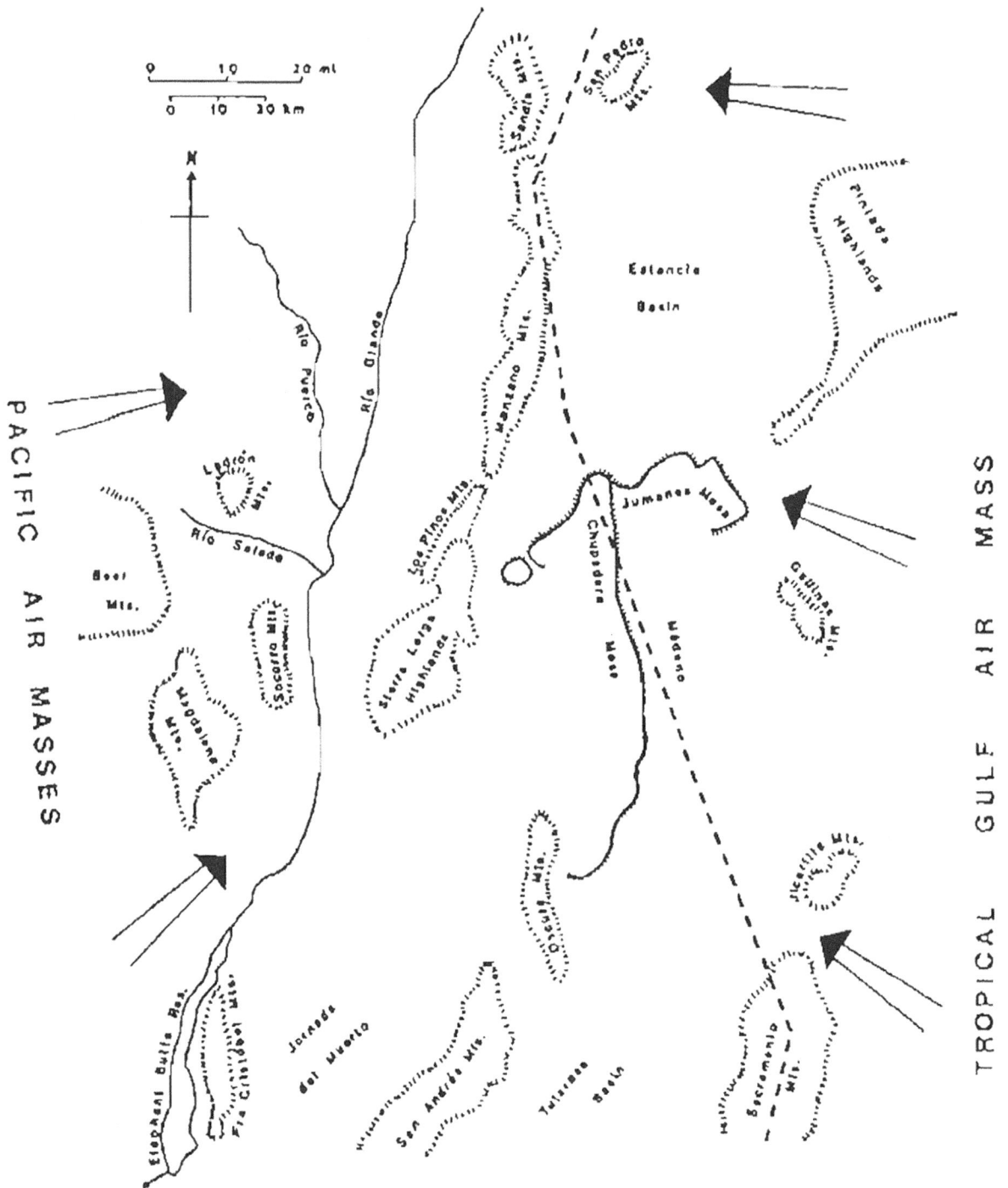

0 10 20 ml

0 10 20 km

N

PACIFIC AIR MASSES

TROPICAL GULF AIR MASS

Rio Puerco

Rio Grande

Estancia Basin

San Pedro Mts.

Sandia Mts.

Pinleda Highlands

Ladron Mts.

Rio Salado

Manzano Mts.

Jumanes Mesa

Chupadera Mesa

Gallinas Mts.

Bear Mts.

Socorro Mts.

Los Pinos Mts.

Sierra Larga Highlands

Madano

Magdalena Mts.

Jornada del Muerto

Oscura Mts.

Jicarilla Mts.

Elephant Butte Res.

Fra Cristobal Mts.

San Andres Mts.

Talbanae Basin

Sacramento Mts.

DORROH'S EASTERN AND WESTERN CLIMATIC ZONES

Figure 2-5

Figure 2-5

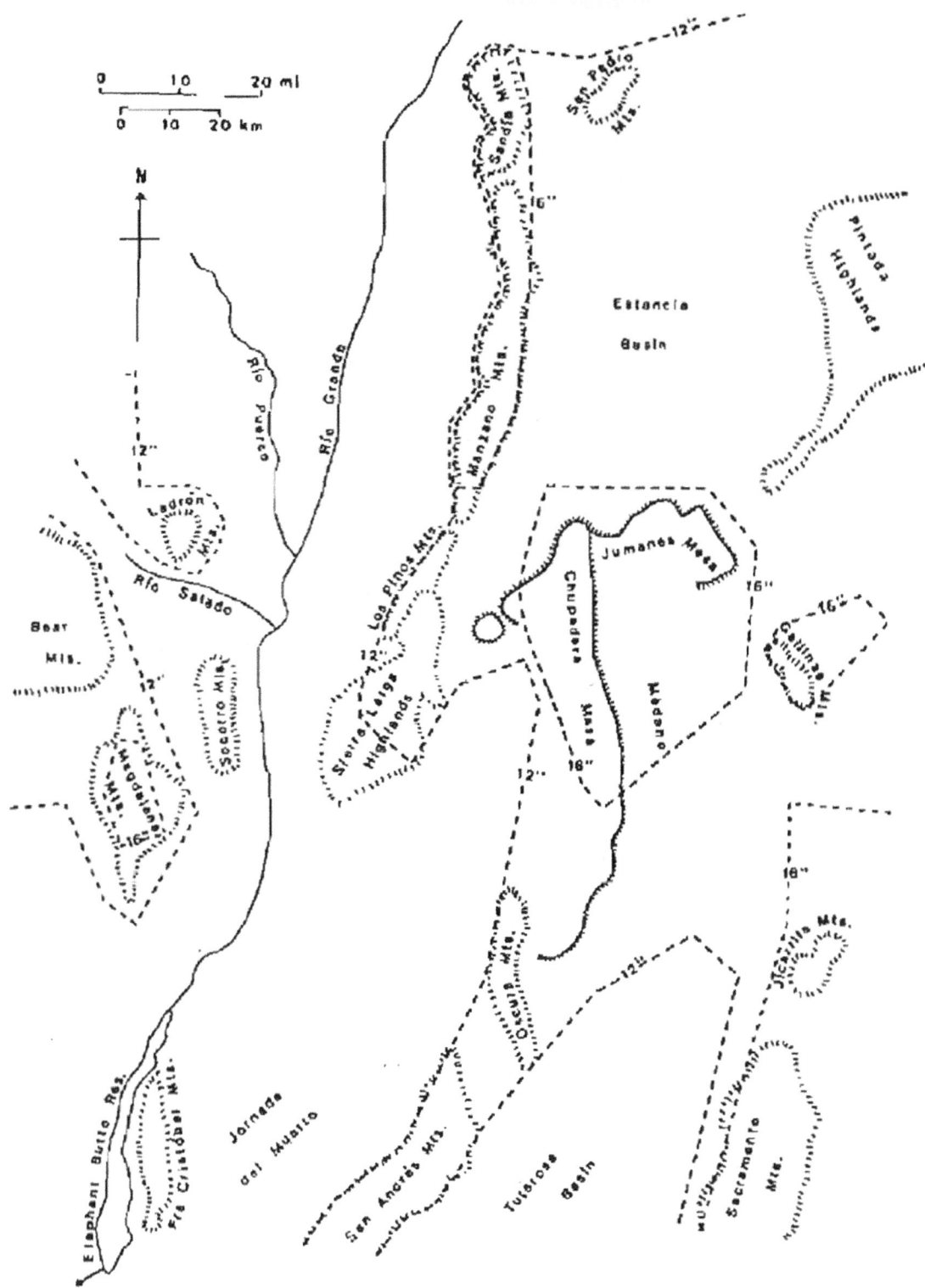

AVERAGE ANNUAL PRECIPITATION

(in inches)

Figure 2-6

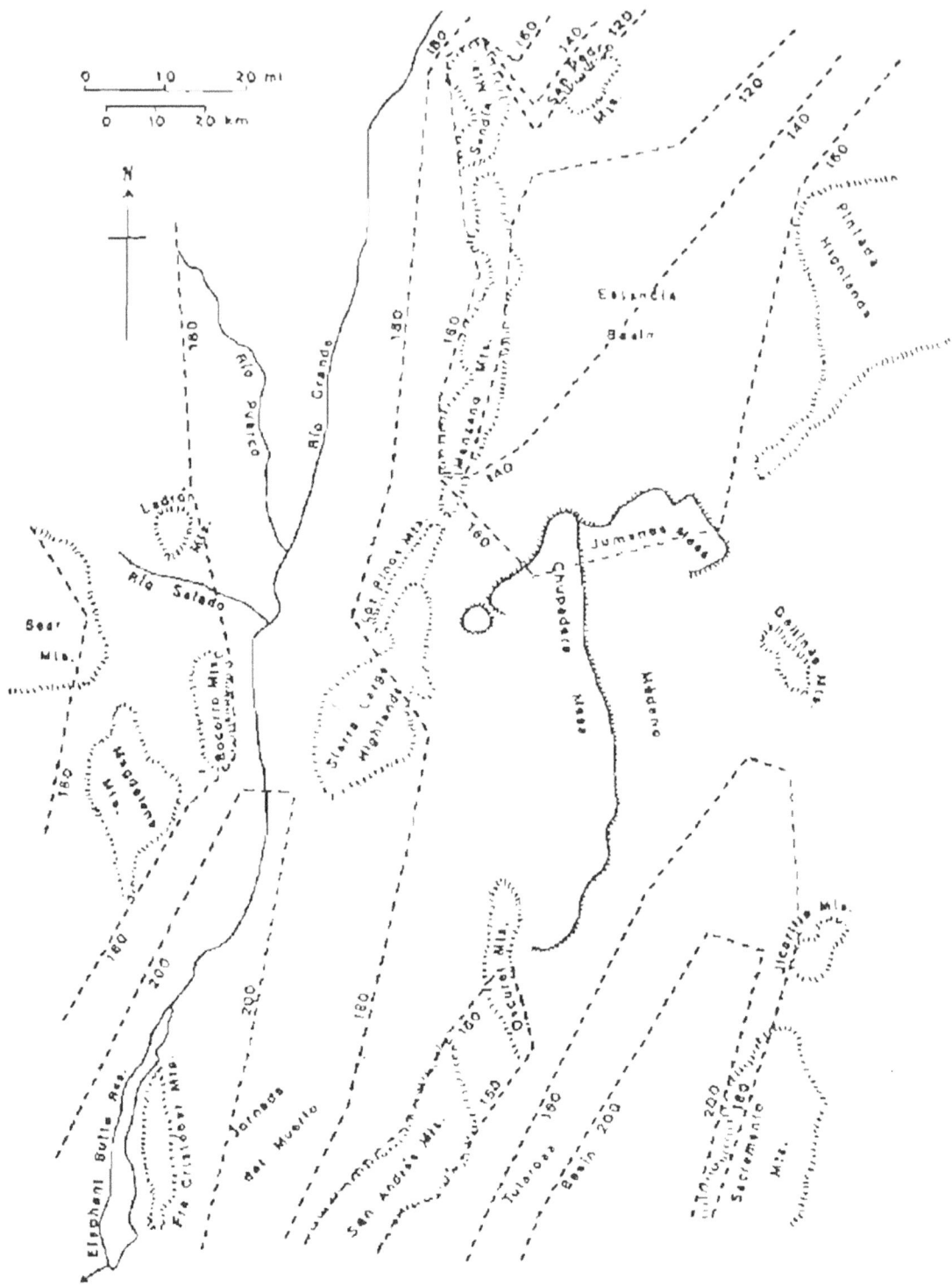

GROWING SEASON LENGTH

(average number of days between frosts)

Figure 2-7   (based on Map 3 in Cordell 1979)

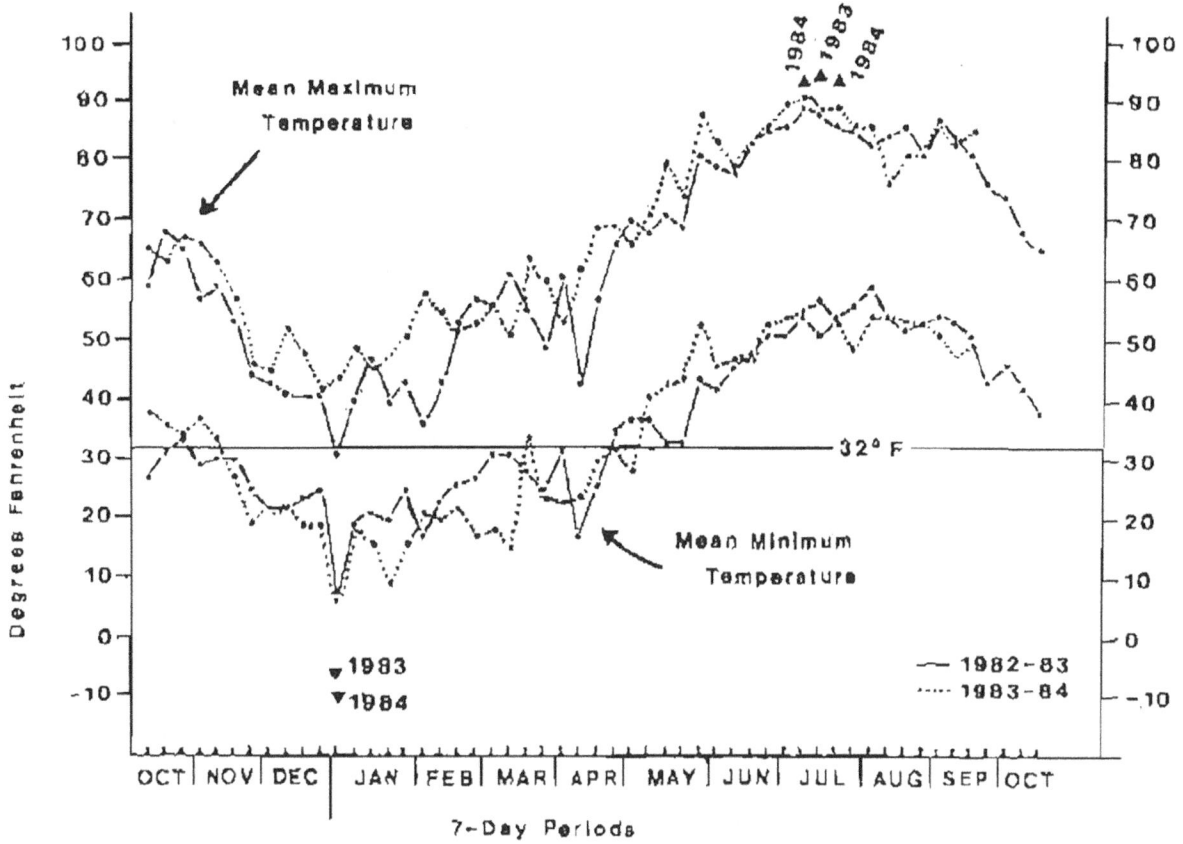

MOUNTAINAIR TEMPERATURE RECORDS

1982-1984 Records from U.S. Forest Service Station, Mountainair

▼ winter extreme low   ▲ summer extreme high

Figure

2-8

Figure 2-8

Table 2-5: PERIODS OF EROSION AND ALLUVIATION

(Based on Table 1 in Bryan 1941: 228-229)

PERIOD	DATE	CHARACTERISTICS
Erosion III	A.D. 1860/1900 to present	Present day arroyo cutting
Deposition III	ca. A.D. 1300 to 1860	Alluviation burying erosion channels
Erosion II	ca. A.D. 1100 to 1300	Arroyos similar to present day features
Deposition II	undated	May represent two or more alluvial periods
Erosion I	undated	Arroyos larger than in Erosion Periods II and III
Deposition I	undated	Alluvium containing extinct fauna (proboscidean & horse)

Table 2-5

Table 2-6: CLIMATIC PERIODS ACCORDING TO SCHOENWETTER

	WEATHER REGIME	MOISTURE REGIME	EVENTS
A.D. 2000	Short Winters:	Relatively dry:	
1900	mild.	Summer-dominant	
1800	Long Winters:	Relatively Moist:	
1700	colder.	Winter-dominant	
1600			
1500			
1400			
1300			"Great Drought"
1200	Short Winters:	Moisture regime	– moist
1100	mild.	like present-day.	period
1000		(relatively dry:	– moist
900		summer-dominant	period
800		precipitation).	
700			
600	Long Winters:	Relatively Moist:	
500	colder.	Winter dominant	
400		precipitation.	
300			
A.D. 200			– Drought

Table 2-6

Palynological data has been brought to bear on pa-leo-climatic problems in the Southwest (for a brief overview of early evidence see Mehringer 1967), but most efforts have been oriented towards paleoenvironments of 2,000 B.P. to 12,000 B.P., which are mainly outside the purview of the present study. Of more immediate value are Schoenwetter's findings. (Schoenwetter 1966, Schoenwetter and Dittert 1968), which are illustrated in Table 2-6. Schoenwetter interprets the pollen record during the past 2,000 years as showing an alternating series of weather regimes character-ized on the one hand by long, cold winters and winter-dom-inant precipitation, and on the other by short, mild winters and summer-dominant precipitation. He further links summer-dominant precipitation, in the form of high-energy rain storms, to erosion cycles, but notes that local conditions caused great variation. (Schoenwetter and Dittert 1968: 49)

Tree-rings have been utilized extensively in the Southwest as a source of chronological information, but they also provide environmental information since ring-width of conifers in arid climates is most strongly effected by available moisture. Climatic summaries based on ten-year averaged periods of tree-ring data are presents for western North America from AD 1501 to 1940 in Fritts (1965: 432-442). These summaries are records of relative wetness versus dryness and do not refer to other climatic factors, such as temperature variations. Since these are averaged periods, they are less useful for archaeological interpretations than are year-by-year indices of tree-growth.

Such a year-by-year tree-ring record is available for the Upper Rio Grande Valley in Smiley, Stubbs and Bannister. (1953: 54-55). This record spans the years AD 908 through 1900. The record for the two hundred years from AD 1500 through 1700 is presented in Chapter 7. As is demonstrated there, there is a good correlation between historically recorded droughts and low tree-ring indices in the AD 1500–1700 record. Presumably such a correlation would hold for the other centuries as well.

Considering the various evidences noted above, it is significant that the historical records, Bryan's most recent period of alluviation, and Schoenwetter's period of win-ter-dominant precipitation from AD 1300 to 1850 all cor-relate positively with the period of glacial advance in Europe and North America known as the Little Ice Age. (See Denton and Karlén 1973.) However, the alluvial and precipitation variations proposed for the earlier portion of the Christian era do not show such a straight-forward correlation with climatic events elsewhere in the world.

Notes:

1. "Eight months of winter and four of Hell."
2. I make no claim to be a competent botanist or zoologist.
3. In the original Spanish: "este rio se hiela muchos anos...en el Nuevo Mexico, y pasan sobre el hielo a caballo y con carretas..."

3

Prehistory in the Southwest and the Salinas Province

This chapter provides a context for understanding the place of the Salinas Province within Southwestern history and prehistory and the place of this project within research on the Salinas Province.

Research Trends in Southwestern Prehistory

Archaeological research in the Southwest began in the 1890s with the large, impressive ruins on the Colorado Plateau and in the northern basin of the Rio Grande. Other areas of southern and western Arizona, Utah west of the Colorado River, most of Colorado, central-southern-eastern New Mexico, West Texas, the Mexican part of the Southwest were unknown and attracted only sporadic interest before ca. 1930. As a consequence, early Southwestern archaeological concepts were almost entirely based on remains of the Anasazi Culture.

Archaeological work at Pecos, on the Pajarito Plateau, and among the Hopi Mesas had made clear the cultural connection between the historic Pueblo Indians and the prehistoric remains at Chaco Canyon, Mesa Verde and elsewhere in the San Juan Basin. It is not surprising, then, that at the time of the Pecos Conference in 1927 the Southwest as a culture area was thought of in terms of a single prehistoric culture, the Anasazi, and that the Pecos System of chronological periods (Table 3-1) was visualized as classifying developments essentially universal in time and space within the Southwest. This conception was supported by concurrent ethnographic concepts of culture areas in North America, where each "culture area" had a developmental center that was a dominant innovative influence throughout its particular culture area. (Wissler 1923, 1926) Within the Southwest, Chaco Canyon was the obvious candidate for being this developmental center.[1]

Shortly after this understanding had been reached and the Pecos System set up, new archaeological work in the 1930s demonstrated that areas south of the Colorado Plateau had been occupied by two major prehistoric cultures that were distinct from the Anasazi: the Hohokam and the Mogollon. (Haury 1932, 1936) Nor did the subdivision of the Southwest stop there: soon smaller prehistoric cultures were recognized in central and western Arizona, including the Sinagua and Patayan (the Yuman Cultures), and a larger one in Utah. i.e. the Fremont. (See Figure 3-1.) Hand in hand with this cultural fragmentation of the Southwest culture areas, tree-ring dating demonstrated synchronic regional heterogeneity within first the Anasazi, and then within the other cultures as well. A general trend, then, has been away from normative conceptions of archaeological cultures and prehistoric sequences and toward recognition of unexpected variations over both time and space. Symptomatic of this was Wendorf's (1954) proposal of a separate chronological sequence for the northern Rio Grande region. (Table 3-1)

I suspect that this process of reassessment of cultural relationships has not yet run its course. For example, it has been suggested that the regional unit known as the Jornada Branch of the Mogollon Culture should be separated from the Mogollon. (See Wiseman 1983: 17-19.) Personally, I favor this and have used the term "Jornada Culture" instead of Jornada Branch throughout this study. Likewise, the area of central New Mexico labeled with a question mark in Figure 3-1 may or may not contain other as yet undefined prehistoric cultural entities, rather than simply being a "borderland" between the Mogollon and Anasazi cultures. This questionable "borderland" includes the Salinas Province to the east, the Piro area in the center, and the Magdalena-Cebolleta areas to the west.

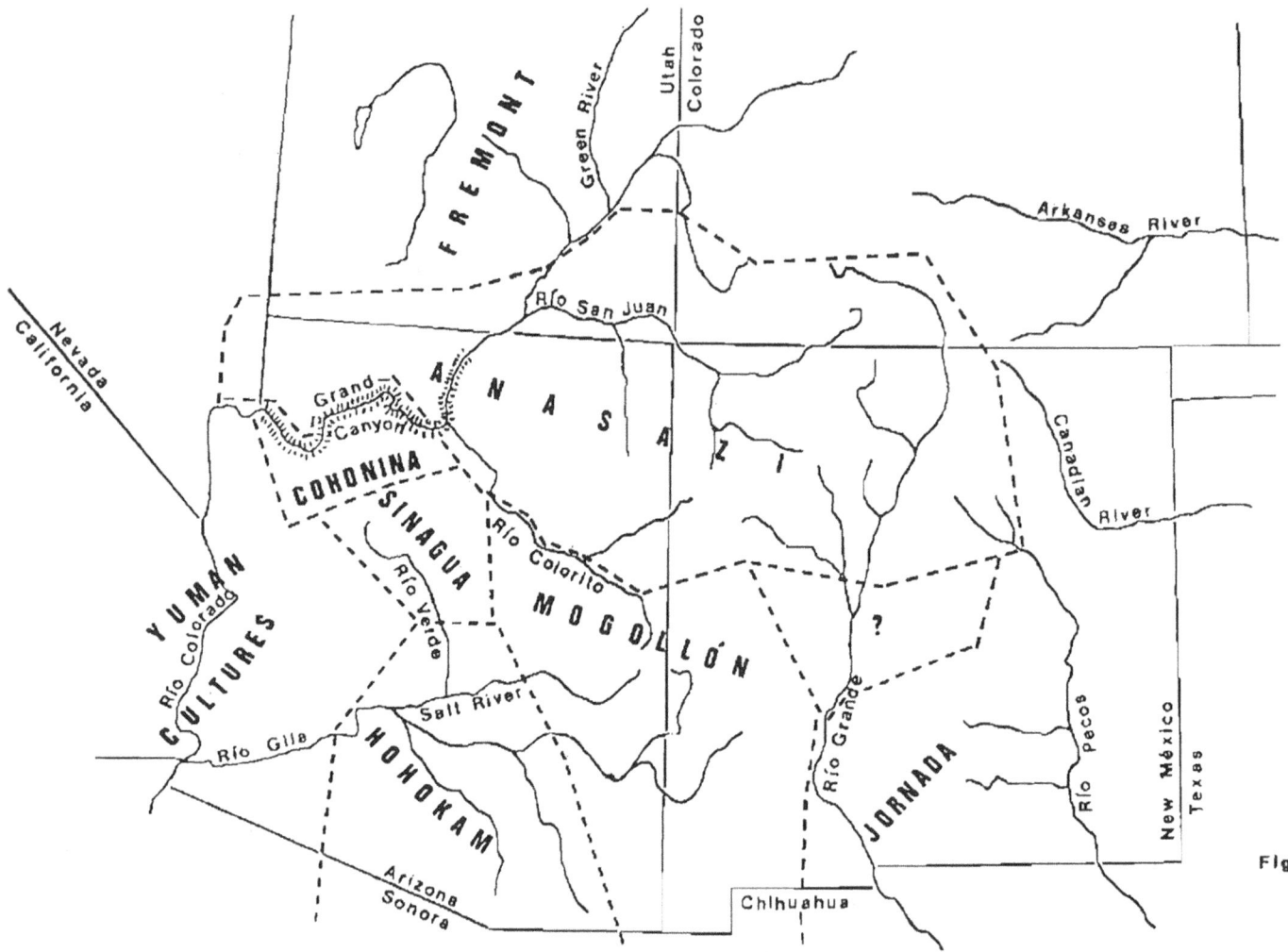

Figure 3-1

Table 3-1: MAJOR CHRONOLOGICAL SEQUENCES

Time	PECOS SYSTEM (Kidder 1927)	RIO GRANDE SEQUENCE (Wendorf 1954)	JORNADA PHASES (Lehmer 1948) NORTH	SOUTH
A.D.1900	Pueblo V	Historic Period		
1800				
1700				
1600				
1500	Pueblo IV	Classic Period		
1400			San Andres	El Paso
1300		Coalition Period		
1200	Pueblo III		3 Rivers	Doña Ana
1100				
1000	Pueblo II		Capitan	Mesilla
900		Developmental Period		
800	Pueblo I		Hueco	
700				
600	Basketmaker III			
500		Preceramic Period		
300	Basketmaker II			
A.D. 1				

Table 3-1

Summary of Anasazi-Mogollon Culture History

The following is a very brief, impressionistic prepis of Anasazi-Mogollon culture history meant to serve as background for the discussion of Pueblo IV and the Salinas Province given below. The Hohokam, Fremont, Sinagua, Patayan, and developments in the Mexican portion of the Southwest are not covered, as they do not have immediate bearing upon Pueblo IV and the Salinas Province. Lengthier summaries with more citations can be found in Reed (1949, 1950), Wendorf (1954), Wendorf and Reed (1955), Ellis (1967), Trager (1967), Ford, Schroeder and Peckham (1972), and Mackey (1977).

AD 1–1150: This period of time can be considered as a period of mainly in situ development for the Anasazi and Mogollon cultures. Movement was mainly by individuals or small groups, and principally for the purposes of trade rather than resettlement. Cultural changes were relatively slow during the first 500 years within both cultures, with the diffusion of pottery-making from the Mogollon to the Anasazi being the main cross-cultural development.

After AD 500 the Central Anasazi entered a period of rapid cultural evolution that was copied to some extent by the Western Anasazi and the Largo-Gallina Anasazi, but had less direct effect upon the Rio Grande Anasazi. These geographic divisions of the Anasazi Culture probably reflect ethno-linguistic groups: The Western Anasazi being the Hopis, the Central Anasazi being Keresans, the Largo-Gallina Anasazi being Towas, and the Rio Grande Anasazi being Tiwas. (See Figure 3-2.)

Also, heavily influenced by Central Anasazi developments were the Mogollon peoples of which only the division living in east central Arizona can be identified with an ethno-linguistic group: the Zunis. (See Reed 1950.) Indeed, by AD 1000 the Mogollon had adopted so many Anasazi characteristics that a separate Mogollon entity could hardly be said to exist.

As part of Central Anasazi developments, the Chaco Phenomenon emerged by ca. AD 1000 and collapsed by ca. AD 1130. This collapse triggered the first major abandonments in the Anasazi Culture, although these may have been site abandonments more than territorial abandonments. It is possible, though, that a first wave of Keresan refugees into the Rio Grande region originated from the ruins of the Chaco Phenomenon, however small that wave might have been.

AD 1150–1300: While in situ development continued in some areas, such as Mesa Verde, population shifts of various sizes marked this period of time and culminated in the last quarter century with abandonments of large tracts of territory. There is still no agreement or certainty as to the causes of this final large scale departure of the Anasazi from territories held by them for over a millennium.

Most of the refugees seem to have gravitated towards the northern Rio Grande basin. The Largo-Gallina Anasazi moved a short distance southeast to become the Jemez. (Mackey 1977) The Keresans moved south and east into their historic territories, with some elements of their population apparently joining the Hopis along the southern fringe of Black Mesa. Other Keresans apparently were taken into Tiwa communities in the Galisteo and Tewa basins in numbers so large that the native Tiwa speech was pidginized, resulting in a new language known as Tewa. (See Trager 1967, who would reverse the roles of the Tiwa and Keres.)

AD 1300–1525: This period marks the last major population movements of the series beginning ca. AD 1130: the movement of the Zunis from east central Arizona a short distance northeast to their historic location. The mixing of peoples caused by the migrations during the preceding period seems to have produced a Grand Synthesis of the Disparate Anasazi groups and an impressive cultural florescence.

AD 1525–1700: A new period of change may have begun in 1525 with the possible occurrence of the first epidemic of European-introduced smallpox. This was followed by the Vazquez de Coronado Expedition of 1540–1542, the Spanish explorations of the 1580s, and Spanish colonization of New Mexico in 1598. Almost simultaneously, the Apacheans appeared from the northeast and quickly spread into uninhabited areas surrounding the Pueblo Indians. Distribution of the native language groups ca. AD 1600 is shown in Figure 3-3. Caught between the Spaniards and the Apacheans, the Pueblo Indians lost their independence and declined in numbers. (See Chapter 7.) After staging several abortive revolts against Spanish rule, the Pueblo Revolt of 1680 succeeded in freeing the Pueblo Indians for 12 years. The revolt and its aftermath resulted in the displacement of the Piros, Tompiros, Southern Tiwas, and Tanos.

AD 1700–1846: By 1700 the reestablishment of Spanish rule had been accomplished (except over the Hopis) and an accommodation was reached between Spaniards and Pueblo Indians that allowed peaceful co-existence thereafter. Pueblo Indian population stabilized at a low level. The Hopis retained their independence from the Spanish, and the Zunis a semi-independent status.

AD 1846-present: Conquest of the Southwest by the United States brought political and legal changes; also, the Hopis lost their independence. Pueblo Indian land holdings were recognized and guaranteed by the U.S. government, and encroachments on them by Hispanic settlers was halted. Modern medicine and other factors promoted a rise in Pueblo Indian population. Anthropological study began.

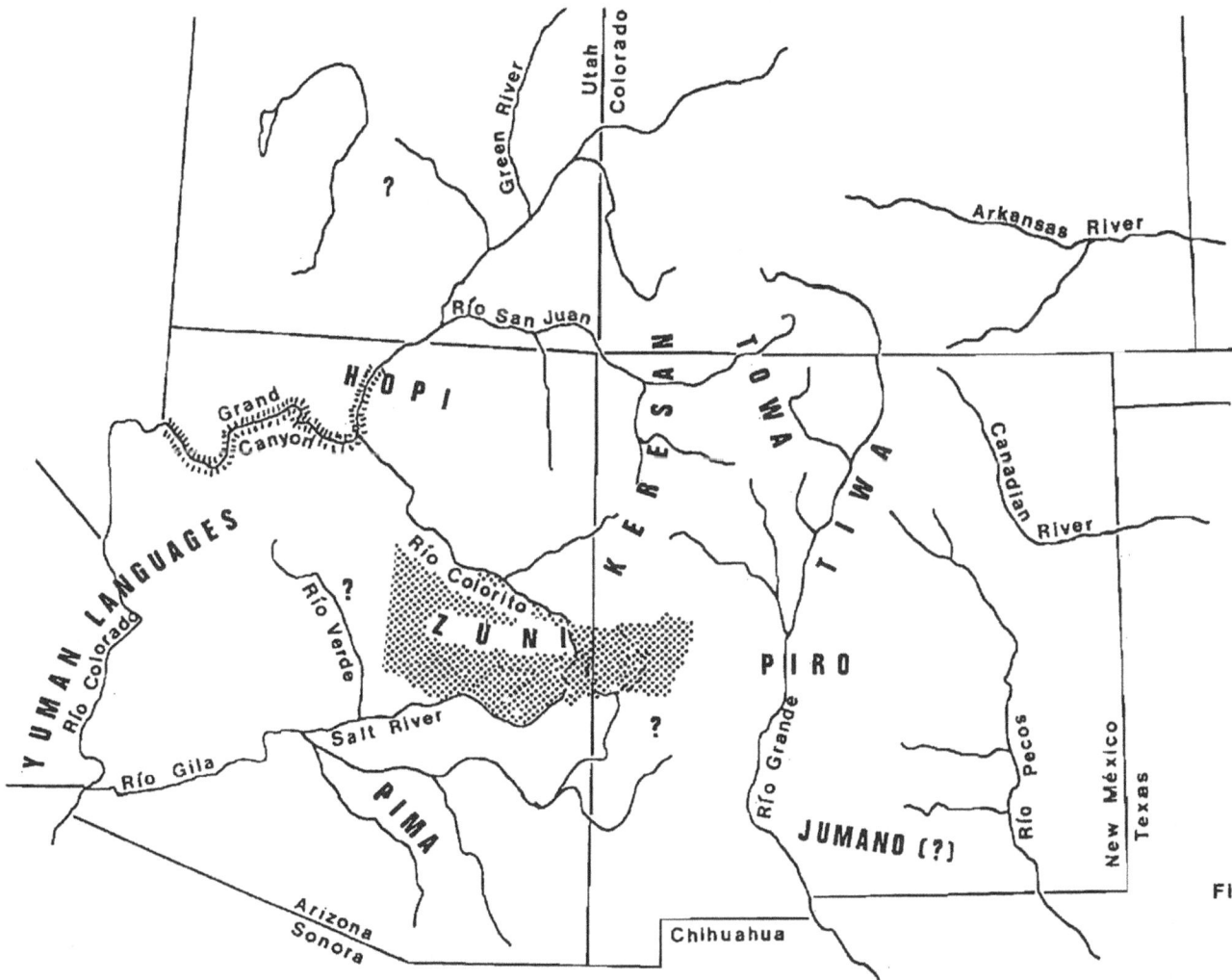

Figure 3-2

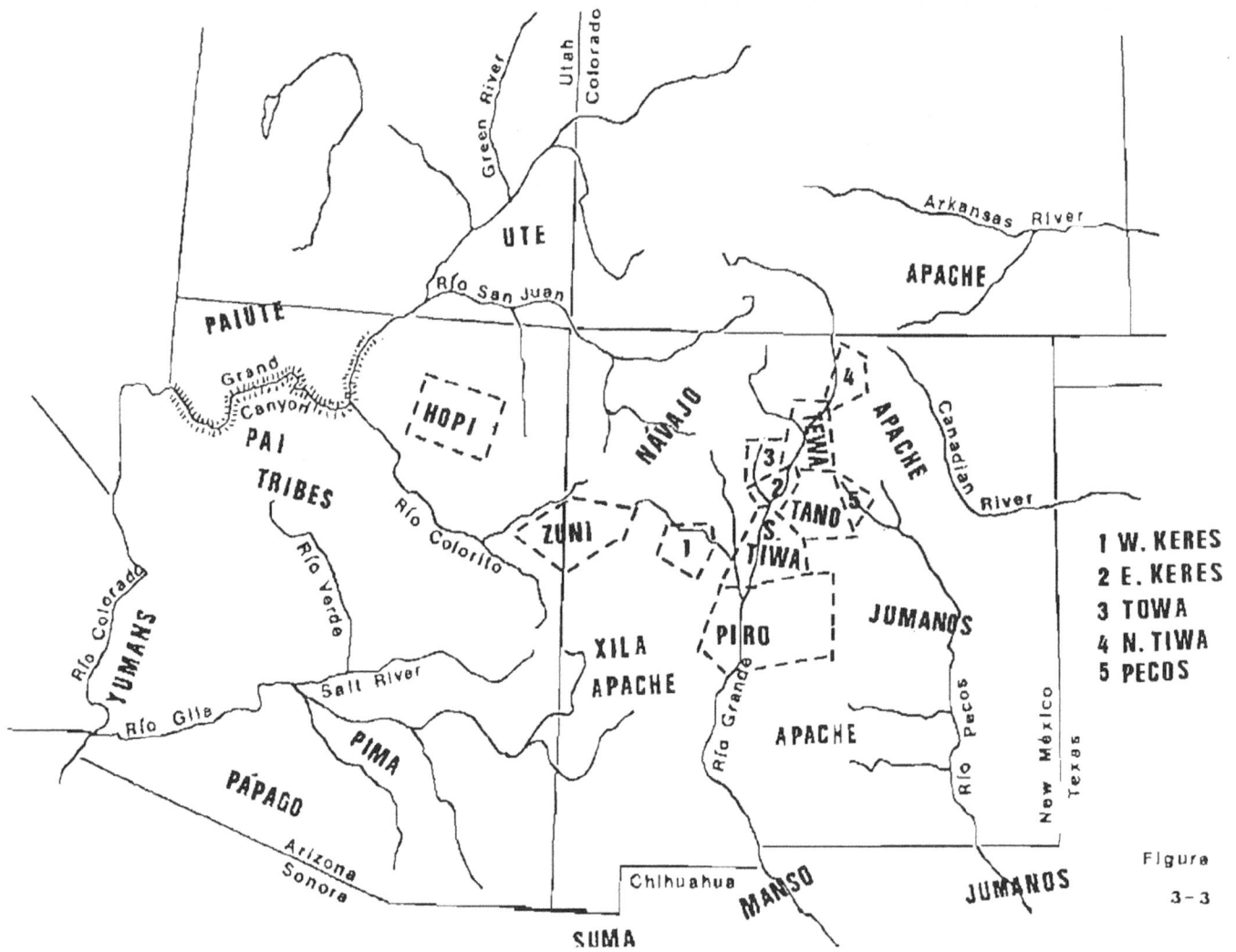

Figure 3-3

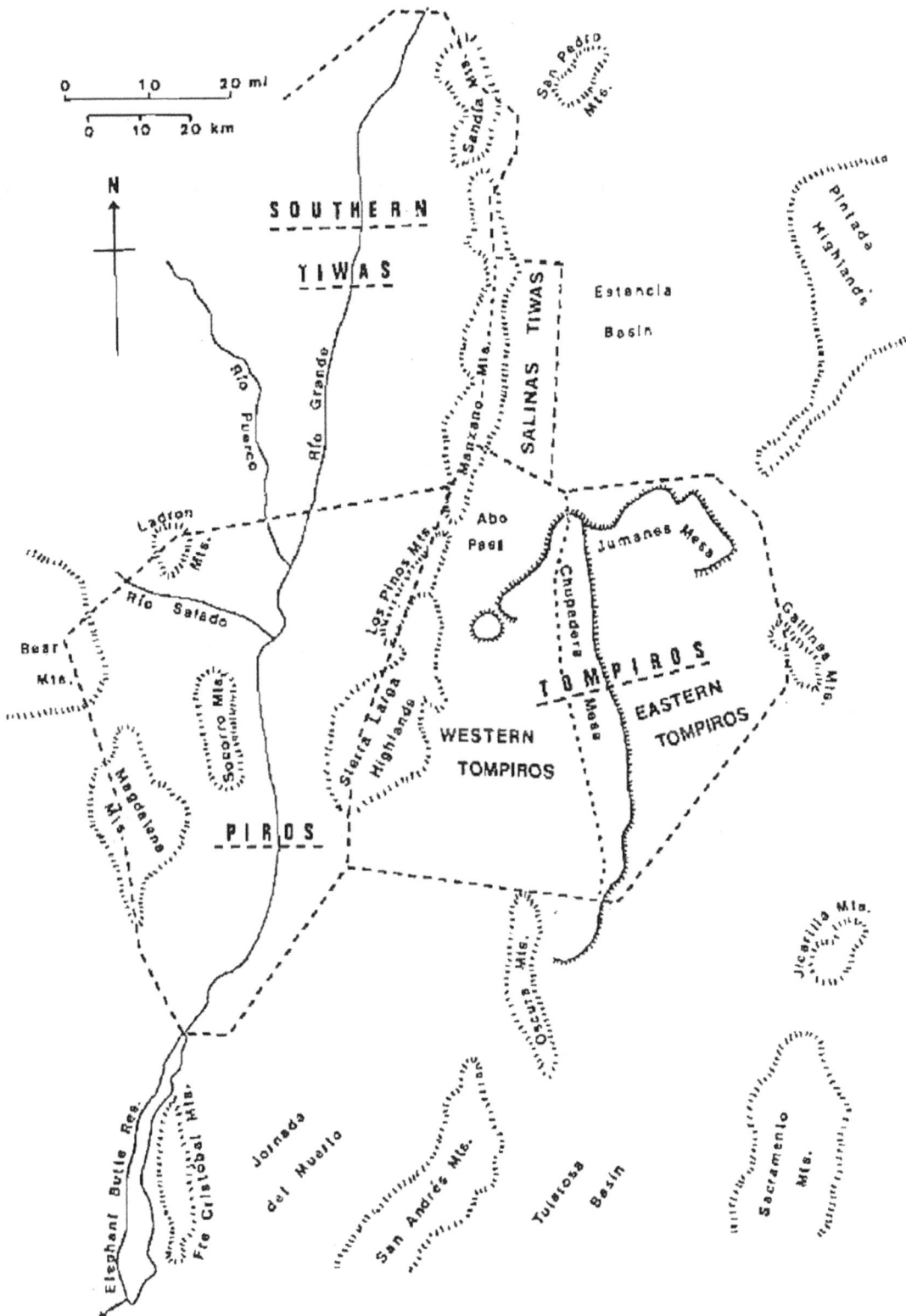

Figure 3-4

Pueblo IV: A Discussion

Pueblo IV is the Pecos System time period encompassing the four centuries from AD 1300–1700. It thus spans the transition from prehistory to history in the Southwest. Compared to most other time periods of the Pecos System, Pueblo IV has had relatively little research. It seems that, once early research at Pecos and on the Pajarito Plateau had established the cultural continuity between the historic Pueblo Indians and the prehistoric Anasazi, that Pueblo IV, was no longer considered important in terms of research problems. Since Pueblo IV material culture was so much like that of the historic Pueblo Indians, the attitude seems to have been "well, it's all the same, let the ethnographers study it!"

Historians, who were only concerned with documented periods, had no interest in times earlier than about AD 1539, and then concentrated on the history of the Spaniards, leaving the Indians to be a sort of background "given". Ethnographers, who should have followed Bandelier's lead in the use of historical documents as well as "ethnographic present" observations, failed to make more than desultory use of the historical sources available.

A new spate of archaeological work in Pueblo IV sites in the 1930s was only a means of putting the unemployed to work (i.e., WPA projects) and allotted no funds for analysis. Consequently, the results of most of these excavations have gone unreported.

Thus, Pueblo IV, and the first half of Pueblo V (AD 0700–1850), has been left a fallow field, abandoned or ignored for various reasons by all of those who should be taking an active interest in it.

Research Questions on Pueblo IV

The Immigration: archaeologists have spent much research time and spilt much ink over the problem of the cause of major abandonments during Pueblo III (AD 1100–1300). Little consideration has been given to what happened when the refugees produced by the abandonments arrived in the Rio Grande region and elsewhere. Consequently, there have been overlooked a whole range of questions of cultural events and processes that are critical for understanding how historic Pueblo Indian culture came to be what it was. Some of these questions are:

How were the refugees received when they appeared "on the doorstep" of the Rio Grande Anasazi? Were they admitted into existing communities, or turned away and forced to set up on their own? Did they have to conquer a new homeland to live in?

Exactly where did the refugees settle and who are their descendants?

Are there elements of material culture or social organization that were introduced into the Rio Grande region by the refugees? Or, were the refugees completely assimilated by the Rio Grande Anasazi?

Partial answers are suggested by some evidences: the origin of the Tewa language (as a pidginized version of Tiwa) suggests an integration of at least part of the refugee population with at least some of the local Rio Grande population. This leads to questions of how such integration was accomplished, why did the Tiwa language survive in some areas and not in others, if the Keresans were the immigrants (accepted by many scholars) then why did they adopt Tewa (pidginized Tiwa) in some areas but retain their own language in others?

Integration and Cultural Change: Our present knowledge of Pueblo IV indicates that instead of the older societies simply living on side by side in the Rio Grande region, there was a general melding together of immigrant and local cultural traditions in what I call the Grand Synthesis. What emerged from this synthesis was the Pueblo Indian culture as presently recognized, minus a few aspects introduced later through European contact. Some of the elements of this new, revitalized Pueblo Indian culture have origins and early functions that need to be researched. For example:

The origins, history and role of the kachina cult, particularly its integration with older religious elements.

The origins, history and functions of the dual organizations found in many Pueblo Indian societies.

Questions of pre-Spanish social organization, particularly the role of the "cacique."

The origins of intensive irrigation agriculture in the Rio Grande region.

The Spanish Impact: The impact of the Spanish culture on the Pueblo Indians needs more serious consideration that it has had previously. For example:

Is the famous Pueblo Indian conservatism a result of culture shock?

Were there changes in male/female socio-economic roles as a result of stresses on the Pueblo Indian economy by Spanish tribute demands?

How much have the governmental structures of the Pueblo Indians changed under Spanish influence?

It can be seen that these are important questions, for which answers are needed. Many archaeologists, new archaeologists among them, have blithely and uncritically made direct application of ethnographic analogy from modern Pueblo Indians to prehistoric Anasazi without even the pretense of accounting for the possible changes that have taken place between times and mainly in Pueblo IV. That aside, the opportunities for studying cultural processes are abundant for the Pueblo IV period, and it is for this period of time that we can make the best joint uses of the resources and methods of the various subdisciplines of anthropology and history.

I should note that I did not begin this project within all these issues regarding Pueblo IV in mind, but my initial strong interest in Pueblo IV was based on some of them and others have developed over the years. Indeed, I have not attempted to mention all issues and points of interest, nor have I attempted to document above those efforts that have been made towards study of them. My purpose has been more to present an argument demonstrating the research importance of the Pueblo IV period.

The Salinas Province

The Piro-Tompiro Ethnohistory and Archaeology Project

The term Salinas Province is borrowed from Spanish Colonial usage to refer to Abo Pass, the Chupadera Basin, Jumanes Mesa, the eastern Manzano foothills, and the Estancia Basin. (See Figure 2-2.) This area was occupied during Pueblo IV by Tompiros and Salinas Tiwas, while the Rio Grande Valley to the west was occupied by the Piros. (Figure 3-4) It is notable in Wendorf's (1954) summary of the Rio Grande region that the Salinas Province passes almost without mention. This is symptomatic of the general ignorance of the area due to lack of field research. The same holds true for the Piro area of the Rio Grande Valley. What research had been done in these two areas up to 1980 is summarized in Chapter 5. (See also Chapter 9 in Volume II.)

In 1981, the two volumes reporting the archaeological work accomplished at Mount 7 at Gran Quivira were published (Hayes, Young and Warren 1981, Hayes 1981), as was the important summary by Stuart and Gauthier (1981). And in 1984 the survey results for the Piro area were published by Marshall and Walt (1984). But these did not influence the formulation of my original research problems, which occurred in 1980.

In 1980, archaeological knowledge of the Salinas Province was based mainly on the excavations of Spanish mission churches, with only limited work in the contemporary Indian ruins, and some of this was unreported. Even less was known regarding the Piro area. Historiographically, the concentration had been on Spanish activities, particularly church-state squabbles. Clearly, basic work needed to be done in all sectors regarding the Indians.

Thus, it was my intention upon first entering the field to address the following matters:

Piro-Tompiro Ethnohistory: My intent was to compile as complete as possible an ethnohistory of the Piros and Tompiros during the 16th and 17th centuries. An objective was to demonstrate the great potential that I felt lay dormant within the historical records, and that I felt had been only superficially exploited previously.

Abo Pass Prehistory: I felt that excavating at the site of Tenabo without any diachronic context was unsatisfactory, therefore I determined to undertake intensive survey in the area around Tenabo. (See Chapter 9 in Volume II.)

Tenabo Excavations: These were oriented towards providing the needed basic descriptions of material culture at Tenabo during Pueblo IV (AD 1300–1700), with the ultimate objective of comparison to materials from Gran Quivira and Pueblo Pardo, on the one hand, and material from excavations I hoped to conduct in the Piro area. These last did not occur, consequently the comparisons have been less extensive than originally planned.

Some specific research questions kept in mind during the excavations were:

Just how "Puebloan" were the Piros and Tompiros? This question was in part based on the old "Mogollon or Anasazi?" question that had been raised regarding the remains at Gran Quivira. Since I separate the Jornada Culture from the Mogollon, this question needs to be rephrased as "were they Jornada or Anasazi?" It arises in part because of the prevalence of Jornada Brown pottery on some pre-Pueblo IV sites around Gran Quivira, and in part because in attempting to explain the disappearance of Jornada Culture peoples ca. AD 1400 efforts have been made by archaeologists to migrate them into the Salinas Province and the Piro area along the Rio Grande. (e.g., Mera in Scholes and Mera 1940: 296) Thus, an assessment of possible relationships to Jornada Culture peoples needed to be made. The reverse side of this was the closeness of Piro-Tompiro relationships to other Pueblo Indians.

How similar were the Pueblo IV archaeological cultures of the Piro area, Abo Pass, the Chupadera Basin, and Jumanes Mesa? For example, Mera (1940) had lumped the Pueblo IV manifestations in the Chupadera Basin with the Piros of the Rio Grande Valley, while separating out as distinct areas the Abo Pass and Jumanes Mesa areas, all based on supposed territorial extents of the historic ethno-linguistic groups. The validity of these separations had not been tested archaeologically.

What were the origins of the Piro and Tompiro peoples? I did not expect to gather much data relevant to this question, as I tentatively assumed an in-situ development for them, hence the materials relevant to this problem were probably to be found at sites dating before Pueblo IV.

Hence, the original objectives of this project were a mixture of answering the need for basic descriptive research and addressing as far as possible certain broad research questions. As the project progressed, these objectives were modified by circumstances and opportunities not foreseen in 1980.

Chronological Sequences

Major Sequences: The major chronological sequences relevant to this study are showing in Table 3-1. The Pecos System, originally applied to the whole Southwest, is now recognized as being a highly idealized summation of Anasazi-Pueblo Indian culture history, and is now used mainly as a chronological frame of reference. Its only unit of known applicability within the Salinas Province is the Pueblo IV period.

I have not applied Wendorf's Rio Grande sequence (Table 3-1) to the Salinas Province because it implies a particular series of cultural developments, and it is not yet known if developments within the Salinas Province follow that same trajectory.

Lehmer's Jornada sequence (Table 3-1) is of interest as a neighboring series of cultural developments whose

Hueco and Capitan phases may be closely related to early developments in the Salinas Province.

Local Sequences: The first system of chronological periods proposed for the Salinas Province (and for the Piro area) was that advanced by Mera (1935). Mera's sequence of phases (Table 3-2) were based upon the sparse reconnaissance survey information available in the early 1930s, were defined only in terms of ceramic types, and, since none of these types were firmly placed chronologically, the whole sequence was only loosely tied to the Pecos system (Mera 1935). This phase sequence was never elaborated upon and subsequent investigators have not used it, with the exception of the San Marcial Phase which has been utilized for the Rio Grande Valley by Mike Marshall and his co-workers. (See Marshall and Walt 1984: 35-45.)

Mera's Abo, Cedarvale and Bosquecito phases seem to be mostly applicable to the highlands, i.e., the Salinas Province. However, the Polished Red pottery in Mera's Abo phase is apparently Salinas Red, which actually dates much later, hence the "pottery complex" upon which the phase is based is erroneous. Likewise, his Cedarvale phase contains Rio Grande Glaze A, another anachronism since Glaze A does not appear until after AD 1300. His Bosquecito phase, in the light of present knowledge, would only be applicable to Jumanes Mesa.

Table 3-2: LOCAL CHRONOLOGICAL SEQUENCES

TIME SCALE	MERA (after Wiseman 1983)	PIRO AREA (Marshall & Wait 1984)	ABO PASS & CHUPADERA BASIN	JUMANES MESA — CAPERTON (1981)	JUMANES MESA — TOULOUSE (Toulouse & Stephenson 1960)
A.D. 1900			Hispano-Anglo		
1800		Post-Revolt	—1875 → 1850—		
1700		—1680—	Apache		
1600	Bosquecito	Colonial Piro	—1675 → 1650—	Late Masonry	Salinas
1500		—1540—	Pueblo IV		Pueblo Pardo
1400		Ancestral Piro		Early Masonry	Pueblo Colorado
1300			—1350—		Gran Quivira
1200	Cedarvale	Late Elmendorf	Jacal	Jacal	Arroyo Soco / Claunch
1100				—1175—	
1000	Abó / Cañada Cruz	Early Elmendorf	Pithouse	Pithouse	
900		—950—			
800		Tajo			
700			—750—		
600	San Marcial				
500		San Marcial	?		
400			- - - - -		
300					
200					
100		ARCHAIC	ARCHAIC		
A.D. 1					

Table 3-2

Toulouse's focus sequence is also primarily defined in terms of ceramic types and covers only Pueblo IV and late Pueblo III in terms of the Pecos system. (Toulouse and Stephenson 1960: 40-41) Despite the fact that Toulouse's sequence was based on excavation and survey on Jumanes Mesa, later investigators at Gran Quivira (LA 120) seemingly have found no use for his sequence and have ignored it. (Vivian 1964; Hayes, Young and Warren 1981: 12; Caperton 1981). Whatever its suitability for the Jumanes Mesa remains, I do not find it usable in Abo Pass since there are significant archaeological differences between Abo Pass and Jumanes Mesa during Pueblo IV.

Hayes has utilized a three-phase system for classifying the remains in Mount 7 at Gran Quivira, but he used it only for that roomblock and made no claim for its applicability elsewhere. (Hayes, Young and Warren 1981: 12) Caperton (1981) utilizes a combination architecture/ceramic sequence for ordering his survey results, but, again, this is based mainly on the Jumanes Mesa area, and is thus of limited applicability to Abo Pass.

The sequence of horizons I have developed for Abo Pass and the Chupadera Basin is described in detail in Chapter 9 in Volume II.

Notes:

1. Kroeber (1939) produced the most sophisticated version of the culture center/culture area concepts, but by the time his work was published Southwestern archaeologists were already starting to draw away from these conceptions, although they remained influential for many years.

Section II

Ethnography and Ethnohistory

Dexemos a los troyanos,
que sus males no los vimos,
ni sus glorias;
dexemos a los romanos,
aunque oimos y leimos
sus estorias;
no curemos de saber
lo de aquel siglo passado
que fue dello;
vengamos a lo de ayer,
que tan bien es olvidado84
como aquello.
—Jorge Manrique (Cohen 1960: 47)

4

The Language And Ethnography of the Piros and Tompiros[1]

The purpose of this chapter is to collate and present the available ethnographic information on the Piro and Tompiro Indians and to identify them in terms of their language and ethnic divisions. Chronologically, this information falls into two groupings: (a) Ethnographic data from the 16th and 17th centuries, which is found in early Spanish colonial records, and (b) ethnographic and linguistic data from the 19th and 20th centuries, which was recorded by American observers (to the best of my knowledge, 18th century data are limited to historical and demographic aspects only). I feel that it is important to maintain a separation between these two chronologically distinct bodies of data because: (1) while the earlier body of data represents the Piros and Tompiros when they were distinct ethnic entities, living separately in their two regions, the later body of data represents a mixed Piro-Tompiro group, in which original differences have been submerged, and (2) most of the earlier body of data describes the Piros and Tompiros at a time before major European cultural influences had modified their way of life, whereas the later body of data describes the mixed Piro-Tompiro group when they are on the verge of extinction as an ethnic entity separate from the contemporary Mexican-American culture of the Juarez/El Paso area. Hence, this chapter is divided into five major sections: the first section discusses the Piro language, the second describes the ethnic divisions within the Piro-speakers, the third presents 16th and 17th century Piro ethnography, the fourth presents 16th and 17th century Tompiro ethnography, and the last section presents the 19th and 20th century Piro-Tompiro ethnography.

The Piro Language

It is a great misfortune that the Piro language is now extinct, having been displaced by Spanish within the past 150 years. The few records of the tongue are very limited in scope, consisting of a vocabulary of 174 items collected by Jon Russell Bartlett in 1852 at Seneca del Sur, near El Paso, Texas (Bartlett 1909), and secondly a similar vocabulary, never published, recorded in 1897 by James Mooney at an unspecified place (Harrington 1909: 567);[3] a translation of the Christian Lord's Prayer into Piro, published in several 19th-century sources (e.g. Pimentel 11865:253), as well as pueblo names and personal names, none with translations, scattered through Spanish Colonial documents.

Three linguistic analyses of Piro are available. The earliest, by Harrington (1909), is a lexical comparison of Bartlett's Piro vocabulary with Tiwa, Tewa, and Towa vocabularies collected by Harrington, with the result that Harrington classified Piro as a dialect of Tiwa.[2] Unfortunately, this relatively superficial analysis was uncritically accepted over sixty years, with the result that the concept of Piro being only a variety of Tiwa has become entrenched in the literature. A more recent analysis of Bartlett's vocabulary by Leap (1971) demonstrates that Piro is not a dialect of Tiwa, and suggests that it is not even a Tanoan language.

The most recent analysis by Shaul (1984), utilizing both the Bartlett and Mooney vocabularies, concludes that while Piro is a Tanoan language, it is also quite distinctive and forms a separate branch within the family. As will be seen, there is evidence in Spanish Colonial documents of a definite distinction (i.e., lack of mutual intelligibility) between Piro and Tiwa that supports the analyses of Leap and Shaul.

References to the Piro language in the Spanish Colonial records are infrequent, but clearly indicate that two dialects were spoken, one called "lengua Pira" among the pueblos of the Rio Grande Valley, and a second called "lengua Tompira" among the pueblos of Abo Pass, at "Last Humanas" (Cueloce, now called Gran Quivira), and at

Tabira. The clearest statement is by Fray Nicolas de Freitas before the Inquisition in Mexico City in 1661: "...it must be explained that Fray Garcia de San Francisco is the only religious who knows and preaches in the Piro language, the language of the Indians of the pueblo of El Socorro and of the pueblos of Senecu, El Alamillo, and Sevilleta; he can also make himself understood by the Indians of the pueblos of Umanes, Abo, and Tabira." (Hackett 1937; 163)

This indicates that the two dialects (Piro and Tompiro) were mutually intelligible. Other references to the Piro language are as follows:

1) Vetancurt (1697: 98), speaking of the inhabitants of the pueblo of Socorro, refers to them as being "of the Piro nation, of the same tongue as those of Senecu";

2) Fray Nicolas de Freitas, in a statement before the Inquisition in Mexico City on February 21, 1661, states that the alcalde mayor of the Salinas Province, Nicolas de Aguilar, made an announcement to the assembled inhabitants of "Las Humanas" (Cueloce) in Spanish and, through an Indian interpreter, "en lengua Tumpira" (Kessel n.d.: 54-55);

3) On December 19, 1681, Governor Antonio de Otermin interrogated "an Indian prisoner of the Piro nation, a native of the pueblo of Socorro, who said he was named Lucas," and who stated, "nor does he understand the languages (of the other Pueblo Indians), or any other except his own, which is Pira" (Hackett 1942, II: 243-244) Lucas was interrogated through "interpreter Raphael Tellez Jiron, a soldier who speaks the said Pira language, and Castilian as his mother tongue" (Hackett 1942, II: 242); and

4) Don Juan Manso, in a statement before the Inquisition in Mexico City on January 13, 1661, refers to the Tompiro dialect at the pueblo of Abo, noting "that language is very difficult to learn and there is no grammar for it as is also true for all the other languages of New Mexico..." (Kessell n.d.: 56)

There are also two statements in the Spanish records, which make it clear that Piro and Tiwa were considered to be separate languages:

1) Diego Perez de Luxan, chronicler of the Espejo Expedition (1582–1583), states that when, traveling from the south, they reached the Piro pueblo, later to be known as Sevilleta, "We named this place El Termino de Puala (the Boundary of Puaray, i.e., of the Tiwas), for the Puala are a different nation from this and speak a different tongue" (Hammond and Rey 1966: 174)[3]; and

2) When Governor Antonio de Otermin captured the pueblo of Isleta at dawn of December 6, 1681, he found it inhabited by its native Tiwas and by "others from outside who were there, of the Piro nation, from the pueblos of El Socorro, Alamillo, and Sevilleta." (Hackett 1942, II: 208) The next day, December 7, 1681, as soon as it was light, the señor governor and captain-general ordered the (Indian) governor and captains...to assemble all the people of this said pueblo and the others who were attached to it, and the very reverend father visitador (Fray Francisco de Ayeta)...in a loud voice delivered a sermon to all the apostates through an interpreter, as there were people of different tongues present. (Hackett 1942, II: 210)

The need for an interpreter was clearly because the Tiwa and Piro languages were not mutually intelligible.

The distinction between Piro and Tiwa is confirmed in a statement by a number of Isletans, native speakers of Tiwa, to Bandelier on May 4, 1882: They acknowledged that they understand the Taos somewhat, but principally the Picuries. They have no knowledge of the Tano pueblos, and no names for them in their own idiom. They say that those of Senecu (del Sur) are Piros, but those of the Isleta del Sur are Tiguas and speak their own language. (Lange and Riley 1966: 277)

Names And Ethnic Divisions Of The Piro-Speakers

There is a consistent distinction drawn by the Spanish between the Piros of the Rio Grande Valley and the Tompiros of the highlands east of the river, and sometimes, but not consistently, the Tompiros are further divided into a western group in Abo Pass and an eastern group centered on the pueblo of Cueloce (now called Gran Quivira). During the 16th and 17th centuries, the Spanish record and use several names for these ethnic divisions before finally settling on the terms "Piro" and "Tompiro."

Although the Piros of the Rio Grande Valley are noted in the documents of the Coronado Expedition of 1540–1542 (Hammond and Rey 1940: 220, 245, 309), no name was recorded for them. Similarly, neither the

Rodriguez-Chamuscado (1582) nor the Espejo Expedition (1582–1583) record any name for the Piros. However, the Espejo Expedition did record a name for the inhabitants of the pueblos of Abo and Tenabo in the Abo Pass, variously spelt as "Maguas" (by Espejo, see Pacheco et alia 1871a: 114, 176), "Manguos" (by Obregon: Hammond and Rey 1928: 322), and "Magrias" (by Luxan, in Hammond and Rey 1966: 175). It is uncertain which of these forms should be considered correct (except that it is probably not the second form as Obregon is a secondary source), nor is it clear from what group the Spaniards obtained the term (the possibilities include the Rio Grande Valley Piro-speakers, the Tompiros of the Abo Pass themselves, or the Tiwas of the Albuquerque area), nor is it even certain whether or not the term refers just to the people of Abo Pass or also the other Tompiros. None of the three forms, nor anything reasonably similar to them, are ever recorded again in later documents.

A generic term for the Piros of the Rio Grande Valley first appears in the two documents relating to Oñate's colonization of New Mexico, as follows:

> 1) In the "Obedience and Vassalage" sworn at the pueblo of San Juan on September 9, 1598 (Hammond and Rey 1953: 342-347), the missionary field assigned to Fray Juan Claros includes the provinces of the Tiwas, the Hopis, and "the province of Atzigues down the river" of which the pueblos are listed, the list containing the known names of Piro pueblos, as well as a good number of others[4]; and
>
> 2) In a letter written by Oñate to the Viceroy of New Spain on March 2, 1599, he mentions "the province of the Tziguis, which one passes (through) on the way from New Spain." (Hammond and Rey 1953: 483)

We have, then, a term given in two forms, "Atzigues" and "Tziguis" (plus the form "atzigui" used in reference to the Piro language, see below) which is applied to the Piros of the Rio Grande Valley. This term is not mentioned during the colony's journey through Piro territory, but only after the colony had reached its permanent headquarters at the Tewa pueblo of San Juan. Thus, it seems quite possible that the term does not originate with the Piros themselves, but with some other Pueblo Indian group.[5] I suggest that it is the Keresan term for the Piros, specifically the one used at Santo Domingo in the 16th century. This suggestion is based upon Oñate's heavy reliance on the interpreters Tomas and Cristobal, Mexican (Aztec) Indians who had been left in New

Mexico by the Castaño de Sosa Expedition of 1591, and who were residing at Santo Domingo in 1598. (Hammond and Rey 1953: 319, 338; Espinosa 1933: 142-143) It seems likely that the languages known to Tomas and Cristobal were their native Nahuatl, Spanish, and the Keresan of their adopted home. Since no Piros were present at the obedience ceremony held at San Juan on September 9, 1598, it is likely that Tomas, who was acting as an interpreter, used the Keresan term with which he was familiar for reference to the Piros. This term was used by Oñate in his letter to the Viceroy and, as will be seen, in reference to the language of the Tompiros.

The documents of Oñate's time use the term "Xumanas," and variants thereof, for reference to the inhabitants of three pueblos forming the eastern group of Tompiros, e.g.:

> 1) In the Decreto de Oñate (Scholes and Mera 1940: 276) of September 8, 1598, the three eastern Tompiro pueblos are referred to as "llamados de los xumanes rrayados";
>
> 2) In the "Obedience and Vassalage" taken at San Juan on September 9, 1598, these same pueblos are called "los tres pueblos Grandes de xumanas o rrayados llamados en su lengua atzigui genobey, quellotezei, pataotzei." (Scholes and Mera 1940: 276) It is in this passage that specific reference is made to the "atzigui" (=Piro) language being spoken at these pueblos.
>
> 3) In the report of Oñate's trip to the South Sea, the eastern Tompiro pueblos are referred to as "los Xumas...son tres pueblos(,) uno grande de como cia (Zia) y dos pequeños (;) y los dhos pueblos de Salinas y Xumanas dieron obediencia a su magd." (Scholes and Mera 1940: 276)
>
> 4) In Oñate's "Itinerary" this visit to the Eastern Tompiros is recorded in these words: "a los pueblos de los Xumanes o rrayados q. son tres (,) uno muy grande." (Scholes and Mera 1940: 277)
>
> 5) In Oñate's letter to the Viceroy of March 2, 1599, he refers to this visit in the following terms: "fui en persona a la provincial de Abo y a la de los Xumanas." (Scholes and Mera 1940: 277)

During the same period, the Western Tompiros, those resident in Abo Pass, were referred to under the phrases "province of Abo" or "pueblos of Abo." Precisely why Oñate distinguished between the Western and Eastern Tompiros is never stated, but the reason may lie in Oñate's use of the term "rayados" (= "striped ones") as a synonym for "Xumanas."

Scholes has suggested that there was a second, "striped" (or tattooed) element in the population of Cueloce (now called Gran Quivira) in addition to the Tompiros. (Scholes and Mera 1940: 285) The source of this population element would seem to be a plains-roving group, called the "Xumanas," or "Jumanos," who traded at Cueloce (Benavides, 1634, in Hodge, Hammond and Rey 1945: 66) and who may have intermarried with the Tompiros of Cueloce.[6]

Be this as it may, it is certain that the term "Xumanas" became entrenched as a referent for the pueblo of Cueloce (LA 120) so far as to supplant the pueblo's true name in Spanish usage during the 17th century. While Oñate always seems to have restricted his use of the term "Xumanas" to the Easter Tompiros, other Spaniards extended the term to include the Tompiros of the Abo Pass, as well. For example, on October 2, 1601, Capitan Geronimo Marquez prepared an interrogatory to be sworn to by various witnesses, which included the question "Seventeenth, if he knows the governor (Oñate) commissioned Sargento Mayor Vincente de Zaldivar to go to the Juamanas pueblo of Abo to punish the offenders who had killed Castañeda and Santillan..." (Hammond and Rey 1953: 704-705)

One further point must be brought forward regarding the terms "Xumanas" and "rayados": both terms are used by Oñate before he, or anyone else in his expedition, had ever visited the Eastern Tompiro pueblos. This suggests that the source of the terms may have been the interpreters Tomas and Cristobal, which further suggests that they have an ultimate source within the Keresans of Santo Domingo.[7]

The terms "Piro" and "Tompiro" are not known to be used by the Spanish before the middle of the 1620s.[8] There is no direct indication as to the origin of these two terms, but they could be Piro since the known phonology of Piro would permit such forms. (See Leap 1971: 324.)[9] The first record of these terms is to be found in Benavides' monographs of 1630 and 1634 (see Ayer 1916 and Hodge, Hammond and Rey 1945, respectively), which implies use of the terms in New Mexico during the period 1626–1629 while Benavides was custodian. Thereafter, Piro is the only term used for Piro-speakers in the Rio Grande Valley and Tompiro is used in reference to the Piro-speakers of the Abo Pass and those previously called "Xumanas." (This survived in the form "Las Humanas" as the 17th century name for Cueloce.) After the mixing of valley and highland Piro-speakers caused by the abandonment of the Tompiro pueblos in the 1670s, the term "Tompiro" fell from use and all Piro-speakers were referred to simply as "Piros."

In this study, I use the term "Piro" to refer to the Piro-speakers of the Rio Grande Valley, the term "Western Tompiro" to refer to the Tompiros of Abo Pass and the Chupadera Basin, and the "Eastern Tompiro" to refer to the Tompiros of Jumanes Mesa.

Piro Ethnography of the 16th and 17th Centuries

The first Spanish contact with the Piro Indians of the Rio Grande Valley apparently came in July 1541, when an unnamed "captain" explored 80 leagues (ca. 208 miles or 335 km) south from Tiguex along the Rio Grande, passing four pueblos on the way. (Hammond and Rey 1943: 245) However, since none of the surviving records of the Vasquez de Coronado Expedition provide any description of the Piros, Piro ethnography beings with the Rodriguez-Chamuscado exploring party of 1581–1582 and the follow-up Espejo expedition of 1582–1583. In fact, the majority of Piro ethnographic data comes from the records of these two expeditions.

An explanation for the relative fullness of the ethnographic data on the Piro provided by these two expeditions seems to lie in the fact that both expeditions approached New Mexico from the south by the way of the Rio Grande Valley, hence the Piro were the first Pueblo Indian group to be encountered by both parties and thus received the most thorough description. This can be seen in the descriptions of subsequently encountered groups (e.g., the Tiwa and the Tompiro) where the Spanish chroniclers simply state that they are more or less like the first people encountered, except for certain distinguishing characteristics.

Subsistence Activities

Agriculture: Like other Pueblo Indians, the Piros appear to have depended mainly upon agriculture. Aboriginal crops reported are maize, beans, squash (and/or gourds), tobacco, and cotton. (Gallegos 1582, in Hammond and Rey 1966: 82; Espejo 1583, in Hammond and Rey 1966: 220; Luxan 1583, in Hammond and Rey 1966: 172) Fields were on the flood plain of the Rio Grande, where they were watered by both rainfall and irrigation, and the sandy soil was noted as being particularly good for growing corn. The fields were worked using a digging stick (specifically compared to the digging stick of the Aztecs) and each worker (apparently men) spent the full day in the fields, retiring to a four-post ramada at noon to rest during the hot part of the day and eat a meal brought out to him from the pueblo. (Espejo 1583, in Hammond and Rey 1966: 220-221; Luxan 1533, in

Hammond and Rey 1966: 172; Gallegos 1582, in Hammond and Rey 1966: 82; Obregon 1584, in Hammond and Rey 1928: 291, 320) The corn stubble was left in the fields over the winter. (Luxan 1583, in Hammond and Rey 1966: 172)

After the arrival of Oñate's Spanish colony in 1598, the Piros added Spanish crops. (Benavides 1630, in Ayer 1916: 16-17.) Gaspar Perez de Villagra, in his epic tale of the founding of the New Mexico colony, states that Spanish vegetables adopted by the Pueblo Indians included "lettuce, cabbage, peas, chickpeas, cumin-seed, carrots, turnips, garlic, onions, artichokes, radishes, and cucumbers." (G. Espinosa 1933: 144) In addition, the Franciscan missionaries apparently introduced wine grapes after about 1630, as grape arbors producing wine are noted for both the pueblos of Socorro and Senecu (Vetancurt 1697: 98, 1698: 7), and fruit trees were also introduced, as witnessed by mention of peach trees at the ten-deserted pueblo of Socorro in 1760. (Tamaron y Romeral 1937: 333)

Domestic Animals: Dogs are never mentioned in connection with the Piros, but they almost certainly had them since dogs were present among all other Pueblo Indian groups. Turkeys, however, are frequently mentioned and apparently were numerous. (Gallegos 1582, in Hammond and Rey 1966: 82; Luxan 1583, in Hammond and Rey 1966: 172) It is not clear whether the turkeys were eaten, or were just raised for their feathers, as is the case with most modern Pueblo Indians. (Parsons 1939: 22)

Hunting, Fishing, and Collecting: Collecting of wild plants is never specified directly, but may be inferred from the mention of yucca fibre cord (Luxan, 1583, calls it "maguey," in Hammond and Rey 1966: 172) and the mention of piñon (Pinus edulis) on two occasions. (Espejo 1583, in Hammond and Rey 1966: 221; Benavides 1630, in Ayer 1916: 17) However, the collection of firewood is specifically noted. (Espejo 1583, in Pacheco et alia 1871: 110, 173)

Hunting and fishing are specifically noted: "very great hunts of deer, cottontail rabbits, jackrabbits, and may sorts of fish in the river" (Benavides 1630, in Ayer 1916: 16) and, with specific reference to the inhabitants of the pueblo of Alamillo, "they catch trout, pampanos, and salmon (?) among the abundant diversity of fish (in the Rio Grande)." (Vetancurt 1697: 98)

Foods and Food Preparation: Maize-based foods are the only ones specifically described. Pinole, made from toasted and ground corn mixed with water, is the only known beverage, and tortillas and "other kinds of bread" made from ground corn are mentioned. (Luxan 1583, in Hammond and Rey 1966: 172-173; Espejo 1583, in Hammond and Rey 1966: 219-220) Tortillas may have been cooked on a pottery comal. (Gallegos 1582, in Hammond and Rey 1966: 82)

Diego Perez de Luxan gives a very complete description of Piro mutates and metate bins:

Their mills are of the following type: four or five and even eight mill are placed together, depending on the capacity of the house. They are a yard long and two-thirds wide. They are made of whitewashed stones, built low, right on the ground, and resemble (Aztec) metates, with a border one span high and in the center and indented stone like the metate (of the Aztecs), about half a yard in length and a third wide. The Indians grind with another stone (the mano). (Hammond and Rey 1966: 172)[10]

Antonio de Espejo adds that five or six women would work together at one time. (Hammond and Rey 1966: 219)

Clothing And Hair Styles

Hair Styles: Luxan, speaking of the men, states that "they wear their hair in the shape of a queue" (Hammond and Rey 1966: 172); this is almost certainly the Pueblo Indian hairstyle presently known as a chongo where the hair is caught into a bun at the back of the neck, which, interestingly, is a hairstyle recorded by Bandelier (Lange and Riley 1970: 158) for the Piro men of Senecu del Sur in 1883!

"The women wear their hair tied up on their heads" (Luxan 1583, in Hammond and Rey 1966: 172), to which Espejo adds "the women wear their hair well combed and arranged, with the hair neatly wrapped around moulds at both sides of the head." (Pacheco 1871: 111, 173)[11] These "moulds" may have been some sort of wooden framework; the whole description strongly reminds one of the Hopi "butterfly" hairstyle for adolescent girls.

Clothing: The Rodriguez-Chamuscado expedition visited the Piros at the height of the summer heat in the late August of 1582, and the only description of clothing given by members of their party is that found in Obregon (1584, in Hammond and Rey 1928: 291): "Both men and women are clothed, largely with cotton cloth, fine, well tanned deerskins, and cowhides (bison hides). They wear shoes and some have caps of tanned leather."

The Espejo expedition reached the Piro area in February 1583, hence the clothing described is probably full winter garb. Luxan presents the following description of male attire:

Most of the men cover their privy parts with small pieces of cotton cloth (i.e., loincloths); others leave them uncovered, tied near the prepuce with a cord of maguey (yucca) fiber. Some wear tanned deerskin jackets and other tanned deerskins tied to their bodies. Most of them have, especially for sleeping, quilts made of turkey feathers. (Hammond and Rey 1966: 172)

In contrast, Espejo provides the most complete description of female clothing:

> The women have cotton skirts, often embroidered with colored thread, and over the shoulders a blanket like that worn by the Mexican Indians (as a serape), fastened at the waist by a strip of embroidered material, with tassels, resembling a towel (i.e., a Pueblo woman's sash). The skirts are worn like slips, next to the skin, the lower portion loose and swishing. Each woman displays such an outfit to the best of her ability. (Hammond and Rey 1966: 220)

To this description, Luxan adds tanned deerskin clothing (skirts, probably) and "feather quilts in place of cloaks." (Hammond and Rey 1966: 172) Ewers (1980) has recently compared the Piro woman's combination of skirt and serape with similar woman's clothing of Indian groups of the Southern Plains and Northern Mexico and makes a tentative correlation between such an outfit and southern temperate climate.[12]

Concerning footwear, Espejo states that "everyone, man or woman, wears shoes or boots with soles of buffalo hide and uppers of dressed deerskin." (Hammond and Rey 1966: 220)

The Spaniards' overall impression of the Piros is put succinctly by Luxan (Hammond and Rey 1966: 172): "They are clean and tidy, and do not smell, as is the case with other Indian nations (referring, probably, to the nomadic Indians of Nueva Vizcaya)."

Crafts, Tools and Weapons

Pottery: Hernan Gallegos, 1582, states: "the inhabitants have a great deal of crockery, such as pots (ollas), large earthen jars (tinaias), and flat pans (comales), all decorated and of better quality than the pottery of New Spain." (Hammond and Rey 1966: 82)

Weaving: There is no direct mention of weaving, but since the Piros grew cotton (See Agriculture, above) and wore cotton clothing (See Clothing, above) it seems reasonable to infer that they also did cotton weaving. Likewise, since the Piros are noted to raise turkeys (See Domestic Animals, above) and to wear feather garments (See Clothing, above) we may infer the weaving of feather-cloth as well.

Skinning and Tanning: Again, there is no direct mention of these activities; however, since the Piros are recorded to have hunted deer (See Hunting, etc., above) and are noted to wear tanned buckskins (See Clothing, above), they may be inferred.

Weapons and Warfare: The basic description is given by Espejo in 1583: "As arms they have bows and arrows, macanas and chimales; the arrows are fire-hardened wooden shafts with points of chipped flint which can easily pierce leather armour; the chimales are made of bison hide and are like oval leathern shields; the macanas are clubs half a vara long and very large at the head. It is not known whether or not they are at war with any other province." (Pacheco et alia 1871: 174-175)[13] To which Luxan adds, "hide-wrapped stone bludgeons about half a yard long. They have few and poor Turkish bows and poorer arrows." (Hammond and Rey 1966: 173)

Luxan's reference to "Turkish bows" is difficult to evaluate. A true "Turkish bow" is a composite bow: compounded from wood, horn and sinew. (Stone 1934: 130, 133) Such composite bows are known ethnographically from the Plateau, Great Basin, and western Great Plains, but in the Southwest only "self-bows" (single piece wooden bows) and sinew-backed reflex wooden bows are known. (Driver and Massey 1957: 349-351; Underhill 1944: 108-111; Stirling 1942: 96, 123) Hamilton (1982: 64-66) has discussed this problem of "Turkish bows" in the Southwest. His conclusion is that some of the bows referred to were sinew-backed reflex bows (which show a double-curved shape when strung), while others, the Piro bows specifically, were probably double-curved self-bows. It is possible, however, that the Piro bows were also sinew-backed reflex bows, but just not of very good quality. See Chapter 10 for petroglyphic evidence on Tompiro bows.

Architecture and Settlement Pattern

It is clear from the various descriptions that Piro pueblos were very similar to those built by other Pueblo Indians: "They have houseblocks (casas) of two and three and four storeys and with many apartments in each houseblock (casa), and in many of their households (casas) they have stoves for the wintertime." (Espejo 1583, in Pacheco et alia

1871: 110, 173)[14] Luxan, 1583, gives us the most detailed description:

Their houses are of mud, built by hand, the walls like small adobes half a yard wide. They contain upper and lower floors and have bedrooms. The people climb to the upper floors by means of moveable hand ladders; and the lower part of the pueblo can be dominated from above...in the lower part they have their granaries, pantries, and kitchens.

At the end of these (kitchens) they have mills where they grind the corn, as for making tortillas...The rooms are small and whitewashed. The doors are shaped like a "U" so as to allow only one person to go through at a time. (Hammond and Rey 1966: 172-173)

Details added by other sources include the presence of stone as well as adobe walls, of terracing of the upper stories, and of galleries[15] facing on the plazas. (Obregon 1584, in Hammond and Rey 1928: 288-289; Benavides 1630, in Ayer 1916: 16, 94-95) Preliminary archaeological inspection of historic Piro pueblos confirms the use of both adobe and adobe-and-cobble masonry construction.

The historic documents indicate Piro pueblo ground plans of houseblocks grouped around plazas containing two kivas. (See Religious Organizations, etc., below, for details of kiva construction.) This is confirmed by the ground plans of the historic Piro archaeological sites, which show a regular central plaza ground plan. (See definition in Stubbs 1950: 14.)

All historic Piro pueblos are either on the floodplain of the Rio Grande (Quaternary alluvium), Socorro (LA 791), Qualacu (LA 755), San Pascual (LA 757), and probably the pueblo of Alamillo (the latter possibly destroyed by changes in the channel of the Rio Grande), or on the edge of the Quaternary/Tertiary conglomerate bench (the Santa Fe Group) overlooking the floodplain, Sevilleta (LA 744), Teypana (LA 283), Penjeacu (LA 282?), and Senecu (LA 19266). In either case, the Piro pueblos are situated in defensible locations permitting a view of their surroundings and not dominated by higher land (in contrast, the Spanish estancia recorded as LA 286 is in a highly indefensible position with its back against a high mesa).

Luxan, 1583, notes the presence of sweathouses in the plazas (Hammond and Rey 1966: 173), but does not describe them nor the method of sweating.

Kinship And Marriage

The Spaniards record no information regarding kinship and descent among the Piros. Since at least two different systems are present among the other Pueblo Indians (bilateral and matrilineal systems), it is not possible to make any valid assumptions regarding the Piro system.

Gaspar de Villagra has the following to say about marriage and female adolescence among the Piros: "We discovered a very base and vile custom of these people. It seems that their damsels are common property for all while they are single. As soon as they marry they lead a chaste life and are satisfied with their husband only." (G. Espinosa 1933: 140) The first part of Villagra's statement seems to be an exaggeration of the sexual freedom permitted unmarried adolescent girls among some of the Pueblo Indian groups; the latter part, however, seems to accurately reflect the idealized behavior expected of Pueblo married women. A further statement by Villagra claiming the presence of male homosexuality (G. Espinosa 1933: 141) is difficult to evaluate since, even if true, it may not refer to Piros, but to other Pueblo Indians.

Political Organizations

There is only one good descriptions of the Piro political organization, namely that given by Espejo: Each pueblo has leaders agreed to by the people of that pueblo; thus there are the caciques, who have their tequitatos which are like policemen that execute within the pueblo whatever the caciques command, exactly as in the case of the Mexican (Aztec) people. When the Spaniards asked the caciques of the pueblos for something, the caciques told it to the tequitatos and these latter called it out through the pueblo, at the top of their voices, and then the people very quickly brought whatever had been asked for. (Pacheco et alia 1871: 111, 173-174)[16]

This description is clearly that of the well-known system of townchief with two lieutenants (sometimes known as "war captains"), which is characteristic of the native governments of other Pueblo Indian groups in New Mexico. (See Dozier 1970: 187-189, 198.) If the Piros followed the known practice of other Pueblo Indians, then the cacique served for life, but his lieutenants for only a year or so. The former, at least, seems likely since Fray Alonso de Benavides describes the death-bed conversion of "the principal chief" of Pilabo. (Hodge, Hammond and Rey 1945: 63)

It seems that a Spanish civil government had been imposed on the Piros living at El Paso in the 1680s since a "governor of the Piros of El Socorro (del Sur)" is mentioned on November 10, 1681 (Hackett 1942, II: 200); however, it is not clear if this system was in existence prior to the removal of the Piros to El Paso in 1680. In the same document, a "war captain" (capitan de guerra) of the Piros is noted, which official could have belonged to either the native or Spanish civil governments.

It seems that each Piro pueblo was autonomous and self-governing, as was typical for the historic Pueblo Indians.

Religious Organizations, Beliefs, and Kivas

Religious Organization: Among the modern Pueblo Indians, the townchief and his lieutenants have religious, as well as political, functions, but it is not clear if this was always so; certainly, in the case of the Piro townchiefs and their lieutenants noted above, we haven no information to indicate one way or the other. Indeed, for the Piros, we have no direct information on religious organization at all.

Religious Beliefs and Practices: The most complete statement available is that provided by Espejo: In each of these pueblos they have a house where they bring food to feed the devil, and they have small stone idols where they worship. And as the Spaniards have crosses along the roads, so they have midway between one pueblo and another, in the middle of the trail, small cairns like shrines built of rocks where they place painted sticks and feathers, saying that the devil will come there to rest and speak to them. (Pacheco et alia 1871: 111, 174)[17]

This one passage provides information of considerable importance! The first statement is clearly a reference to the ritual feeding of kachina masks and/or fetishes, while the second statement makes it clear that small stone fetishes similar to those used by the modern Pueblo Indians were present among the Piros and may have been kept on permanent altars (regarding the feeding of fetishes and masks, see Parsons 1939: 303-304). The reference to a house where the "devil" is fed inclines me to think that kachina masks are the subject of the remark, as some modern Pueblo Indian groups in New Mexico store their masks together in a special room. (Parsons 1939; Lange 1959: 284-285) That kachina impersonations and dances were a part of Piro religious life is clear from the written declaration of a capitan Andres Hurtado, made in Santa Fe in September 1661, where he states that during the tenure of Governor Lopez de Mendizabal (1659–1661) the Piros of Alamillo had danced the catzinas and their priest, Fray Francisco de Azebedo, had confiscated the masks. (Hackett 1937: 186)[18]

The remainder of Espejo's description is clearly of shrines where prayer-sticks and prayer-feathers were deposited as offerings to spirits. (See Parsons 1939: 270-299.)

It appears that in this case, the shrines may have served as community boundary markers, probably on the agricultural bottomlands along the Rio Grande where the three pueblos of Penjeacu (LA 282?), Pilabo (LA 791, Socorro), and Teypana (LA 283) were not far apart.

Kivas: The kivas (ceremonial rooms) of the Piros are reasonably well described: "In each pueblo, in the center of the plazas, are some very large cellars (kivas) two and one-half estados deep, with an entrance in the shape of a trap door and with a stepladder. They are all whitewashed and provided with stone benches all around. Here the people perform their games and dances." (Luxan 1583, in Hammond and Rey 1966: 173)[19] and "In each plaza of these pueblos they have two estufas (kivas), which are houses built below ground, within well-warmed and circled with benches for sitting; and at the entrance of each estufas they have a ladder for the descent and a great quantity of communal firewood, because here visitors are lodged." (Espejo 1583, in Pacheco, et alia 1871: 110, 173)[20]

Among the present-day pueblos, it is customary to lodge visitors with Pueblo families in the houseblocks, but it is possible that in the 16th century a different practice was followed as the Spaniards report being lodged in kivas when visiting several different groups. However, it should be kept in mind that from the Pueblo Indian point of view, Spanish explorers were arrogant and dangerous guests and might be best lodged at some remove from the Indians themselves; certainly the Piros were well aware of the mistreatment inflicted on the Tiwas by the Spaniards of the Vazquez de Coronado exploring party of 1540–1542. The reference to games probably means ritual performances. The physical descriptions could be duplicated by many present-day Pueblo Indian kivas of the Rio Grande area. The point regarding the presence of two kivas is intriguing since among the modern Eastern Keres, the presence of the two kivas is linked to dual ceremonial and social divisions within each pueblo; however, as Dozier (1965: 44) notes, among other Pueblo groups (e.g., the Tewa) there is no link between dual divisions and number of kivas.

There is some further information which may refer to Piro kivas: Hernan Gallegos, 1582, mentions "houses" which are "whitewashed inside and well decorated with (pictures of) monsters, other animals, and human beings." (Hammond and Rey 1966: 82) This passage may refer to kiva murals, such as are well-known from prehistoric and historic pueblos in the Rio Grande area and elsewhere. (See Smith 1952, Dutton 1963, and Hibben 1975.)

There is a second possible record of Piro kiva murals,

that by Gaspar Perez de Villagra referring to the Oñate Entrada of 1598: "On the walls of the rooms where we were quartered were many paintings of the demons they worship as gods. Fierce and terrible were their features. It was easy to understand the meaning of these, for the god of water was near the water, the god of the mountains was near the mountains, and in like manner all those deities they adore, their gods of the hunt, crops, and other things they have." (G. Espinosa 1933: 140)

There are two difficulties with this account, the first being Villagra's artistic license. He was writing an epic account of the Oñate Entrada and takes considerable liberty with the known facts. In this case, Villagra collapses the visits of the Oñate party to three pueblos (San Pascual, Sevilleta, and San Juan Bautista) into one event. Now, from the other Oñate Entrada documents, we know that the Spaniards were quartered in only two of these pueblos, Sevilleta and San Juan Bautista, so Villagra's account of the painted rooms should refer to one or the other (or both). Here, however, we encounter the second difficulty: while we know that Sevilleta (LA 774) was a Piro pueblo, there is uncertainty as to the ethnic affiliation of the pueblo called San Juan Bautista. This pueblo was a new foundation (apparently built after the 1582–1583 exploring expeditions) four leagues north of Sevilleta, which would place it near the mouth of Abo Arroyo.[21] This location is about a midway between the known contemporaneous pueblos, Piro Sevilleta (LA 774) to the south and two Tiwa pueblos (LA 81 and LA 953) to the north (Mera 1940). So, to which ethnic group, Piro or Tiwa, did this new pueblo of San Juan Bautista belong? At present, we cannot be sure; hence we are not sure if Villagra was referring to Piro or to Tiwa murals.

Miscellaneous Religious Data: There is further religious data recorded from this doubtful pueblo of San Juan Bautista: Don Juan de Oñate, in his Discurso de las Jornadas recounting the colonizing journey in 1598, found at San Juan Bautista "so many painted idols that in two rooms alone I counted sixty." (Hammond and Rey 1953: 319)

Don Antonio de Otermin, a Spanish governor (1677–1683), records an interesting ceremonial deposit at the pueblo of Sevilleta in 1681: "A short distance away from it (the pueblo) were found some deep subterranean chambers, in four parts, full of maize, most of it spoiled, earthen jars, calabashes, and some pots. On top of everything was a very curious sort of vessel made of clay, and carved on it was a figure with the face of an Indian and the body of a toad. Inside of it were many powered idolatrous herbs, two pieces of human (?) flesh, feathers, and other superstitious things made by the idolaters, who offer them to that figure so that it will guard their maize." (Hackett 1942, II: 207)

If the pottery figure was not a true toad, but instead was a horned-toad, then perhaps there is a link here to an Acoma tale where Horned-toad guards the entrance to the underground corn stores of the Twin Wargods. (See Parsons 1939: 247, 966; White 1932: 150-154.) Horned toad would make a good guard for buried stores of corn since he is a "devourer of ants," which might carry off the stored grain. (Parsons 1939: 886) It should be noted that Otermin had Piros with him at the time he uncovered the ceremonial deposit, hence the maize-guarding function of the Spirit represented on the vessel may be an interpretation offered by the Piros themselves.

The only other information on religious beliefs available for the Piros is a statement made by Fray Alonso de Benavides concerning his first visit to the pueblo of Pilabo: "the devil had persuaded them that if a friar only looked at them, they would become Christians, and if this happened all would go wrong with them. Because of this, they all hid or hurried away." (Hodge, Hammond and Rey 1945: 63) This sounds as though a witchcraft accusation had been made against the Spanish friars, rather than that the people had an actual fear of conversion.

Miscellaneous Observations

Care of Sick Persons: Obregon, 1584, records the following observation made by members of the Rodriguez-Chamuscado party: "While they were searching the houses (of San Pascual) for people to talk with they found a sick Indian with food by the side of his head. He was so near the end of life that he was unable to give any account of himself and could not flee." (Hammond and Rey 1928: 289)

External Relations: None of the historical sources known to me indicate that the bison (*Bison bison*) existed in Piro territory, nor does Roe (1970: 257-282) find any evidence of bison along the Rio Grande in the Piro area. All contemporary (16th and 17th century) accounts place the bison in the plains east of the line formed by the Manzano Mountains, Chupadera Mesa, and the Sacramento Mountains. Hence, it is likely that the bison hides and leather mentioned as being in the possession of the Piros were obtained through trade, either with the Tompiros or with eastern Apache groups.

Hernan Gallegos, 1582, records "that further on was another nation with which they were at war" (Hammond and Rey 1966: 82), which appears to be a reference to the

Tiwas. The hostilities and other relations between the Piros and the various Apache groups are dealt with in Chapters 7 and 8.

Tompiro Ethnography of the 16th and 17th Centuries

There is much less ethnographic data on the Tompiros than on the Piros. To some extent, we may be able to supplement the Tompiro data by reference to Piro ethnography (above), since the early explorers visiting the Western Tompiros (the pueblos of Abo and Tenabo) were of the opinion that they were much like their valley-dwelling cousins. (Luxan 1583, in Hammond and Rey 1966: 175) There are, however, obvious environmental differences between the valley-dwelling Piros and the highland-dwelling Tompiros, with known important effects with regard to architecture and subsistence activities, hence we should be cautious about assuming too close a resemblance between the two groups without more evidence than is presently available.

While Abo and Tenabo apparently were briefly visited by the Rodriguez-Chamuscado expedition of 1581–1582, their records do not provide any details other than the size of the pueblos. The most detailed information comes from the Espejo Expedition of 1582–1583, with some information added at the time of Oñate (ca. 1598–1601) and in 1661–1663 at the Inquisition hearings on the conduct of Nicolas de Aguilar and Governor Bernado Lopez de Mendizabal.

Subsistence Activities

Accounts of the Espejo Expedition of 1582–1583 note that turkeys and maize were supplied to the Spaniards by the inhabitants of Tenabo. (Luxan and Espejo 1583, in Hammond and Rey 1966: 175, 222) Obregon, 1584, in his account of the Espejo Expedition adds, "They sow in the rainy season. No river was found in their settlement... the water and climate are good. They till the soil with hoes like the Mexicans." (Hammond and Rey 1928: 322)[22] The references to "no river" and to planting "in the rainy season" suggest that the Western Tompiro pueblos of Tenabo and Abo made do with dry-farming dependent upon rainfall. It should be noted, however, that the Espejo Expedition was in the area in February 1583, when there would have been no farming activity to be observed.

Regarding the Eastern Tompiros, the alcalde mayor of the Salinas region, Nicolas de Aguilar, stressed the lack of water in the vicinity of Cueloce, alleging that "the scant water supply is in a few wells a quarter of a league from the place (Cueloce) and forty or fifty estados deep (that is, 220 to 275 feet deep (67 to 83 meters))" (Inquisition hearing of May 11, 1663, in Hackett 1937: 142.) Aguilar's facts are countered by the testimony of Fray Nicolas de Freitas: "the deepest well is about ten estados deep (about 55 feet deep (17 meters)) and no more, and there are wells which are only from four to five estados deep (about 22 to 27.5 feet deep (6.7 to 8.3 meters)); the whole number of wells is thirty-two." (Hackett 1937: 162)[23] While such wells may have provided water for the hand-watering of kitchen gardens or a few maize plants, the major reliance must have been placed on dry farming dependent upon precipitation. These wells, dry farming, and the reports of irrigation ditches by American explorers at Cueloce in the AD 1800s are discussed in detail by Howard (1959). The agricultural situation at Pueblo Pardo (LA 83, probably Pataotzei), just 4.25 km south of Cueloce, is undoubtedly the same. There is no information on aboriginal agriculture at Tabira (LA 51, Pueblo Blanco; probably Genobey).

No specific mention is made of hunting by the people of any of these pueblos. Plant collecting is mentioned only in the context of the gathering of piñon nuts (Pinus edulis) on behalf of the mission at Abo. (Hackett 1937: 192)

Clothing and Adornment

Espejo, 1583, states regarding the Western Tompiros "the Maguas province borders on the land of the so-called Cibola Cattle (bison). The natives clothe themselves with the hides of these animals, cotton blankets, and chamois skins." (Hammond and Rey 1966: 222) The reference to "chamois skins" could be to deerskins and/or to the skins of pronghorn. (*Antilocapra americana*)

The only specific mention of adornment of any sort is made by Gines de Herrera Horta in 1601 who, in reference to a visit by Adelantado Oñate to Cueloce, states "his aim also was to visit a pueblo of the Jumanes, which means striped Indians, those who have a stripe painted across the nose." (Hammond and Rey 1953: 650) France V. Scholes, in the course of discussing the term "Jumano" and its application to the Eastern Tompiros and other groups, states that this is probably a reference to tattooing. (Scholes and Mera 1940: 274)

Crafts and Weapons

Pottery: Although no specific mention of pottery is made, Espejo in 1583 notes that "in this province we found metals in the houses of the Indians" (Hammond and Rey 1966: 222), which may refer to the metallic ores for mineral glaze paints used in decorating pottery.

Weapons: The most complete statement is in Obregon's account of the Espejo Expedition and refers to the Western Tompiros: "The weapons which they bear are a small bow, arrows, a cowhide (bison hide) shield, wooden and stone bludgeons loaded at the end. These people are more warlike than those formerly encountered (the Piros)." (Hammond and Rey 1928: 322)

In 1601, Oñate's nephew, Vicente de Zaldivar, led a punitive expedition into the Salinas region to punish the murderer of some Spanish soldiers at Abo. A resistance force of Tiwa and Tompiro warriors met the Spanish at Cuarac, where the Spanish besieged them and it was latter reported by several witnesses that arrows and thrown stones were used against the Spanish forces. (Hammond and Rey 1953: 705, 792, 796, 799, 803, and 806) The reference to stones is undoubtedly to loose stones hurled from the rooftops, a well-known Pueblo Indian defensive measure. See Chapter 10 in Volume II for further discussion of Tompiro weapons and warfare.

Architecture and Settlement Patterns

Luxan, 1583, gives this description of the pueblo of Tenabo (LA 200): "There were two large plazas in this pueblo. The houses were of slabs and rocks, well built and white washed inside" (Hammond and Rey 1966: 175), to which Obregon, 1584, adds "the houses were two and three stories high, the walls being of stone and adobe." (Hammond and Rey 1928: 322. The sister pueblo of Abo is noted by Luxan to have the same characteristics as Tenabo. Preliminary archaeological observations confirm the adobe and slab masonry construction of both Tenabo and Abo and the presence of two (or more) plazas at Tenabo. The data on kivas are given below, but it can be noted here that at least three kiva depressions can be seen at Tenabo. (Luxan mentions four kivas there.)

There are no documentary descriptions of Eastern Tompiro architecture other than Nicolas de Aguilar's possible exaggeration that "indeed the lack of water is so acute (at Cueloce) that they are accustomed to preserve their urine to moisten the earth the make walls" (Inquisition hearing on May 11, 1663, in Hackett 1937: 142), and passing mentions of such architectural features at the pueblo of Cueloce as "the plaza" (Fray Nicolas de Freitas 1661, in Hackett 1937: 135), and "groups of houses" and "terraces." (Gines de Herrera Horta 1601, in Hammond and Rey 1953: 651) Archaeological information shows that all three Eastern Tompiro pueblos, Cueloce (LA 120, Gran Quivira), Pataotzei (probably Pueblo Pardo, LA 83), and Tabira (LA 51, Pueblo Blanco, Genobey), are of adobe and masonry construction.

Tenabo, Cueloce and Pueblo Pardo are all situated on high ridges or benches, which are highly defensible; Tabira, while not on a ridge, was probably able to visually dominate the surrounding terrain. Abo, however, is in a narrow and shallow valley, which does not seem a particularly favorable location for defense.

Political Organization

There is very little information on Tompiro political organization. Espejo, 1583, simply states of the Western Tompiros that "they are governed like the people of the provinces already mentioned. (Piro and Tiwas)" (Hammond and Rey 1966: 222) In the "Act of Obedience and Vassalage by the Indians of Cueloze" on October 17, 1598, there is mention of "captains" representing Abo and each of the three Eastern Tompiro pueblos (Hammond and Rey 1953: 351), which are probably townchiefs, such as possessed by the Piros and other Pueblo Indians. In this regard, it is important to note the absence of a townchief representing Tenabo; this circumstance, plus reference to the "pueblos" (plural) of Abo in some contemporary documents suggests that the two pueblos, Abo and Tenabo, may have been under the same leadership, an unusual but not inconceivable departure from the more common "one pueblo, one chief" Pueblo Indian pattern.

Fray Alonso de Benavides, 1634, mentions a "war captain" and "principal captains" at Cueloce (Hodge, Hammond and Rey 1945: 67), which may be references to, respectively, an assistant to the townchief and a council of religious leaders such as is known for modern pueblos. (Dozier 1970: 187-189, 198) Likewise, Fray Nicolas de Freitas, 1661, mentions "the fiscales, or (and) the captains" of Cueloce and Tabira (Hackett 1937, 135) in conjunction with the keeping of public order, which appears to be reference to the war captains and the townchiefs.

Religious Organization, Beliefs and Kivas

Religious Organization: There is no clear description of religious organization among the Tompiro; Fray Alonso de Benavides does make reference to what may be a council of religious leaders (See Political Organizations, above) and mentions "sorcerors" at Cueloce. (Hodge, Hammond and Rey 1945: 66-67) Beliefs and Kivas: Espejo, 1583, reports that the Western Tompiros "have idols which they worship in the same manner as those other Indians (Piros and Tiwas)." (Hammond and Rey 1966: 222) Luxan, 1583, expands upon this, as follows:

> The people are idolatrous, for that pueblo (Tenabo) had four caverns (kivas) in the plazas where they have their dances and their baths; and these places served as a community center and lodging place for strangers. In front of each one, outside the entrance, is a black stone (basalt?) four fingers in thickness (ca. 7 or 8 cm), three spans wide (ca. 66 cm), and one estados (ca. 1.67 m) above ground; and on each kiva (?) is a badly painted figure of an Indian with a flaming crown. Everyone has these idols in his house. (Hammond and Rey 1966: 175)[24]

The description of a figure with "a flaming crown" is highly reminiscent of the pictographs near Tenabo which show masks surmounted by headdresses of standing red feathers. (See descriptions an illustrations in Schaafsma 1976: 131-133.) I suspect that the pictograph masks and Luxan's figures with a "flaming crown" are representations of kachinas.

External Relations

It appears that Cueloce, at least, served as a center of trade between Pueblo Indians and groups from the southern Great Plains: "that pueblo (Cueloce) is the most populous one in those provinces (the Salinas province), whither they gather together from all parts to trade antelope skins and corn." (Fray Nicolas de Freitas 1661, in Hackett 1937: 135) According to Nicolas de Aguilar, alcalde mayor of the Salinas province in 1660, the Apaches of the Siete Rios area (southeastern New Mexico between Artesia and Carlsbad) had agreed with the Spanish "that they should not pass beyond the pueblos of Humanos (Cueloce) and Tavira, where they come to barter." (Inquisition hearing of May 11, 1663, in Hackett 1937: 143) Earlier, in 1634, Fray Alonso de Benavides calls Cueloce "Xumanas" (a name which was used both before and after his time to refer to the Eastern Tompiros) "because this nation often comes there to trade and barter." (Hodge, Hammond and Rey 1945: 66) The "Jumanos" were a group of Plains Indians apparently living along the Pecos River and friendly to the Tompiros, but enemies of the Apaches. (See discussion of the Jumanos in Chapter 6) The Tompiros' own hostilities with the Apaches will be described later, as will their apparently close relations with the Tiwas of the Salinas area.

Piro-Tompiro Ethnography of the 19th and 20th Centuries

Due to the events discussed in Chapter 8, the Piro and Tompiro populations merged in the AD 1670s, and then were removed to the Juarez/El Paso area in the 1680s. With their merger, the distinction between the two groups was lost and they were commonly referred to thereafter as the "Piros." The term Tompiro almost never appearing in records post-dating 1680. In the section, therefore, the term "Piro" will be used to refer to this mixed population residing the El Paso area.

The ethnographic information of this period comes from two small pueblos, Senecu del Sur and Socorro del Sur, located a short distance downstream from El Paso, Texas. Even in the 1850s, the time of our earliest data, these two pueblos were greatly Mexicanized, to the extent that Spanish was the everyday language and the Piro tongue incompletely remembered (as witnessed by the substitution of Tiwa words for some of the vocabulary items collected by Bartlett in 1853), and by the end of the first decade of the 20th century, all persons even knowing individual words had died. (Harrington 1909: 568-570) What information there is comes from three sources: (1) John Russell Bartlett, an American boundary commissioner visiting the El Paso area in the early 1850s, (2) Adolph F. Bandelier, an early American ethnologist who visited the El Paso area in 1883, and (3) Jesse Walter Fewkes, another American ethnologist who visited the Piros in 1901.

Subsistence Activities

Agriculture: There is no direct information on agriculture at the two pueblos although both Bandelier (Lange and Riley 1970: 163) and Harrington (1909: 568) make casual mention of "farms," "cultivation," and "acequias" (irrigation ditches) on the flood plain of the Rio Grande. Maize was presumably the staple crop.

Hunting: Fewkes (1902a: 73) briefly mentions rabbit hunts at Senecu del Sur, where Bandelier records the following on November 10, 1883:

Tomorrow they will have the rabbit hunt, with (rabbit) sticks and bows and arrows. They have not exactly the same customs as at Cochiti, but they pay for each rabbit, one medio (1/2 real); for each hare, one Real. The skins do not go to the cacique. (Lange and Riley 1970: 163)[25]

Clothing and Hairstyles

There is little information recorded as to clothing, the only record being that made by Bartlett of the clothing worn during a dance. (See quotation given below under Religious Beliefs and Ceremonies.) As to hairstyles, Bandelier states, "The women wear their hair loose; the men have 'chungo' and 'melotes.'" (Lange and Riley 1970: 153) The "chungo" or chungo is a bun of hair tied at the back of the neck, while the significance of "melotes" (literally meaning "molasses") is not clear.

Crafts and Weapons

Pottery: Bandelier found the pottery made at Ysleta del Sur, Senecu del Sur, and El Paso del Norte (present-day Juarez) by descendants of the Tiwas, Piros, and Mansos to be of uniform character, which he describes in the following terms: "The recent pottery looks very much like that of the Pimas. It has the same paint and color. Only it is a little lighter in(side?) here, but the designs are remarkably similar." (Lange and Riley 1970: 161, 163, 164) This description should be compared to that of archaeological pottery recently recovered from the vicinity of the mission of Socorro del Sur (Scheutz 1980: 32-33) and the historic pottery of Ysleta del Sur. (Hedrick 1971)

Weapons: Both Bandelier and Fewkes mention bows and arrows, but do not describe them. (Lange and Riley 1970: 163; Fewkes 1902a: 73)

Some other material items are described under Religious Beliefs and Ceremonies, below.

Architecture and Settlement Pattern

Fewkes (1902a: 73) describes Senecu del Sur as "a small cluster of adobe houses, in the midst of which rises an old church," while Harrington (1909: 568) states:

The pleasant road leads through Juarez... and further,

between the small farms which dot the broad, low bank of the river, until it passes the old church of Senecu. If it were not for the church one would hardly know when Senecu is reached, for the river bank is not more thickly populated here than all along the way.

Political Organization

Bandelier records the political organization of Senecu del Sur as consisting of a cacique (or townchief), a governor, "one war captain, one lieutenant (war captain), and five 'alguaziles'" (Lange and Riley 1970: 163), and Fewkes (1902a: 73) records and identical organization, except that he seems to omit the lieutenant war captain and implies that there are only four alguaciles.[26] It is possible that in the time between Bandelier's observations (1883) and those of Fewkes (1901), two of the officers were allowed to lapse. Bartlett, 1853, recorded the term taikhemtsae as meaning "chief" (1909: 432), which is almost certainly the Piro term for the townchief (cacique).

Religious Beliefs and Ceremonies

Religious Beliefs: Bandelier records the following ambiguous piece of information: "He (the lieutenant war captain of Senecu del Sur) told me that, shortly (recently), upon denunciation of a Mexican, they had compelled to bury and conceal 'hasta la madre.' This he said with a wink!" (Lange and Riley 1970: 163)[27] If we are to take this seriously, then the lieutenant war captain may have been confiding to Bandelier the existence of a "corn-mother" fetish, such as is known among many of the other Pueblo Indians. (Parsons 1939: 319-323) On the other hand, he could have been joking with Bandelier, as Pueblo Indian informants are sometimes known to do.

Bandelier also records various statements on Piro religious practices, witchcraft, and other matters made by a Major Van Patten, U.S. Army, residing in 1883 at Las Cruces, New Mexico. (Lange and Riley 1970: 157-159) Unfortunately, there are some aspects of this information which excite doubts as to its authenticity or, at least, its accuracy; these include (1) the denial of the presence of the Montezuma legend among the Piros; (2) the claim to have witnessed an act of witchcraft, supposedly held in a kiva! (Claims which are very doubtful); and (3) Van Patten's claim that the Piro words for "sun" and "moon" are probably words bear no resemblance to the Piro terms recorded in Bartlett's vocabulary (Bartlett 1909: 432), nor, for that matter, to the corresponding Tiwa terms from Ysleta del Sur. (Harrington 1909: 574) Bandelier himself later expresses serious reservations regarding Van Patten's accuracy on another body of data. (Lange and Riley 1970: 167) Hence, I am not prepared to accept at face value most of Van Patten's statements on Piro ethnography, and will not repeat them here.

Religious Ceremonies: Fewkes (1902a: 73) states that at Senecu del Sur in 1901, the "Piros perform dances in the open space before the church building, and are accompanied by a drum and rattles. They are practically secularized pagan dances which have lost all their aboriginal significance," and notes the performances as taking place at Christmas and the Saint's Days of San Antonio de Padua, San Juan, San Pedro, Santa Ana, "and others." Such a performance was described in detail by John Russell Bartlett in 1850, apparently enacted before the church in El Paso del Norte (now Ciudad Juarez, Chihuahua):

The men were chiefly dressed after the manner of the lower class of Mexicans. They wore short jackets, decorated with innumerable bell-buttons, and dark pantaloons with similar buttons, open at the outside from the hip to the ankle, with large white trouser beneath. The women all wore short black dresses, reaching just below the knees, with a thin white muslin mantle thrown over their shoulders. A bright red silk shawl was tied around their waists, and they had bunches or bows of gay ribbons in their hair. All their faces were painted alike, with a spot of vermilion on each cheek, surrounded by a border of small white dots. The women held in each hand a large turkey feather, which they moved up and down, keeping time with their music. The men carried flint muskets, and one of them a drum, on which he was beating constantly. All joined in singing a monotonous tune, and, when they reached the church, stopped and commenced dancing. They formed lines similar to those made for a contra dance by us (i.e., two facing lines), passing through a variety of figures and marchings. From the perfect regularity with which they went through these figures, they must have followed some established forms. (Bartlett 1854: 148-149)

This sounds very much like a Pueblo Indian Harvest Dance (also known as a "corn Dance" or "Tablita Dance") such as is performed in Rio Grande area pueblos in the present days (for exemplary descriptions, see Kurath and Garcia 1970: 22, 46, 169-183; Kurath 1959: 545-556; photographs in Lange 1959: Plates 22 and 23), but with considerable acculturation, especially in the men's costume. Bandelier, 1833, describes a similar performance by the

Mansos of San Lorenzo. (Lange and Riley 1970: 164-165)

Ceremonial Paraphernalia: Fewkes describes the drum used in Senecu del Sur for the dances noted above: It consists of a hollow log with a piece of rawhide stretched over each end, closely resembling those used for the same purpose by the Pueblos higher up the Rio Grande. The drum employed in their secular dances, of which they have many, consists of a jar with skin stretched over the top. (1902a: 73)

Bandelier briefly describes a similar drum for the Mansos of San Lorenzo, then states that the drums of the Piros of Senecu del Sur and the Tiwas of Ysleta del Sur are identical. (Lange and Riley 1970: 161, 164) Recent description and illustration of the Ysleta del Sur drum can be found in Houser (1970: 32-33). Fewkes also notes "hand rattles," but does not describe them.

Miscellaneous: Fewkes (1902a: 73) mentions footraces, probably held in conjunction with feast day celebrations.

Kinship

Bartlett's Piro vocabulary only gives nuclear family kinship terms (Table 4-1), hence descent principles cannot be read from the terminology. Of those terms available I suspect that the term for "daughter" was probably not a true kinship term but simply a descriptive form which his an artifact of the process of elicitation. The term *elamzeuize*, "my child," was probably used for sons and daughters (i.e., the gender of the child was not specified).[28] Such usage is not uncommon among Pueblo Indian kinship systems. (For Hopi and Zuñi, see Eggan 1950: 20-21, 179-180; for Tewa, see Dozier 1955: 255; for Towa, see Parsons 1925: 19.)[29]

Bandelier, speaking of the people of Senecu del Sur, states, "their traditions are so far lost that even the cacique has forgotten the names of the gentes, although they exist." (Lange and Riley 1970: 163) By "gentes," Bandelier means matrilineal clans, such as are found among the Hopi, Zuñi, and Keres. However, Bandelier mistakenly expected to find such matrilineal clans among all Pueblo Indians, hence the cacique's "forgetting" of the clan-names is probably more apparent than real; indeed, it is questionable whether or not the Piros really understood the point of Bandelier's inquiries regarding clans.

Table 4-1: PIRO KINSHIP TERMS

(Source: Bartlett 1909: 431)

All are given with a prefix (elem-, elam, elaan- *) meaning
"my" and a nominal suffix (-e).

elem-tata-e	my father
elem-kia-e*	my mother
elam-antsala-e	my husband
elaam-sun-e	my wife (literally "my woman")
elam-eui-e	my son (literally "my child")
elam-eui-sun-e	my daughter (literally "my female child")
elam-pupu-e	my brother
elam-ququ-e	my sister

* The prefix for "my mother" is given as "etem-", but
this is probably a misprint of "t" for "l".

Table 4-1

Notes:

1. The Piro language referred to here is a North American tongue spoken within the Southwest culture area, and should not be confused with the South American language of the same name spoken in the Amazon Basin.

2. I accept the following classification of the Tanoan languages:

> Tanoan Languages (sub-family):
> Tiwa language:
> Northern Tiwa dialect group:
> Taos dialect, Taos pueblo;
> Picuris dialect, Picuris pueblo;
> Southern Tiwa dialect, Sandia, Isleta, Ysleta del Sur pueblos.
> Tewa language:
> Tewa (Northern Tewa) dialect group, San Juan, Santa Clara, Nambe, Tesuque, San Ildefonso, Pojoaque pueblos;
> Tano (Southern Tewa, Arizona Tewa) dialect, Hano pueblo.
> Towa language, Jemez pueblo.

Pecos is frequently listed as being a Towa dialect, but Trager (1967: 337) notes that, "there has never been any direct evidence that the language of Pecos was indeed Towa, or, for that matter, even Tanoan." The claim that the inhabitants of Pecos pueblo spoke Towa seems to rest mainly on the statement by Fray Alonso de Benavides (Forrestal and Lynch 1954: 23), who is not an especially reliable source. The whole matter cannot be considered settled at this time and needs to be carefully investigated. Irvine Davis (1959) has presented a glotto-chronological assessment of the Tanoan languages, but Trager (1967: 339-340) considers Davis' times for linguistic separation to be "utterly misleading" and presents a different chronology. Kiowa forms the other sub-family of a Kiowa-Tanoan language family, which is distantly related to Uto-Aztecan. (Trager 1967: 338)

3. Antonio de Espejo, the leader of this expedition, confirms the usage of the term "Puala" for Tiwas by Luxan when he states in his own relacion "we found another (province) which is called the province of the Tiguas, with 16 pueblo, one of which is called Puala." (See Pacheco et alia 1871a: 112, 175.)

4. A detailed discussion of this list is found in the next chapter.

5. However, the Piro term, *atsihem* for "Indian; people' has an intriguing resemblance to "atzigui." (See Bartlett 1909: 431.)

6. Further consideration of the Plains Indian "Jumanos" and their relationships with the Tompiros of Cueloce is found in Chapters 7 and 8.

7. The source of the name Jumano appears to have been the Tewas, as witnessed by the following statement made by Juan Rodriguez on April 26, 1602 during the Valverde Inquiry in Mexico City: "The Indians around the San Gabriel (i.e., the Tewas) called these people from the settlement (the Wichitas of central Kansas) Jumanos; in fact, they gave this name to all of the Rayados." (Hammond and Rey 1953: 867) It appears then, that all tattooed or striped Indians (Rayados), were known indiscriminately to the Tewas as "Jumanos."

8. "Piro" and "Tompiro" were treated as common Spanish noun and adjective forms, i.e., with masculine and feminine, singular and plural forms: Piro (-os, plural), Pira (-as, plural); Tompiro (-os, plural), Tompira (-as, plural). The variation "Tumpiro" is also found.

9. Recently recorded terms for Piro which resemble the Spanish "Piro" are (1) a Southern Tiwa form recorded by Harrington at Ysleta del Sur (Harrington 1909: 594; 1916: 575) using two different orthographies but both phonetically equivalent to (piru) (see Trager 1942 regarding Tiwa phonology); (2) a Towa form recorded by Harrington (1916: 575) at Jemez as (p' lo); and (3) a Northern Tiwa form recorded by Spinden at Picuris and glossed as meaning "Pecos people," but which Harrington (1916: 473, 575) thinks is really a term for Piros, (*pe lo ine*). (See Trager 1942) No other terms for "Piro" are known from Southwestern Indian languages.

10. The Spanish vara (yard) is 33 inches (83.6 cm) long. The Spanish palmo (span) is about 9 inches (22 cm) long.

11. Hammond and Rey (1966: 220) translate this passage as: "The women arrange their hair neatly and prettily, winding it with care around moulds at each side of the head," which I feel does not quite capture the full meaning of Espejo's statement.

12. In present-day Mexican Spanish a serape is a blanket with a hole in the center through which the head can be put; in American and Canadian English such a garment is called a poncho (e.g., in Ewers 1980), but that usage conflicts with the Mexican usage of poncho to mean a serape which has been sown together on the sides, leaving two arm-holes, to produce a kind of jacket. To avoid possible confusion over the term poncho, in this work I am using the term serape in the sense defined above.

13. I present a different translation from that given by Hammond and Rey (1966: 221) since I believe that they have made a considerable error in translating macanas as "flint-edged wooden clubs." The term macanas, borrowed from the Taino of the Island Hispaniola, was widely used by the Spanish in the New World to indicate a large, hardwood club (Corominas 1954, III: 167) As Espejo makes no mention of flint edging, but simply uses the world macanas with no elaboration, I suspect that Hammond and Rey are confusing a simple wooden macanas with he obsidian-edged Aztec macahuitl. (See discussion in Salas 1950: 77-81.) The term chimale (plural, chimales) is a Hispanized form of the Nahuatl chimalli, "shield." (Molina 1571)

14. The traditional dwelling pattern among Pueblo Indians is for a group of relatives, known as an extended family or "household," to live together in a set of interconnected rooms called an "apartment," sometimes also called a "household." Houseblocks are compact groups of apartments, and there are usually several houseblocks within a given pueblo. The Spaniards used the word casa (literally "house") for both the social unit (the household) and its architectural equivalent (the apartment) on a regular basis, and sometimes also used casa in reference to the houseblocks, as is the case in the quotation from Antonio de Espejo.

15. Historians unfamiliar with Pueblo architecture have translated the term corridor as either "corridor" or "balcony." (Ayer 1916: 16; Forrestal and Lynch 1954: 14; Hammond and Rey 1928: 289, 291), but this term should be rendered as "gallery," in the sense of a covered porch, which is open on one or more sides. Such galleries are familiar features of historic Pueblo architecture. (See discussion by Kidder 1958: 91, 93-95, 98; mention and illustration in Mindeleff 1891: 187, plate LXXIX; photographs in Lange 1959: plate 19, upper, and in Dozier 1970: 149.)

16. The term cacique, borrowed from the Taino of the Island of Hispaniola, was used throughout the New World by the Spanish to mean "Indian chief, Indian leader." (Corominas 1954, I: 564)

Tequitato is a Spanish modification of an Aztec term, which was used for various subordinate officials in the Indian towns of central Mexico. (See discussion in Gibson 1964: 182.)

The quoted text is my own translation, which I consider to better render the sense of Espejo's statement than does the translation provided by Hammond and Rey (1966: 220). My main difference with Hammond and Rey is over the translation of the phrase "conforme a" which they read in the sense of "in proportion to," where as I read it in the sense of "agreeable to."

17. Hammond and Rey (1966: 220) give a slightly different translation, which, while good, misses a couple of subtle points of ethnographic importance.

18. This statement was presented as evidence before the court of the Inquisition in Mexico City during hearings on the church-state conflicts in New Mexico during the administration of Governor Mendizabal. The Spanish term catzina (katsina), which appears at various points in the Spanish records, in the 1660s, is clearly modeled on the Keresan term (k'atsina). The modern English term "kachina" is modeled on the Hopi term (qatsina). The Piro term for kachina is not recorded.

19. The estado is a rough measure, being equivalent to the height of a man. This, I am arbitrarily placing at 5.5 feet (1.67 m), which would make the Piro kivas approximately 13.75 feet deep (4.19m). For the definition of the measure, see Cobarruvias Orozco (1979: 561).

20. As in other cases, I read Espejo's passage differently from the translation given by Hammond and Rey (1966: 219).

21. Mera (1940) does not record any site in this area, but this pueblo may have been one of those destroyed by the Rio Grande prior to the present day.

22. In place of "hoes," read, "digging sticks." (See discussion of Piro agriculture.)

23. The discussion of wells and water was centered on a controversy reading the livestock herds of the Franciscan missions and the adequacy of the local water supply for these herds. As to the depth of the wells, the figures given by Freitas seem the most likely.

24. The question mark was introduced by Hammond and Rey to indicate uncertainty as to referent. I suspect that the referent is to "each stone slab" rather than to "each kiva," but without the Spanish text, this cannot be checked.

24. The real currency of Mexico consisted of copper and silver coins valued at 1/16, 1/8, ¼, ½, , 2, 4, and 8 reales (8 reales = 1 peso). The last of the real coinage was minted in 1897. (Yeoman 1970: 314-316) By "rabbits," Bandelier no doubt means cottontails, and by "hares," he means jackrabbits.

26. The term *alguacil*, of Arabic origin, is used in Spanish to mean a policemen or constable, generally of the lowest rank.

27. "Hasta la madre" is Spanish for "even the mother."

28. It should be kept in mind that the terms were elicited through the medium of the Spanish language, where hijo means "child" in the generic sense, as well as "son," while hija means only "daughter." It is clear, then, that Bartlett's Piro informants, when asked for the Piro equivalent of hijo, responded with their kinship term for "child," and when asked for the Piro equivalent of hija, they responded with a descriptive modification of the generic term.

29. On the other hand, both the Keres and Tiwa do have sex specific terms for "son" and "daughter." (See Hawley 1950: 509, and Trager 1943: 560-567.)

5

Correlation of Piro and Tompiro Historic Pueblos with Archeological Sites

In the past, various attempts have been made at correlating historic pueblos with archeological sties in the Piro and Tompiro areas, with variable results and, in the sum, indifferent success, particularly in the Piro area. The lack of firm correlations up to the present can be blamed on two factors: (a) the lack of intensive archaeological and historical work on the Piros and Tompiros, and (b) older Euro-American scholarship with discipline overspecialization. To elaborate on this latter factor, we have seen historians speculating on the locations of historic pueblos without recourse to the details of archeological evidence, and archaeologists speculating on historic identifications of archaeological sites without careful appraisal of the historical evidence. The muddle is particularly acute for Piro territory in the Rio Grande Valley, where lack of archaeological excavation has compounded the problem of general disinterest by historians in the early Spanish Colonial history. The Tompiros of Abo Pass and the Salinas Province have been better served by both archeologist and historian, but only in comparison to the fate of the Piros. Hence, the purpose of this chapter is to attempt to correct the omissions and errors of the past through a systematic and intensive synthesis of data from those artificially separated disciplines: history and archaeology.

Piro Pueblos and Archaeological Sites

Previous Work

Bandelier: The first effort at correlation is the work of Adolph F. Bandelier (1892: 236-253). Bandelier was the first (and, in reality, the only) scholar to seriously attempt an integration of historical and archaeological data in the Piro area. Some of Bandelier's correlations are correct, in

particular those of Sevilleta and Socorro, but not others. Bandelier's disadvantage was that he was a true pioneer in both fields, history and archaeology, and thus lacked the full resources from either discipline necessary to solve the problems involved. He was especially handicapped by the very limited time available to him fro archaeological survey. Furthermore, it must be remembered that Bandelier was taking on the whole Southwest, not just one short stretch of river valley, so his efforts were necessarily extremely diffuse.

Mecham: In 1917, J. Lloyd Mecham, working under Herbert E. Bolton, produced an M.A. thesis at the University of California entitled "The Rodriguez Expedition into New Mexico." In this thesis, he attempted to identify the pueblos mentioned by the 1581–1582 Rodriguez-Chamuscado Expedition, using historical accounts of that expedition in conjunction with information from the Espejo Expedition and the Oñate Colonization. (Hammond and Rey 1966: 51) His conclusions were later published in Mecham (1926). Although Mecham utilized the archaeological evidence provided by Bandelier (1892: 236-253), there is no hint that Mecham ever set foot in the Piro area to observe the archaeological remains for himself. I find Mecham's conclusions (as presented in Mecham 1926) unsatisfactory on several grounds:[1] Mecham fails to make correlations of historic pueblos with specific archaeological sites, which reduces his locations for pueblos to nothing more than historical speculation unsupported by tangible evidence,[2] Mecham appears to ignore locational evidence within the documents he used, as when he places Piña and Piastla on opposite banks of the Rio Grande in his map (Mecham 1926: facing page 272) when the documents clearly indicate that they are both on the same side of the river, and[3] Mecham has the Rodriguez-Chamuscado party reaching the Piro territory via the west bank of the Rio Grande, while internal evidence suggests that they were on the east bank when they reached the Piros. Mecham was working under two handicaps: (1) he had no more archaeological evidence than that provided by Bandelier, and (2) he attempted to encompass the whole of the Rio Grande and Zuñi areas, with the result that errors in the sequential identities of pueblos in one area were carried over and compounded in the next. The net result is that Mecham's work, while influential in his own time, unfortunately is of no lasting value (in sharp contrast to that of Bandelier).

Hodge: In 1935, Frederick Webb Hodge published an article in the New Mexico Historical Review, correlating and correcting names of pueblos recorded in the documents of the Oñate Colonizations; a slightly revised list was republished later (Hodge 1953) and is the version under consideration here. Hodge's aim in his list was to correct spelling mistakes in transliterations of pueblo names from Spanish documents, to group variations of the same name together, and to correlate the names in the documents with known names of known pueblos. In these objectives, he was reasonably successful, although there remains considerable room for improvement. Unfortunately, Hodge did not attempt the next step: the correlation of the historic pueblos with archaeological sites.

Mera: Working from his base at the Laboratory of Anthropology in Santa Fe, Henry Percival Mera conducted the first archaeological survey of the Piro area since Bandelier's work. The result was a greatly expanded corpus of known sites that could be considered for correlation with historic pueblos. (Mera 1940: 6-13) He also provided a temporal scheme based upon glaze-pottery types which, although flawed, could be used to distinguish prehistoric from historic occupations. Mera himself made little attempt to correlate his sites with historic pueblos, singling but only one (LA 791), which he identified as being the pueblo of Pilabo (Socorro). While demonstrably incomplete, Mera's survey provided a sufficient database to have allowed considerable advances in correlation beyond the effort of Mecham if only historians (or archaeologists) had been willing to apply themselves to the problem. Instead, nothing was done.

Hammond and Rey: From the 1920s through the 1960s, the historians working most intensively with the relevant 16th and early 17th century documents were George P. Hammond and Agapito Rey. (See Hammond and Rey 1928, 1940, 1953, 1966; Hodge, Hammond and Rey 1945.) By and large, these two scholars confided their efforts to pursuits circumscribed by the narrower view of history: transcription, translation, and summation of basic historical documents, with an emphasis on the European invaders and their activities. Native (Pueblo Indian) history received second place in their attentions, hence important considerations of fact, such as pin-pointing the true locations of Piro pueblos, were by-passed, or even dismissed, as being virtually insoluble. (1) Generally, the same assessment can be made for the other historians of the early Spanish Colonial era (with the possible exception of Charles Wilson Hackett) and of Euro-American historical scholarship as a whole, which has led in recent times to the development within Anthropology of that new inter-disciplinarian, the ethnohistorian.

Wilson: In 1971, some archaeological surveying was done in the Piro area by John P. Wilson and Pat Beckett, during which sites previously located by Mera were revisited and some new sites located. There is no publication summarizing the results of this survey, but site forms sent to the Laboratory of Anthropology include correlations of some sites with historic pueblos. The reason for these correlations is not indicated on the site forms. The only correlations with which I can agree at present is that of LA 774 with Sevilleta.

Schroeder: The most recent treatment of the Piro pueblos is that by Albert H. Schroeder (1979: 236-241). While Schroeder does not make explicit archaeological site/historic pueblo correlations in his text, his map (his Figure 2) shows his conception of the positions of several named historic pueblos in the Piro area. While the positions shown for Sevilleta (Seelocu), Alamillo, and Socorro (Pilabo) are approximately correct, his positions for Senecu and Qualacu are not ones I can accept. Furthermore, his attempt at correlating the pueblos reported by the Rodriguez-Chamuscado and Espejo Expeditions (his Table 1) is faulty, and I believe he is mistaken in correlating Coronado's Tutahaco with the Piros since it is more likely that Tutahaco is the southern group of Tiwa pueblos in the Los Lunas/Isleta area.

None of the research reviewed above is satisfactory in the problem area of archaeological site/historic pueblo correlations. Specific correlations are either non-existent, vague, or incomplete, and perhaps worst of all, the methodology or reasons behind the correlations are seldom, if ever, specified. Thus, those correlations presented appear to be merely matters of opinion, with very little empirical basis. The net result is that only two correlations between archaeological sites and historic pueblos can be considered as established through previous work with any degree of certainty and consensus: that of LA 774 with Sevilleta, and that of LA 791 with Socorro/Pilabo.

Methodology of the Present Study

The set of correlations, which I present below, are based upon an explicit methodology, which seeks a detailed integration of archaeological and historical data to arrive at valid correlations. The methodology may be outlined as follows:

I. Data Base:

a. Locational and descriptive data for historic Piro pueblos recorded within Spanish Colonial documents, namely

i. Distances between pueblos and/or named localities,

ii. Relative sequences of pueblos along the Rio Grande in the Piro area,

iii. Descriptions of individual pueblos, and

iv. Maps of the Piro area;

b. Locational and descriptive data for archaeological sites recorded by archaeologists from ca. 1880 to the present day, namely:

i. Locations of archaeological sites with Glaze E and F occupations in the Piro area,

ii. Descriptions of the individual archaeological sites, (2) and

iii. Personal visits to the sites LA 224, 282 (twice), 283 (twice), 285, 286, 287, 755, and 774 (twice) in the summers of 1980 and 1981.

II. Procedures:

a. I have accepted LA 774 and LA 791 as correlating with the historic pueblos of Sevilleta and Socorro/Pilabo, respectively, and hence have used these archaeological sites as fixed points from which to make measurements of distances recorded in the Spanish Colonial documents;

b. Distances, relative positions, and descriptions of Piro pueblos from the documents being measured on U.S. Geological Survey maps, and correlations made with known archaeological sites for several periods within the early Spanish Colonial era, (3) to wit:

i. The period of the Pueblo Revolt and the Reconquest (1680–1693), plus some sources from the 1700s,

ii. The period between 1620 and 1680,

iii. The period of the Oñate Colonization (ca. 1598–1610), and

iv. The period of explorations in the 1580s;

c. In each case above, the positive results for the preceding periods (1 through 4) were used as a framework for understanding each successively earlier period.

The net result is that reasonable correlations have been achieved between most of the historically known Piro pueblos and individual archaeological sites. Contributing greatly to this positive outcome has been Mike Marshall's generous sharing with me of the results of the concurrent archaeological survey of the Piro area. (Marshall et alia 1981) These new archaeological data have greatly supplemented those previously available (collected by Bandelier, Mera, and Wilson, as discussed above) and filled in a number of troubling lacunae. Marshall's final results are presented in Marshall and Walt (1984).

The Archaeological Sites

The archaeological sites in the Piro area, which merit consideration for correlation with historic Piro pueblos, are those exhibiting Glaze E and F ceramics.[4] Figure 5-1 shows these sites in their correct geographical positions while Table 5-1 provides information on their ceramic composition. As noted above, I accept as established correlations between LA 774 and the historic pueblo of Sevilleta, and LA 791 and the historic pueblo of Socorro/Pilabo.

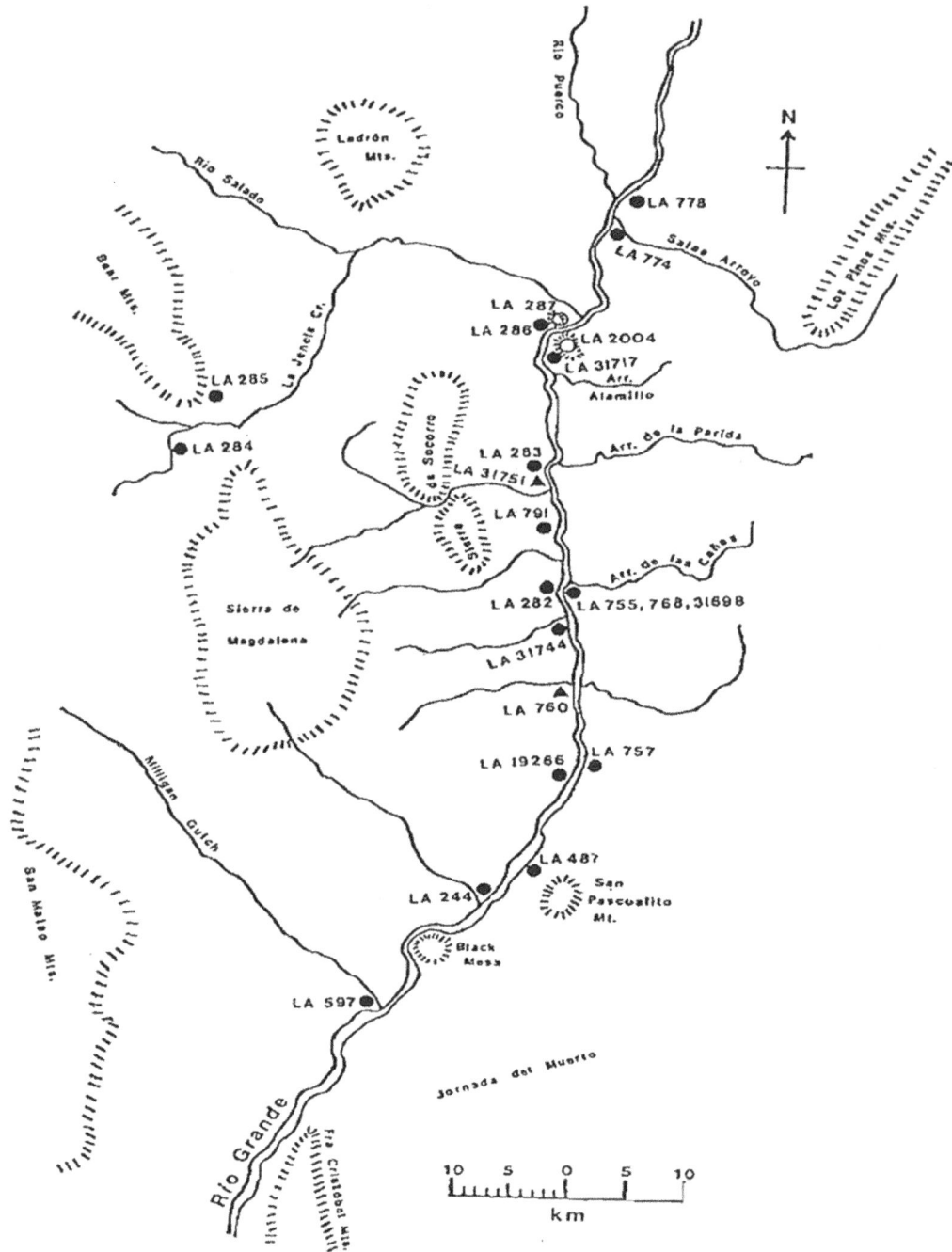

ARCHÆOLOGICAL SITES IN PIRO AREA

Glaze E/F Sites: ● = pueblo; ▲ = small site

O = prehistoric pueblo with traces of Glaze E/F

Figure
5 - 1

Figure 5-1

Table 5-1: LATE GLAZE ARCHAEOLOGICAL SITES

| | | Ceramic Relative Abundance | |
LA No.	Kind of Site	Glaze E	Glaze F
244	pueblo	major	major
282	pueblo	minor	minor
283	pueblo	"	"
284	pueblo	major	major
285	pueblo	"	"
286	estancia	"	"
287*	pueblo	trace	trace
487	pueblo	minor	minor
597	pueblo	major	---
755	pueblo	minor	(present)
757	pueblo	"	minor
760	sherd scatter	"	---
768	isolated rooms	"	---
774	pueblo	major	major
778	small pueblo	"	---
791	pueblo	"	major
2004*	pueblo	trace	trace
19266**	pueblo	major	---
31698	small pueblo	"	(present)
31717	small pueblo	"	major
31744**	pueblo	"	---
31751	isolated rooms	"	major

* The traces of Glazes E and F at these sites probably reflect visitation rather than true occupation.

** The apparent lack of Glaze F at these sites may be an artifact of the very small ceramic samples obtained.

The relative abundances of the ceramic categories are estimations communicated to me be Mike Marshall, with the exception of those in parentheses which are modifications made by me to Marshall's original table.

Table 5-1

Sources: Marshall et alia (1981), Mera (1940), and Marshall (personal communication).

Table 5-2: RETREAT AND RECONQUEST ITINERARIES (1680-1682)

NORTH

Alonso Garcia's Retreat (1680) ↓	Gov. Otermín's Retreat (1680) ↓	Otermin's Northward Trip (1681) ↑	Otermin's Southward Trip (1682) ↓
Isleta (Aug. 14)	Isleta (Aug. 29)	Isleta (Dec. 6) ↑	Opposite Isleta (Jan.1) ↓ (1 league) 1st stop (Jan. 1) ↓ Tome (Jan. 2 to 5) ↓
Pueblo del Alto* (Aug.20)	Las Nutrias (?)	Las Barrancas (Dec.5) ↑	Pueblo del Alto*(Jan.5) ↓ Vega de las Nutrias (Jan.6) ↓ Stop north of Sevilleta (Jan.8) ↓
Sevilleta (?)		Sevilleta (Dec.4) ↑	
	Cerro de Acomilla ↓ (1 league) (Sept.6) Alamillo (Sept.6)	Las Vueltas de Aco-milla (Dec.2) ↑ Alamillo (Dec.1) ↑	Las Vueltas de Acomilla (Jan.9 & 10) (cross Cerro de Aco-milla) ↓ Alamillo (Jan.11-13) Opposite El Nogal (Jan.13) ↓
		La Vuelta de Socorro (Nov.30) ↑	In sight of Socorro (Jan. 14) ↓
Socorro (Aug.24)	Socorro (?)	Socorro (Nov.29) ↑ stop (Nov.28) ↑	Opposite Socorro (Jan. 15) ↓ Hacienda de Luis López (Jan.16 ↓ Qualacú (Jan.17) ↓
		(6 leagues) San Pascual (Nov.27) ↑ Senecu (Nov.26) ↑	San Pascual (Jan.18) ↓ Beyond Senecu (Jan.19) ↓
	(16 leagues)	El Contadero (Nov.25) ↑	El Contadero (Jan.20) ↓
Fra Cristobal (Sept.4)	Fra Cristobal (Sept.13 & 14)	Fra Cristobal (Nov.24) ↑	Fra Cristobal (Jan.21)

SOUTH

Pueblo del Alto apparently was a ruined pueblo on the east bank in the vicinity of Belén; Mera (1940) does not record any glaze-pottery sites in the area.

Sources: (a) Alonso Garcia's Retreat: Hackett (1942,I: 70,71,73,82)
  (b) Gov. Otermín's Retreat: Hackett (1942,I: 27,60,62,63,65,85,88-90,92,94,112,116, 120,121; II: 164)
  (c) Otermin's Northward Trip: Hackett(1942,II: 203-208)
  (d) Otermin's Southward Trip: Hackett (1942,II: 362-364).

Table 5-2

Distance Measurements in the Spanish Documents

The unit of distance measurement used in the early Spanish Colonial period was the legua (league). Unfortunately, there was some variation in the length value of the league: most sources use a league equivalent to 2.6 miles (4.18 km), but Don Diego de Vargas in 1692 used a shorter league equal to ca. 2.2 miles (3.5 km). Unless otherwise indicated, the leagues referred to in this chapter are the 2.6-mile leagues. A problem, which arises in the distance records, is the Spaniards' habit of rounding-off distances to the nearest league, which results in a ±1.3 mile margin of error in all distance figures that must be taken into account when making correlations.

Correlations for the Period of the Pueblo Revolt and After (1680–1692)

At the time of the Pueblo Revolt in 1680, the historical documents indicate that only four Piro pueblos were inhabited: Sevilleta, Alamillo, Socorro (Pilabo), and Senecu. In addition, the revolt-era documents make casual mention of several abandoned pueblos, as well as a number of Spanish estancias and natural landmarks within the Piro area. The main sources consist of the itineraries of Spanish groups passing up and down the camino real. Four of these itineraries are presented in Table 5-2: they are the two retreats by Spanish refugees from the Pueblo Revolt in 1680 and Governor Otermin's journeys up and down the Rio Grande during his attempted Reconquest of 1681–1682. Otermin's southward trip in 1682 is the most detailed in terms of mention of places along the camino real due to his slow progress and frequent stops caused by inclement weather. There is not much information on absolute distances in these accounts, but there is a wealth of data on the relative sequence of pueblos and landmarks.

Among the important landmarks mentioned are "Las Vueltas de Acomilla," "La Vuelta de Socorro," and the "Cerro de Acomilla." The term Vuelta (literally, "turn") seems to be used to mean "entrenched meander," since it is clear that "Las Vueltas de Acomilla" refers to the series of river meanders hemmed in by escarpments which begin just north of present-day San Acacia and end about 4 km (2.5 miles) south of present-day La Joya. La Vuelta de Socorro appears to be the constriction of the Rio Grande's floodplain at present-day Pueblito, just south of the confluence of the Arroyo de la Parida with the Rio Grande. The "Cerro de Acomilla"

appears to be the high ridge on the east bank of the Rio Grande, which runs southeast from the mouth of Las Vueltas de Acomilla. The name "Acomilla" (literally, "Little 'Acoma") sounds like a pueblo site, and was probably a name attached to a pueblo ruin by the Spanish. The most likely candidate would be LA 287, which is located on a mesa reminiscent of the site of 'Acoma just north of present-day San Acacia, but another possibility is LA 2004, which is situated high on the Cerro de Acomilla itself.

An important landmark was the locality called "Fra Cristobal," where the camino real reached the Rio Grande after traversing the Jornada del Muerto from the south. In the records of Gov. Otermin's retreat, the distance along the east bank of the river from a point opposite Socorro to Fra Cristobal is recorded as 16 leagues. (Hackett 1942, I: 105) My measurement of this distance (ca. 41.5 miles) reached a point on the Paraje Well Quadrangle map roughly opposite the mouth of Lumbre Canyon, from which point Paraje Well itself is within the ±1.3 mile margin of error. The Paraje Well locality is at the northwest corner of a large sediment-filled embayment (an old meander?) on the east bank of the Rio Grande; this embayment, or, actually, the portion of it bordering the river, is in my opinion the historic camping spot known as Fra Cristobal. (This is within 3 miles of the northern tip of the Fra Cristobal Mountains.)[5]

North of Fra Cristobal and south of the pueblo of Senecu was a landmark known as El Contadero, "The Narrow Passage," which name probably refers to a point along the east bank of the Rio Grande that was constricted in some fashion; perhaps the reference was to a narrow floodplain bank between the river and the cliffs of Black Mesa. Other landmarks mentioned seem to be the names of Spanish estancias: El Nogal (the Walnut) on the west bank north of La Vuelta de Socorro, and the Hacienda de Luis Lopez on the east bank south of Socorro.

The itineraries of 1680–1682 make it clear that the route of the camino real through the Piro area was from Fra Cristobal north along the Rio Grande's floodplain until past La Vuelta de Socorro, when the road climbed out of the floodplain and passed over the ridge called the Cerro de Acomilla, dropping down onto the floodplain again within Las Vueltas de Acomilla (directly south of the mouth of the Rio Salado) and again following the floodplain north out of Las Vueltas de Acomilla and past Sevilleta. Apparently the reason for the camino real crossing the Cerro de Acomilla is the narrow constriction of the river between basaltic cliffs at the mouth of Las Vueltas de Acomilla. While this constriction would be passable during low water periods, at floodstage in the spring, it would be filled by the river, hence the need to by-pass this dangerous point.

This leaves us with mention of six pueblos in the Piro area: Sevilleta and Socorro, whose locations are already known, and Alamillo, Qualacu, San Pascual, and Senecu. Two of these, San Pascual and Qualacu, both on the east bank between Senecu and Socorro, are noted as being in ruins at the time of the Pueblo Revolt, hence must have been abandoned earlier in the century. On Otermin's northward trip in 1681, it is specifically stated that San Pascual is within sight of Senecu and it is clear from the itinerary that it lay slightly north of Senecu. Since it is equally clear from the records that Senecu was on the western bank of the river, we should look for a pair of pueblos nearly opposite each other, with the eastern pueblo slightly further north. I suggest that LA 19266 and LA 757 fit these requirements and may be identified as Senecu and San Pascual, respectively. Evidence that this identification is correct can be found in the distance between Senecu and Socorro given by Vetancurt (1697: 98) as seven leagues (18.2 miles), which matches perfectly the distance between LA 19266 and Socorro as measured along the floodplain of the west bank.

The correlation of San Pascual with LA 757 then suggests a possible correlation between Qualacu and the three closely associated sites of LA 755, LA 768, and LA 31698. (See Figure 5-1.) The Hacienda de Luis Lopez would then lie somewhere north of the Arroyo de las Cañas and south of a point opposite the pueblo of Socorro (LA 791). For the moment, this will be left as a tentative correlation.

The itineraries clearly indicate that the pueblo of Alamillo is on the east bank of the Rio Grande between Socorro and the Cerro do Acomilla. Vetancurt (1697: 98) gives the distance between Alamillo and Socorro as 3 leagues (7.8 miles) and that between Alamillo and Sevilleta as 5 leagues (13 miles). Remembering the ±1.3 mile margin of error, these measurements converge on a pueblo ruin known as LA 8870, which I would not hesitate to designate as Alamillo if only there were clear evidence of Glaze F occupation. Unfortunately, the ceramic surface collection made by John P. Wilson in 1971 does not give unequivocal evidence of such an occupation. At present, the best I can say is that the pueblo of Alamillo must have existed somewhere in the near vicinity of LA 8870.

Turning now to the information given in the itineraries of the Reconquest and Recolonization of 1691–1693 (See Table 5-3), a problem which confronts the researcher is the length of the leagues used for recording distances: Vargas was using a "short" league equal to 2.2 miles on his

Reconquest journey, but distances recorded for the Recolonization journey are in the familiar 2.6-mile leagues.

Most of the locations mentioned in these itineraries are already familiar from the earlier records of the Pueblo Revolt. The Hacienda de Felipe Romero was just a short distance north of Sevilleta, as witness Vargas' statement: "(I) arrived with the camp at this uninhabited pueblo of Sevilleta, and I continued on to the farm which is said to have belonged formerly to Felipe Romero." (J. M. Espinosa 1940: 66) As Vargas' starting point for that day's march was the pueblo of Alamillo, known to be about five (2.6 miles) leagues (13 miles) south of Sevilleta, then Vargas' march of six or seven (2.2-mile) leagues (13.2 to 15.4 miles) places the Hacienda de Felipe Romero at between 0.2 and 2.4 miles north of Sevilleta. The extreme distance, 2.4 miles, would place the hacienda at the present-day village of Contreras.

Vargas' stopping place "near Socorro" on Sept. 2, 1592 apparently was a point on the east bank about 3.2 miles south of Socorro, or just north of the Arroyo de las Cañas. This would locate the "Place of Juan Garcia" as about 15.4 miles south, or on the east bank roughly opposite the head-quarters of the Bosque del Apache Wildlife Refuge (and LA 19266, Senecu). Another five leagues (ca. 11 miles) brings us to the vicinity of Val Verde, which Vargas refers to as "near Senecu." (Senecu, LA 19266, is about 7.4 miles directly north.)[6] A further five leagues south of Val Verde brings one near to the camping place of Fra Cristobal.

On his journey southward, Vargas returned to the Piro area directly overland from Zuñi, passing through the Sierra de Socorro by means of the canyon now called Cañoncito del Puertecito de Lemitar. From the eastern foot of these mountains, Vargas traveled "two long leagues" (i.e., 2.6-mile leagues) south to the pueblo of Socorro. (J.M. Espinosa 1940: 246) On the next day, Vargas traveled "nine or ten leagues" (2.2-mile leagues) to a spot "in view of, and a short distance from, the pueblo of Senecu." (J.M. Espinosa 1940: 247) Vargas' march of 19.8 to 22 miles would place his camping spot south of Senecu (LA 19266). From there, he continued on south down the west bank of the river.

On considering the Recolonization itinerary, it is clear that 2.6-mile leagues are being used as its total of leagues from Fra Cristobal to the Hacienda de Felipe Romero is 25 to 26 leagues, which compares well with the total of 24 leagues from Fra Cristobal to Sevilleta, derivable from the Pueblo Revolt period documents.[7] A problem arises, however, in the distance from Socorro to the Hacienda de Luis Lopez, which is given as "3 leagues" (Bailey 1940: 93): this would place the Hacienda de Luis Lopez south of Arroyo de las Cañas, about halfway between Bosquecito and Gallegos Well. In contrast, Otermin's 1682 itinerary south from Isleta (See Table 5-2) clearly places the Hacienda de Luis Lopez between Socorro and Qualacu, and Qualacu is tentatively identified with LA 755 and other sites at the mouth of Arroyo de las Cañas. One solution would be to assume that LA 755 is not Qualacu, which would then place Qualacu somewhere south of Gallegos Well. Such displacement southwards for Qualacu is hard to justify since (as will be seen) distance data from the Oñate Colonization strongly support a correlation between Qualacu and LA 755 and associated sites. The question then becomes one of the correct location for the Hacienda de Luis Lopez: north or south of LA 755? As will be seen from data from Tamaron's 1760 itinerary, which supports the location for the hacienda given in Vargas' itinerary; hence, the problem may lie with Otermin's placement of the hacienda. (There is no data confirming Otermin's placement. Did he reverse the positions of Qualacu and the hacienda?)

One more facet needs to be mentioned: Bailey (1940: 93) gives the distance from Fra Cristobal to the Hacienda de Luis Lopez as a mere two leagues, whereas J.M. Espinosa (1942: 133, footnote) gives the distance as twelve leagues. I have checked the reading of the Spanish text on this point and can confirm that twelve leagues is the true distance recorded.[8]

Before turning back to earlier 17th century accounts, it is worth examining three 18th century itineraries to see how they compare with those already given above. These itineraries are presented in Table 5-4. The original tables of Tamaron's journeys appear to include several typographical errors relating to distances, which complicates matters. Tamaron's distance from Fra Cristobal to the Hacienda de Luis Lopez (13 leagues) agrees well with the 12 leagues given by Vargas (See above), but the component distances (from Fra Cristobal to San Pascual to Luis Lopez) seem faulty since they would place San Pascual two leagues south (at LA 487) of its previously determined location at LA 757. Since Tamaron refers in his text (Tamaron y Romeral 1937: 332) to the journey between San Pascual and Luis Lopez as "short," we should probably read "3" or "4" leagues instead of "6" and, correspondingly, "9" instead of "7" leagues for the distance between San Pascual and Fra Cristobal.

Tamaron's locality called "Alamitos" or "Alamo" is apparently not the ruins of the pueblo of Alamillo, but a camping spot almost opposite the mouth of Rio Salado, very near the confluence of the Arroyo Rosa de Castilla with the Rio Grande. Of his next day's journey northward, Tamaron states: "On the following day, in the middle of the journey, we found the site where the pueblo of Servilleta (sic) used to be, and a little further on the ruined estancia of Felipe Romero, both of which were lost along with the kingdom (in the 1680 Revolt)." (Tamaron y Romeral 1937: 333)[9] This confirms the location of the Hacienda de Felipe Romero indicated in Vargas' northbound itinerary.

The itinerary of Anza's journey south in 1780 is less equivocal in its distance entries, as they are given twice in the text: once as the distance traveled in a particular day, and again as the total distance traveled from Santa Fe up to that particular day. Traveling south from Las Nutrias, Anza's party reached a point near present-day La Joya, which is referred to as being "in the Vueltas de Romero." (Thomas 1932: 198) It appears that the stretch of the Rio Grande, known as Las Vueltas de Acomilla in the 17th century, had been renamed in the 18th century after the Hacienda de Felipe Romero near its northern end. Five leagues travel on the next day brought the party into the "region of Alamillo," probably almost to the mouth of the Arroyo de la Parida. Another five leagues south from there brought the party to "Pueblito," which corresponds with the location for the Hacienda de Luis Lopez given in the earlier itineraries. Four leagues more brought the party to a spot about 1.5 miles south of San Pascual (LA 757), which Anza refers to as both "the spring of the Apaches" and "Apache Wood" (Thomas 1932: 198), recognizable as the modern Bosque del Apache. From there, the party traveled four leagues to Val Verde. (The distance is almost precisely correct when measured on the maps.) The last five leagues on the itinerary brought the party to the embayment previously identified as Fra Cristobal, and so they call it.

Maps for 1680 and after are not very accurate in their locations for pueblos, with the major exception of the maps made by Bernardo de Miera y Pacheco in the mid-18th century. An example of these latter is Miera's 1758 map of New Mexico (published in Kessell 1979: 3) which clearly shows Sevilleta, Alamillo, Socorro, Senecu, and San Pascual in their correct respective positions (Sevilleta and Alamillo on the east bank of the Rio Grande north of Socorro, Socorro and Senecu on the west bank, and San Pascual on the east bank across from, and slightly north, of Senecu). The other two maps are unfortunately of little use due to their inaccuracies, namely:

1) A French map prepared by Nicholas de Fer in 1700 (Plate 12 in Leonard 1932) is the better of the two since it shows Sevilleta, Alamillo, Socorro, and Senecu in their correct order from north to south

and on the correct banks of the Rio Grande, however their position in relation to other features (such as the Rio Puerco and Isleta pueblo) leaves much to be desired; and

　　2) The Coronelli map of 168(?) (Published in the New Mexico Historical Review, Vol. 2, No. 4; October 1927) shows Alamillo and Senecu on the wrong sides of the Rio Grande.

The pueblos and landmarks of the late 17th century (ca. 1680–1700) in the Piro area are shown in Figure 5-2.

Correlations for the Period 1620–1680

There is not a great amount of relevant information for the period 1620 and 1680, most of what there is being confirmatory of correlations made on the basis of the later documentation discussed above.

It is apparent that in the 1660s, the Hacienda de Felipe Romero belonged to an individual named Diego de Guadalajara on the basis of two statements: (a) In 1661, capitan Andres Hurtado stated that the hacienda of Diego de Guadalajara was "but one league" distant from the pueblo of Sevilleta (Hackett 1937: 189), and (b) Fray Joseph de Epeleta in 1660 stated that this same hacienda was "six leagues from the pueblo of Alamillo" (Hackett 1937: 148), which two distances would place the hacienda a league north of Sevilleta, and thus identify it with the one later known as belonging to Felipe Romero. Chavez (1954: 43) records that Diego de Guadalajara's daughter, Jacinta Bernardo y Quiros, married Felipe Romero, which would explain his later ownership of the hacienda.

In the accounts of the hurried journey of the Frailes Alonso de Posada and Salvador de Guerra from the pueblo of Alamillo to the pueblo of Isleta in 1662 for the purpose of arresting Nicolas de Aguilar and other persons, it is twice stated that the distance from Alamillo to Isleta is 18 leagues. (Kessell n.d.: 133, 138) It is also clear from these accounts (as well as from the accounts from the Pueblo Revolt period) that Isleta was on the west bank of the Rio Grande. Thus, a distance of 18 leagues north from LA 8870 (near the position of Alamillo) and crossing to the west bank of the Rio Grande north of the Rio Puerco brings one almost precisely to the archaeological site known as LA 81. (See Mera 1940: 18.) Therefore, I correlate 17th-century Isleta with LA 81, in contradistinction to those scholars who assume that present-day Isleta is on the site of the 17th-century pueblo. (e.g., Vivian 1932: 44-47.) This correlation is supported by Mera's

inability to locate any significant glaze-pottery occupation at present-day Isleta. (Mera 1940: 20)

The previously established correlations for pueblos in the Piro area are supported by Fra Alonso de Benavides' definition of the Piro province in 1630:

> This province of the Piros extends along up the Rio del Norte from the first pueblo of San Antonio de Senecu up to the last, San Luis de Sevilleta, fifteen leagues, where there are fourteen pueblos, on one and the other side of the river. (Ayer 1916: 19)

Fifteen leagues perfectly encompasses the distance from LA 19266 to LA 774, confirming the correspondence of Senecu with LA 19266, and thus that of San Pascual with LA 757. It also strengthens the probably of a correlation between Qualacu and LA 755 and associated sites. Other significant information given by Benavides includes the Piro names for Socorro and Sevilleta, "Pilabo" and "Seelocu" respectively. (Ayer 1916: 17; Hodge, Hammond and Rey 1945: 64)

Maps available from this period are not detailed and/or are very inaccurate in their placement of pueblos:

　　1) French map by Pierre Du Val dating to 1670, which only shows the pueblo of Socorro on the west bank of the Rio Grande, with the river flowing southwest into the Gulf of California. (Bloom 1945: 276-278, frontispiece);

　　2) The "Peñalosa Map" of 1665 (or later), apparently prepared by a French cartographer from information supplied by the renegade Spaniard, ex-governor of New Mexico, Don Dionisio de Peñalosa (Bloom 1934), which map shows Senecu, Socorro, and Sevilleta in approximately their correct positions, but wrongly placed Alamillo on the west bank of the Rio Grande; also incorrectly sited is the estancias of Las Barrancas, placed between Senecu and Socorro, which was actually located just south of Isleta; and

　　3) The Sanson Map of 1657 (Bloom 1936), prepared by French cartographer Nicolas Sanson d'Abbeville, shows only two pueblos, Socorro (correctly) and Sevilleta (incorrectly) on the west bank of the Rio Grande, which, as in the du Val Map (above), is flowing into the Gulf of California.

Table 5-3: RECONQUEST AND RECOLONIZATION ITINERARIES

NORTH

```
 Vargas' Reconquest Journey*    Recolonization Journey**

Northbound (1692) Southbound      _____(1693)_____

Hacienda de Felipe                Hacienda de Felipe
  Romero (Sept. 4)                  Romero
    |                                 |
    | (6/7 leagues)                    |
    |                                 |
Alamillo (Sept. 3)                  | (13/14 leagues)
    |                                 |
    | (5 leagues)                      |
    |               Socorro (Dec. 9)  |   Socorro
    |                   |             |     |
near Socorro (Sept. 2)  |             |     | (3 leagues)
    |                   |             |     |
    | (7 leagues)       |             Hacienda de Luis Lopez
    |                   |               |     (Nov. 4)
    |               (9/10 leagues)     |
    |                   |             |
Place of Juan Garcia    |             |
      (Sept. 1)         |             |
    |                   |             |
    |           In sight of Senecu    |
    |               (Dec. 10)         |
    |                                 |
    | (ca. 5 leagues)                 |
    |                                 | (12 leagues)
near Senecu (Aug. 31)                 |
    |                                 |
    | (ca. 5 leagues)                 |
    |                                 |
Fray Cristobal                    Fray Cristobal (Oct. 31)
```

SOUTH

* On the Reconquest Journey Vargas is using a "short" league
equal to ca. 2.2 miles.

** Distances of the Recolonization Journey apparently were
recorded in 2.6-mile leagues.

Sources: Northbound Reconquest Journey: J.M. Espinosa
(1940: 64-66).   Southbound   Reconquest   Journey:
J.M. Espinosa (1940: 246-268).   Recolonization Journey:
Bailey   (1940: 93-94),   J.M. Espinosa   (1942: 133-134).

Table 5-3

93

Table 5-4: ITINERARIES OF TAMARON AND ANZA (1760 AND 1780)

NORTH

```
Nutrias (May 18)    Nutrias (July 8)    Las Nutrias (Nov. 15)
  |                   |                    |
  | (9 leagues;  should be 7?)            | (3 leagues)
  |                   |                    |
  |                   |                   Vueltas de Romero
  |                   |                    |          (Nov. 16)
Alamitos (May 17)   Alamo (July 9)       | (5 leagues)
  |                   |                    |
  | (8 leagues)       | (3 leagues;      region of Alamillo
  |                   |  should be 8?)     |          (Nov. 17)
  |                   |                    | (5 leagues)
  |                   |                    |
Hacienda de Luis    Hacienda de Luis    Pueblito (Nov. 18)
  | Lopez (May 16)    | Lopez (July 10)   |
  |                   |                    | (4 leagues)
  | (6 leagues;       | (8 leagues;       |
  | should be 3?)     | should be 3?)     Spring of the Apaches
  |                   |                    |          (Nov. 19)
San Pascual         San Pascual          | (4 leagues)
  |       (May 15)    |       (July 11)   |
  |                   |                   Valverde (Nov. 20)
  | (7 leagues;  should be 9?)            |
  |                   |                    | (5 leagues)
  |                   |                    |
(Fra Cristobal)     (Fra Cristobal)     Fray Cristobal
                                                  (Nov. 22)
```

SOUTH

Sources: Tamaron's Northbound Trip: Tamaron y Romeral
(1937: 332-333, 382-383); Tamaron's Southbound Trip:
Tamaron y Romeral (1937: 382-384); Anza's Journey: Thomas
(1932: 198-199)

Table 5-4:

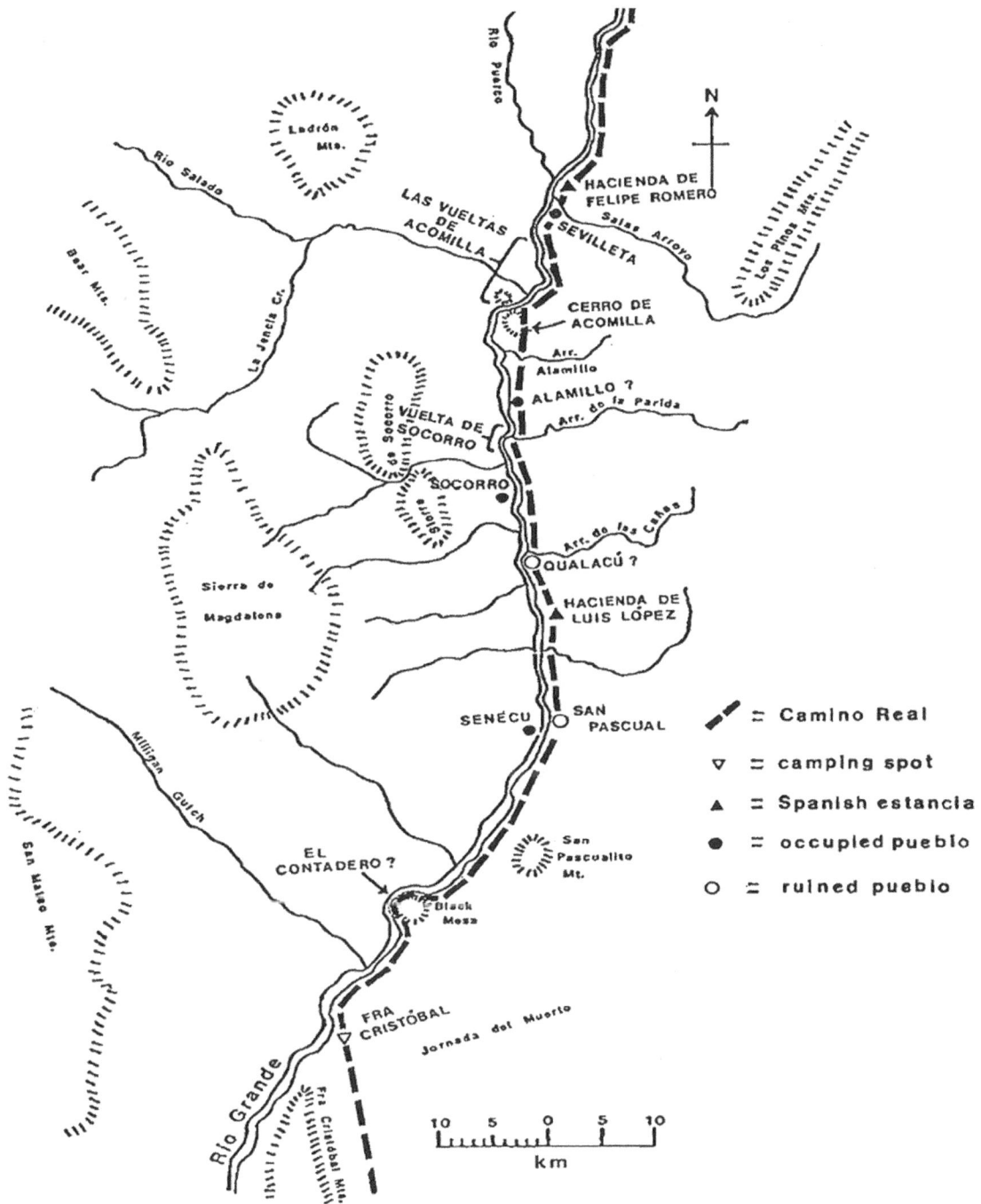

PIRO PUEBLOS AND PLACENAMES: 1680s

Figure

5 – 2

Figure 5-2

Table 5-5: ONATE COLONY ITINERARY AND MARTINEZ MAP

NORTH

Oñate_Colony_Itinerary_(1598)___ ___Martinez_Map_of_1602___

west_bank   east_bank   west_bank   east_bank

               San Juan Bautista   7) San Juan:
               | (June 22)   1 symbol
               |
               | (4 leagues)
               |
               Nueva Sevilla   6) Nueva Sevilla:
               | (June 16)   3 symbols
               | (4 + 3 leagues:
               | June 15 and 16)   5) no name:
               | 1 symbol
               beyond Teipana
Teipana | (June 14)
               | (3 leagues)   4) Socorro:
               | 1 symbol
               beyond Qualacu
               | (May 28)
               | Qualacu   3) no name: 2) Calicu:
               | 3 symbols   1 symbol
               | (almost 4 leagues)
               |
               La Cienega de la
               Mesilla de Guinea
               | (May 27)   1) no name:
               | 1 symbol
               | (7 + over 2
               | leagues: May
               | 26 and 27)
               |
               Place of reaching
               the Rio Grande (Fra
               Cristobal) (May 25)

SOUTH

Localities on the Martinez map were numbered; the informants
could not remember all of the names for pueblos.

Table 5-5

Table 5-6: LISTS OF PUEBLOS (1598)

NORTH

Decreto de Oñate (bank not specified)	Obedience and Vassalage at San Juan	
	West bank	East bank
	Pencoana	
	Quiomaqui	
	Peixoloe	
	Cumaque (Zumaque)	
	Teeytzaan	
	Puguey <-------->	Puguey
	Canocan	Tuzahe
	Geydol	Aponitze
	Quiubaco	Vumaheyn
	Tohol	Quiaoo
	Cantemachul	Cunquili
	Tercao	Pinoe
	Poloaca	Calziati
	Tzeyey	Aquiabo
	Quelquelu	Emxa
	Ategua	Quiaguacalca
	Tzuia	Quialoo
	Tzeygual	Izeiagui
	Tecahan	Puquias
	Guatahamo	Ayqui
(others not named)	Piloque (Piloque)	Yanano
Teypana	Penjeacu	Teyaxa
Tzenacu	Teypama	Qualacu
Qualaqu	Izenaguel de la	Texa
el de la Mesilla	Mesilla	Amo

The underlined names in the "Obedience and Vassalage" lists are those recognizable as known Piro pueblos.

Sources: Decreto de Oñate: Scholes and Mera (1940: 277). Obedience and Vassalage: Hammond and Rey (1953: 342-347), Pacheco et alia (1871b: 108-117).

Table 5-6

97

Correlations for the Period of the Oñate Colonization (1598–1610)

Data on the Piro area for this period consists of (a) the Oñate colony's itinerary north along the Rio Grande in 1598 (Table 5-5), (b) the Martinez Map of 1602 (Also in Table 5-5), and (c) two lists of Piro pueblos made in 1593. (Table 5-6)

The Oñate Colony's itinerary is particularly important since it gives distances between points along the Rio Grande in the Piro area. Working backwards from north to south, the first point identified is a "new" pueblo name by Oñate's party, "San Juan Bautista,"[10] four leagues north of Sevilleta, which should place it near the mouth of Abo Arroyo. Unfortunately, no archaeological site is known at present in that locality. It is not clear whether this was a Piro or Tiwa pueblo. South of San Juan Bautista is the pueblo named by the Oñate party, "Nueva Sevilla," later modified to "Sevilleta." This may be correlated with LA 774, as previously noted. South of Sevilleta, no pueblo is mentioned for a distance of some seven leagues (two day's march), with the first three leagues south from Sevilleta placing Oñate's party at a camping spot within Las Vueltas de Acomilla, probably near Arroyo Rosa de Castilla at more or less the same spot Tamaron was to rest at 162 years later. For the remaining four leagues south of this spot, Oñate states, "We always kept to the bank of the river,"[11] meaning that instead of crossing the Cerro de Acomilla like later travelers, Oñate's party passed through the mouth of Las Vueltas de Acomilla. (This was the middle of June, late enough for subsidence of the spring floodwaters to make this passage practical.) Thus, measuring south from Arroyo Rosa de Castilla via the mouth of Las Vueltas, one reaches a spot about one mile north of the mouth of Arroyo del la Parida: this is the camping spot where Oñate states "We slept (at a spot) beyond Teipana, the pueblo we call Socorro."[12] The itinerary does not make clear on which bank Teipana lay, but the Martinez map and the list of pueblos in the "Obedience and Vassalage" both clearly indicate the west bank; this would strongly suggest LA 283 as being the archaeological site correlating with Teipana. Three leagues south of the camp beyond Teipana brings us to a point 1.2 miles north of the mouth of Arroyo de Las Cañas where Oñate's party camped and recuperated between May 23 and June 14. This spot is a short distance "beyond" the pueblo of Qualacu, which clearly correlates Qualacu with LA 755 and its associated sites, which lie just south of Arroyo de las Cañas; this confirms the tentative correlation made on the basis of Pueblo Revolt period documents.

Qualacu is referred to as "the second pueblo," which I take to mean "the second pueblo on the east bank" as there is no indication in the itinerary that Oñate was aware of Senecu on the west bank. The first pueblo, therefore, would almost certainly be San Pascual (LA 757). To continue the itinerary, almost four leagues south of the camp "beyond Qualacu" brings one almost to the Vigil Brothers' Well, a spot at the northern end of the wide, marshy section of Rio Grande, now known as the Bosque del Apache, but referred to by Oñate as "La Cienega de la Mesilla de Guinea," the Mesilla de Guinea being his name for Black Mesa, which marks the southern end of the Bosque del Apache marsh. (As Oñate was approaching from the south, it is understandable that he would use the name for Black Mesa to also refer to the marsh beyond.) The remainder of the itinerary gives 9+ leagues as the distance to the point where the colony had descended from the Jornada del Muerto to the Rio Grande (the spot later to be known as Fra Cristobal).[13] The seven league journey on May 27 would have started south of Black Mesa and passed the first pueblo on the east bank (San Pascual, LA 757) on the way north.

The itinerary does not make specific mention of the locations of pueblos other than Qualacu, Teipana, Sevilleta, and San Juan Bautista, but off-hand reference is made to others. (Pacheco et alia 1871b: 251) The Martinez Map of 1602 augments this slightly, showing at (1) an unnamed pueblo which probably represents San Pascual, at (2) a pueblo named Calicu (=Qualacu), at (3) three triangles which may represent west bank pueblos (perhaps LA 31744, LA 282, and LA 791) at (4) a pueblo named Socorro (Teipana), at[5] an unmade pueblo, possibly representing Alamillo or the small site at LA 31717, at[6] three pueblos, one of which is Nueva Sevilla (Sevilleta), another of which may be LA 778, the third unidentified (but possibly representing the pueblo known as La Pedrosa to the Rodriguez-Chamuscado Expedition?, see discussion above), and at[7] the pueblo of San Juan (Bautista).

Passing on to the two lists in Table 5-6, it is quite clear that the "Obedience and Vassalage" list must include non-Piro pueblos further north along the Rio Grande, indeed only the southern dozen or so names yield any which can be definitely recognized as Piro. Among these, on the east bank, are "Tzelaqui," which compares well with the Piro name "Seelocu" recorded by Benavides for Sevilleta, and Qualacu; while on the west bank "Pilogue (or Pilooue)" compares well with the name "Pilabo" recorded by Benavides, "Teypama" is recognizably a variant of "Teipana," and "Tzenaquel de la Mesilla" can be recognized as Senecu when it is realized that it should be read as "Tzenaqu, el de la Mesilla."[14] However, the order of the pueblos, at least in the west bank list, seems to be somewhat scrambled since "Teypama" is listed as south of "Pilogue," whereas it should be north (i.e., Teipana = LA 283, Pilabo = LA 791). "Penjeacu" and "Qualahamo" may be names for the other two pueblos south of Teipana, at LA 31744 and LA 282, but which is which is anyone's guess since the names are mentioned only this one time in the Spanish Colonial records. The names "Tecahan" and "Tzeygual" may refer to LA 284 and LA 285 in the La Jencia Creek drainage west of the Rio Grande, but again, this is the only known mention of these names. The rest of the west bank list, from "Tzula" on, probably does not refer to the Piro pueblos at all. Returning to the east bank, I suspect that the two names "Texa" and "Amo" should really be read as one, that is, "Texahamo" (modeled on "Qualahamo," where the silent Spanish "h" would represent a glottal stop), which should then be the Piro name for San Pascual (LA 757). This leaves four pueblo names arranged between "Qualacu" and "Tzelaqui": since the 1602 Martinez Map shows four symbols (at "5" and "6") which are otherwise unaccounted for, I suggest that the four names from the list can be matched with the four symbols on the map. (See discussion above as to the possible identities of these four places.) Does "Quialpo" then represent the native name of San Juan Bautista? Possibly, but not certainly, and the remainder of the east bank list are probably not Piro pueblos at all.

The new correlations which emerge from the documents of the Oñate Colony may be summarized as (a) Teipana, the original Socorro, is correlated with LA 283; (b) Qualacu is confirmed as correlated with LA 755 and its associated sites; (c) a possible correlation is established between LA 282 and LA 31744 and the pueblos named Qualahamo and Penjeacu; (d) a more tentative correlation may be suggested between LA 284 and LA 285 and the pueblos named Tecahan and Tzeygual; (e) Tzelaqui and Texahamo are established as the probable Piro names for Sevilleta and San Pascual, respectively; (f) Alamillo (LA 8870?), LA 31717, LA 778, and an un-located site tentatively may be correlated with pueblos named Teyaxa, Yanamo, Ayqui, and Puquias without any certainty as to which name is associated with which site; and (g) San Juan Bautista may have been named Quialoo. These correlations are summarized in Figure 5-3.

A final point of some significance is that apparently none of the archaeological sites south of LA 19266 and LA 757 were occupied as late as 1598.

Correlations for the 1580s

The first two Spanish expeditions to reach New Mexico by ascending the Rio Grande, and thus to traverse the Piro area, were the Rodriguez-Chamuscado expedition of 1581–1582 and the Espejo Expedition of 1582–1583. Both expeditions provide itineraries listing, in more or less detail, the pueblos encountered and their locations. (See Tables 5-7 and 5-8) One problem unique to these itineraries is the fact that each expedition assigned arbitrary names of Spanish and Nahuatl origin to the pueblos encountered, resulting in two sets of names, which do not correlate with each other, nor with later names. Thus, the correct correlation of these sets of names has been one of the unsolved historical puzzles of the Piro area. I propose a solution to this problem below.

First, while it is clear that the Espejo Expedition arrived in the southern part of the Piro area via the west bank of the Rio Grande, it has not been certain upon which bank the Rodriguez-Chamuscado Expedition was traveling. I believe that the latter expedition ascended the east bank, which conclusion I arrived at by working backwards (i.e., from north to south) through the itineraries of the expedition while making comparisons to the itinerary of the Espejo Expedition.

The first task is to establish a specific point at which the itineraries of the two expeditions unequivocally correspond. This is found at the locality described by Luxan, the chronicler of the Espejo Expedition, "as where they camped at the said river (Rio Grande) between two pueblos two harquebus shots apart, they belonged to the same nation and had the same characteristics as the other, except that the walls are of stone from the river. The one had about sixty houses and other twenty...We named this place El Termino de Puala, for the Puala are a different nation from this and speak a different tongue." (Hammond and Rey 1966: 174)

Two harquebus shots would equal a distance of about 160 to 300 paces (about 400 to 750 feet, or 122 to 299 meters). (Salas 1950: 209) The reference to "Puala" is clearly to "Puaray," and thus to the Tiwas, [15] which places the two pueblos at the northern boundary of the Piro area. Turning to the Rodriguez-Chamuscado Expedition, we find reference to two pueblos, El Oso of 50 houses and La Pedrosa of 14 houses, the first of which is located "on a high hill" and the second "near El Oso, on the same side (of the Rio Grande) and in a bend formed by the bank of the river." (Hammond and Rey 1966: 103, 116) Since the relative sizes of El Oso and La Pedrosa are very close to those recorded for the pueblos of El Termino de Puala, I suggest that they are the same. The reference to stone construction immediately brings to mind the cobble construction of Sevilleta (LA 774) and, according to information of the Rodriguez-Chamuscado Expedition, El Oso and La Pedrosa are on the same side of the Rio Grande as Elota, which is "on the same side of the Sierra Morena," the name used for the Sandia-Manzano Range by that expedition (Hammond and Rey 1966: 103, 116), thus placing them on the east bank. There is now no second pueblo down on the floodplain near Sevilleta, but it very well may have been washed away by the Rio Grande.[16] I think, then, that El Oso (and La Pedrosa) and El Termino de Puala can be correlated with Sevilleta (LA 774).

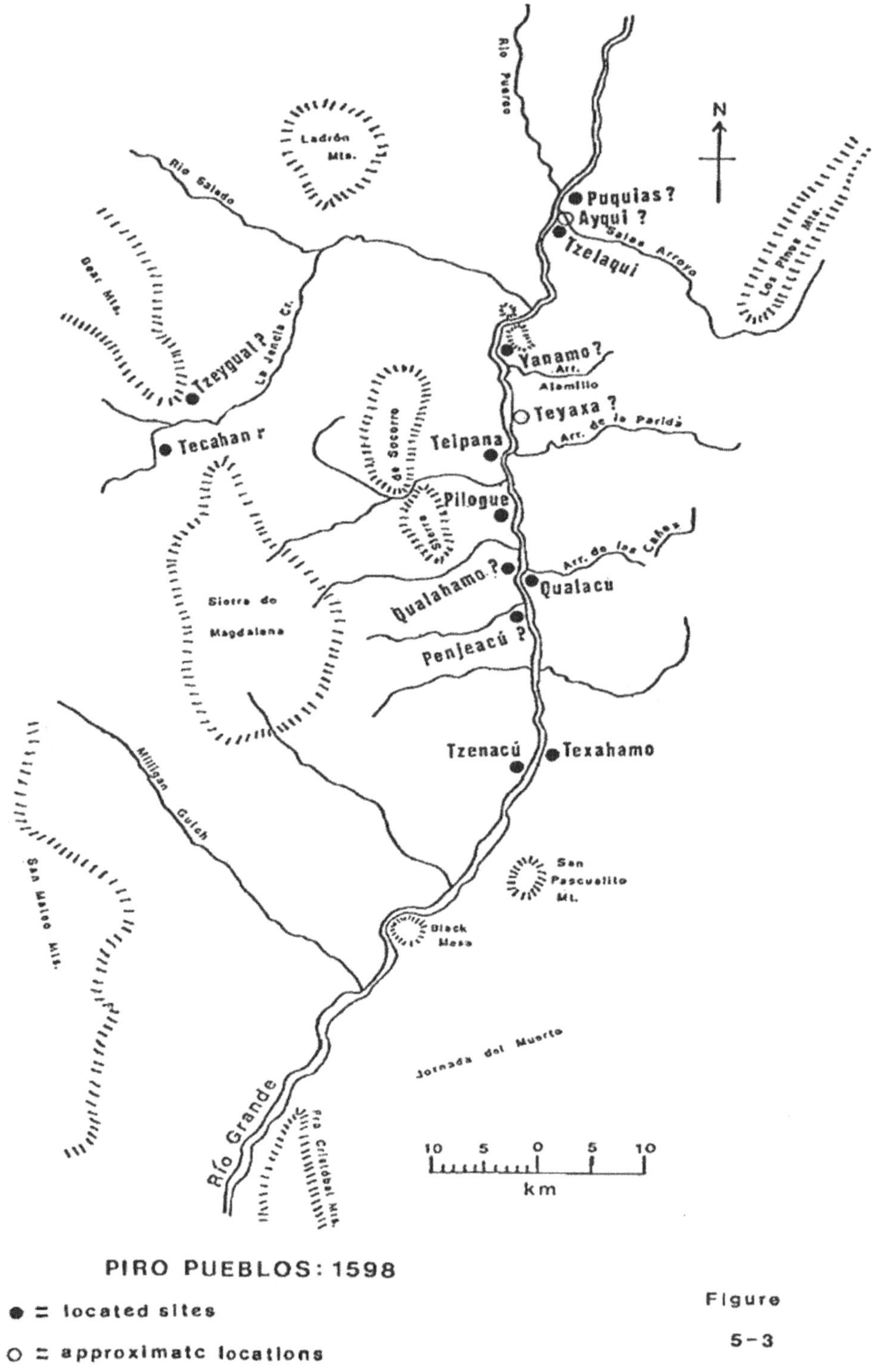

PIRO PUEBLOS: 1598

● = located sites

○ = approximate locations

Figure 5-3

Table 5-7: ITINERARIES OF THE RODRIGUEZ-CHAMUSCADO EXPEDITION

NORTH

Gallegos' Account of Itinerary		The Pedrosa List of Pueblos	
west bank	east bank	west bank	east bank
	Pueblo Nuevo (25)		Ponsitlán (25)
	Ponsitlán (25)		Pueblo Nuevo (20)
	{ El Hosso (50) { La Pedrosa (14)		{ El Oso (50) { La Pedrosa (14)
	Elota (14)		Elota (14)
Piña (85)		Piña (85)	
Piastla (35)	San Juan (40)	Piastla (35)	San Juan (40)
Santiago (25)	San Miguel (47)	Santiago (25)	San Miguel (47)
	↑ (ca. 2 leagues)		↑ (2 leagues)
	San Felipe (45) (ruined)		San Felipe (45) (ruined)

SOUTH

The numbers in parentheses are the number of "houses" (house-holds) per pueblo.
West bank and east bank pueblos on the same line are said in the itineraries to be on opposite sides of the river from each other.

Sources: Hammond & Rey(1928: 267-314), Hammond & Rey (1966: 67-114, 115-120)

Table 5-8: ITINERARY OF THE ESPEJO EXPEDITION

Source: Hammond and Rey (1966: 171-175)

```
El Corvillo (Feb. 13)                    NORTH
        |
        |    (4 leagues)
        |
 El Termino de Puala (Feb. 8) = 2 pueblos
        |                           (60 + 20 houses)
        |    (3 leagues)
        |
Jueves de las Comadres (Feb. 7) = camping spot
        |
        |    (5 leagues; pass 4 large ruined pueblos
        |     and a "small hamlet" of 20 houses)
        |
El Gallo (Feb. 6 ?) = last of the 5 pueblos?
        |
        |    (In midst of 5 pueblos: 4 of 50 houses
        |     each, 1 of 100 houses; went from pueblo
        |     to pueblo, no recorded distances)
        |
no name (Feb. 4) = first of the 5 pueblos?
        |
        |    (3 leagues)
        |
no name (date ?) = 2nd pueblo (50 houses),
        |                near San Felipe?
        |    (distance ?)
San Felipe (Feb. 1) = 1st occupied pueblo
        |
        |    (2 leagues)
        |
2nd ruined pueblo (Feb. 1)
        |
        |    (3 leagues)
        |
El Malpais (Jan. 31) = camping spot
        |
        |    (1 league)
        |
1st ruined pueblo (Jan. 31)
        |
        |    (3 leagues)
        |
La Punta de Buena Esperanza (Jan. 30)    SOUTH
```

Table 5-8

Four leagues north of El Termino de Puala is the pueblo called El Corvillo (The Halberd), which may be the same as the San Juan Bautista of Oñate's time. (See above..) In the itineraries of the Rodriguez-Chamuscado Expedition, there are two pueblos listed north of El Oso and La Pedrosa, buttheir order is given differently. (See Table 5-7.) However, there is internal evidence in Gallegos' account that Ponsitlan should actually be north of Pueblo Nuevo. (See Hammond and Rey 1966: 103.) Thus, Pueblo Nuevo is likely to be the same as El Corvillo and should be correlated with San Juan Bautista.

Returning now to El Termino de Puala, Luxan states that the Espejo party had camped at a spot three leagues to the south called Jueves de las Comadres, which seems to be just south of the mouth of Arroyo Rosa de Castilla, the same camping spot used by Oñate and Tamaron! To reach this spot, the Espejo party had traveled five leagues from the south, apparently keeping to the river bank so that they would pass through the mouth of Las Vueltas de Acomilla (it was mid-winter, hence the river would be low), and passing on their way "four large pueblos in ruins and abandoned, and a small hamlet of twenty houses." (Hammond and Rey 1966: 173) The "small hamlet" would be the same as Elota, which probably correlates with LA 31717, which is the right size. The four large ruined pueblos may correlate with LA 1999 at the mouth of Las Vueltas de Acomilla, LA 8870, LA 761/762, and another ruin presently unidentified (but probably not LA 2004, as it is high above the river bank and probably would have been missed by Espejo's party).

To reach Jueves de las Comadres, Espejo's party started from a place called El Gallo, apparently one of the group of five pueblos, which the party had reached two days before. The only Glaze E/F pueblo of the right size (at least 5 houses) and about the right distance from Jueves de las Comadres (five leagues) is LA 283 (Teipana) on the west bank. If El Gallo is to be correlated with LA 283, then it means that Espejo's party crossed the river from the west bank to the east bank at the Vuelta de Socorro, that is, at present day Pueblito.

Previous to this crossing, Espejo's party had spent two days (February 5 and 6, 1583) among the group of five pueblos, four of 50 houses in size, one of 100 houses. In the itineraries of the Rodriguez-Chamuscado Expedition, there are three pueblos which seem to be of roughly the correct size and location to correlate with the pueblos mentioned by Espejo's party: Piña with 85 houses and Piastla and San Juan with 35 and 40 houses, respectively.[17] (Santiago is too small;

hence, it and San Miguel are probably not to be included here.) Piña and the 100-house pueblo mentioned by Luxan are probably one and the same, and probably correlate with Pilabo (LA 791) on the west bank of the Rio Grande. Therefore, Piastla (on the same bank and below Piña) would be correlated with LA 282, and San Juan, across from Piastla, would correlate with Qualacu (LA 755 and associated sites), which lies across the river from LA 282. Qualacu and LA 282 thus account for two of the 50-house pueblos mentioned by Luxan. This leaves two more 50-house pueblos to identify: one is certainly El Gallo (LA 283), and the other should then be LA 31744.

The question then arises as to how did the Rodriguez-Chamuscado party manage to miss these last two pueblos? I suggest that it was because they were traveling on the east bank (as is clear from the records for the stretch from Elota north), hence they would have by-passed LA 31744 altogether, arriving at Qualacu to visit LA 282, perhaps then traveling north on the west bank to visit Pilabo (Piña) before crossing back to the east bank, and continuing northward, in which case they would also by-pass LA 283 (Teipana). In contrast, the Espejo party by traveling up the west bank, would encounter four of the five pueblos (LA 31744, LA 282, LA 791, and LA 283) as a matter of course, and could easily have learned of the fifth (Qualacu) on the east bank without crossing to visit it. In fact, Luxan states that at this point in their journey, they went "from pueblo to pueblo" accompanied by a crowd of Indians. (Hammond and Rey 1966: 173)

On the Espejo party's itinerary, the next location south is a pair of pueblos, or so I read the record at this point. The problem here is a certain ambiguity in the published text (Hammond and Rey 1966: 171-172), which has the Spaniards arriving at the first occupied pueblo, called by them San Felipe, and then, after some ethnographic description of the inhabitants, a second pueblo of 50 houses is noted without any indication of how far way it is from the first. If the correlations made in the preceding paragraph are correct, then these two pueblos should correlate with Senecu (LA 19266) and San Pascual (LA 757), respectively.

The distance of three leagues given by Luxan reaches, when measured from LA 31744, almost to San Pascual (LA 757), but is not long enough to reach Senecu (LA 19266). I take this to mean that the Espejo party reached Senecu on the west bank first, naming it San Felipe, then crossed to the east bank to visit San Pascual (not named by them), then crossed back to the west bank, and continued north to LA 31744.

Turning now to the Rodriguez-Chamuscado Expedition, it is apparent that San Miguel (47 houses), stated to be on the same bank of the river as San Juan (i.e., the east bank), matches well with the unnamed pueblo of 50 houses described by the Espejo party, and Santiago (25 houses, west bank) would therefore be the same as Luxan's San Felipe. A correlation of Santiago/San Felipe with Senecu is strengthened by the statement that Santiago "is situated on the top of a little hill, close to a meadow (cienega) formed by the river" (Hammond and Rey 1966: 115), which mention of a hilltop location corresponds with site locations for Senecu given in later documents.

About two leagues south of San Miguel on the east bank, the Rodriguez-Chamuscado party describe an abandoned adobe pueblo that was crumbling into ruins, but was still intact enough to be judged to have been three stories high, with 45 households; it was named San Felipe by the expedition. The size and construction of the archaeological site called LA 487 corresponds well with this description and it is on the east bank, but the distance from San Miguel (San Pascual) is closer to three leagues than to two. However, the distance was described as "about two leagues," which could easily mean "greater than two leagues." Thus, I think it is reasonable to correlate the San Felipe of the Rodriguez-Chamuscado Expedition with LA 487.

The Espejo party, ascending the west bank, missed LA 487, but instead, encountered two other abandoned and ruined pueblos. The second of these was two leagues south of Senecu (LA 19266, the San Felipe of the Espejo party), which distance reaches almost to LA 244. This site, then, can be correlated with the second ruined pueblo. Three leagues south of LA 244 is the camping spot called El Malpais (The Badland) by Espejo's party, described as "a marsh...close to some badlands." (Hammond and Rey 1966: 171) The distance brings one to a spot on the west bank, just north of the ruins of Fort Craig and opposite the lava flow south of Black Mesa on the east bank; this lava flow is obviously the "badland" referred to. Another league, south of this spot, brings us to the first ruined pueblo and to LA 597 just south of the mouth of Milligan Gulch: the correlation between these two is thus obvious. La Punta de Buena Esperanza, three leagues south of LA 597, appears to lie at approximately the mouth of Silver Canyon, just across the Rio Grande from the northern tip of the Fra Cristobal Mountains.

Finally, it is significant that Antonio de Espejo mentions in his relacion that in the Piro area, his party "found ten inhabited pueblos on both sides of the river and close to its banks (which number agrees with the pueblos listed by Luxan), in addition to others which seemed to be off the beaten track (my italics)." (Hammond and Rey 1966: 219) The italicized parts of Espejo's statement may be a reference to LA 284 and LA 285 in the La Jencia Creek drainage west of the Rio Grande and/or reference to pueblos east of the Rio Grande in the Chupadera Mesa internal drainage. (These last will be discussed with the Tompiro pueblos.)

Figure 5-4 summarizes the pueblos mentioned by the expeditions of the 1580s and Tables 5-9 and 5-10 give a concordance of pueblo names and my correlations.

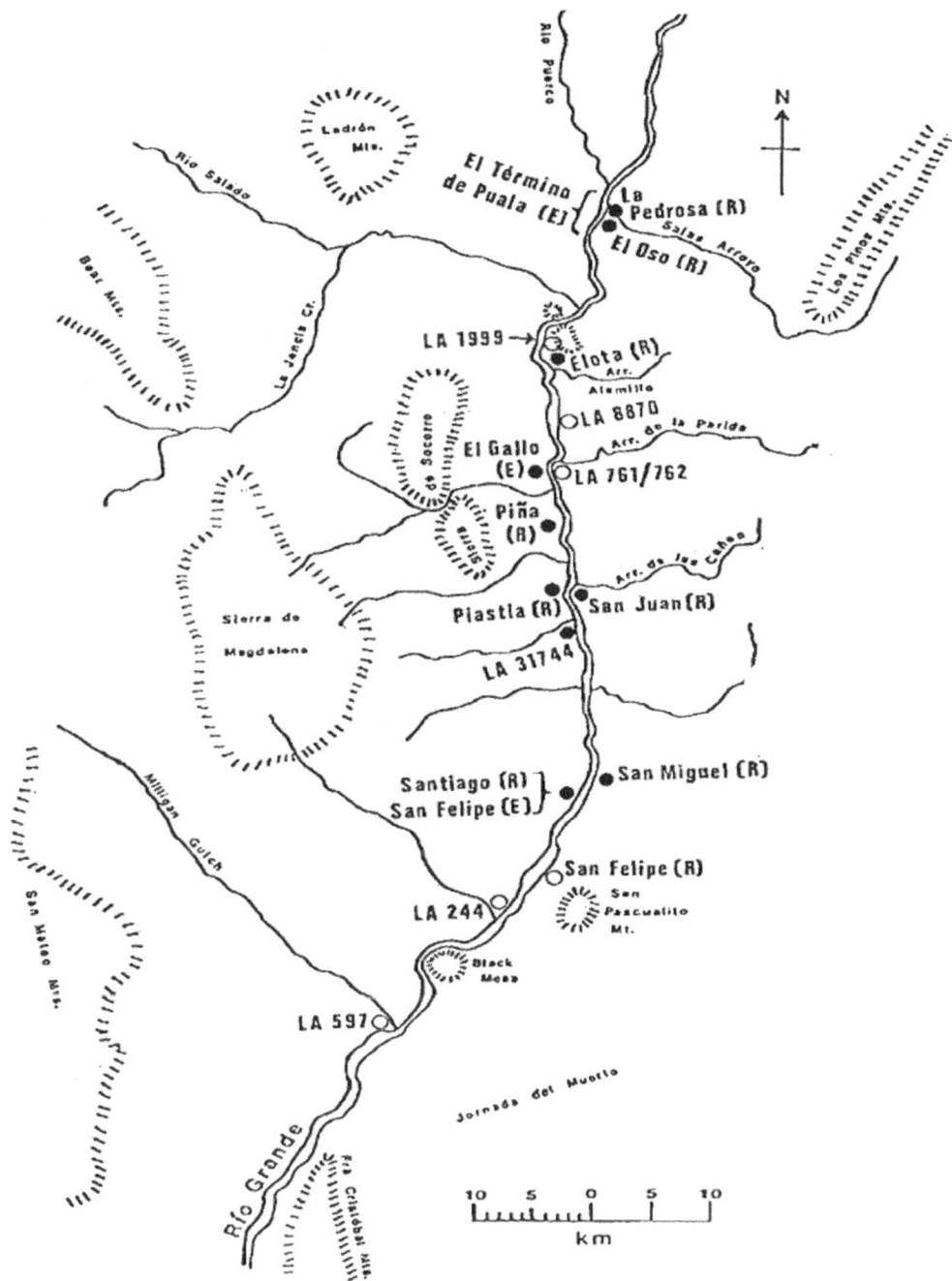

Río Puerco

Ladrón Mts.

Río Salado

El Término de Puala (E) {

La Pedrosa (R)

El Oso (R)

Salas Arroyo

Los Pinos Mts.

N

Bear Mts.

La Jencia Cr.

LA 1999 →

Elota (R)

Arr. Alemillo

LA 8870

Arr. de la Parida

Sierra de Socorro

El Gallo (E)

LA 761/762

Piña (R)

Arr. de las Cañas

Sierra Ladrón

Piastla (R)

San Juan (R)

Sierra de Magdalena

LA 31744

Santiago (R) } San Felipe (E)

San Miguel (R)

San Mateo Mts.

Milligan Gulch

San Felipe (R)

San Pascualito Mt.

LA 244

Black Mesa

LA 597

Jornada del Muerto

Río Grande

Fra Cristóbal Mts.

10 5 0 5 10
|ılıılıılı|ıılı|ı|ıılı|
km

PIRO PUEBLOS: 1580s

● = occupied pueblos   O = ruined pueblos

Names given by: [E] Espejo Expedition

[R] Rodríguez – Chamuscado Expedition

Figure 5-4

Figure 5-4

Table 5-10: PIRO PUEBLOS ON EAST BANK OF RIO GRANDE:
A CONCORDANCE OF HISTORIC NAMES

LA #	Rodríguez-Chamuscado: 1581	Espejo: 1583	Oñate: 1598	Benavides: 1620s	1630-1682
778	-----	-----	Puquias ?	-----	-----
774	El Oso	El Término de Puala (the	Nueva Sevilla/ Tzelaqui	Seelocu/ Sevilleta	Sevilleta
-----	La Pedrosa	boundary of Puaray)	Ayqui ?	-----	-----
2004	-----	-----	-----	-----	Acomilla ? (prehistoric)
1999	-----	"large ruin" ?	-----	-----	-----
31717	Elota	"small hamlet"	Yanamo ?	-----	-----
8870	-----	"large ruin" ?	Teyaxa ?	-----	Alamillo ?
761/762	-----	"large ruin" ?	-----	-----	-----
755/768/ 31798	San Juan	(mentioned, no name)	Qualacu, second pueblo	-----	Qualacu
757	San Miguel	(mentioned, no name)	first pueblo, Texahamo ?	-----	San Pascual
487	San Felipe (ruin)	-----	-----	-----	-----

Table 5-9

Table 5-9: PIRO PUEBLOS ON WEST BANK OF RIO GRANDE:
A CONCORDANCE OF HISTORIC NAMES

LA #	Rodriguez-Chamuscado: 1581	Espejo: 1583	Oñate: 1598	Benavides: 1620s	1630-1682
287	-----	-----	-----	-----	Acomilla ? (prehistoric)
286	-----	-----	-----	-----	-----
283	-----	El Gallo	Teipana (Socorro)	-----	-----
31751	-----	-----	-----	-----	-----
791	Piña	(mentioned, no name)	Pilogue (Pilopue)	Pilabo/Socorro	Socorro
282	Piastla	(mentioned, no name)	Penjeacu or Qualahamo ?	-----	-----
31744	-----	(mentioned, no name)	Penjeacu or Qualahamo ?	-----	-----
760	-----	-----	-----	-----	-----
19266	Santiago	San Felipe	Tzenacu,"el de la Mesilla"	Senecu	Senecu
244	-----	2nd abandoned pueblo	-----	-----	-----
597	-----	1st abandoned pueblo	-----	-----	-----

Note: The Espejo Expediton ascended the west bank of the Río Grande, while the Rodríguez-Chamuscado Expediton ascended the east bank.

Table 5-10

The Chronological Position of Late Glaze Pottery

The evidence and correlations presented above provide a new perspective on the absolute chronological positions of late glaze pottery in the Piro area, especially for Glaze F ceramics. If my correlations of LA 597, LA 244, and LA 487 with ruined pueblos mentioned by the Spanish expeditions of the 1580s are correct, then we are presented with the difficulty of explaining the presence at LA 244 and LA 487 of Glaze F pottery since, according to Mera's chronology of the glazes (1940: 5), Glaze F pottery is not supposed to be present before AD 1650? This could be explained by assuming a late 17th century reoccupation of these two sites, but this would have to remain an assumption since there is no historical evidence that such reoccupations ever occurred.

It has already been noted (chapter note 4, q.v.) that Mera's beginning date for Glaze F is considered too late. I would suggest, on the strength of the correlations presented above, that Glaze F must have begun prior to 1580 in order for there to be such pottery at two sites already abandoned in the early 1580s! Indeed, for there to be a "major" abundance of Glaze F at LA 244 (See Table 5-1), this pottery must have been present for an appreciable period of time prior to 1580. I tentatively suggest that a beginning date of AD 1550 for Glaze F ceramics would be reasonable given the above considerations.

Finally, I should stress that I do not envision a complete replacement of Glaze E ceramics by Glaze F types at AD 1550! Rather, these two forms must have existed side-by-side for a considerable period, with Glaze E ceramics probably persisting into the 17th century.

Tompiro Pueblos and Archaeological Sites

The discussion and correlations given below will include consideration of those Southern Tiwa pueblos east of the Manzano Mountains since the pueblos of the "Salinas Province" are frequently listed together in the Spanish colonial documents without direct reference to the two linguistic groups present, with the result that any attempt at correlation of Tompiro pueblos with archaeological sites must also deal with the Tiwa pueblos of the Estancia Basin.

Previous Work

Site correlations by previous investigators in the Salinas Province have been made more frequently and more accurately than in the Rio Grande Valley due to the use of masonry architecture by both Indians and Spaniards. This difference in architectural medium resulted in the survival of several large mission churches (those at Abo, Cuarac,[18] and Gran Quivira) as imposing landmarks, which were more easily identifiable without excavation than the melted adobe mounds in the Rio Grande Valley. Indeed, the sites of many of the 17th century pueblos were correctly known by name to the Spanish-American settlers of the 1800s, whose knowledge formed the initial basis for the site identifications by scientific investigators. This is not to say, however, that all sites were correctly known and named: the confounding of Gran Quivira with Tabira, discussed below, and the confusion over the location of Cuarac being contrary cases. In addition, archaeological excavation has provided confirmation of early Spanish colonial occupation of five major pueblos: Abo, Tenabo, Cuarac, Las Humanas (= Gran Quivira), and Tabira.

American Military Expeditions, 1846 and 1853: Early in November 1846, Lieutenant J. W. Albert led the first American reconnaissance to the Salinas Province, entering from the Rio Grande Valley via Hells Canyon and visiting Chilili, "Tagique," Torreon, Manzano, "Quarra," and Abo before leaving by way of Abo Pass. (Abert 1848: 64-77) Abert notes the ruins at Tajique, Cuarac, and Abo and provides brief description for the mission churches of the latter two, correctly concluding that, "The present ruins of the buildings that we find at Abio (sic), Quarra, and (Gran) Quivira, were erected by Indians under the direction of the Spanish priest." (Abert 1848: 74)

In December of 1853, Major James Henry Carleton led an American military exploring party into the Salinas Province that visited the sites of Abo, Cuarac, and Gran Quivira. (Carleton 1855) Carleton provides descriptions of the mission churches at all three sites and, on the basis of his observations of the pueblo ruins, debunks some of the fanciful and fantastic accounts of Gran Quivira, then current in New Mexico and elsewhere, namely the apparently hearsay description published in 1844 by Josiah Gregg (Gregg 1954: 116-117), the likelihood that the site had any relationship to the "Quivira" of Coronado, and the likelihood of an Aztec origin for the ruins at Gran Quivira, Cuarac, and Abo. Carleton also correctly concluded that the mission churches belonged to the period of the Spanish Colony prior to the Pueblo Revolt of 1630. (Carleton 1853: 312)

Bandelier: As for the Piros, Bandelier (1892: 253-292) is the first scholar to attempt a correlation of historic pueblos with archaeological sites. In the Manzano foothills, Bandelier visited and identified the sites of Chilili (LA 847),

Tajique (LA 381), and Cuarac (LA 95), and also mentions the site called Los Ojitos (LA 45853), which does not seem to appear in the historical records. In Abo Pass, he visited and identified Abo (LA 97) and a ruin he calls "Torneada" which from his description seems to be LA 9008 (1892: 275), but he did not reach Tenabo. He also visited Gran Quivira (LA 120), but misidentified it as the historic pueblo of Tabira: his mistake not being corrected by other scholars until 1939. His ground plans for Cuarac, Gran Quivira, and Abo are published in Kubler (1972: plates 45, 48, and 49).

1913 Excavations at Cuarac: Edgar Lee Hewett conducted the first excavations in the Salinas Province at Cuarac (LA 95) in 1913 (Senter 1934: 173). These have never been reported, hence have made no contribution to our knowledge of the Salinas Province.

Mecham: Mecham (1926: 287-288) identifies the five pueblos visited by the Rodriguez-Chamuscado Expedition as being Tiwa sites, including Chilili, Tajique, and Cuarac, but he does not attempt any specific pueblo/site correlations. He considers the three large pueblos reported to the exploring party by the Tiwas to be Abo, Tenabo, and Tabira, but here he is, apparently accepting Bandelier's misidentification of the name Tabira with LA 120 (Gran Quivira).

Hewett: From 1923 through 1926, Edgar Lee Hewett and various individuals under his supervision conducted excavations in the pueblo and in the mission church of San Buenaventura and its convento at LA 120 (Gran Quivira). Disappointingly, Hewett failed to prepare or publish a comprehensive report, hence our knowledge of the results is limited to the information contained in a few brief notices (Hewett 1923, 1924; Anonymous 1925, 1926; Halseth 1926) and an incomplete summary compiled much later by Gordon Vivian (1964: 5, 46, 54-57, 84-93), which only covers the years 1923 through 1925. Hewett carried on his work under the mistaken assumption that he was excavating the remains of historic Tabira.

Stallings: In 1931, W.S. Stallings of the Laboratory of Anthropology collected tree-ring samples from original timbers in the mission churches of Abo, Cuarac, and Las Humanas (Gran Quivira). Due to the shaping of the beams, thus eliminating exterior rings, few of the samples produced cutting dates, but the evidence generally supported the 17th century construction of the churches. The results were first published by Stallings (1937: 5), were republished in 1953 (Smiley, Stubbs and Bannister 1953: 40, 43, and 46), and now corrected dates are available. (Robinson, Hannah and Harrill 1972: 83-88)

Excavations at Cuarac: 1934–1936, 1939–1940, 1944:

In the middle and late 1930s, a series of excavations were carried out at Cuarac by investigators from the University of New Mexico, Museum of New Mexico, and School of American Research. Apparently, the mission church and parts of the convento were excavated and various stratigraphic and room excavations were conduced in the pueblo, but again, the work was poorly reported: only a few brief notices (Senter 1934; Ely 1935a; Anonymous 1936, 1944) being published and a master's thesis (Ely 1935b) and two unpublished manuscripts (Baker 1936, Hurt n.d.) being available. Recently, however, Hurt (1986) has prepared an updated report on his excavations for the U.S. Park Service.

Toulouse: Joseph Toulouse headed the excavation and stabilization of the mission church, convento, and a kiva in the garth of the convento at Abo (LA 97) in 1938 and 1939, and he is notable as the first archaeologist in the Salinas Province to carry through his professional obligations by publishing a comprehensive report. (Toulouse 1949)

He followed the Abo project with a summer's field-school excavations for Washington and Jefferson College at Pueblo Pardo (LA 83) in 1941, the first of a projected series of field seasons, which unfortunately were cut short by World War II. Again, Toulouse and his co-author produced a comprehensive report (Toulouse and Stephenson 1960) and, although publication was delayed for some seventeen years, it was still only the second archaeological report to be published on the Salinas Province. Toulouse mistakenly thought Pueblo Pardo might have been visited by the Espejo Expedition in 1582, but his contention that the site was occupied up into the early years of the Spanish colony is almost certainly correct. (Toulouse and Stephenson 1960: 3)

Kubler: In 1939, George Kubler made the first breakthrough in historic pueblo/archaeological-site correlation since Bandelier's time with his identification of Gran Quivira (LA 120) as the historic pueblo of Las Humanas (Kubler 1939). This corrected Bandelier's mistaken identification of the site as historic Tabira, opening the way for the later correct correlation of Tabira with La 51 (Pueblo Blanco).

In 1940, Kubler published the first edition of his architectural study of churches and chapels in New Mexico (the revised edition, Kubler 1972, contains the original text of 1940, plus an additional preface), in which he reviewed the information on such structures in the Salinas Provinces. (See Kubler 1972: 87-92.) In this work, he incorrectly states that 17th century Chilili is at a different location from the modern town; he is troubled by the 18th century confusion over the sites of Tajique and Cuarac, but ends up correctly adhering to the identifications made by Bandelier, and he correctly sorts out the historical associations of the chapel and later mission church as Las Humanas (Gran Quivira).

Scholes and Mera: In 1940, France V. Scholes and H. P. Mera published "Some Aspects of the Jumano Problem," which incorporated two individually authored papers dealing respectively with historical and archaeological evidences. Scholes reviews and resolves the interpretive problems caused by the various usages of term "Jumano," which had been instrumental in Bandelier's misidentification of Gran Quivira as Tabira. Scholes agrees with Kubler's identification of Gran Quivira as historic Las Humanas, and goes further to suggest LA 51 (Pueblo Blanco) as the probable site of Tabira. (Scholes and Mera 1940: 284) Scholes is also the first scholar to suggest the correlation of historic Tenabo with LA 200 (1940: 284-285). Scholes gives considerable discussion to identification of pueblos mentioned in the documents of Oñate's time, with most of which I am in agreement and will be discussing in more detail below.

Mera's paper provides a broad overview of the prehistory of the southeastern quarter of New Mexico, and briefly discusses several pueblo ruins in the Gran Quivira area, which might be historic pueblos, but makes no correlations for them. In passing, Mera does accept the correlations of Abo with LA 97 and Cuarac with LA 95 previously made by other scholars. In a separate publication, he provides his survey data for sites exhibiting glaze-decorated pottery in the Salinas Province (Mera 1940: 6-17, 21-23), in which he makes the same correlations mentioned just above.

Dutton: In 1944, Berta P. Dutton conducted test excavations at various points in the pueblo ruins at Abo (LA 97), the results of which have recently been published. (Dutton 1981, 1985) While the published results do not have direct bearing on problems of site correlation, pottery from Dutton's Test 1 is dominated by Glaze F sherds, which supports the 17th century occupation of the site already suggested by Mera's surface collection.

Vivian: In 1951, Gordon Vivian conducted excavations in three areas of Las Humanas (LA 120): a pueblo roomblock (House A), a kiva, and the Spanish chapel of San Isidro, which unfortunately had already been seriously damaged by treasure-hunters. The results of these excavations were published in Vivian (1964), which, as noted above, also included the data Vivian was able to salvage from Hewett's unreported earlier work.

1953 Pipeline Survey: In 1953, an archaeological survey of a gas pipeline route crossed the Jumanes Mesa and Abo Pass portions of the Salinas Province. While mainly restricted to the pipeline right-of-way, in which only prehistoric sites were encountered, a visit was also made to LA 200, "an enormous stone masonry pueblo usually known as Tenabo." (Fenenga and Cummings 1956: 221) Unfortunately, their assessment, "The site is believed to have been abandoned before Spanish occupation", is incorrect.

Stubbs and Howard: In 1959, two Spanish chapel structures were excavated by the Museum of New Mexico: (1) An almost featureless small chapel at Cuarac (LA 95), which may be a forerunner of the large 17th century mission church, and (2) another small chapel at Pueblo Blanco (LA 51), which is certainly of 17th century date. (Stubbs 1959) In his article, Stubbs correlates Pueblo Blanco (LA 51) with the historic pueblo of Tabira. This was followed up by an article by Richard M. Howard (1960), which discusses the historical evidence supporting the correlation of LA 51 with Tabira.

Schroeder: Albert H. Schroeder (1964) has argued that the identification of Cuarac, Tajique, and Chilili as Tiwa pueblos by Bandelier, Scholes, and others is incorrect; he argues, instead, that they were Tompiro pueblos. I find his argument faulty and unconvincing on both historical and archaeological grounds, and have prepared a detailed rebuttal. (Baldwin n.d.) Other recent investigators of the Salinas Province have either disputed Schroeder's position (e.g., Alden C. Hayes, in Hayes, Young and Warren 1981: 6-7), or have ignored it. (Wilson 1973) In a more recent article, Schroeder has repeated his conclusions (1979).

Hayes: From 1965 through 1967, Alden C. Hayes directed major excavations in Mound 7 at Las Humanas (LA 120), which proved to contain both prehistoric and historic Indian occupations, as well as a number of Spanish-converted rooms, which are identified as the convento used by Fray Francisco Letrado, the missionary responsible for the construction of the chapel of San Isidro. (Hayes 1968) After considerable delay, a comprehensive report on the excavations has been published (Hayes, Young and Warren 1981), accompanied by a volume of special studies (Hayes 1981), which includes an archaeological survey of the area around Gran Quivira. (Caperton 1981)

Wilson: John P. Wilson has published a brief history of Cuarac (Wilson 1973) which, while not an exhaustive treatment of the available historic materials, is the best such summary for any of the historic pueblos in the Salinas Province. In it, he suggests a possible correlation between Cuarac (LA 95) and the pueblo name "Acolocu" appearing in documents of Oñate's time. In a second work (Wilson, Leslie and Warren 1983) is presented the surviving archaeological data from an amateur excavation in a refuse mound at LA 51 in 1957, which include European metal and majolica, thus adding further confirmation to the correlation of this site with Tabira. In this latter publication, Wilson suggests that the name Tabira, applied to the pueblo by the Spanish, and not resembling any of the recorded Indian names of pueblos in the area, was borrowed from the Portuguese city of Tavira. (Wilson, Leslie and Warren 1983: 91-92)

As can be seen from the above review, a much more satisfactory situation exists with regard to correlation of archaeological sites with historic pueblos in the Salinas Province than in the Piro area. Four positive correlations have been made based on a combination of historical and archaeological data: that of Abo with LA 97, Cuarac with LA 95, Las Humanas with LA 120 (Gran Quivira), and Tabira with LA 51 (Pueblo Blanco). Other correlations based on historical data have been made and generally accepted: Tenabo with LA 200, Tajique with LA 381, and Chilili with LA 847. My archaeological data from LA 200 (reported later in this study) also support its identification with historic Tenabo. On the other hand, most correlations are only for pueblo names recorded in about AD 1620 and after (with the exception of Abo). Thus, my major task here is, after systematically reexamining the evidence for the pre-existing correlations, to attempt further correlations for the time of Oñate and the Spanish expeditions in the 1580s.

Methodology of the Present Study

Essentially, the same methodology is used here as in establishing correlations for the Piro pueblos in the Rio Grande Valley. The methodology may be outlined as follows:

I. Data Base:
a. Locational and descriptive data for historic Tompiro and Tiwa pueblos recorded within Spanish Colonial documents, namely:
b. Distances between pueblos and/or named localities;
c. Relative sequences of pueblos along lines of march by Spanish parties, and other relative sequences (as described in the course of the correlations);
d. Descriptions of individual pueblos; and
Maps of the Salinas Province and adjoining areas.
e. Locational and descriptive data for archaeological sites recorded by archaeologists from ca. 1880 to the present day, namely:
f. Locations of archaeological sites with Glaze E and F occupations in the Salinas Province;
g. Descriptions of the individual archaeological sites; Personal archaeological investigations at Abo (LA 97) and Tenabo (LA 200); and

h. Personal visits on several occasions to Cuarac (LA 95), Tajique (LA 381), and Gran Quivira (LA 120); plus one or more visits apiece to Tabira (LA 51), Pueblo Colorado (LA 476), Pueblo Pardo (LA 83), LA 9008, Los Ojitos (LA 45853), LA 1250, LA 1259, LA 474, LA 782, LA 33035, and many earlier (i.e., prehistoric) sites in the

II. Salinas Province.
a. Procedures:
i. I have accepted prior identifications of LA 97 with Abo, LA 95 with Cuarac, LA 120 with Las Humanas, and LA 51 with Tabira as established beyond reasonable doubt, and hence have used these archaeological sites as fixed points from which to make measurements;
ii. Distances, relative positions, and descriptions of Tompiro and Tiwa pueblos from the documents were compared between sources, the distances being measured on U.S. Geological Survey maps (following the topography, not as airline routes), and correlations made with known archaeological sites for several periods within the early Spanish Colonial era,[19] to wit:
iii. The period from 1650 to the abandonment of the pueblos (ca. 1672–1677);
iv. The period between 1610 and 1650;
v. The period of the Oñate Colonization (ca. 1598–1610); and
v. The period of explorations in the 1580s.
b. In each case above, the positive results for the preceding periods (1 through 4) were used as a framework for understanding each successively earlier period.

The Archaeological Sites

The archaeological sites in the Salinas Province that merit consideration for the correlation with historic Tompiro and Tiwa pueblos are those exhibiting Glaze E and F ceramics. Figure 5-5 shows those sites in their correct geographical positions, while Table 5-11 provides information on their ceramic composition.

Correlations for the Period 1650 to Abandonment (Ca. 1672–1677)

During this period, there is mention in the Spanish Colonial documents of only six inhabited pueblos in the Salinas Province: three Tiwa pueblos (Chilili, Tajique and Cuarac) and three Tompiro pueblos (Abo, Las Humanas and

Tabira), plus a "pueblo de Las Salinas", the identity of which will be discussed below. Our greatest source of information for this period consists of a large group of documents laid before the Inquisition in Mexico City, dating to ca. 1660–1664, and associated with cases brought against Nicolas de Aguilar and former governor Bernardo Lopez de Mendizabal by the religious authorities. (Hackett 1937: 131-227; Kessell n.d.)

Table 5-12 gives a summary of distance measurements between pueblos stated in the Inquisition documents. Given LA 95 (Cuarac) and LA 120 (Las Humanas) as fixed points, the measured distance on maps between LA 95 and LA 120 was found to be 26.73 miles (10.28 leagues), which corresponds very well with the distance given by Fray Freitas on February 21, 1661. Likewise, the distance from LA 95 to LA 381 (Tajique) measured 11.24 miles (4.3 leagues), and from LA 381 to LA 847 (Chilili) it measured 10.67 miles (4.1 leagues), for a combined distance from Cuarac to Chilili of 8.4 leagues. These distances correspond quite well with those given by Fray Freitas on February 26, 1661. Furthermore, the total distance between Las Humanas and Chilili (presumably by way of Cuarac) given by Nicolas de Aguilar on October 22, 1663 corresponds exactly with a sum of Freitas' figures of the distances from Chilili to Cuarac and Cuarac to Las Humanas (i.e., 18 leagues).[20]

The above distance figures support the correlations reached by previous investigators. As a consequence, it is clear that the distance figures given Vetancurt, a secondary source, are grossly incorrect: Cuarac to Chilili as being three leagues and Cuarac to Tajique as being two leagues. (Vetancurt 1697: 103) Vetancurt's erroneous figures, and also the implication within them that Cuarac lay between Tajique and Chilili, led to later confusion over the true site of Cuarac, as has been discussed by Kessell (1979a).

While Abo is mentioned in the documents laid before the Inquisition, there is no information on its distance or geographical relationship to the other pueblos. Vetancurt (1697: 103) states: "From here (Abo) the administration (of the priest at Abo) stretches towards the east; however, fifteen leagues from there (Abo) there are some Xumanas who are ministered to from Quarac."[21] This passage appears to refer to Las Humanas, but a direct route from Abo to Las Humanas (southeastward along Deer Canyon, over the escarpment of Chupadera Mesa, across the mesa top, and to Las Humanas via North Canyon) is only 8.34 leagues (21.68 miles). However, if the passage is interpreted to mean a journey from Abo via Cuarac to Las Humanas, a total distance of 15.16 leagues (39.43 miles), then the passage fits the map measurements. This suggests that the Spaniards' most frequently used route between Abo and Las Humanas was via Cuarac during this period.

Tabira is briefly mentioned in the Inquisition documents and by Vetancurt, but with no mention of location or distances. In 1695, subsequently a number of maps appeared showing a pueblo named Tavira at varying locations in the general vicinity of Las Humanas, most of these locations being technically incorrect in respect to their positions relative to Las Humanas and other features of the Salinas Province. (See extensive discussion above of these maps in Wilson, Leslie and Warren 1983: 101-104.) Two French maps, both crediting information provided by Don Diego De Peñalosa (a former Spanish governor of New Mexico, 1661–1664) and dating to the 1680s, show a pueblo named S. Diego (San Diego) northeast of Las Humanas, in the right position to represent LA 51 (Anonymous 1927; Bloom 1934). Howard (1960: 69-70) suggests a correlation between this San Diego and the pueblo of Tabira, with the chapel structure excavated at LA 51 by Stubbs (1959) being dedicated to San Diego (St. James).

Wilson has suggested that the name Tabira (which is unlike any of the Indian names recorded for pueblos in the Salinas Province) was derived from the Portuguese city of Tavira, which, among other industries, is noted as producing salt, hence:

Some early New Mexico padre may have seen the proximity between the salt lakes in the Estancia Valley and the nearest occupied pueblo as reason enough to give the pueblo an appropriate Hispanic (sic) name, Tabira. (Wilson, Leslie and Warren 1983: 92)[22]

I have further investigated this possible derivation of the name Tabira with the following results:

1) The usual Portuguese spelling of the city's name is Tavira, but it is recorded that the Moorish name for the original settlement was Tabira; and both spellings are found in documents or on maps for the pueblo in New Mexico.

2) Portuguese Tavira was re-conquered from the Moors in AD 1242 by Dom Paio Peres Correia, who was a master of the Order of Santiago. Two years after the Reconquest, King Sancho II made a grant of the city to the Order of Santiago, and the city's coat of arms still carries a red Cross of Santiago.

3) Furthermore, the city contains a parish and church of Sant'Iago. (The above information comes from the Grande Enciclopedia Portuguesa e Brasileira n.d.)

These close associations between Sant'Iago (in Spanish: Santiago or San Diego) and Portuguese Tavira serve to link Howard's interpretation of the maps with Wilson's interpretation of the origin of the pueblo's name, thereby giving credence to both interpretations.[23]

A final problem for this time period is the identity of the "pueblo de Las Salinas," which is only mentioned in the "Petition" by Fray Francisco de Ayeta, dated May 10, 1670, in which he reports to the viceroy of New Spain the abandonment of the pueblos in the Salinas Province sometime between the end of 1672 and 1677. These pueblos are specifically listed as being Las Humanas, Abo, Chilili, Cuarac, and the "pueblo de Las Salinas." (Hackett 1937: 298; Maas 1929: 52) It is notable that neither Tajique nor Tabira are mentioned by name in the document, indicating that one of them must be this "pueblo de Las Salinas."

Wilson has recently assumed that Tabira is to be identified with the "pueblo de Las Salinas" (Wilson, Leslie and Warren 1983: 98), while Scholes had earlier suggested an identification with Tajique. (Scholes and Mera 1940: 283) A completely satisfactory answer cannot be arrived at from the evidence available, but I would note that Tajique is specifically mentioned as an inhabited pueblo as late as 1672 (Bloom and Mitchell 1938: 113), whereas Tabira is not specifically mentioned after the early 1660s, and there was a period of serious droughts, famines, epidemics, and Apache attacks between 1666 and 1672 that might have caused the abandonment of Tabira. (Hackett 1937: 271-272, 301; Maas 1929: 57) Thus, I feel that Tajique is the more probable identification for the "pueblo de Las Salinas."

Figure 5-6 shows the pueblos of the Salinas Province for the period AD 1650 to abandonment (ca. 1672–1677).

Correlations for the Period 1610 to 1650

During this period, there is mention of seven inhabited pueblos in the Salinas Province: the six surviving past 1650, plus the Tompiro pueblos of Tenabo. There is also archaeological evidence for a small-inhabited pueblo on the Arroyo de Manzano.

Tenabo is mentioned twice by Vetancurt (1697: 103; 1698: 81-82) as being a "small" pueblo, with a chapel, and being a visita of Abo, but with no locational data. The only other mention of this pueblo is in a letter written at Chilili on October 4, 1622 by Fray Alonso de Peinado, in which he mentions "those (Indians) of the warlike pueblo of Abo and Penabo." (Scholes and Bloom 1945: 68)[24] One significant

point is that the pueblo's name is given as "Penabo" rather than "Tenabo," which suggests that the form given by Vetancurt may be misspelt. Secondly, it appears that Abo and Penabo are spoken of as a single community. It is this last point that is very favorable to a correlation of LA 200 with Penabo, since LA 200 is very close to Abo (only 4.63 miles distant following valley bottoms), and in terms of archaeological remains, is virtually identical to Abo. Furthermore, there is archaeological evidence from LA 200, in the form of excavated Spanish metal and a "soup plate" pottery vessel, that indicates a Spanish Colonial Period occupation.

At the site of Los Ojitos (LA 45853) on the Arroyo de Manzano north of Cuarac, there is a small pueblo mound (the west mound), which has yielded Glaze E and F pottery, including "soup-plate" forms indicative of Spanish contact. This small site overlooks good agricultural land and may have been a summer residence for farmers from Cuarac (LA 95). The name "Los Ojitos" was that current in the 1880s when it was recorded by Bandelier (Lange and Riley 1966: 386-387; Lange, Riley and Lange 1970: 10), and should not be taken to be a 17th century name.

The only distance measurement available for this time period is Benavides' statement that the "Tompiro Nation," as he called the Salinas Province, "extends for more than fifteen leagues through these regions" (Hodge, Hammond and Rey 1945: 65), which approaches the 18 league distance between Chilili and Las Humanas previously noted. Benavides' claim of "fourteen or fifteen pueblos" in the late 1620s (Hodge, Hammond and Rey 1945: 65) is double the number actually documented from other sources, and should be regarded with skepticism, although it is possible that some sites in the Chupadera Basin might have been inhabited as late as the 1620s. (So far, however, there is no proof of this.)

It is during this period that the names by which the pueblos were to be known to the Spaniards were established: only Abo, Penabo and Cuarac have a clear relationship to Indian names recorded during the Oñate period. (See below.) Tajique is of doubtful derivation from any earlier name, nor does Chilili have any apparent connection to previous names. Las Humanas is derived from the ethnic name "Jumano," and Tabira was apparently borrowed directly from the Portuguese city of that name. This establishment of Hispanic names for the pueblos appears to have accompanied the missionization of the Salinas Province, which began at Chilili in 1613 or 1614. (Scholes and Bloom 1944: 335)

Figure 5-7 shows the pueblos of the Salinas Province for the period AD 1610 to 1650.

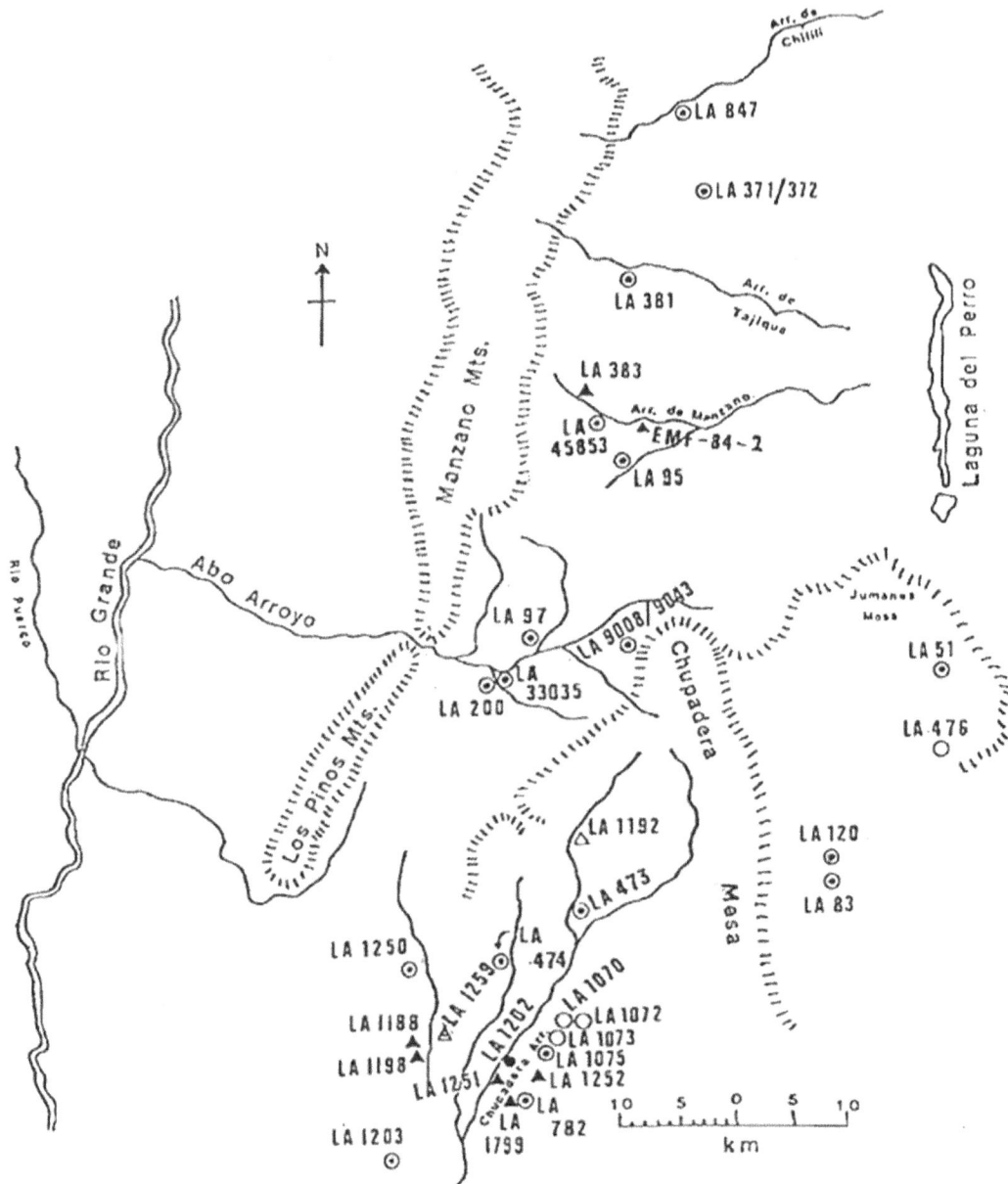

LATE GLAZE ARCHÆOLOGICAL SITES IN
THE SALINAS PROVINCE

Glaze E only (?): O = pueblo; △ = small site

Glaze F only (?): ● = pueblo; ▲ = small site

Glazes E & F: ⊙ = pueblo; △ = small site

Figure
5-5

Figure 5-5

Table 5-11: LATE GLAZE ARCHAEOLOGICAL SITES
IN THE SALINAS PROVINCE

			Ceramics Present	
LA No.	Kind of Site	Locations*	Glaze E	Glaze F
51a,b,c	pueblo	Jumanes	x	x
83b	pueblo	Jumanes	x	x
95b,c	pueblo	Manzano	x	x
97b,c	pueblo	Abo	x	x
120b,c	pueblo	Jumanes	x	x
200b,c,d	pueblo	Abo	x	x
371e	pueblo	Manzano	x	x
372e	pueblo	Manzano	x	x
381	pueblo	Manzano	x	x
383	fieldhouse?	Manzano	x	x
473	pueblo	Chupadera	x	x
474	pueblo	Chupadera	x	x
476	pueblo	Jumanes	x	-
782	pueblo	Chupadera	x	x
847	pueblo	Manzano	x	x
1070	pueblo	Chupadera	x	-
1072	pueblo	Chupadera	x	-
1073e	pueblo	Chupadera	x	-
1075	pueblo	Chupadera	x	x
1188	fieldhouse?	Chupadera	-	x
1192	fieldhouse?	Chupadera	x	-
1198	fieldhouse?	Chupadera	-	x
1202	small pueblo	Chupadera	-	x
1203	small pueblo	Chupadera	x	x
1250	small pueblo	Chupadera	x	x
1251	small pueblo	Chupadera	-	x
1252	small pueblo	Chupadera	-	x
1259	fieldhouse	Chupadera	x	x
1799	fieldhouse?	Chupadera	-	x
9008	pueblo	Abo	x	x
9043e	pueblo	Abo	x	-
33035	small pueblo	Abo	x	x
45853	small pueblo	Manzano	x	x
EMF-84-2	fieldhouse	Manzano	?	x

* Localitiy: Abo = Abo Pass; Chupadera = Chupadera Basin;
Jumanes = Jumanes Mesa; Manzano = Manzano foothills.
a LA 572 (see Mera 1940: 14) is considered by the Laboratory
of Anthropology to be a duplication of LA 51.
b Sites for which there are excavation data.
c Sites yielding Spanish artifacts and/or structures.
d Immediately surrounding LA 200 are a number of associated
Glaze E/F fieldhouses, etc. which are too numerous for
inclusion on the map. See Chapter 9.
e Reported sites that could not be relocated.

Table 5-11

Table 5-12: DISTANCES BETWEEN PUEBLOS
GIVEN IN THE INQUISITION DOCUMENTS

Individual, Document, Date	Distance Stated and Source
- Fray Nicolas de Freitas, Testimony before the Inquisition, February 21, 1661.	- Cuarac to Las Humanas: 10 leagues (Hackett 1937: 135; Kessell n.d.: 56).
- Fray Nicolas de Freitas, Testimony before the Inquisition, February 26, 1661.	- Chilili to Cuarac: 8 leagues (Kessell n.d.: 61). - Tajique to Cuarac: 4 leagues (Kessell n.d.: 62).
- Nicolas de Aguilar, Testimony before the Inquisition: October 22, 1663.	- Las Humanas to Chilili: 13 leagues (Kessell n.d.: 215-207).

Table 5-12

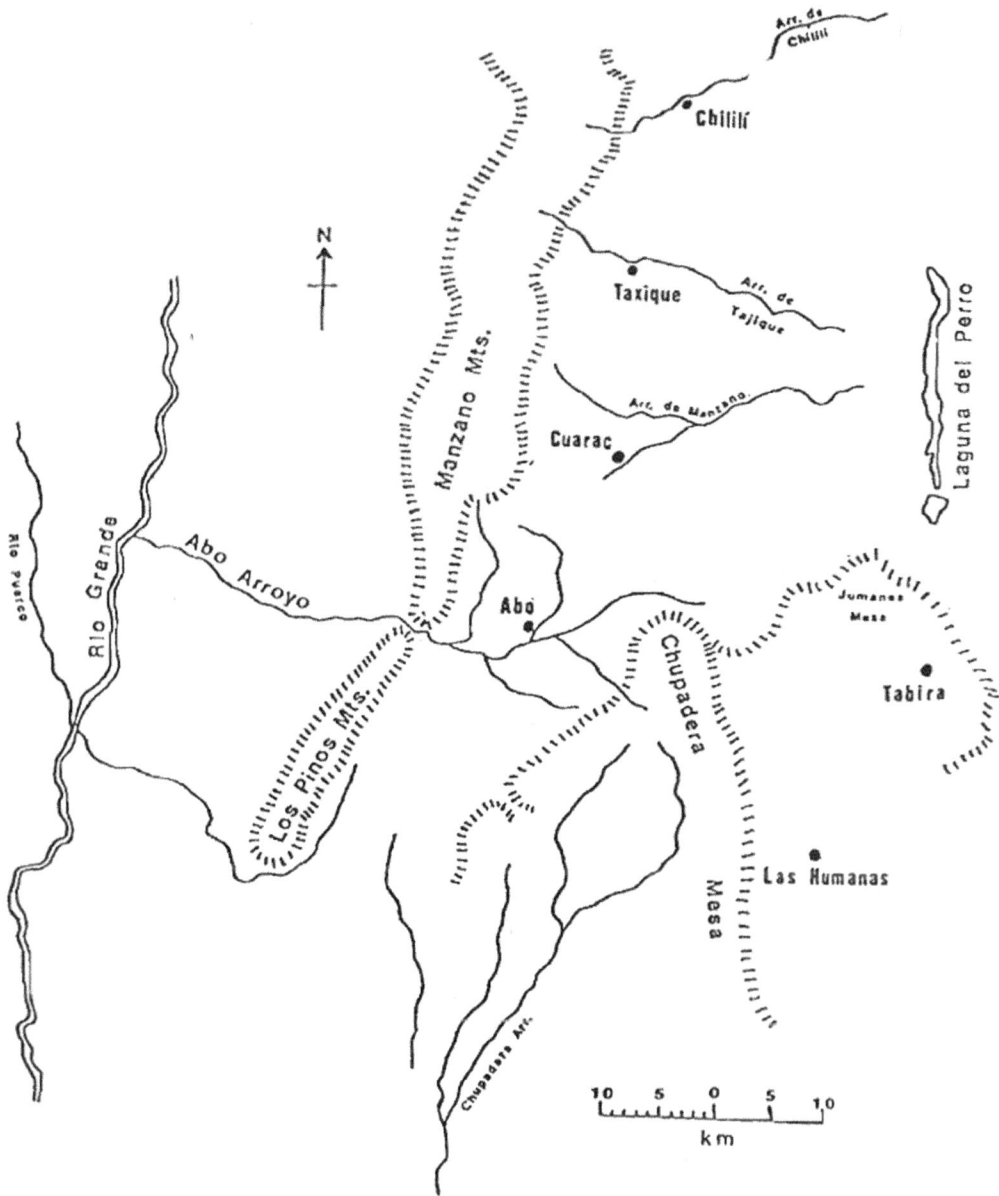

SALINAS PROVINCE PUEBLOS: 1650-1670s

Figure

5 - 6

Figure 5-6

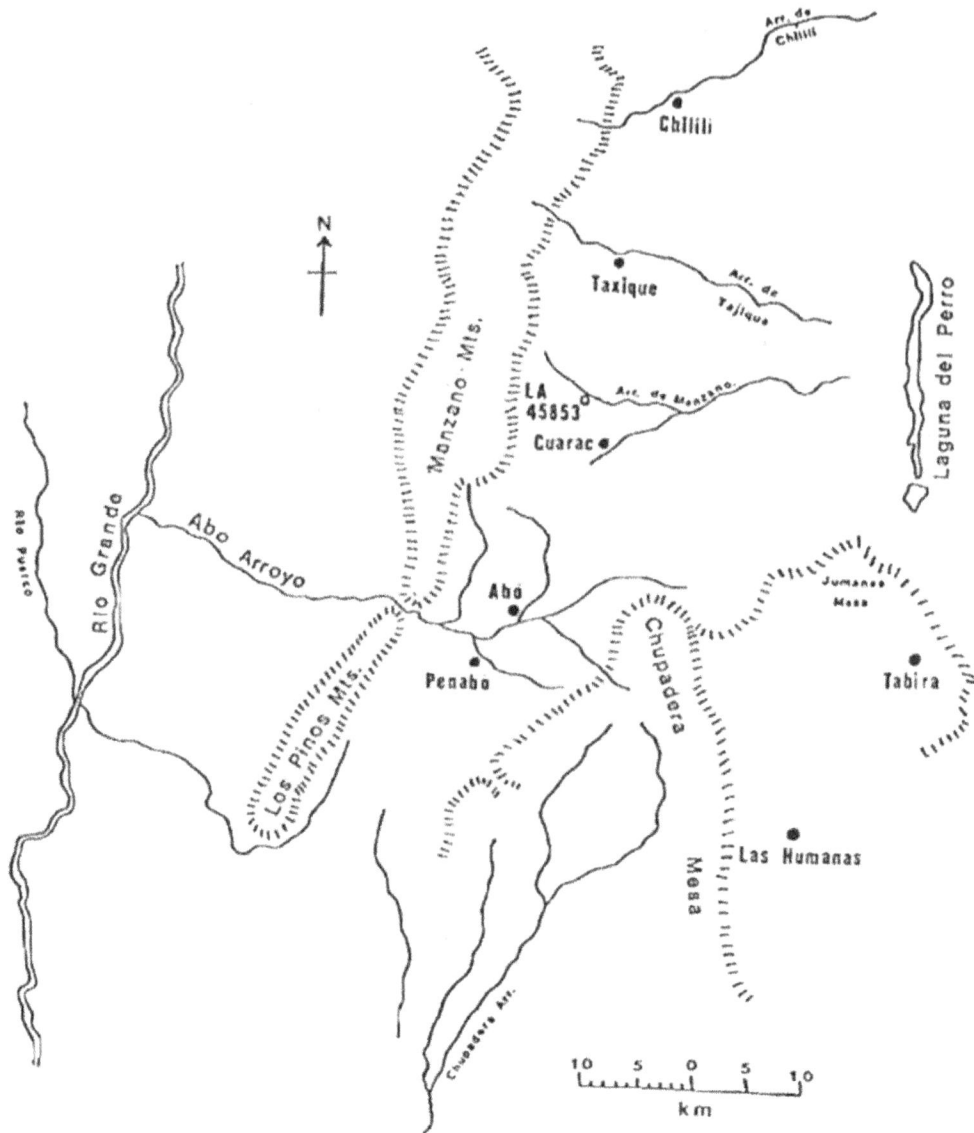

SALINAS PROVINCE PUEBLOS: 1610-1650

● = major pueblo

○ = seasonal site ?

Figure
5-7

Figure 5-7

Correlations for the Period of the Onate Colonization (1598–1610)

Data for the Salinas Province in this period consist mainly of (a) two lists of pueblos made at San Juan in September 1598, (b) the itinerary of Oñate's visit to the Salinas Province in October 1598, and (c) lists of pueblos contained in two Obediences taken during the aforesaid journey.

The first mention of any pueblos in the Salinas Province for this period is during the colony's march north along the Rio Grande in June 1598, the colony reaching the Piro pueblo of Nueva Sevilla (later known as Sevilleta) on June 16, and remaining there until June 22 "to wait for the supply of maize brought by Villagran and because of the exploration of the pueblos of Abo by the maese de campo and the sargento mayor." (Hammond and Rey 1953: 319)[25] This mention of "pueblos of Abo" appears to refer to both Abo and Penabo (Tenabo), located in Abo Pass to the east of Sevilleta.

The next mention of Salinas Province pueblos is in the two official documents drawn up by the Spaniards at the Tewa pueblo of San Juan: (1) a decree by Oñate on September 8, 1598 giving possession of various areas of New Mexico to the Franciscan Order for missionary purposes (see Scholes and Mera 1940: 276) and (2) an Obedience and Vassalage on September 9, 1598, wherein the mission fields for the various priests were listed. (See Scholes and Mera 1940: 276; Hammond and Rey 1953: 342-347; Pacheco et alia 1871b: 108-117.) The lists of pueblos in these documents are compared in Tables 5-13 and 5-14, which also include for comparison the pueblos listed in the Obedience and Vassalage documents dating to October 1598.

Considering first the Obedience and Vassalage taken at San Juan, Scholes states that the printed version given in Pacheco et alia (1871b) contains misspellings of the pueblo names. (Scholes and Mera 1940: 276) Perusal of Table 5-13 reveals that Hammond and Rey read some manuscript entries differently from Scholes, my impression being that Scholes' readings are more correct.

My first observation regards the pueblo names lying above the dashed line on Table 5-13: I regard these names as referring to Tano pueblos in the Galisteo Basin because the fifth of these, Xaimela, has a very close resemblance to the names (Ximena, Xameca, Jumea) given by earlier Spanish explorers to a pueblo probably to be identified as Galisteo Pueblo. (See Reed 1943: 262-263.)

Turning to the pueblos listed below the dashed line on Table 5-13, the name "abbo" is immediately recognizable

as a spelling variant of Abo. Immediately below it is "apena," which I correlate with Penabo (Tenabo). Given these identifications, and the fact that Abo and Apena (Penabo) lie in a north/south geographical relationship to one another, plus the identifications of Xaimela and the names above it as pueblos in the Galisteo Basin, it becomes clear that this list is essentially a north-to-south listing of pueblos.

If this relative ordering is correct, then the pueblo above (north of) Abo should be Cuarac: Acoli/Accole/Acolocu; this will be demonstrated later using distance measurements given in Oñate's itinerary to the Salinas Province.

The next pueblo north of Cuarac is listed in a variety of ways. (See Table 5-13.) Comparing these renditions, I conclude that the forms "cutzalitzontegi" and "cutzalitzontezi" are, in fact, two names run together, and should be read "cutzal(i) y tzontegi" or "cutzal(i) y tzontezi," which would render them comparable to the other forms. There then remains the problem of the names listed in the Decreto de Oñate, where it should be noted that the list of pueblo names is given in reverse order (i.e., from south to north),[26] producing the sequence "tziu tzi cuyzay" as rendered by Scholes. (Scholes and Mera 1940: 276) In this case, Cuyzay clearly corresponds to Cutzal (i) and Cuzaya in the other documents, and I suggest that "tziu. tzi" is a single name that was erroneously divided, and that the "u" in the first syllable is a misreading of "n" (a common error in transcription of 16th and 17th century documents), giving Tzintzi as a name comparable to Tzontegi/Tzontezi and Junetre/Junctre. Furthermore, the "tr" in these last forms may be a misreading "tz" (another frequent transcription error), which would give the forms Junetze/Junctze.

Given the above consideration, there are two pueblo names north of Cuarac for which correlations are needed: possibly Tzontegi/Tzintzi/Junetze/Junctze should be correlated with Tajique and Cutzal (i)/Cuyzay/Cuzaya correlated with Chilili. Such a correlation is complicated by two factors: (a) the presence on the lists of a third pueblo named north of the two discussed above, and (b) the archaeological record of two more sites (LA 371 and LA 372) that have to be considered as candidates for correlation. (See Figure 5-5.)

Taking up the matter of LA 371 and LA 372 first, these two sites are recorded as being very close to each other (Mera 1940: 22), hence would probably have been considered as only one pueblo, which might suggest a correlation of Aggei with Chilili, Cutzal(i) et alia with LA 371-372, and Tzontegi et alia with Tajique. However, the status of LA 371-372 is rather uncertain: (1) the sites have not been revisited since they were first reported in the 1930s; (2) we searched for these sites without success and no local informants seem to know of their existence; and (3) inspection of the pottery in surface collections from these sites at the Laboratory of Anthropology reveals an assemblage much more like that of Pecos or a Galisteo Basin pueblo than what one would expect from the Salinas Province. Thus, do LA 371-372 actually exist in the Manzano foothills, or are they Galisteo Basin sites mislocated as being in the Salinas Province? There is no answer to this problem at present.

Turning now to the problem of the third pueblo north of Cuarac, I suspect that the Aggei of the Obedience and Vassalage taken at San Juan and the Paaco of the Obedience and Vassalage taken at Acolocu may not be the same pueblo. It seems possible that Paaco may be LA 24 near Tijeras (north of the Salinas Province), this point will be argued later during discussion of Oñate's itinerary to the Salinas Province. Aggei may be another pueblo of the Galisteo Basin since the Obedience and Vassalage taken at San Juan refers to "the province of the Pecos with the seven pueblos of la cienega which lies to the east,"[27] where, counting the Pecos as one of the seven, the pueblo names from Quanquiz to Aggei would make up the other six.

Returning again to the two pueblos north of Cuarac, since even the existence of LA 371-372 is questionable, I am inclined to ignore them and to postulate the correlation of Cutzal(i) et alia with Chilili and Tzontegi et alia with Tajique.

Below, Abo and Apena on Table 5-13 are seven pueblo names, which appear to be associated with sites in the Chupadera Basin. There appear to be twelve possible sites within the basin, which might correlate with the names: LA 473, 474, 782, 1070, 1072, 1073, 1075, 1202, 1203, 1250, 1251, and 1252. Among these, sites with both Glaze E and F ceramics would be most likely to have been occupied in 1598, namely LA 473, 474, 782, 1075, 1203, and 1250, which leaves one pueblo unaccounted for, perhaps because of deficiencies in the surface collection data, or perhaps LA 9008 in the Abo Pass should be considered as being represented among the seven names. There is no record of any Spanish visitation of pueblos south of Apena (Penabo). As these sites are not geographically distributed in a neat north-south line, it is not possible to make unequivocal correlations between sites and names at this time.

Passing on now to the pueblos of the Jumanes Mesa area, these are listed from the same documentary sources in Table 5-14. Again, the geographic order in the Obedience and Vassalage taken at San Juan appears to be north/south and the reverse is seen in the Decreto de Oñate. This clearly puts Cueloce intermediate between the other two pueblos, corresponding to the position of LA 120 (Las Humanas), which lies between LA 83 and LA 51 (Tabira). Xenopue is thus to be correlated with LA 51 (Tabira) and Pataoce with LA 83 (Pueblo Pardo).

A check upon these lists of pueblos and the correlations based upon them can be made by an analysis of Oñate's journey to and through the Salinas Province in October 1598. (See Table 5-15.) For some reason not stated in the available records, distances on this journey were measured using the legua de diecisiete y medio al grado, equal to 3.94 miles (Real Academia Española 1956: 795), instead of the usual 2.6-mile league. Oñate and his company set out from San Juan on October 6, and traveled four leagues to the "primer pueblo de la Cañada de los teguas," then on the next day, six more leagues to San Marcos. The "primer pueblo de la Cañada de los teguas" was probably Cuyamungue (LA 38) on the lower Rio Tesuque, which contains both Glaze E and F ceramics (Mera 1934) and is about the right distances from both San Juan and San Marcos. From San Marcos (LA 98), Oñate traveled another six leagues to the "pueblo del Tuerto,"[28] which distance agrees well with the 6.34 leagues measured on maps to LA 162. (See Figure 5-8 for Oñate's route.) Subsequently, Oñate traveled two more leagues to the "first pueblo behind the sierra (the Sandia Mountains), the last pueblo of the Puaray," which when measured on maps, identifies this pueblo with LA 24 north of Tijeras. The phrase "postrer pueblo del puaray" indicates this to be a Tiwa pueblo associated with the Puaray group of pueblos in the Albuquerque area.

Table 5-13: SALINAS PROVINCE PUEBLOS (1598)

(except Jumanes Mesa)

Obedience Taken at San Juan (Sept.1598)			Decreto de Oñate (Sept. 8, 1598) (Scholes and Mera 1940)	Obedience Taken at Acolocu October 12, 1598	
Pacheco et alia (1871b) Version	Hammond and Rey (1953) Version	Scholes Version (Scholes and Mera 1940)		Hammond and Rey (1966) Version	Scholes' Version (Scholes and Mera 1940)
Quanquiz y Hohotà	Quauquiz Yhohota	quanquiz y hohota			
Yonalùs	Yonalu	yonalu			
Xatòe	Xotre	xotoe			
Xaimela	Xaimela	xaimela	xaimela		
Aggéy	Aggei	aggei	cuyzay	Paaco	Paaco
Cuzà	Cutzalitzon-	cutzalitzon-	tzi	Cuzaya	Cuzaya
Cizentetpı	tegi	tezi	tziu	Junetre	Junctre
Acoli	Acoli	acoli	accole	Acolocu	Acolocu
Abbo	Abbo	abbo	abbo		
Apena	Apona	apena	apena		
Axauti	Axauti	axauti	axauti		
Amaxa	Amaxa	amaxa	amaxa		
Couna	Cohuna	cohuna	cohuna		
Dhiu	Chiu	chiu	chiu		
Alle	Alle	alle	ale		
Atuyama	Atuya	atuya	atta		
Chein	Machein	machein	amactin		

Table 5-13

Table 5-14: SALINAS PROVINCE PUEBLOS ON JUMANES MESA (1598)

Obedience Taken at San Juan (Sept. 1598)			Decreto de Oñate (Sept. 8, 1598) (Scholes and Mera 1940)	Obedience Taken at Cueloce- October 17, 1598	
Pacheco et alia (1871b) Version	Hammond and Rey (1953) Version	Scholes' Version (Scholes and Mera 1940)		Hammond and Rey (1966) Version	Scholes' Version (Scholes and Mera 1940)
genobey	Genobey	genobey	genouey	Xenopue	xenopue
quelotetrey	Quellotezei	quellotezei	quelotzey	Cueloze	cueloce
pataotrey	Pataotzei	pataotzei	patuozey	Patasci	pataoce

Table 5-14

Table 5-15: ONATE'S JOURNEY TO AND THROUGH THE SALINAS

PROVINCE (OCTOBER 1598)

I follow the Spanish text given by Scholes (Scholes & Mera 1940: 276); an English translation
is available in Hammond and Rey (1953: 393-394).

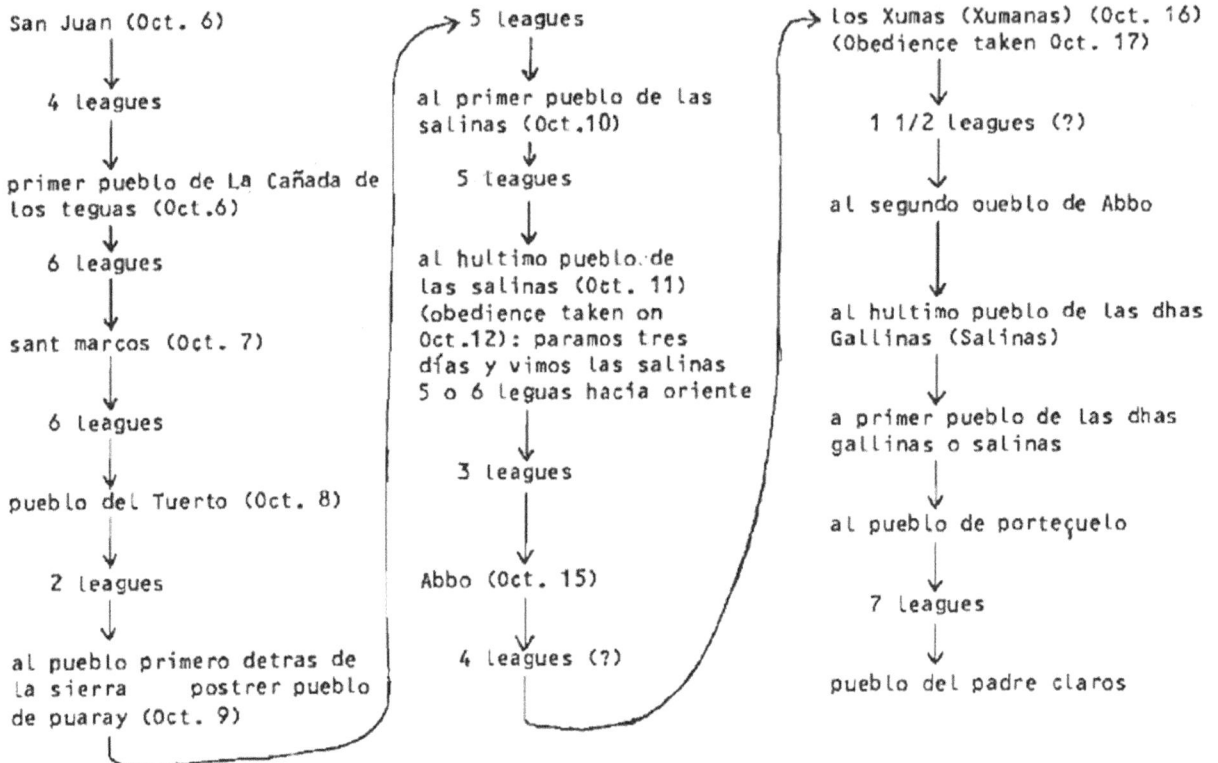

San Juan (Oct. 6)

↓
4 leagues
↓

primer pueblo de La Cañada de
los teguas (Oct.6)

↓
6 leagues
↓

sant marcos (Oct. 7)

↓
6 leagues
↓

pueblo del Tuerto (Oct. 8)

↓
2 leagues
↓

al pueblo primero detras de
la sierra   postrer pueblo
de puaray (Oct. 9)

5 leagues

↓

al primer pueblo de las
salinas (Oct.10)

↓
5 leagues
↓

al hultimo pueblo de
las salinas (Oct. 11)
(obedience taken on
Oct.12): paramos tres
días y vimos las salinas
5 o 6 leguas hacía oriente

↓
3 leagues
↓

Abbo (Oct. 15)

↓
4 leagues (?)

los Xumas (Xumanas) (Oct. 16)
(Obedience taken Oct. 17)

↓
1 1/2 leagues (?)
↓

al segundo oueblo de Abbo

↓

al hultimo pueblo de las dhas
Gallinas (Salinas)

↓

a primer pueblo de las dhas
gallinas o salinas

↓

al pueblo de porteçuelo

↓
7 leagues
↓

pueblo del padre claros

Table 5-15

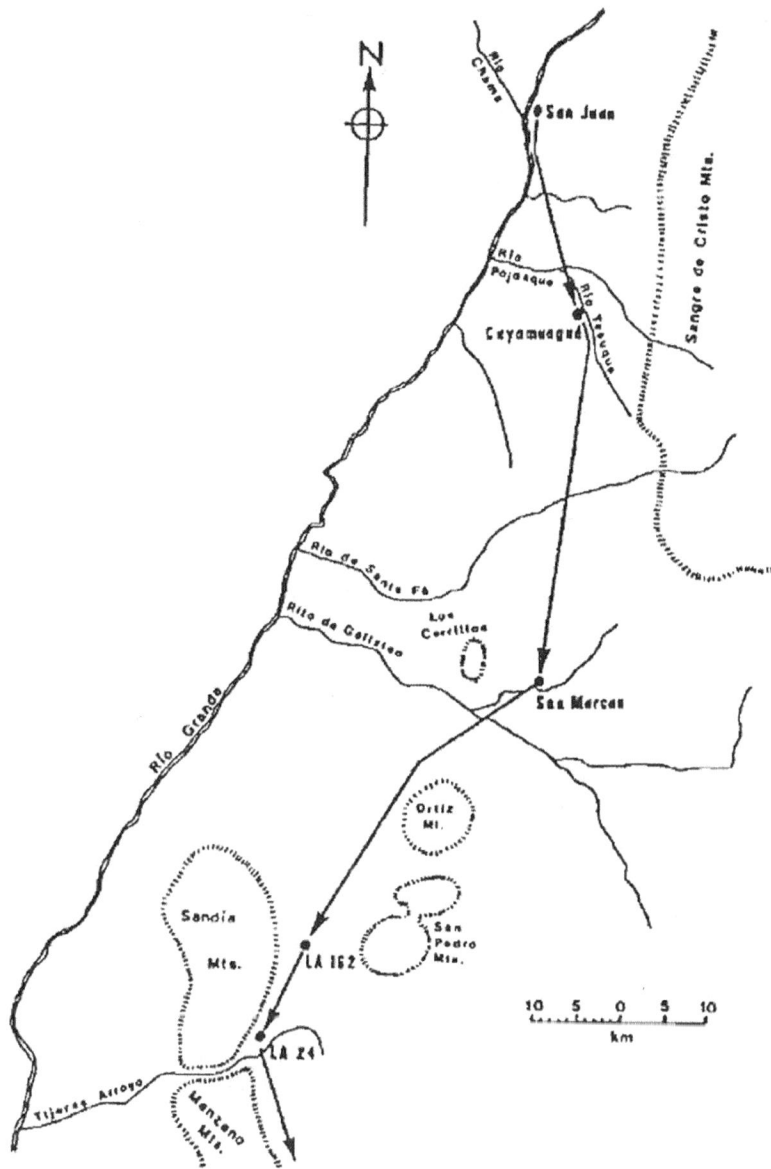

N

Rio
Chama

San Juan

Rio
Pojaque

Rio Tesuque

Cuyamaugué

Sangre de Cristo Mts.

Rio de Santa Fé

Rio de Galisteo

Los
Cerrillos

Rio Grande

San Marcos

Ortiz
Mt.

Sandia

Mts.

San
Pedro
Mts.

LA 162

10 5 0 5 10
km

Tijeras Arroyo

LA 24

Manzano
Mts.

OÑATE'S ROUTE TO THE SALINAS
PROVINCE FROM SAN JUAN (1598)

Figure
5 - 8

Figure 5-8

Leaving LA 24, Oñate traveled five leagues to the "first pueblo of Las Salinas," which distance is a very good approximation of the distance from LA 24 to Chilili (LA 847) via Cedro Canyon. The next day's journey took Oñate another five leagues to the "last pueblo of Las Salinas," which distance is only a half league short of the measured distance (via Tajique) to Cuarac (LA 95), if Tajique was bypassed by Oñate, a slightly straighter route to Cuarac would result, giving a closer approximation to Oñate's figure of five leagues. Counting the days recorded for Oñate's trip to LA 95 places his arrival there on October 11, 1598. The party stayed there for three days (October 12 through 14), with at least some members taking a side trip east to the saline lakes, said to be "five or six leagues" away, but actually only 4.69 leagues by a route east along the Arroyo de Manzano.

Also while at LA 95, on October 12, 1598, an "Obedience and Vassalage to His Majesty by the Indians of the Pueblo of Acolocu" was taken. (Spanish text in Pacheco et alia 1871b: 117-122; English translation in Hammond and Rey 1953: 348-350.) This clearly associates the name Acolocu with this "last pueblo of Las Salinas," which the above distance measurements have identified as LA 95 (Cuarac).

This brings up the question of languages and translations and how they relate to the various recorded forms of pueblo names. Take, as a case in point, this pueblo at LA 95, the name of which was variously recorded as Accole/Acoli/Acolocu/Agualagu in documents of Oñate's time, and later was known as Cuarac. The obvious similarities between these forms allow their correlation with one another as variants of the same name, and some variants (Accole/Acoli and Acolocu/Agualagu) probably resulted from the Spaniards' unfamiliarity with the phonological nuances of the Indian languages, thus precluding complete consistency in the rendition of these sounds into Latin letters. Admitting this source of error, there are still other variations which need explanation. The name Cuarac, although no doubt somewhat Hispanicized, is still a reasonable rendition of Southern Tiwa sounds; however, the forms recorded in the documents of Oñate's time all give variants of this name, which have an "l" in place of the "r." This observation calls for explanation when it is known that Southern Tiwa lacks an "l" phone, replacing it with "r". (See Trager 1942: 3.) Add to this the fact that Acolocu is a very Piro-like form, [29] and that Accole/Acoli were recorded at San Juan before the Spaniards visited the Salinas Province and the dimensions of the problem begin to come into focus.

An aspect that needs consideration is how the Spaniards acquired knowledge of these names. When Oñate's colony entered New Mexico, it was accompanied by only one person who could speak a language of the Pueblo Indians: the Mexican (Aztec) Indian, Juan de Dios, who knew the language of Pecos Pueblo. (See Kessell 1979b: 43-45, 77, 81 for information on this interpreter and the circumstances of his learning the Pecos language.)

After arriving at the Keresan pueblo of Santo Domingo, Oñate acquired the interpretive services of two Mexican Indians, known as Don Tomas and Don Cristobal, who had been left in New Mexico by the expedition of Castaño de Sosa in 1591, and who could speak their native Nahuatl, Spanish, and the Keresan dialect of Santo Domingo. (For the circumstances of the Spaniards' discovery of these two interpreters, see G. Espinosa 1933: 141-143, Pacheco et alia 1871b: 252-253; Hammond and Rey 1953: 319.)

The three persons mentioned above were the only interpreters available to the Spaniards during the first few months of the colony in New Mexico. For the Obedience and Vassalage taken at San Juan on September 9, 1598, it is specifically noted that Don Tomas, Don Cristobal, and Juan de Dios all assisted as translators.[30] Presumably, then, communication between Pueblo Indians and Spaniards was carried out through the media of the Keresan and Pecos languages. As there is no indication that any natives of the Salinas Province were present, the names of the pueblos there were probably obtained from either Keres, Pecos, or Tewa speakers (in the case of the latter, from Tewa speakers who could also understand Pecos or Keres). The upshot of this is that the names given in the Obedience and Vassalage taken at San Juan are Keresan, Pecos, or Tewa forms passed on to the Spaniards by the translators and inscribed as he heard them by the notary, Juan Peres de Donis.

In the case of the Obedience and Vassalage taken at the pueblo of Acolocu on October 12, 1598, the only interpreter noted as being present was Don Tomas, who must have spoken to the assembled leaders in the Keresan language. In this case, different forms of the pueblo names were elicited. (See Table 5-13.) Presumably, either the pueblo leaders understood Keres, which was not their native tongue, or they relied upon a local interpreter. In this regard, the Piro-like for "Acolocu" is suggestive: perhaps a Piro or Tompiro served as interpreter. What I visualize is this: the Spaniards spoke Spanish to the assembled leaders, Don Tomas provided an interpretation from Spanish into Keres, the local interpreter provided an interpretation from Keres into Tiwa, which was the language of the leaders; the leaders then responded to the Spanish in Tewa, the interpreter (our putative Piro or Tompiro) then translated from Tiwa into

Keres, but rendered the pueblo names in Piro forms, then Don Tomas translated from Keres into Spanish, retaining the Piro placename forms, which were then copied out as part of the Spanish text by Oñate's secretary, Juan de Velarde. An alternative would be that the local interpreter translated from Keres into the Piro language, which the local leaders may have been able to understand, given the apparently close relationships between Tiwa and Piro speakers in the Salinas Province, and was responded to in that language by the leaders.[31]

To return to tracing the Spaniards' itinerary: after leaving Cuarac, the party traveled three leagues to Abo, which matches well the 3.22 leagues measured by maps. However, beyond Abo, there is a lack of correspondence in distance measurements: the document records a distance of four leagues to "los Xumas" (Las Humanas), which is presumably the pueblo of Cueloce at which an Obedience and Vassalage was taken on October 17, 1598. The problem is that the shortest reasonable route from Abo to Las Humanas, southeast from Abo via Deer Canyon, crossing the escarpment of Chupadera Mesa at the head of Deer Canyon, thence in a fairly straight line across Chupadera Mesa to Las Humanas via North Canyon, is a minimum of 5.5 leguas de 17.5 al grado (21.68 miles). The only way I can explain this discrepancy is to suggest that a copyist's error substituted the word "cuatro" in place of "cinco."

There is indeed evidence that the document is a copy rather than an original: (1) The document used by both Scholes and by Hammond and Rey is cited as being in the Archivo General de Indias in Sevilla, Spain, hence is likely to be a copy rather than an original document; and (2) there are several places within the document where "salinas o gallinas" is written (meaning "salines or chickens/hens"), as if the writer was uncertain of which word to use, I suggest that a copyist was having difficulty reading the handwriting of the original, or a copy of the original, and therefore felt compelled to render the equivocal word in the two alternatives.

Given, then, that the document is a defective copy, certain other problems may be accounted for. The next of these is the one and a half league journey from Cueloce to "the second pueblo of Abo," which must be a reference to Tenabo. The problem comes when the distance from Cueloce (LA 120) to Tenabo (LA 200) is measured, the shortest possible route, from Cueloce west-north-west through North Canyon and across the top of Chupadera Mesa, descending the mesa's escarpment at the head of the east branch of Saladito Canyon, thence west-northwest down Saladito Canyon to LA 200, comes to 6.15 leguas de 17.5 al grado (24.22 miles).

I can only suggest that a copyist wrote "legua y media" when he should have written "seis leguas y media."

Oñate's party probably arrived at Cueloce on the evening of October 16, 1598: the Obedience and Vassalage taken at Cueloce is dated to October 17, 1598; thus, I would suggest that the journey to "the second pueblo of Abo" occurred on October 18, 1598. The document does not mention spending a whole day at Cueloce (October 17), but by working back from dates given later in the itinerary (specifically in the Zuñi area and at 'Acoma), I found that October 18 was the most likely date for the journey away from Cueloce.

The next day (October 19), Oñate's party returned to the last pueblo of Las Salinas (Cuarac), probably by way of Abo (no distance is given). The party passed on to the first pueblo of Las Salinas (Chilili), and then on to the "pueblo of Portecuelo" (i.e., "the pueblo of the mountain pass," apparently a reference to the pass made by Tijeras Canyon between the Rio Grande Valley and the Estancia Basin). I suspect that this pueblo is LA 24, the same pueblo that had been referred to earlier in the trip as "the last pueblo of the Puaray." From there, the party traveled another day for seven leagues to "the pueblo of Padre Claros."

Padre Claros had been assigned the missionary province of the Tiwas and Piros in the Obedience and Vassalage taken at San Juan on September 9, 1598, so apparently the missionary was already at work in one of these pueblos. If we assume that Oñate's party traveled from LA 24 to the "pueblo of Padre Claros" westward via Tijeras Canyon, then the figure of seven leagues could bring them either to the cluster of Tiwa pueblos between Bernalillo and Albuquerque, or to the cluster of Tiwa pueblos near Los Lunas. Since the Oñate party then traveled on westward to 'Acoma, a distance of 13 leguas de 17.5 al grado (ca. 51.22 miles), the pueblo of Padre Claros must be in the Los Lunas cluster since from there to 'Acoma measures about 50 miles, whereas from near Bernalillo to 'Acoma, the distance is about 75 miles.

Before leaving the Oñate party's itinerary, the identification of the pueblo named Paaco in the Obedience and Vassalage taken at Acolocu should be discussed. Scholes (Scholes and Mera 1940: 277) has argued that the Pueblo Indian leaders taking part in this oath-taking were all from Tiwa-speaking pueblos. If Paaco is the pueblo visited twice by the Oñate party (LA 24) just north of the Salinas Province, which appears to have been a Tiwa pueblo affiliated with the Puaray group, then Scholes' argument receives further support from a different perspective. The point is of some importance since the name Paaco has previously been assigned to LA 162 (e.g., Bandelier 1892: 112-115; Lambert 1954), but LA 162 correlates with the "pueblo del Tuerto" on the basis of distance measurements. (See above.)

Figure 5-9 shows the pueblos of the Salinas Province for the period of the Oñate colonization (AD 1598–1610).

Correlations for the 1580s

Both the Rodriguez-Chamuscado Expedition of 1581–1582 and the Espejo Expedition of 1582–1583 penetrated into the Salinas Province, but the latter did not reach the Tiwa pueblos in the Manzano foothills, and neither expedition reached into the Chupadera Basin or onto Jumanes Mesa.

The entry of the Rodriguez-Chamuscado Expedition into the Pueblo Indian area in late August 1581 was via the Rio Grande Valley from the south, the expedition first passing through the Piro area (as discussed in the first half of this chapter), then going on north to the Tiwas and other Pueblo Indians. The expedition spent most of the autumn of 1581 exploring in various directions from a base of operations in the Puaray group of pueblos between Bernalillo and Albuquerque. Finally, in December 1581, the party heard of the saline lakes of the Salinas Province and set out to visit them.

While the route from the Puaray group of pueblos to the Salinas Province is not specified in any of the documents, the distance is mentioned as 14 leagues by two members of the expedition. (Testimonies of Pedro de Bustamante and Hernan Gallegos on May 16, 1582: Pacheco et alia 1871a: 86-87, 93-94, Hammond and Rey 1966: 131-132, 137.) I have considered several alternative routes for this journey: (1) Around the north end of the Sandia Mountains, then south to Chilili by the route traveled later by Oñate; (2) from Puaray to Chilili via Tijeras and Cedro Canyons; (3) from Puaray to Chilili via Hells and Gotera Canyons; and (4) from Puaray to Tenabo via the Rio Grande Valley and Abo Pass. I find that only the second route fits the distance of 14 leagues, I measured 13.85 leagues (36.02 miles) for this route on maps.

This indicates that Chilili was the first pueblo encountered, and thus allows a straightforward correlation of the five pueblos listed by the expedition with Chilili, Tajique, Cuarac, Abo, and Tenabo (See Table 5-16.) I discount LA 371-372 as a possible correlation for the reasons previously discussed. While among these pueblos, the party heard of "three very large pueblos beyond the salines," which are probably the three pueblos of Jumanes Mesa. (Hammond

and Rey 1966: 107, 119, 132, 137) These were not visited due to heavy snowfall; there is no mention of pueblos in the Chupadera Basin.

The only penetration of the Salinas Province by the Espejo Expedition was a side-trip into Abo Pass by Espejo and two other Spaniards, February 10-12, 1583, during which two unnamed pueblos were visited. (Hammond and Rey 1966: 175-176, 222-223; Pacheco et alia 1871a: 114-115, 176-177) From the descriptions given, it is clear that these two pueblos are Tenabo and Abo, visited by Espejo in that order. While he never visited all of them, Espejo mentions a total of eleven pueblos as belonging to the Salinas Province. (Hammond and Rey 1928: 322; Hammond and Rey 1966: 222; Pacheco et alia 1871a: 114, 176) Counting the two visited (Tenabo and Abo), plus the Tiwa pueblos (Chilili, Tajique, Cuarac), and the pueblos of Jumanes Mesa (Tabira, Las Humanas, Pueblo Pardo), there is only a total of eight, leaving three pueblos unaccounted for, but possibly referring to sites in the Chupadera Basin.

Figure 5-10 shows the pueblos of the Salinas Province for the period of explorations in the early 1580s. Table 5-17 presents a concordance of pueblo names from the different periods.

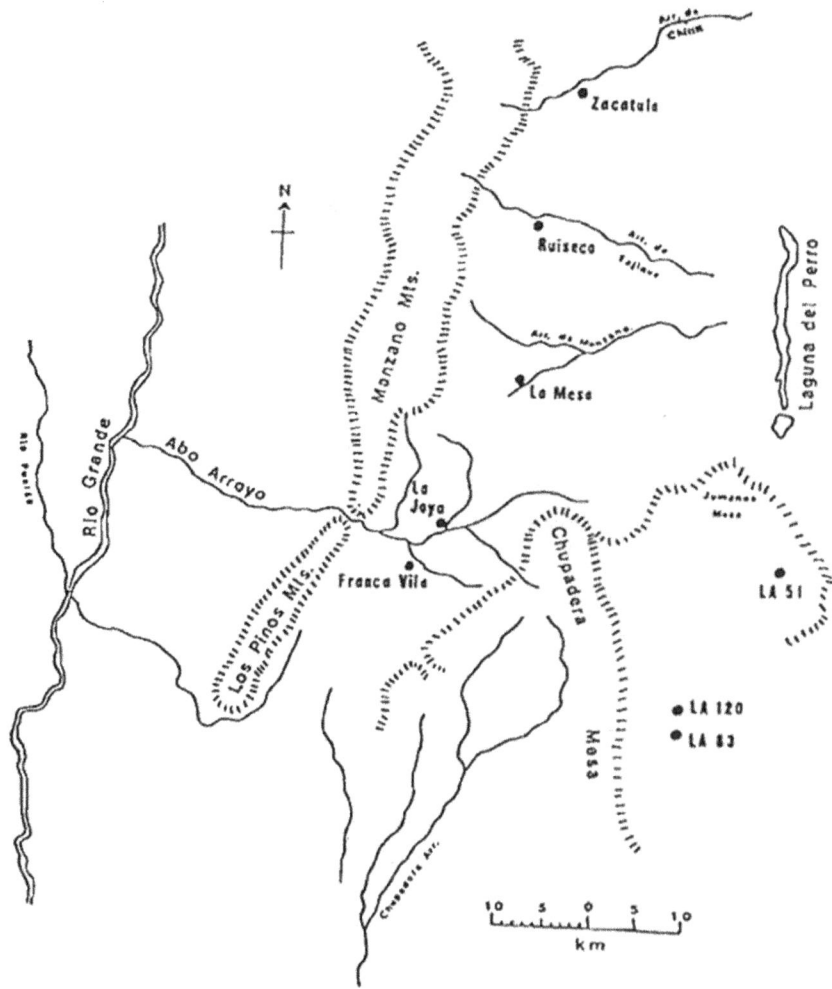

SALINAS PROVINCE PUEBLOS: 1580s

Figure

5 - 10

Figure 5-9

Table 5-16: SALINAS PUEBLOS VISITED BY

RODRIGUEZ-CHAMUSCADO EXPEDITION (December 1581-January 1582)

Gallegos' List_____   Pedrosa's List_____   Correlations____

Zacatula: 125 houses   Zacatula: 125 houses   Chilili (LA 487)

Ruiseco: 200 houses   Ruiseco: 200 houses   Tajique (LA 381)

La Mesa: 90 houses   La (blank): 90 houses   Cuarac (LA 95)

La Hoya: 95 houses   La Joya: 95 houses   Abo (LA 97)

Franca Vila: 65   Franca Vila: 65   Tenaoo (LA 200)

       houses   houses

Sources: Gallegos' List: Hammond and Rey (1966: 107)

      Pedrosa's List: Hammond and Rey (1966: 119).

Table 5-16

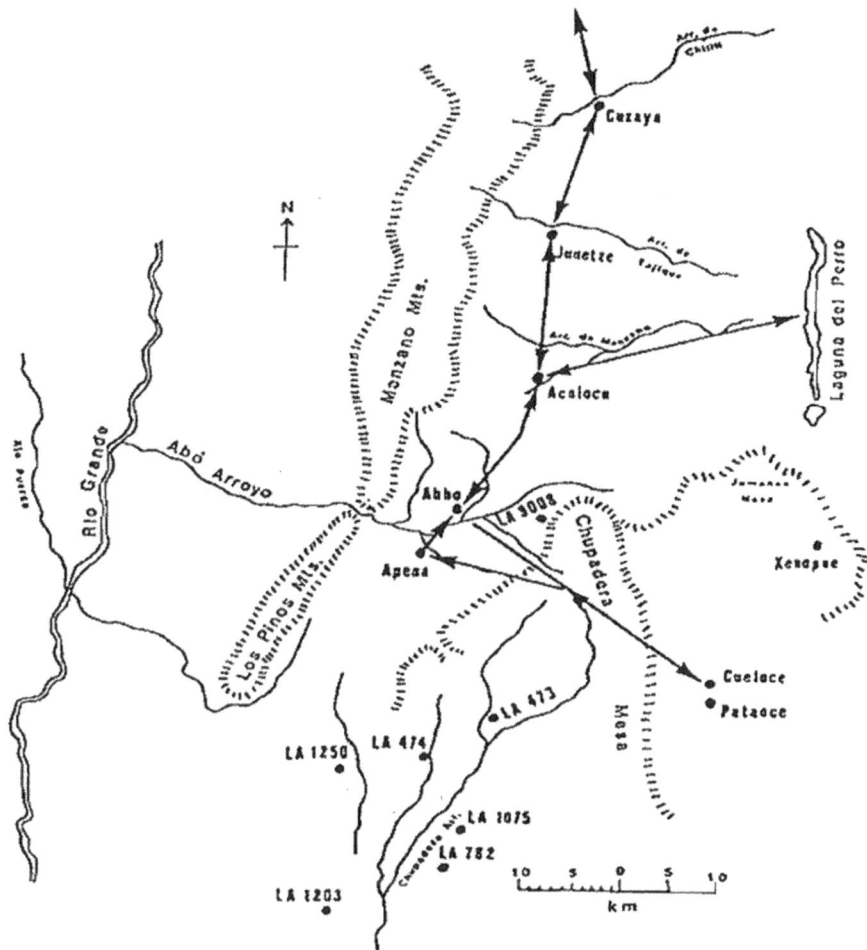

SALINAS PROVINCE PUEBLOS: 1598~1610

(arrows show Oñate's route: Oct. 1598)

Figure
5-9

Figure 5-10

Table 5-17: A CONCORDANCE OF HISTORIC NAMES
FOR PUEBLOS OF THE SALINAS PROVINCE

LA #: Modern Name	Rodriguez-Chamuscado (1581)	Espejo (1583)	Oñate (1598)	1610-1670s
847: Chilili	Zacatula	- - -	Cuzaya, etc.	Chilili
381: Tajique	Ruiseco	- - -	Junetze, etc.	Taxique
95: Quarài	La Mesa	- - -	Acolocu, etc.	Cuarac
97: Abo	La Joya	mentioned, no name	Abbo	Abo
200: Tenabo	Franca Vila	mentioned, no name	Apena	Penabo (Tenabo)
51: Pueblo Blanco		- - -	Xenopue, etc.	Tabira
120: Gran Quivira	mentioned, no name	- - -	Cueloce, etc.	Las Humanas
83: Pueblo Pardo		- - -	Pataoce, etc.	- - -

No unequivocal correspondences can be made for other sites in the Salinas Province.

Table 5-17

Notes:

1. In their last work, Hammond and Rey (1966: 51-63) discuss the matter of correlation of archaeological sites with historic pueblos, with particular reference to the Rodriguez-Chamuscado Expedition of 1581–1582, and excuse themselves from any serious attempt at doing so with the following words:
In fact, we believe that it is possible to identify specifically only a few of the pueblos mentioned in 1581, and to suggest locations for some others. In general, however, it is feasible to locate them only as nations or linguistic groups. (Hammond and Rey 1966: 53)

2. As only one scientific excavation of a Piro pueblo has yet occurred, at LA 282 in the summer of 1981, and the results are not yet available, the archaeological descriptions are limited to surface indications and analyses of small surface sherd collections.

3. The reader is invited to replicate my correlations by using the data from the historical sources and making measurements on topographic maps. The J.S.G.S. maps used were the most detailed available, namely 1:24,000 quadrangles (Paraje Well, Fort Craig, Socorro, Loma de las Cañas, Mesa del Yeso, Lemitar, San Acacia, La Joya, Abeytas) where possible, and 1:62,500 quadrangles (Val Verde, San Antonio, Magdalena) elsewhere. In addition, the new 1:100,000 metric maps (San Mateo Mountains, Socorro, Belen) were also consulted.

4. Mera (1940: 5) dates Glaze E ceramics to ca. AD 1515 to 1650, and Glaze F ceramics to ca. AD 1650 to 1700. It has been apparent for some time that Mera's beginning date for Glaze F is too late (see discussion in Hayes, Young and Warren 1981: 98-99) and that is overlaps the span for Glaze E. (for example, see Warren 1980: 159, table 16.) Precisely what ending date for Glaze E and beginning date for Glaze F we should use in the Piro area is uncertain at present, but it is at least clear that both ceramic groups at least partly overlap the Spanish Colonial era.

5. This historic camping spot probably lies below the high-water mark of present-day Elephant Butte Reservoir.

6. This might be read to suggest that LA 244 is really Senecu, but LA 244 is too far from Socorro.

7. That is: 16 leagues from Fra Cristobal to opposite Socorro, three leagues from Socorro to Alamillo, five leagues from Alamillo to Sevilleta, for a total of 24 leagues. If the Hacienda de Felipe Romero were one league further, then the total would be 25 leagues, quite comparable to the Recolonization itinerary.

8. The Spanish text reads: "dho Govr y cappan Genl llegue con dho campo a esta hazienda despoolada y cayda que dizen fue de Luis Lopez que se alla doze leguas del puesto dho de fray Christobal." (Spanish Archives of New Mexico, microfilm role 1, frame 835.)

9. The Spanish text reads: "al dia siguiente, en medio de la jornada, se encontro el sito donde estuvo el pueblo de la Sevilleta, y poco mas adelante la estancia arruinada de Felipe Romero, que uno y otro se perdieron con el reino."

10. This should not be confused with the Tewa pueblo of San Juan Bautista (now known as just "San Juan") far to the north near present-day Española.

11. The Spanish text reads: "siempre paramos a la orilla del Rio." (Pacheco et alia 1871b: 251)

12. Previous translators (e.g., Hammond and Rey 1953: 318) have translated the phrase "frontero de" as meaning "opposite, across from," therefore meaning "on the opposite bank from." I believe that this is incorrect, and that "frontero de" means "beyond" in the sense that the spots referred to are further along the route of the colony than the pueblos named; thus, the June 14th camping spot is "beyond" or slightly to the north of Teipana, and the camping spot occupied between May 28 and June 14 is "beyond" or slightly to the north of Qualacu. See the Spanish text in Pacheco et alia (1871b: 250-251).

13. Fra Cristobal was named for Fray Cristobal de Salazar, a cousin of Don Juan de Oñate, who had accompanied the colony to New Mexico in 1598 and who died in the next year while on his way back to New Spain, apparently near the spot and mountains named for him.

14. Senecu is consistently described in the Spanish Colonial records as being situated on a hill or small mesa, hence it is clear that "el de la Mesilla" is a descriptive phrase relating directly to Senecu and should not be considered a separate name (as is implied in the list in the Decreto de Oñate).

15. This is confirmed by Antonio de Espejo in his own relacion where he states: "we found another (province) which is called the province of the Tiguas, with 16 pueblos, one of which is called Puala." (Pacheco et alia 1871a: 112, 175)

16. The existence of a second, small pueblo near Sevilleta may help explain the presence of three symbols on the Martinez Map of 1602 at this point: one for LA 778, one for Sevilleta (LA 774), and one for this small vanished pueblo. LA 778 itself is too far away to be La Pedrosa if the two harquebus-shot distance is to be taken seriously.

17. In general, the size estimates for pueblos given by the Rodriguez-Chamuscado Expedition seem to be more modest (i.e., more realistic) than those given by the Espejo party. The latter have a marked tendency to round up to a larger figure (for example, 85 houses is rounded up to 100 houses by the Espejo party).

18. Cuarac is the 17th century Spanish name for the archaeological site now known as Quarai. As this study is concerned with the living Indian pueblo of the 16th and 17th centuries, I will use the contemporary name in preference to the modern corruption.

19. The reader is invited to replicate my correlations by using the data from the historical sources and making measurements on topographic maps. The U.S.G.S. maps used were the most detailed available, namely 1:24,000 quadrangles (Scholle, Abo, Chupadera, Bigbee Draw, Gran Quivira, Mesa Draw, Round Top, Torreon, Tajique, Milbourn Ranch, and Chilili) where possible, and 1:62,500 quadrangles (Mountainair, Estancia, Torreon) elsewhere. In addition, the new 1:100,000 metric maps (Socorro, Belen, Corona, Albuquerque, Los Alamos) were also consulted.

20. The distance from LA 95 (Cuarac) to LA 51 (Tabira) measures 31 miles or 11.66 leagues, adding to the distinction to be drawn between Tabira and Las Humanas.

21. The Spanish text reads: "Hasta aqui llega la administracion azia el Oriente, aunque quinze leguas de alli ay algunos Xumanas, que eran de Quarac administrados."

22. LA 51 is only about 9 miles (ca. 3.5 leagues) from the southern-most large salt lake in the Estancia Basin.

23. There is another Tavira on the Iberian Peninsula: it is an old name for the city of Durango in Vizcaya; but the name Tavira seems to have been eclipsed by that of Durango long before the 16th century, hence is an unlikely source for the pueblo name. (Enciclopedia Universal Ilustrada 1928a, 1928b)

24. The Spanish text reads: "y los del pueblo de guerra de Abo y Penabo."

25. The Spanish text given in Pacheco et alia (1871b: 252) reads: "estobimos...por el socorro de maiz que hizo Villagran, y el descobrimiento de los pueblos de abo, que hicieron el Maese de Campo y Sargento mayor."

26. The Spanish text given by Scholes is as follows: "yten los pueblos de amactin. atta. ale. chiu. cohuna. amaxa. axauti. apena. abbo. accole. tziu. tzi. cuyzay. con todos los demas Pueblos de las salinas cienega y sierra que caen a aquella cordillera del oriente en derecera de los pecos..."

27. The Spanish text given by Scholes is as follows: "la prouincia de los Pecos con los siete pueblos de la cienega que cae al oriente."

28. "Pueblo del Tuerto" means "pueblo of the one-eyed (man)," presumably a comment on the physical condition of the concurrent townchief of that pueblo.

29. Acolocu looks very much like Piro pueblo names in the Rio Grande Valley (e.g., Tzenacu, Qualacu, Seelocu, etc.) where it appears that "-cu" is a locative suffix (probably meaning "place," but perhaps meaning "town"). Applying this to Acolocu: acolo-cu, the resulting root "acolo" very closely resembles the forms acoli/accole recorded at San Juan.

30. There is also a Don Juanillo mentioned as a translator near the beginning of the document; but he is not mentioned at the end, where instead Don Cristobal is mentioned. Presumably, "Juanillo" is a mistake for "Cristobal."

31. In this regard, Vetancurt (1697: 103) specifically states of Cuarac that the people were "de nacion Tiguas, que hablan el idioma de los Piros," meaning, I believe, that the Tiwas at Cuarac were bilingual.

6

Non-Puebloan Neighbors of the Piros and Tompiros

This chapter discusses the non-Puebloan peoples of the Southwest and Southern Plains with whom the Piros and Tompiros are known to have interacted. Specific information on such interaction is relatively skimpy; consequently a full evaluation will be deferred until after presentation of relevant archaeological data in later chapters. (See also the immediately following chapters.) However, the two major non-Puebloan groups interacting with the Piros and Tompiros, namely the Apacheans and the Plains Jumanos, have been imperfectly defined and sometimes confused in the past, especially since Forbes' (1959a) ill-founded attempt to subsume under the rubric "Apachean" a number of poorly known ethnic groups of the Southern Plains and northern Chihuahua. Consequently, I find it necessary to define these groups and their territorial holdings in this chapter, especially since the territories were undergoing drastic changes during the time period of interest.

The Apacheans

The term "Apacheans" encompasses the Athabaskan-speaking peoples historically known to have inhabited portions of the Southwest and the Central and Southern Plaines; they are also known as the "Southern Athabascans," and by the terms "Navajo and Apache." (See Opler 1983 and Young 1983)

It has long been accepted that the Apacheans have migrated into the Southwest from the north, and that their arrival is relatively recent in comparison to the Pueblo Indians, the Yumans, and the Uto-Aztecans of Arizona and Sonora. However, much discussion and divergence of opinion has occurred concerning the specific immigration route(s) and time(s) of arrival. I do not propose to review the various arguments put forward, nor the evidences used to support them, as they are beyond the subject of this work.

For a recent comprehensive review, see Wilcox (1981), and also Brugge (1981, 1983) and C. Schaafsma (1981).

For my part, however, I have always been skeptical of the suggested Intermontaine Route of immigration (west of the Rocky Mountains) and of any date earlier than AD 1400 for entry of the Apacheans into the Southwest. This is basically because the earliest historical evidence places the Apacheans in the extreme northeastern corner of the Southwest and subsequent historical evidences suggest general westward and southward movements by the Apacheans from that area. Hence, I would favor a gradual Apachean movement south along the eastern foothills of the Rocky Mountains, with concurrent use of plains and mountain environments to the east and west, and an arrival on the northeastern perimeter of the Southwest (southeastern Colorado and northeastern New Mexico) by ca. AD 1500 or slightly earlier. It is at this point that historical documentation begins.

AD 1541

The first documentation of the Apacheans comes from the Vasquez de Coronado Expedition, in particular that expedition's excursion onto the Southern Plains in 1541. There has been some dispute over the route taken through the plains by the expedition. I have not attempted a detailed plotting of this route, but from my reading of the documents, I would tend to agree with the analyses by Bolton (1964) and Swanton (as reported in Wedel 1970) that the route ran south of the Canadian River until the meeting with the Teya Indians, rather than with Schroeder's (1962) contention that the route was north of that river.

Given the above, the expedition marched eastwards from the Pecos River for some eight to ten days before reaching the first representatives of a bison-hunting Indian group called the Querechos on the Llano Estacado in the general vicinity of the present New Mexico/Texas boundary.

The name "Querecho" is stated to be that given to these Indians by the Pueblo Indians. (Winship 1896: 440, 504, 588; Pacheco et alia 1870b: 310) It seems likely that "Querecho," (kereco), is a rendition of the term used at Pecos, which may derive from the same source as the Keresan term "Kirauash," (kirawas), recorded by A. Bandelier (1892: 116-117, 119) and the Jemez term (k'yalats'a a), "Navajo-person," perhaps originally used for any Apachean. (Harrington 1916: 573) These Querechos are generally acknowledged as being Apacheans.

Beyond the Querechos, the expedition reached a series of barrancas (canyons), which were probably part of the eastern escarpment of the Llano Estacado. There, a second bison-hunting group was encountered: the Teyas. Some scholars have accepted the Teyas as being a second Apachean group (e.g., Harrington 1940: 512), while others have suggested a Caddoan affiliation entailing a close relationship with the Wichita (e.g., Schroeder 1962: 7-9). I consider the Teyas to be Plains Jumanos for very specific reasons that are discussed below. (For concurring opinions, see Bolton 1964: 260 and Wilcox 1981: 220.)

Returning to the Querechos, their culture is briefly described in several of the Spanish documents pertaining to the expedition, but, unfortunately, some of the longer descriptions are generalized lumpings of the Querechos and Teyas. Selecting only those descriptions definitely pertaining only to the Querechos, there emerges a picture of a nomadic, bison-hunting people, utilizing tanned bison hides for clothing and tipi covers, conversant in sign language, and utilizing pack-dogs for carrying their possessions and dragging tipi poles (Winship 1896: 440, 504, 580-581; Pacheco et alia 1870a: 262-263, 1870b: 310). Winship (1896: 527: footnote 5) mistakenly attributes the dog-travois to these people, but a close reading of the Spanish text reveals that only dog-packing and pole dragging are described.

Referring equally to both Querechos and Teyas, Pedro de Castañeda states:

As I have related in the first part, people follow the Cows (bison), hunting them and tanning the skins to take to the settlements in the winter to sell, since they go there to pass the winter, each company (band) going to those which are nearest, some to the settlements at Cicuye (Pecos), others toward Quivira (the Wichita), and others to the settlements which are situated in the direction of Florida. (Winship 1896: 456, 527)

There is no direct information regarding possible contacts between the Apacheans and either the Piros or Tompiros.

The Vasquez de Coronado Expedition does not refer to any non-Puebloan peoples in areas surrounding the Pueblo Indians except for the Querechos and Teyas east of Pecos. It is possible that in 1541, the Apacheans had only recently appeared from the north and were confined to that area shown on Figure 6-1 for the later Apaches Vaqueros (and possibly further north).

There is some equivocal archaeological evidence, which might be indicative of an early AD 1500s Apachean intrusion west of the Rio Grande into the area later known to be occupied by the Navajo. These consist[1] of three tree-ring dates ranging between 1491+ and 1541+ from a hogan in the Gobernador drainage (E.T. Hall 1944: 100), which specimens could not later be relocated for redating (Robinson, Harrill and Warren 1974: 3); and[2] of tree-ring cutting dates of 1526 and 1548 from un-described excavations at Grotto Cave, a site in the Mesa Mountains between 'Animas and Pine Rivers in New Mexico. (Robinson, Harrill and Warren 1974: 65) No firm conclusions as to an Apachean presence or absence can be drawn from these dates at present.

AD 1581–1583

In August of 1581, the Rodriguez-Chamuscado Expedition was approaching the Piro area from the south, having followed the Rio Grande northwards from La Junta de los Rios. (See Figure 6-1.) After fifteen days' march along the river without seeing human beings, the expedition reached a point about two days' march below an abandoned Piro pueblo (LA 487). As I have indicated in Chapter 5, I believe the expedition to have been ascending the east side of the river. At this point, a side exploration was made in search of Indians to act as guides. I presume this exploration to have been on the east bank since that was the bank traveled, and also because, following a trail inland, the party reached the base of a mountain range after traveling not much more than two leagues (5.2 miles). (Hammond and Rey 1966: 80) At this point, the San Mateo Mountains west of the Rio Grande are more than ten miles from the river, while to the east, the Fra Cristobal Mountains are less than three miles distant. Given that an Indian trail was being followed, which might well have run at a diagonal between the river and the mountain range, only the Fra Cristobal range is likely to be that mentioned.

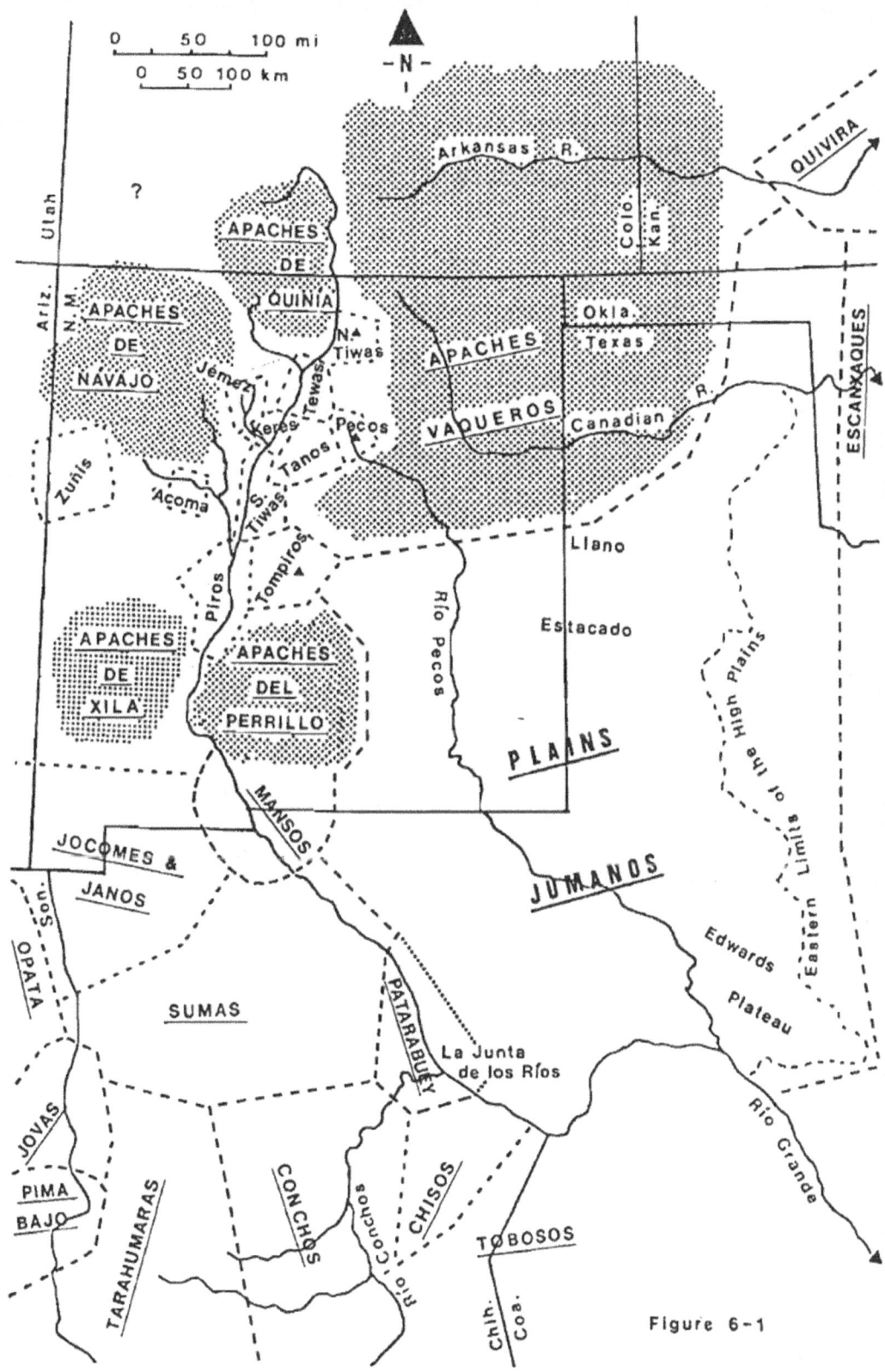

Figure 6-1

Upon reaching these mountains, the Spaniards saw "an Indian brave and two inhabited huts...and discovered many people, who fled towards the mountains." (Hammond and Rey 1966: 80-81; see also Hammond and Rey 1928: 286) Failing to capture any of these people, the Spaniards then returned towards the river when "It was God's will that, on our way back to camp, we should meet an Indian about forty years of age." (Hammond and Rey 1966: 81) This Indian used sign language to tell the Spaniards about the Piros farther up the river, but the Spaniards considered him to be "of a different nation" than the Piros. (Hammond and Rey 1966: 81-82, 141; Pacheco et alia 1871a: 147) A somewhat differing account of the securing of this guide is given in Obregon. (Hammond and Rey 1928: 286-287)

In late January of 1583, the Espejo Expedition was approaching the Piro area from the south, following the west bank of the Rio Grande along which they noted the remains of many rancherias (camps). (Hammond and Rey 1966: 170) On January 26th, "we halted at an arm of this river which we named Los Humos, because there were many smoke columns on a high sierra on the opposite side of the river." (Hammond and Rey 1966: 171) Fifteen leagues (39 miles) north of Los Humos, the Espejo Expedition encountered the first abandoned Piro pueblo, which I have identified as LA 597. (See Chapter 5) Measuring 15 leagues south from LA 597 brings one to present-day Truth-or-Consequences, New Mexico. On the opposite bank of the Rio Grande from Truth or Consequences is the northern end of the Caballo Mountains, which must be the "high sierra" mentioned by Espejo.

The above information suggests an Apachean presence in the Fra Cristobal and Caballo Mountains and along the adjacent portion of the Rio Grande in the early AD 1580s. This territory was later known to be inhabited by the Apaches del Perrillo (See Figure 6-1), the smoke columns sound very much like Apache smoke-signals as described by Mallery (1881: 538-539), (1) the use of sign language by the guide is consonant with Querecho abilities in 1541, the "huts" could be the Apachean form of wickiup used in mountainous areas (Opler 1983: 371), and it is my general impression that the Mansos did not range north of the southern tip of the Caballo Mountains.

It would seem then that Apacheans had moved south and west by the 1580s to at least occupy the above mentioned mountain ranges, and probably the basin of the Jornada del Muerto to the east and possibly the San Andres Mountains further east. Such a distribution would make them southern neighbors to the Piros and to the Tompiros of the Chupadera Basin. Unfortunately, no information as to the actual interactions between these peoples is present in the written records.

In early October of 1581, the Rodriguez-Chamuscado Expedition ventured out onto the plains of New Mexico in search of the bison. Before reaching the herds, they encountered a large camp of Apacheans along the Rio Pecos, probably in the general vicinity of modern Santa Rosa. The camp was composed of over 400 warriors and a total of 2,000 persons. (Hammond and Rey 1928: 303, 1966: 89-90) There is some discrepancy in the number of "huts and tents" reported for the encampment: only 50 noted in Gallegos' relacion (Hammond and Rey 1966: 89), but over 500 reported in Obregon. (Hammond and Rey 1928: 303) If the figures for persons are to be accepted, then the figure of over 500 "huts and tents" would be most realistic (yielding an average of four persons per dwelling, in contrast to an unlikely average of 40 persons per dwelling in only 50 dwellings were present).

The "huts and tents" are described as being covered with tanned bison hides. The people are noted to be "semi-naked" and to wear bison and "deer" skins (2), and shoes and caps made of skins. Communication with the Spaniards was by sign language. Bows and arrows were the weapons in evidence and pack-dogs, tied together in trains and capable of traveling three to four leagues (eight to ten miles) per day, were noted as transporting the Indians' supplies. (Hammond and Rey 1928: 303-305, 1966: 89-90, 131, 136; Pacheco et alia 1871a: 86, 93)

The Tanos, the Pueblo Indians of the Galisteo Basin among whom the Spaniards had been prior to their venture onto the plains, had described these Apacheans as hunting the bison except "during the rainy season they would go to the areas of the prickly pear and yucca" (Hammond and Rey 1966: 87), and Pedro de Bustamante stated that the Apachean's pack-dogs "carried their provisions of corn and yucca." (Hammond and Rey 1966: 131; Pacheco et alia 1871a: 86) If the "rainy season" was essentially the same as that of the present day (ca. July through early September), then it would roughly coincide with the bison's rutting season, when the meat is rank with hormonal secretions, and when the prickly pear cactus fruit would be maturing. Furthermore, green corn would be available in the fields of the Pueblo Indians at this time.

The datil, or yucca mentioned in these accounts, may be reference to the eating of the central leaves of Yucca baccata, which is specifically known for the Apaches. (Bell and Castetter 1941: 19) Both the prickly pear cactus and the yucca would be available in the Pintada Highlands west of Santa Rosa, from which the cornfields of the Tompiros at Tabira (LA 51), Cueloce (LA 120), and Pueblo Pardo (LA 83) could be raided for green corn.

The time, early October, of the Spaniards' visit to this large Apachean camp would be after the end of the rainy season and during the time of the autumn bison hunt. This would account for the large number of people gathered together at this time: the camp was probably being used as a homebase for hunting parties. Also, the camp was located near the probable southern periphery of Apachean territory (See Figure 6-1), so there would be safety in numbers given the possibility of attack from the Plains Jumanos to the south.

The Tanos described these Apacheans as enemies, but enemies with whom there was a regular trade of corn and cotton blankets in exchange for bison and pronghorn skins and meat. (Hammond and Rey 1966: 87) Again, there are no specific data on relations between these Apacheans and the Tompiros.

In July of 1583, the Espejo Expedition descended the Rio Pecos without encountering any Apacheans. As they were passing through Apachean territory early in the month, it is probable that the Apacheans were further east on the Llano Estacado, where they would be finishing off their summer bison hunt before the beginning of the rutting season.

The Rodriguez-Chamuscado Expedition did not encounter Apacheans elsewhere in the Southwest, but the Espejo Expedition found a group called "Querechos" in the area near 'Acoma. They were described as being warlike mountain dwellers who traded salt, game (deer, rabbits, hares), and dressed deerskins to the people of 'Acoma in return for cotton blankets and other goods. (Hammond and Rey 1928: 332-333, 1966: 224; Pacheco et alia 1871a: 117, 180) The reference to mountain dwelling presumably refers to the Mount Taylor area north of the Rio San Jose, and this may be the first mention of the Navajos as a separate group. Luxan speculates that 'Acoma's position on its mesa top was for protection against these Querechos (Hammond and Rey 1966: 182), but archaeological evidence shows that 'Acoma was established in the late AD 1200s, too early to reflect an Apachean presence, and has continued to be inhabited until the present day. (Dittert 1959: 171-178)

The Espejo Expedition visited the Hopi pueblos in April 1583, and found that the Hopis were planning to resist, and had called to their aid "many Chichimecos, who are called Corechos." (Hammond and Rey 1966: 189, see also Hammond and Rey 1928: 328) Were these "Corechos/Querechos" Apacheans? I suspect not, since other nomadic Indians (the Yavapais of the Verde Valley) were subsequently called "Querechos," indicating that the term was being applied generally to any previously unknown nomads by the Espejo Expedition. (See Hammond and Rey 1928: 330.) I suspect that the "Corechos" at the Hopi pueblos may have been Southern Paiutes, who many have already begun to settle the Kaibito Plateau northwest of the Hopi Mesas. (See the recent summary on Paiute "proto-history" by Fowler and Fowler 1981.)

To summarize then, by 1581-1583, the Apacheans appear to have at least spread into parts of the areas later known to be inhabited by Navajos and the Apaches del Perrillo, and the latter would definitely have made contact of some sort with the Piros and Tompiros.

AD 1590-1594

In December of 1590, the illegal colonization party led by Castaño de Sosa approached Pecos Pueblo by traveling north up the Rio Pecos. During the last two weeks of December, the party passed through what was probably Apachean territory without encountering any Indians. (Hammond and Rey 1966: 265-269; Schroeder and Matson 1965: 72-77; Pacheco et alia 1865: 312-318, 1871a: 220-226) The Apacheans were probably in winter camps in the foothills of the mountains away from the river.

However, on January 13, 1591, the Castaño de Sosa party visited the Tewa pueblo, later to be known as San Juan, where they found some "gente forastera" (foreign people) camping in some huts "a long harquebus shot" from the pueblo (about 150 paces distance, according to Salas 1950: 209). These "foreign people" had come to trade with the Tewas of San Juan, and were probably Apacheans from either the west, north, or east. (Hammond and Rey 1966: 284; Pacheco et alia 1865: 339, 1871a: 245-246)[3]

The disastrous expedition by Leyva and Humaña to New Mexico in 1593-1594 is recorded only in the statement of an Indian servant, which records the presence of the Apaches Vaqueros on the plains east of Pecos Pueblo in 1594, but gives no details. (Hammond and Rey 1966: 323-325)

AD 1598–1601

In the Vassalage of San Juan, taken by the Spaniards on September 9, 1598, mission assignments of pueblos were made to the various missionary priests, including three mentions of adjacent Apachean peoples, as follow:

> To Father Fray Francisco de San Miguel, the province of Pecos with the seven pueblos of the cienega (the Galisteo Basin) to the east and all of the Vaquero (Apache) Indians of that (mountain) range (and district (4)) as far as the Sierra Nevada (Sangre de Cristo Mountains)...

> To Father Fray Francisco de Zamora, the province of the Picuries, together with all the Apaches from the Sierra Nevada toward the north and east, (5) and the province of Taos...

> To Father Fray Alonso de Lugo, the province of Emmes (Jemez)...and, in addition, all of the Apaches and Cocoyes of the neighboring sierras and settlements. (6) (Hammond and Rey1953: 345; Spanish text in Pacheco et alia 1871b: 113-114).

If we take the Spanish text as more authoritative in the case of chapter note 5, then Fray Zamora clearly was to administer to Apaches north and west of Taos, those later known as Apaches de Quinia (See Figure 6-1), while Fray San Miguel had the Vaquero Apaches of the plains, and Fray Lugo the Apacheans later to be known as the Navajos. Oñate later states in a letter to the viceroy dated March 2, 1599 that the Cocoyes are "a very numerous people who dwell in jacal huts and who farm." (Hammond and Rey 1953: 485, Pacheco et alia 1871b: 309) This would indicate that the Navajos had already adopted agriculture, one of the traits that were later to distinguish them from other Apacheans.

Two trips out onto the plains were made by members of the Oñate colonizing party: (1) An exploration led by Vicente de Zaldivar from late September through early November 1598, which appears to have visited the plains of northeastern New Mexico north of the Canadian River, and (2) an exploration led by Juan de Oñate from late June to late November 1601, which followed the Canadian River eastwards into the Texas panhandle, then turned northwards and eventually reached Quivira (the Wichitas). On both occasions, Vaquero Apaches were encountered before or just after reaching Canadian River, and were found continuously for some distance to the east.

A summary of the descriptions of these Vaquero Apaches gives the following picture: they used the bow and arrow, leather shields, and war clubs; the bison was hunted and provided hides, fat, tallow, and meat, some of which was eaten raw, but some made into jerky; hide tipis, some painted red and white, were erected on poles, with the most common size being large enough for four sleeping pallets[7]; clothing of bison hides and buckskin, but with use of cotton blankets acquired from the Pueblo Indians; and use of pack-dogs in trains to carry belongings and drag tipi poles. (Hammond and Rey 1953: 398-401, 403-404, 749, 838-839, 852-854, 864) Trade relations with the pueblos of Taos, Picuris, Pecos, and the Tewa pueblos are specifically noted, with the Vaqueros trading salt, meat, skins, fat and tallow for cotton blankets, pottery, turquoise, corn, and tobacco. (Hammond and Rey 1953: 400, 838-839, 852, 864) In 1598, the Vaqueros asked Vicente de Zaldivar for aid against their enemies, the Plains Jumanos. (Hammond and Rey 1953: 399-400) There is still no specific information on Apachean relations with the Piros and Tompiros.

AD 1626–1630

The positions of the various Apachean groups shown in Figure 6-1 is based primarily on the information provided by Fray Alonso de Benavides in his two accounts. (Ayer 1916; Forrestal and Lynch 1954; Anonymous 1962: 1-77; Hodge, Hammond and Rey 1945) However, it is clear from the above review of information from AD 1581 through 1601 that the Apachean groups known to Benavides were almost all in place or moving into place between those dates. The only group not previously mentioned is the Apaches de Xila, who Benavidez notes as living in the Gila wilderness (as it is known today), 14 leagues west of the Piro pueblo of Senecu. (Forrestal and Lynch 1954: 43; Anonymous 1962: 41; Hodge, Hammond and Rey 1945: 82) According to Benavides, Sanaoa, a chief of the Xila Apaches, was accustomed to come to Senecu to gamble (and probably also to trade), but the Apaches del Perrillo, east of the Rio Grande, were not particularly friendly with the Piros, although they sometimes visited at Senecu. (Hodge, Hammond and Rey 1945: 82, 84-85)

It is at this time that the name Navajo, associated with cultivation of fields, first appears. (Forrestal and Lynch 1954; Anonymous 1962: 43) There is no mention in Benavides' accounts of relations between any of the Apacheans and the Tompiros.

AD 1660–1680

The approximate distributions of Apacheans in the Southwest and on the Southern Plains for this period are shown in Figure 6-2. These distributions are based mainly on the information given in the relacion by Fray Alonso de Posada. (Tyler and Taylor 1958; Spanish text in Anonymous 1962: 460-484) However, since Posada frequently did not given the current names for Apachean divisions, I have in some places utilized names current in the 1690s, which may or may not have been used earlier; these are "Apaches de El Cuartelejo," "Apaches Faraones," and "Apaches Lioanes."

As is apparent from Figure 6-2, the Apacheans made substantial movements to the south and west, and somewhat to the east, between AD 1630 and 1680, displacing various groups, particularly the Plains Jumanos. The Apaches de los Siete Rios, probably a combination of the earlier Apaches del Perrillo and southwestern bands of the Vaquero Apaches, replaced the Plains Jumanos in the middle Pecos drainage, breaking the Jumanos' contact with the Tompiros, and apparently usurping their trading relationship with the Tompiros. (This is discussed in more detail below.) The Tompiros and Salinas Tiwas suffered from hostile action by the Apaches de los Siete Rios, and the Piros maintained varying relations with their Apachean neighbors, at times hostile, at other times, in conspiracy against the Spaniards. (See the historical narrative in Chapter 8.)

The only yielding of territory at this time by Apacheans is a possible slight southern retraction of the northern boundary of the Navajos, reflecting the impact of the Yuttas (Utes), who make their historical appearance in the second half of the 17th century.

The Plains Jumanos[8]

Of all the terms for ethno-linguistic groups in the Southwest and Southern Plains, the tem "Jumano" (Sumana, Xumano, Jumana, etc.) has been one of the most discussed and least understood. I will not attempt to recapitulate in detail the whole history of scholarly discussion on this point, for the basics of which see A. Bandelier (1890: 80-81, 167-169), Hodge (1911), Bolton (1911), Scholes and Mera (1940), J.C. Kelley (1955: 982-984; 1986), Forbes (1959a: 128-139), and Newcomb (1961: 225-245). The basic solution to the "Jumano Problem" is that arrived at by Scholes, namely that the term "Jumano" was applied to several different Indian groups whose common characteristic was the use of "pattern tattooing or dyeing." (Scholes and Mera 1940: 275)

However, it is also clear that there was a distinct ethno-linguistic group on the Southern Plains who were consistently known by the name "Jumano," as is acknowledged by Scholes, who refers to them as the "true Jumanos" or "plains Jumanos." (See also J.C. Kelly 1955: 982-984.) It is following this latter usage that I employ the term "Plains Jumanos" to refer to the nomadic bison-hunters of New Mexico and Texas, so as to especially distinguish them from the several sedentary farming groups to whom the name "Jumano" was also occasionally applied.

Just who were these "Plains Jumanos?" First, it appears that they were linguistically related to the sedentary peoples of La Junta de los Rios, who were known by the name Patarabueyes. This relationship was so close that the two groups were considered to speak the same language by the Patarabueyes, as Hernan Gallegos states in 1581:
We asked them through our interpreter what kind of people there were beyond, in the territory bordering theirs. They replied that in their own land there were many people of their tongue, and from what they indicated their nation extended for more than one hundred leagues; that many more (nations) were to be found beyond their land... (Hammond and Rey 1966: 73-74)

As the Rodriguez-Chamuscado Expedition in 1581 was approaching La Junta de los Rios along the Rio Conchos, i.e., from the south and west, the "beyond" about which the Spaniards inquired was probably the territory north and east of their position at La Junta. On Figure 6-3, I have drawn an arc of 100 leagues' radius to cover that northern and eastern sector. The resulting quadrant encloses an area, which can probably be considered the core of Plains Jumano territory. (Compare Figures 6-3 and 6-1.)

The close linguistic affiliation is confirmed during the Espejo Expedition as the chronicler, Diego Perez de Luxan, had with him a Patarabuey boy named Pedro who could speak his native language and Spanish, and who was able to speak with Plains Jumanos encountered along the Rio Pecos in 1583. (Hammond and Rey 1966: 158-159, 209) The approximate spot where the Espejo Expedition met the Plains Jumanos is marked in Figure 6-3 by a black diamond and the letter "A." This spot is within a zone, shown by dots along the Rio Pecos on Figure 6-3, where the Castaño de Sosa Expedition found rancherias (camp sites) of the Plains Jumanos in 1590.

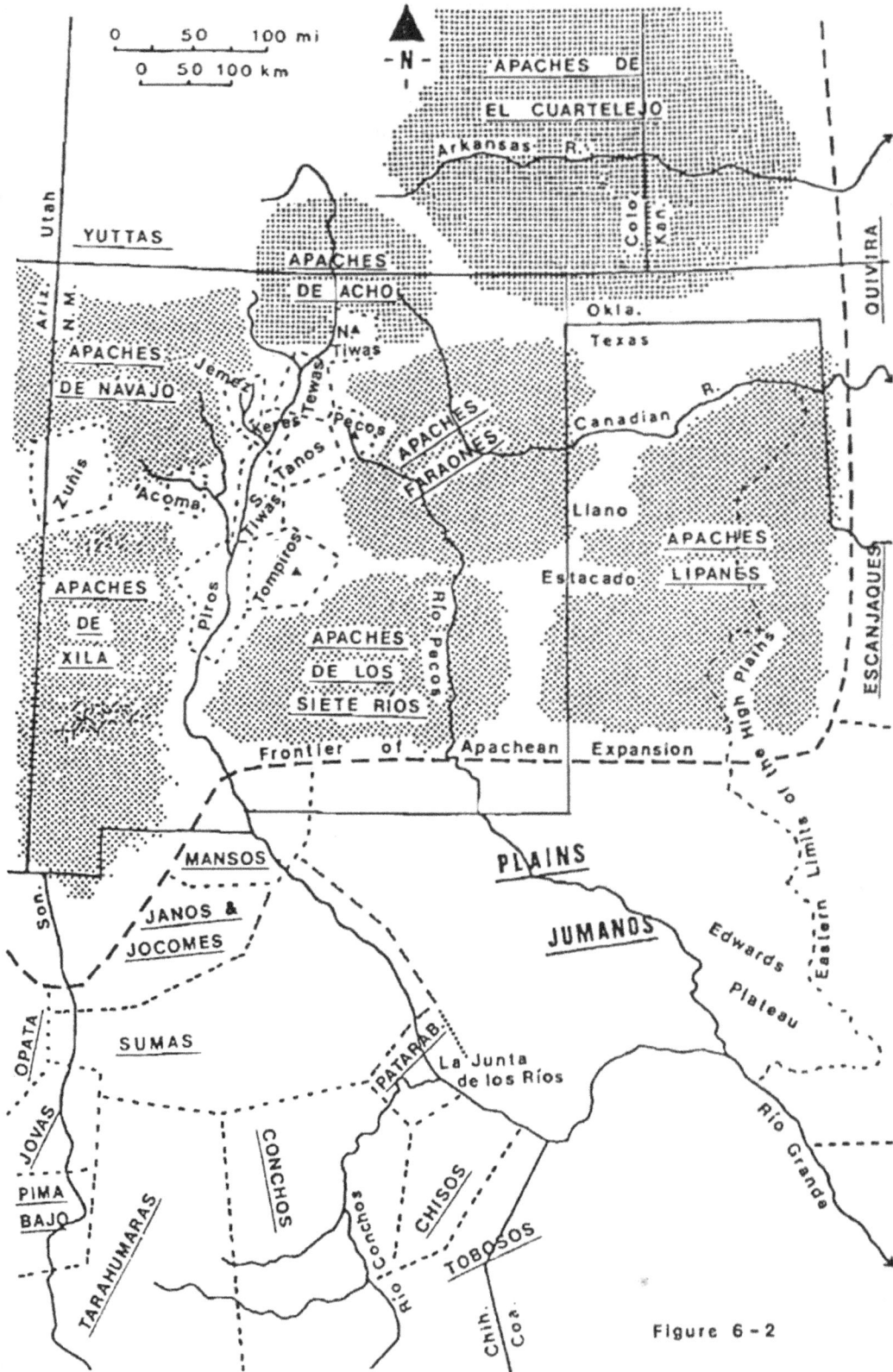

Figure 6-2

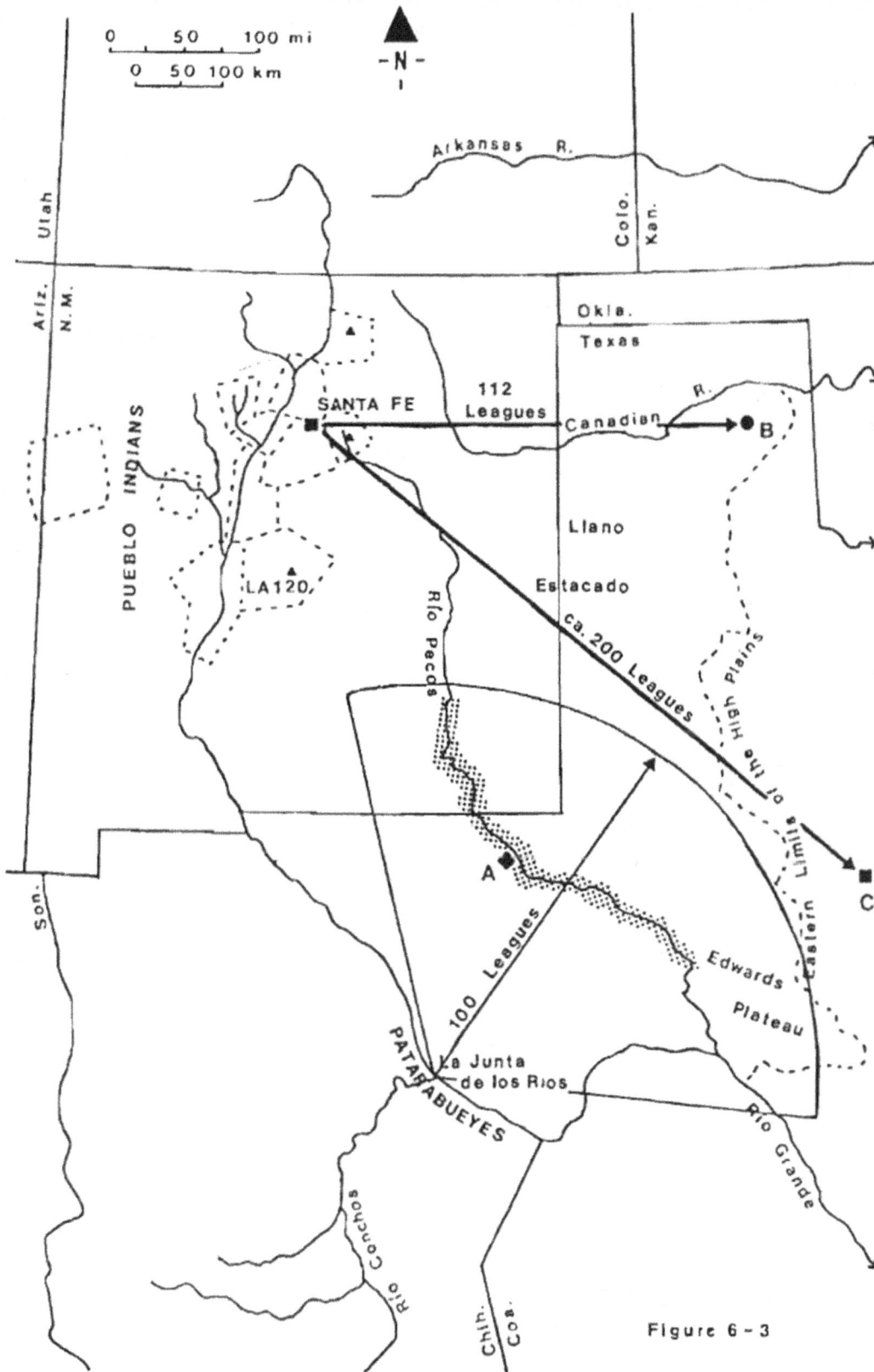

Figure 6-3

It is also clear that the language of the Plains Jumanos and Patarabueyes was not intelligible to the Piros or any other Pueblo Indians of New Mexico, as both the Espejo Expedition and the Rodriguez-Chamuscado Expedition had with them Patarabuey natives as interpreters (a man named Juan Cantor in the case of the latter expedition, see Hammond and Rey 1966: 162), but neither expedition could find any Pueblo Indian who could understand the interpreters. However, neither expedition visited Cueloce (Gran Quivira), where the Plains Jumanos traded and which surely would have had some persons conversant in the language.

The broader relationships of Patarabuey/Plains Jumano are uncertain at present, but may lie with Uto-Aztecan. Naylor (1981) has demonstrated that Suma is definitely Uto-Aztecan, and possibly closely affiliated to Tarahumara, and it has been claimed that Suma and Plains Jumano/ Patarabuey are closely related, if not the same language. (See Scholes and Mera 1940: 285-289; Kroeber 1943b: 15; Miller 1983: 332.) It is clear, however, that Plains Jumano is not Athapaskan, as claimed by Forbes (1959a).

Descriptions of the Plains Jumanos and their relationships with other groups are covered chronologically below. First, however, I wish to summarize our evidence regarding the territories occupied by the Plains Jumanos up to ca. AD 1660. (See Figures 6-1 and 6-3.) (1) There is the statement in Gallegos (quoted above) concerning the extension of Patarabuey/Plains Jumanos ethno-linguistic group 100 leagues beyond La Junta de los Rios in 1581; (2) there is the encounter between the Espejo party and Plains Jumanos at the point marked "A" in Figure 6-3 in 1583; [3] there is the zone of Plains Jumano rancherias along the Rio Pecos encountered by the Castaño de Sosa party in 1590;[4] there is the mention of Plains Jumanos trading at Gran Quivira (LA 120) and having a territorial range near the Estancia Basin by Benavides for the late 1620s;[5] there is further mention by Benavides of a northern group of Plains Jumanos 112 leagues east of Santa Fe at the point marked "B" on Figure 6-3; and (6) there is the mention by Fray Posada of two Spanish expeditions to a favorite rendezvous of the Plains Jumanos on the Colorado River of Texas about 200 leagues southeast of Santa Fe in 1650 and 1654, a point "C" on Figure 6-3. These points and localities pretty well delineate the Plains Jumano territory I have shown in Figure 6-1, except for the extension up to Quivira, which is suggested by the information from AD 1541.

Leading into the chronological discussion, a brief consideration of Patarabuey/Plains Jumano prehistory is in order. The Patarabuey are the easiest to trace due to their sedentary nature: J. Charles Kelley has determined that sedentary occupation of La Junta de los Rios began as an extension of settlement down the Rio Grande from the north. Essentially, the area was colonized by Jornada Culture peoples, probably during the Doña Ana Phase (ca. AD 1100–1200), and produced a local derivative of the Jornada Culture termed the La Junta Focus (Phase), AD 1200–1400 (J.C. Kelley 1952a: 358-363). Due to the disappearance of sedentary settlement in the areas of the Jornada Culture to the north and of the Casas Grandes culture to the west, by AD 1400 (Lehmer 1948: 87; DiPeso, Rinaldo and Fenner 1974, 3: 758-759), the Conceocion Focus (Phase) at La Junta de los Rios, AD 1400–1700, lost direct contact with other sedentary peoples. (J.C. Kelley 1952a: 362-366) Thus, the Patarabueyes appear to be an isolated remnant of the prehistoric Jornada Culture, which survived into historic times. Detailed discussion of the histories of the various Patarabuey pueblos can be found in J.C. Kelley's works (1952a: 366-382, 1952b, 1953).

But what of the Plains Jumanos? Carl Sauer considered the Plains Jumanos to be groups of Patarabueyes from La Junta de los Rios who gave up agriculture to become bison hunters (Sauer as cited in Scholes and Mera 1940: 287), and this view has also been suggested by Newcomb (1962: 227). Such a scenario is analogous to the Crow/Hidatsa split well known from the Northern Plains, where a nomadic bison-hunting group (the Crow) split off from a sedentary farming group (the Hidatsa), but maintained close trade and social contacts. (See Wood and Downer 1977, Taylor 1969, Hanson 1979, Heidenreich 1979, and Matthews 1979.)

An alternative prehistoric origin for the Plains Jumanos would be to consider them the descendants of the Jornada Culture peoples of southeastern New Mexico, as has been suggested by W. A. Dodge (1980: 52). The fate of Jornada Culture peoples after AD 1300–1400 has not been solved archaeologically: at best, it is known that sedentary occupation ceases, and it has sometimes been assumed that there was an abandonment with migration to and absorption by nearby agricultural groups to the north and west, such as the Piros and Tompiros (e.g., W.A. Dodge 1980: 52; Mera in Scholes and Mera 1940: 296; Vivian 1964: 145-146). At this point, I can say that I find no archaeological evidence among the Tompiros for the absorption of a large population from the south around AD 1400, and Tainter (1985) has also cast doubt on this hypothetical migration. Consequently, an alternative, that a sedentary and agricultural mode of life was abandoned in favor of a nomadic bison-hunting existence, must be given serious consideration, as has already been suggested by a number of scholars. (Jelinek 1967: 162-163; Stuart and Gauthier 1981: 274-277) However, Jelinek's attempt to derive the historic Kiowa from the prehistoric population of the Middle Pecos Valley is clearly untenable to anyone familiar with Kiowa traditions and the historical evidence, which sources concur in placing the proto-historic Kiowa homeland in the Northern Plains near the Black Hills of South Dakota and the Kiowa's arrival in the Southern Plains as no earlier than the late AD 1700s. (See Harrington 1939; John 1985.)

Following the hypothesis of a change to a nomadic, bison-hunting life, a reasonable connection can be made between the historic Plains Jumanos and the prehistoric Jornada Culture. On geographic grounds alone, the considerable overlap of Plains Jumano territory with the eastern sectors of the Jornada Culture, it would seem reasonable, but when the close linguistic relationship between the Plains Jumanos and the Patarabueyes is considered (given that the Patarabueyes are a southern remnant of the Jornada Culture), then the suggestion is considerably strengthened. For the moment, I will leave it as being the hypothesis which I favor over any other that has yet been advanced.

Ca. AD 1535

Alvar Nuñez Cabeza de Vaca, along with his Spanish companions and a host of accompanying Indians, approached the lower Rio Pecos from the east, crossed it and apparently traveled through the mountains of the Big Bend country to reach the Patarabueyes at La Junta de los Rios. (F. Bandelier 1905: 144-151) While no name is given for them, there is little doubt from Cabeza de Vaca's descriptions that they were indeed the Patarabueyes. (F. Bandelier 1905: 149-154) The Spaniards were probably at La Junta de los Rios during the autumn since they were given squash, beans and gourds, probably of that year's crop, and much of the population was stated to be away hunting bison. (F. Bandelier 1905: 149, 153) According to the Patarabueyes, 1534 and 1535 had both been drought years, during which people had gone to hunt bison (F. Bandelier 1905: 152), presumably in company with the Plains Jumanos. Unfortunately, however, there is no mention of this latter group.

AD 1541

Beyond the Querechos, the Vasquez de Coronado expedition reached a group of nomadic bison-hunting Indians called the Teyas, which seems to be that used for them at Pecos Pueblos. (See the description of the Teya attack on Pecos and the Galisteo Basin pueblos in Chapter 8.)[9]

I consider the Teyas to be the Plains Jumanos because: (1) They are distinguished from the Querechos by the Spaniards as being tattooed on their bodies and faces (Winship 1896: 441-442, 500, 581)[10]; (2) the locality where the Teyas were first encountered by the Spaniards seems to be in the vicinity of point "B" on Figure 6-3, where Plains Jumanos were known to be in AD 1629-1630 (see below); (3) the Teyas had persons with them, specifically an old man, who had seen Cabeza de Vaca's party six years before far to the south, perhaps at the Patarabuey pueblos at the other end of Plains Jumanos territory (Winship 1896: 441, 505-506, 588-589); (4) the Teya guides of the main "army" of the Spaniards correctly described the geography of the Rio Grande and Rio Pecos to beyond their point of junction, indicating a first hand knowledge of the territory involved, as would be expected of the Plains Jumanos (Winship 1896: 441, 510); (5) these same guides led the main "army" to the Rio Pecos at a point 30 leagues (73 miles) south of the place bridged by the Spaniards on the outward journey, that is: 30 leagues south of Anton Chico, which would be the vicinity of Fort Sumner, inside Plains Jumano territory. (Winship 1896: 444, 510)

Unfortunately, most of the descriptions of the Teyas just state that they are culturally the same as the Querechos. (See above.) Those specific items noted for the Teyas include tattooing, the use of trains of pack-dogs, the bow and arrow, buckskin clothing and shoes, and the eating of raw meat. (Winship 1896: 441-442, 506-507, 581; Pacheco et alia 1870a: 263)

However, we can at least be sure that tattooing is meant when the Plains Jumanos are described as being Rayados ("striped") due to a fortunate passage in Pedro de Castañeda's narrative: "se hallo una india tam blanca como muger de castilla saluo que tenia labrada la barua como morisca de berberia que todos se labran en general de aquella manera por alli se ahogolan los ojos," in English: "there was an Indian woman as white as a woman of Castile, except that she had her chin decorated like a Moorish woman of Barbary; in general they all decorate themselves in this manner there (and) they decorate their eyes." (Winship 1896: 441-442, 500)[11] "Berberia," Barbary, refers to the Mediterranean coastal zones of Morocco and Algeria occupied by Berbers, and where the Spanish had coastal enclaves in the early 16th century, beginning with the capture of Melilla by the Duke of Medina-Sidonia in 1497. (Elliot 1966: 52-52) Facial, especially chin, tattooing is still practiced by Berbers in the area around Melilla. (See Coon 1931: 86-88, Plate 29.) And Vasquez de Coronado specifically states: "y otra nacion de gente que se llaman los teyas, todos labrados los cuerpos y rostros..." (Pacheco et alia 1870a: 263), in English: "and another nation of people who are called the Teyas, all of whom are decorated (on) their bodies and faces."

The Teyas are noted to be enemies of the Querechos (Apacheans) (Winship 1896: 581; Pacheco et alia 1870a: 263) and These (Teyas) know the people in the settlement (the Pueblo Indians), and were friendly with them, and they (the Teyas of the plains) went there to spend the winter under the wings of the settlements. The inhabitants do not dare to let them come inside, because they can not trust them. Although they are received as friends, and trade with them, they do not stay in the villages over night, but outside under the wings. (Winship 1896: 453-454, 524)

It is not clear which pueblos the Teyas visited, but the above information seems to have been acquired at Pecos. Later, Castañeda notes that the Teyas also wintered at Quivira (the Wichitas) and at settlements to the southeast, possibly other Caddoan groups of the Wichitas. (Winship 1896: 456, 527)

AD 1581–1583

The Rodriguez-Chamuscado Expedition passed through the Patarabuey settlements on the way north to the Pueblo Indians in 1581. (Hammond and Rey 1928: 276-234, 1966: 73-79) I will not repeat the recorded details, but will note that the Patarabueyes are called rayados, which term is commonly used thereafter by Spaniards for tattooed peoples, and are specifically noted to "mark their faces." (Hammond and Rey 1928: 276, 278; 1966: 73) It was at this time that the Patarabueyes claimed that people speaking their language were to be found for 100 leagues beyond La Junta de los Rios (Hammond and Rey 1966: 73-74), which I consider to be a reference to the Plains Jumanos.

The Patarabueyes know of the Pueblo Indians to the north, calling them Allaguabas (phonetically, this would be (ay wa as) or (alya wa as)), but their knowledge was second-hand, coming from "the men who hunted the buffalo", which must be a reference to the Plains Jumanos. (Hammond and Rey 1928: 277, 281; 1966: 74, 76)

The Espejo Expedition of 1582–1583 gives a few details about the Patarabueyes. (Hammond and Rey 1928: 317-319; 1966: 158-168, 210-211, 215-218, 229) Significant among them, however, is the mention of facial striping by Espejo and the use of the term "Jumana" for the Patarabueyes.

(Hammond and Rey 1928: 317; 1966: 216, 229) Scholes (Scholes and Mera 1940: 275-276, footnote 30) has discussed the original Spanish passages containing this term "Jumana." Despite Scholes' reservations, it seems clear from the passage in Obregon that "Jumana" was the self-name of the Patarabueyes, at least. I would argue that if "Jumana" was also used as a self-name by the Plains Jumanos, then the reported Tewa use of the term to mean any tattooed people (Hammond and Rey 1953: 867) could have derived from the self-name of the tattooed group best known to the Tewas, the Plains Jumanos.

Diego Peres de Luxan gives us a few tidbits of ethnographic detail on the Plains Jumanos. (Hammond and Rey 1966: 209-210):

The Espejo party met three Plains Jumanos hunting along the Rio Pecos in early August, thus probably not hunting bison since that period was the rutting season.

Shortly afterwards, they met a rancheria (camp) of Plains Jumanos traveling down a tributary "on their way to the river (Rio Pecos), to the mesquite trees", apparently to harvest mesquite beans. The distribution of the mesquite, Prosopis chilensis, closely follows the Rio Pecos in southeastern New Mexico and northernmost trans-Pecos Texas, and "P. chilensis is found at its best on the flood plains bordering rivers." (Bell and Castetter 1937: 2, 11)

"Tents" are mentioned for this rancheria, presumably bison-hide tipis, and a dance "held amid the tents" is noted; Another Plains Jumano rancheria served the Spaniards "roasted and raw calabashes (squash, or possibly yucca pods?) and prickly pears"; And most intriguing is the following passage: "On our way we found settled people of this nation (Plains Jumanos), who in their clothing, appearance, and habitat are similar to the Patarabueyes." The terms "settled" and "habitat" suggest jacal dwellings like those described for the Patarabueyes. The location of this settlement appears to have been on Toyah Creek, less than 23 miles upstream from its confluence with the Rio Pecos. Could this be a 16th century survival of late Glencoe Phase architecture (see J. H. Kelley 1984: 382-385) transposed to trans-Pecos Texas?

AD 1590

During October, November, and December of 1590, the illegal colonizing expedition led by Gaspar Castaño de Sosa was traveling north into New Mexico by way of the Rio Pecos. Along a large stretch of this river, these Spaniards found rancherias, both inhabited and abandoned, traveling bands of Indians, and other evidences of occupation by the Plains Jumanos. This area is indicated by the dotted zone in Figure 6-3. Most of the rancherias are described as "recently constructed," even when not occupied, which leads me to suspect that brush frameworks, such as wickiup frames, must have been present.[12]

A few specific cultural items are mentioned: trains of pack-dogs, use of the bow and arrow, and use of sign language. (Schroeder and Matson 1965: 50-66; Hammond and Rey 1966: 256-262; Pacheco et alia 1865: 299-307; 1871a: 207-215) An especially important item is a structure, which is clearly a bison, or pronghorn, pound, indicating a form of communal game hunting. (Schroeder and Matson 1965: 62; Hammond and Rey 1966: 260-262; Pacheco et alia 1865: 305; 1871a: 213)[13] Another important item was the Spaniards' discovery in a cottonwood grove of a pottery olla containing corncobs recently cleaned of their kernels, probably in the general vicinity of Hagerman or Greenfield, New Mexico. (Schroeder and Matson 1965: 64; Hammond and Rey 1966: 262; Pacheco et alia 1865: 307; 1871a: 215)[14] This is probably an indication of trade between the Plains Jumanos and a nearby Pueblo Indian group, such as the Tompiros.

The time of year is important here: the autumn bison hunt would be in progress in October and November, with a probable use of rancherias along the Rio Pecos as staging bases for hunting parties. The lack of people in these rancherias may have been a result of temporary abandonment but of distrust of the Spaniards' intentions. Such distrust was certainly manifested in the two clashes between the Spaniards and Plains Jumano war parties on November 1 and 2, which occurred just after the Spaniards' capture and temporary detention of four Plains Jumanos on October 31. The smoke signal in the mountains west of the river on November 20 may also relate to Indian observation and communications concerning Spanish movements.

AD 1598–1601

There is very little mention of the Plains Jumanos in the documents of the Oñate Colonizations. In a statement dated February 23, 1599, Vicente de Zaldivar recounted his exploration east of Pecos Pueblo between late September and early November 1598, which appears to have taken his party into northeastern New Mexico, north of the Canadian River. The only Indians met in this area were Vaquero Apaches, who "asked him for aid against the Xumanas, which is the name they give to a nation of Indians who are striped like the Chichimecos." (Hammond and Rey 1953: 399-400) I take this to be a reference to the Plains Jumanos; here it is important to note that the name "Xumana" was used by the Apaches, thus is not one imposed by the Spaniards.

During the Valverde Inquiry, held in Mexico City in 1602, Juan Rodriguez, a soldier who had participated in the colonization, states: "The Indians around San Gabriel (the Tewas) called these people from the settlement (Quivira, i.e., the Wichitas) Jumanos; in fact, they gave this name to all of the Rayados." (Hammond and Rey 1953: 867) This is the evidence that suggests to me that the term "Jumano" is a self-name of the Plains Jumanos, which was generalized by the Tewas for application to any tattooed group. Clearly, it is in this way that the name "Jumano" became first applied to the Tompiros of Gran Quivira (LA 120) and their neighbors.

When Oñate made his trip to Quivira, he encountered an Indian group called the Escanjaques, (eskanhakes), east of the Vaquero Apaches and south of Quivira (the Wichitas). (Hammond and Rey 1953: 751-753, 756-758) I am convinced that the Escanjaques are not Plains Jumanos, but represent a Caddoan group out hunting on the plains west of the area where their settlement would be. (See Figure 6-1.) The name "Escanjaque" resembles the term "Ascani," "Iscani," and others by which a tribal division of the Wichitas was later known to the Spanish and French, and which was known to the Americans as the Wacos. (see Newcomb and Field 1974: 355, 366.) More important than the name similarity, however, is the close cultural similarity between the Escanjaques and the Wichita groups (see Newcomb 1961: 247-277, and Newcomb and Field 1974: 343-364 for descriptions of Wichita culture). The fact that one tribal division of the Wichitas should be at war with another in 1601 (the Escanjaques-vs.-the Quiviras) should not be a reason to doubt this identification since there are many known instances of closely related Indian group being bitter enemies (for example, the Taos and Picuris in New Mexico and the Assiniboines and Dakota on the Northern Plains).

AD 1629–1630

In the 1630 version of his book, Fray Alonso de Benavides gives us two geographic facts about the Plains Jumanos: (1) Their territory is said to lie beyond that of the Vaquero Apaches at a distance east from Santa Fe of 112 leagues, which would place it about point "B" on Figure 6-3, the same area where Vasquez de Coronado encountered the Teyas in 1541; and (2) the territory of the "Xumanas" is said to border on that of the Tompiros and Salineros (Salinas Tiwas). See Figure 6-1. (Forrestal and Lynch 1954: Anonymous 1962: 57)

It seems that over a period of years, the Plains Jumanos had been asking Fray Juan de Salas, who was making visits to the Salinas Tiwa pueblos from his post at Isleta, to come with them out onto the plains. Salas and his companion priest at Isleta, Fray Diego Lopez, finally visited the Plains Jumanos in 1629 at the locality 112 leagues east of Santa Fe. (Forrestal and Lynch 1954: 57; Anonymous 1962: 57-58) After their return, Fray Ascensio de Zarate Salmeron and Fray Pedro de Ortega also went out onto the plains to be with the Plains Jumanos, but the latter died from either overwork or poison, Benavides contradicts himself on this point. (Hodge, Hammond and Rey 1945: 98-99, 164) It is Benavides who informs us that LA 120 (Gran Quivira) was named Las Xumanas "because this nation often comes there to trade and barter." (Hodge, Hammond and Rey 1945: 66)

AD 1650–1680

Information on the Plains Jumano for this period comes mainly from Fray Alonso de Posada's relacion of 1686. Posada notes an expedition in 1650 to the Plains Jumanos at a spot ca. 200 leagues southeast of Santa Fe, on a "Rio Nueces" which is probably the headwaters of the Colorado River of Texas. (Tyler and Taylor 1958: 293-294; Anonymous 1962: 466-467) It is notable that the Escanjaques are mentioned as a separate people living to the east of the above location (which is marked "C" on Figure 6-3), which supports the identification I have made of this group. (See above.) In 1654, a second Spanish party was sent to this location, again meeting there with the Plains Jumanos, and again the Escanjaques are mentioned as a separate, more eastern group. (Tyler and Taylor 1958: 295; Anonymous 1962: 468-469)

As a comparison of Figures 6-1 and 6-2 suggests, after 1630, the Apaches moved south and slightly east in the Southern Plains, dispossessing the Plains Jumanos of much of their former northern territories. (See Tyler and Taylor

1958: 300-302; Anonymous 1962: 457-477.) It is possible, however, that some compensating expansion of Plains Jumano territory occurred towards the east in southern Texas, as is suggested by the journeys of the band led by Juan Sabeata in the 1680s. (See J.C. Kelley 1955.)

The Mansos

While the Mansos occupied the portion of the Rio Grande Valley around El Paso and adjacent mountain and desert areas, thus being not far south of the Piros, I know of no evidence of direct or frequent contacts between the two groups. However, it is clear from Oñate's account that the Mansos were aware of their northern neighbors, even if they did not have much contact. (Hammond and Rey 1953: 315)

As it is beyond the scope of this work to describe non-Puebloan groups that had little or no contact with the Piros or Tompiros, I will not deal with the many groups in Chihuahua shown in Figures 6-1 or 6-2. For information on them, see the works of Griffen (1969, 1979, 1983).

Notes:

1. According to Mallery (1881: 538) three or more columns of smoke signifies danger or the approach of an enemy. This could very well have been a warning of the approach of the Espejo Expedition meant to be seen by Apachean bands farther north in the Fra Cristobal Mountains.
2. Probably meaning "pronghorn."
3. Schroeder and Matson (1965: 124) translate the passage as "who had come to this pueblo for refuge." However, both available Spanish texts read "que venia a rescata este pueblo" (Pacheco et alia 1865: 339; 1871a: 246), which I would translate as "who had come to trade at this pueblo," thus agreeing with the translation given by Hammond and Rey.
4. The Spanish text in Pacheco et alia (1871b: 113) has the extra phrase y comarca ("and district") which is not rendered in the translation by Hammond and Rey.
5. The Spanish text in Pacheco et alia (1871b: 114) gives Norte y Poniente ("north and west") where Hammond and Rey show "north and east."
6. The Spanish text in Pacheco et alia gives sierras y comarcas ("mountain ranges and districts") where Hammond and Rey show "sierras and settlements."
7. This information regarding the size of Vaquero tipis in 1598 confirms my calculation of an average of four persons per tipi from the information provided by the Rodriguez-Chamuscado party in 1581. (See above.)
8. After this chapter had been written, J.C. Kelley's dissertation was published (J.C. Kelley 1986). I will only make the following brief comments on this work: (1) Kelley does not recognize that the

Teyas are the Plains Jumanos; (2) Kelley's historical coverage includes materials from later in time than mine; however, (3) Kelley has come to conclusions regarding the identify and relationships of the Plain Jumanos that are compatible with mine: "that the (Plains) Jumanos...were ethnically distinct from the Patarabueyes of La Junta, though culturally, politically, and possibly linguistically related to them." (J.C. Kelley 1986: 9)

9. Harrington (1940: 512) states: "My discovery that Teya is the Pecos-Jemez word for eastern Apache, that is, Lipanan, proves that at least the Teya band mentioned by Castañeda was Lipanan..." He gives no citation, but presumably is referring to this discussion in Harrington (1916: 573) where the Jemez term for Apache is (togokyala) "east Navajo," from (togo) "east" and (k'yala) "Navajo," and which he says can be abbreviated to just (togo). Unfortunately, I see no adequate similarity between (teya) and (togo) to merit their equation, hence I cannot see Harrington has demonstrated what he claims.

10. To complete matters, I must note that some historic Apache groups are known to utilize tattooing (see Gifford 1940: 37), but we must keep in mind the time differences involved. The AD 1541 descriptions precede by 100 to 200 years the known absorption by the Apaches of groups such as the Yavapai and Plains Jumanos known to practice tattooing. I therefore argue that these population amalgamations are the likely source of the non-universal presence of tattooing practices among 20th century Apache groups. In essence, I am arguing that Apacheans have added cultural traits, which they did not possess when they first entered the Southwest.

11. Winship translates labrada as "painted" and se labran as "paint," which is misleading since labrar means "to decorate" without specifying "how."

12. Schroeder and Matson translate the phrase recien alzadas as meaning "recently built," which seems to me correct, whereas Hammond and Rey translate it as "recently abandoned," which seems incorrect. This phrase is repeatedly used for the rancherias in the Spanish texts.

13. Forbes (1956b: 195) attempts to use this structure as evidence for the possession of domesticated livestock (cattle and/or horses) by plains nomads at an early date, which is surely the least likely interpretation of this structure.

14. The Spanish text reads: "fuimos a dormir a una muy grande alameda, donde se hallo una olla y elotes recien desgranados," which I translate as: "we went to sleep in a very large cottonwood grove, where there was found an olla and corncobs recently stripped of their kernels." Curiously, Hammond and Rey translate the last phrase as "and some fresh cornhusks," which seems completely inappropriate. On the other hand, I find Hammond and Rey's estimations of the expedition's day-to-day geographical position along the Rio Pecos as more reasonable than the positions given by Schroeder and Matson.

7

Piro-Tompiro Ethnohistory: The Population Decline and Its Causes

A major element in the historical experience of the Piros and Tompiros during the 17th century was a drastic decline in their population, an experience in which the other Pueblo Indians shared equally. The task of this chapter is first to document the population decline, and then to investigate its causes. Discussion of the social impact of the population decline will be integrated with other materials in the chronological history presented in Chapter 8.

The Overall Pueblo Indian Population

This discussion and its conclusions are but a step along the way to comprehensive knowledge of the Pueblo Indian population in the 16th and 17th centuries. I believe that such comprehensive knowledge of the subject can only result from intensive ethnohistorical work on all Pueblo Indian groups comparable to what I am attempting here for the Piros and Tompiros. Consequently, this present summary of the overall Pueblo Indian population can only be considered a stop-gap, rather than a definitive statement expected to stand for all time. Such a stop-gap is, however, greatly needed since there is no previous statement that is at all adequate for my purposes, which necessitate a kind of standard or general pattern of population change against which to compare population changes of the Piros and Tompiros.

Previous Work

Bandelier: Adolf Bandelier (1890: 120-121) states: "The aggregate population of the pueblos in the sixteenth and seventeenth centuries did not exceed twenty-four thousand souls." In an extensive footnote, Bandelier explains his reasoning in this matter, from which it is clear that he was over-reacting negatively to the inflated figures present by Espejo for 1582–1583 and by Benavides for 1626–1629. Furthermore, Bandelier does not recognize the existence of a population decline in the 17th century.

Kidder: In 1924 A. V. Kidder (1962: 144) stated: "At the time of the Spanish conquest the Pueblo Indians numbered about 20,000...," but does not indicate how he arrived at this number. Dobyns (1966: 402) suggests that Kidder simply subtracted 5,000 persons from the figure given by Bandelier (above), and rightly points out the temporal imprecision of Kidder's statement. I suspect that Kidder may have had in mind Pedro de Castaneda's figure of 20,000 Pueblo Indians in 1540 (see Winship 1896: 454); I would add that Kidder also does not recognize the problem of the 17th century population decline.

Mooney and Kroeber: In 1928 a posthumously published study of North American aboriginal population by James Mooney appeared in which a figure of 33,000 persons for AD 1680 was provided, not in summary, but broken down into figures for various Pueblo Indian groups, with F. W. Hodge being cited as the source for the figures (Mooney 1928: 21-22). Mooney assumes (incorrectly) that Pueblo Indian population increased up until 1680, and he only recognizes the effects of epidemics during the 19th century. A. L. Kroeber (1934a: 2-3) adopted Mooney's sum for the Pueblo Indians, stating: "Mooney's figures are probably mostly too high rather than too low, so far as they are in error."

Spicer: As part of a larger study, Edward Spicer wrote the first overall ethnohistory of the Pueblo Indians, in which he suggested a figure of less than 40,000 persons for the Pueblo Indians of the Rio Grande (excluding the Zunis and Hopis) at the time of first contact and 25,000 to 30,000 persons in 1680. (Spicer 1962: 155, 162) While he apparently recognized some population decrease, he does not discuss causes or systematically study population figures.

Spicer treats the western Pueblo Indians (Zunis and Hopis) separately (1962: 187-209), where he mentions population figures occasionally but does not give summary figures comparable to those he provided for the eastern Pueblo Indians and does not discuss population changes in the 16th and 17th centuries.

Zubrow: In 1969 Ezra Zubrow wrote an MA thesis on population change among the Pueblo Indians of New Mexico (thus excluding the Hopis) which was published five years later. (Zubrow 1974) Zubrow attempted to analyze population change among the Pueblo Indians from the 17th through the 20th centuries against several possible causal variables. I do not propose to present or analyze his results here because I doubt they could possibly be valid since his data base was poorly constructed. I say "poorly constructed" for the following reasons: (1) his 16th and 17th century population figures were drawn from two secondary sources (Zubrow 1974: 11-13) which, from a 1960s perspective, were already obsolete (i.e., he ignored readily available published population data in the historical scholarship of the 1920s, 1930s, 1940s, and 1950s); (2) he biased his study of causal relationship by only considering Pueblo Indian communities which survived into the 20th century and ignoring those communities which failed to survive; and (3) by ignoring the failed communities, he thus did not control for immigration into his sample from the failed communities. In sum, Zubrow's study demonstrates nothing because of its defective data base.

Dozier: As part of his overall study on the Pueblo Indians, Dozier (1970: 122, 125, 130) provides the best brief summary on population to date, particularly in his diagram of the overall population changes among the Pueblo Indians and their neighbors. His effort is both more comprehensive and essentially just as accurate as the more detailed later sources discussed below.

Simmons and Schroeder: As part of a brief article on the history of Pueblo Indian-Spanish relations up to 1821, Marc Simmons (1979: 185) presents a population table for the Pueblo Indian communities which is not very satisfactory since it gives only two sets of figures for the 17th century, ignores the communities which failed prior to AD 1700, ignores the Hopis altogether, and does not present summary figures for the whole Pueblo Indian population. These failings are somewhat ameliorated through discussion in the text, but the whole result can scarcely be considered an adequate portrayal of 17th century Pueblo Indian population. Albert H. Schroeder (1979) notes population figures for the 16th and 17th centuries in the course of his discussion of

pueblo abandonments, but no clear framework emerges (i.e., there is a mass of data without systematic synthesis).

Riley: Most recently, Carroll Riley has published an ethnohistorical study of the Greater Southwest covering what he calls the Protohistoric Period (AD 1400–1700) and containing sections on the Pueblo Indians. (Riley 1982: 86-139) He discusses the population figures for the Hopis and Zunis in more detail than other sources (Riley 1982: 92-96) but does not utilize 17th century sources other than Fray Benavides' figures. For the Rio Grande pueblos, Riley (1982: 129) relies on Kessell's recent summary of population data for Pecos (see Kessell 1979b: 489-492), and for the rest gives only a general summary, again not using 17th century sources other than Benavides. (Riley 1982: 113-117) Riley recognizes the general decline in population and the role of disease in it, but once again there is no truly systematic synthesis.

Providing an Estimate of the Overall Pueblo Indian Population

Population estimates for North America as a whole, and for the New World, have mainly been projections based upon simple assumptions. (See Ubelaker 1976 for a recent review.) At different times, there have been "conservative" and "liberal" tendencies which have controlled such estimates:

Individual estimates...probably reflect more academic fashion than objective presentations of data. As new information is compiled, it becomes increasingly clear that considerable variability existed in both population density and in the rate of depopulation with the Western Hemisphere. The projection methods...are useful to provide general estimates of possible population size, but since they do not adequately accommodate this variability, they cannot be expected to yield highly accurate estimates. (Ubelaker 1976: 663)

My own approach to the overall Pueblo Indian population is to ignore such "academic fashions" and projection methods, and to concentrate upon empirical data, however fragmentary or formally unsatisfying these data may be. These data consist of a series of population figures or estimates given within the Spanish Colonial documents between 1598 and 1680, which are shown in Figure 7-1 and Table 7-1. Each of these population figures is discussed below, beginning with the 1678–1680 figures and working backwards in time since the 1643 figure is partly dependent upon discussion of the 1656 figure. Some population figures which are considered too inaccurate for use are also discussed.

1678 and 1680: The figure of 17,000 Pueblo Indians is given by Fray Francisco de Ayeta, procurador general in charge of the supply caravans to New Mexico, in a petition to the viceroy of New Spain dated May 10, 1679, but probably citing information current as of 1678. (See Spanish text in Maas 1929: 53, English text in Hackett 1937: 299.) I suspect this was a "rounded up" figure since Ayeta later states that the Pueblo Indians "exceed 16,000" in a letter of September 11, 1680 to the viceroy regarding the Pueblo Revolt. (Hackett 1942, I: 107) This latter statement is the basis for the figure of 16,500 for 1680 in Table 7-1. I am there assuming that at least that number of Pueblo Indians existed in order to allow the rounding up to 17,000 by Ayeta for 1678.

ca. 1656: The population figure for this year is given as the total of a census of the Pueblo Indians in a document published in translation by France V. Scholes (1929: 45-51). The document is a copy of an original, with the copy dated to May 24, 1664, but unfortunately no date is given for the composition of the original. Scholes (1929: 45) at first considered the document to be part of a relacion dating to the 1620s, but later revised his estimation of the date to 1641 (Scholes 1944: 246) on the basis of internal evidence. I have recently reconsidered the dating of this document and on the basis of further internal evidence I have suggested a date of approximately 1656. (Baldwin 1984c).

The date aside, Scholes misread the population figure for Santa Clara Pueblo as 993 in 1929, hence changed the population total in his translation to 20,181 (Scholes 1929: 47, 50), which he corrected later. (Scholes 1944: 246) However, his corrected total is 19,741, while Scholes notes that the manuscript of the document gives a total of 19,951, which higher figure he attributes "to mistakes of addition in the original." (Scholes 1944: 246) Despite the apparent logic of this, I have used the document's original total of 19,951 in table 7-1 because I suspect that this copy of May 24, 1664 inadvertently omits a paragraph listing the mission of Senecu, with the difference of 210 persons (between the document's total and the sum of the mission populations actually listed) representing the missing information on Senecu. Scholes himself comments on the absence of Senecu from the list (194: 245-246), but does not connect that fact with the "high" total given in the document.

1643: Scholes (1944: 246) notes that Spanish governor Alonso Pacheco de Heredia reports a Pueblo Indian population 19,870 persons in 43 pueblos for 1643, the 43 pueblos not including the Zunis who apparently were not under mission control at the time. (See my discussion in Baldwin 1984c.) Hence, Pacheco's figure of 19,870 is incomplete. Assuming that the Zunis were likely to form about the same percentage of the total Pueblo Indian population in 1643 as in 1656, I calculated the percentage of the 1656 population represented by 1,200 Zunis, for a result of 6.01%. Then, taking the 19,870 reported by Pacheco as representing 93.99% of the total Pueblo Indian population, I added 1,270 Zunis (= 6.01%) for a corrected total of 21,140 Pueblo Indians in 1643.

1640: Scholes (1936: 324) states that in 1640 "a pest spread among the Indians taking a toll of three thousand persons, or more than ten percent of the total Pueblo population." I have added these 3,000 persons to the 1643 figure to provide an estimate for 1640 before the epidemic. Of course, the actual pre-epidemic figure for 1640 may have been higher as I have not allowed for possible further losses between 1640 and 1643, but it must be less than 30,000 in order to conform to Scholes' statement that the 3,000 victims represented over 10% of the total population.

ca. 1635: In response to a royal cedula of 1637 requesting information on New Mexico, Fray Juan de Prada, comisario general of the Franciscan Order in New Spain, addressed a letter to the viceroy dated September 26, 1638 in which he described the Pueblo Indian population in these terms:

The people that may be counted to-day in these settlements will total forty thousand or a little less, for, although there must have been more than sixty thousand baptized, to-day these conversions are diminished to that extent on account of the very active prevalence during these last years of smallpox and the sickness which the Mexican called cocoliztli. (Hackett 1937: 108; see also Spanish text in Maas 1929: 21.)

Taking into account the phrase "or a little less" in the above passage, I have placed the population figure at 39,500 persons. Although the letter is dated to 1638, the information contained in it is probably two or three years old due to the slowness of communication, hence my date of ca. 1635.

1598: A population figure of more than 60,000 Pueblo Indians is reported in several places in documents of the Onate Colonization (Onate's letter to the viceroy of March 2, 1599; testimony of Jusepe Brondate, July 28, 1601; testimony of various individuals taken October 3 through 6, 1601; for these see Hammond and Rey 1953: 483, 629, 702-736) which figure seems to be the "official" estimate of population. Other, competing figures were given by persons critical of the colonial venture (from less than 10,000 to less than 20,000), but these figures were being cited to justify the desertion from the colonial effort (hence are suspect) and do not seem at all likely given the later population figures. (Hammond and Rey 1953: 614, 695) There are, however, several figures of from 22,000 to "more than 30,000" which appear to be only fractional population figures, probably referring only to the Rio Grande pueblos to the exclusion of the Hopis, the Zunis, the Salinas Province and perhaps other "peripheral" groups. (Hammond and Rey 1953: 639, 652, 782-783, 1095) I consider these last to be "fractional" figures because again they are smaller than later total population figures. The "more than 60,000" figure I am placing at ca. 62,000 on Table 7-1 and Figure 7-1.

In addition to the population figures I have used, there are those given by Vetancurt and Benavides. Vetancurt claims that in 1660 there were "more than twenty-four thousand persons, great and small, Indians and Spanish" in New Mexico (1697: 99). The total Spanish population in the twenty years prior to the Pueblo Revolt is variously estimated as 2,500 to 2,800 persons (see Hackett 1942, I: xx) which, when deducted from Vetancurt's figure, would leave more than 21,200 to 21,500 Pueblo Indians. This seems too high a figure compared to that for 1656 in Table 7-1, hence I am doubtful of its validity and do not use it here.

Fray Alonso de Benavides, a former Franciscan custodian of New Mexico, gives population figures in two versions of a book on New Mexico published in 1630 (Ayer 1916, Forrestal and Lynch 1954) and in 1634. (Hodge, Hammond and Rey 1945) Unfortunately, I and most other scholars consider these figures to have been inflated for propaganda purposes. (Benavides was trying to convince the Spanish king and his advisors to increase royal support of the mission effort in New Mexico.) Table 7-2 shows Benavides' two sets of population figures for the Pueblo Indian groups, with totals of 68,500 and 64,500 persons for the 1630 and 1634 editions respectively. Neither of these totals seem at all reasonable to me, nor do the component figures for the Piros and Tompiros, given that epidemics famines, and warfare with the Spanish and Apacheans had already begun to take a toll of a population probably no higher than 62,000 in 1598. The dubiousness of the figures is increased by conflicting total figures given in the same works which are even higher than the sums of the lists, e.g., "80,000 souls" in the 1630 edition (Forrestal and Lynch 1954: 34), and "100,000 souls" in the 1634 edition. (Hodge, Hammond and Rey 1945: 161)

I originally hoped that I could convert Benavides' figures into useable ones, but his inflations appear to be too irregular to permit application of any systematic correction factor. Consequently, there seems to be no choice but to ignore them.

There are some population data for the Pueblo Indians from the 1580s and 1540s, but they are incomplete for any particular date and need to be analyzed keeping in mind the possible effects of the hypothesized New World pandemic of the 1520s. Such considerations will be left for the last section of this chapter.

Returning to Figure 7-1 and Table 7-1, it is clear that between 1598 and 1678 a great depopulation occurred among the Pueblo Indians: a loss of 72.58% of the 1598 population in a period of 80 years (an averaged decrease of 0.91% or 562 persons per year). However, it is clear from Figure 1 that the depopulation did not take place at an even rate over that period, but can be separated into three different rates covering three different periods of time: (1) an averaged decrease of 1.01% or 625 persons per year for the 36 years between 1598 and 1635; (2) a more drastic averaged decrease of 4.93% or 3,060 persons per year for the six years from 1635 through 1640; and (3) a slackened averaged decrease of 0.18% or 109 persons per year for the 38 years from 1640 through 1678. (All percentages being based upon the 1598 population figure.)

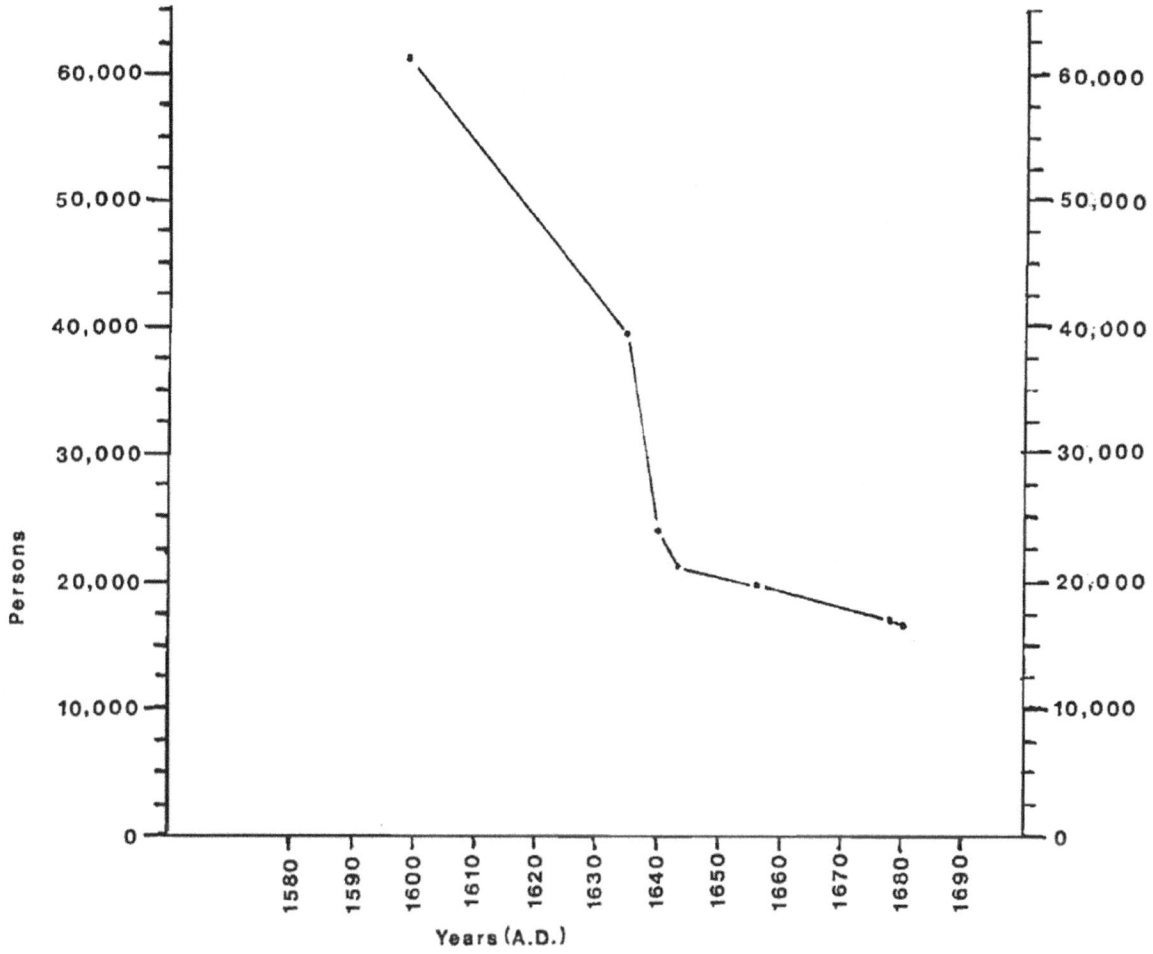

Persons

Years (A.D.)

PUEBLO INDIAN POPULATION: 1598-1680

Figure

7-1

Figure 7-1

Table 7-1: OVERALL PUEBLO INDIAN POPULATION: 1598-1680

Year	Population Figure	Change from Previous Figure	Change from 1598 Figure
1598	ca. 62,000	- - -	- - -
ca. 1635	ca. 39,500	-36.29%	-36.29%
1640	ca. 24,140	-38.87%	-61.06%
1643	ca. 21,140	-12.43%	-65.90%
ca. 1656	19,951	-5.62%	-67.82%
1678	ca. 17,000	-14.79%	-72.58%
1680	ca. 16,500	- - -	- - -

Table 7-1

Table 7-2: BENAVIDES' POPULATION FIGURES

1630: Forrestal and Lynch (1954: 17-32).

1634: Hodge, Hammond and Rey (1965: 64-75).

Pueblo Indian Group	1630 edition		1634 edition
Piros	6,000	<------>	- - -
(S.) Tiwas	7,000		7,000
Queres	4,000		4,000+
Tompiros (+ Salinas Tiwas)	10,000+		10,000+
Tanos	4,000		4,000
Pecos	2,000		2,000
Tewas	6,000		6,000
Jemez	3,000+	<------>	6,000+
Picuries	2,000		2,000+
Taos	2,500		2,500
'Acoma	2,000	<------>	1,000+
Zuñis	10,000+		10,000+
Moquis	_10,000_		_10,000_
Totals:	68,500		64,500

<------> = major discrepancies between the two lists.

Table 7-2

Table 7-3: SIZES OF THE PIRO PUEBLOS (1581-1583)

(See Tables 5-9 and 5-10 for the correlation of pueblos reported by the two expeditions).
E = Espejo Expedition (Hammond and Rey 1966: 171-174).
R = Rodriguez-Chamuscado Expedition (Hammond and Rey 1966: 102-103, 115-116).
* casas = houses, but meaning "households".

Piro Pueblos: LA No.	Name(s)	Aug. 1581: pueblo sizes (Gallegos[R])	Feb. 1583: pueblo sizes (Luxan [E])
283	El Gallo(E)	- - -	50 houses*, 400 persons
791	Piña(R)	85 houses*	100 houses, 800 persons
282	Piastla(R)	35 houses	50 houses, 400 persons
31744	(none)	- - -	50 houses, 400 persons
19266	Santiago(R)	25 houses	- - -
774	El Oso-La Pedrosa (R); El Termino de Puala (E)	50+14 houses	60+20 houses
31717	Elota(R)	14 houses	20 houses
755/768/ 31798	San Juan(R)	40 houses	50 houses, 400 persons
757	San Miguel(R)	47 houses	50 houses, 400 persons

Table 7-3

Table_7-4: POPULATION ESTIMATE FOR PIRO PUEBLOS (1582)

Pueblo	_Households_	Estimated_Population
LA 283	41*	205 persons
LA 791	85	425 "
LA 282	35	175 "
LA 31744	41*	205 "
LA 19266	25	125 "
LA 774	64 (50+14)	320 "
LA 31717	14	70 "
LA 755/768/31798	40	200 "
LA 757	47	235 "
Totals:	392 households	1,960 persons

* Estimated from figures given by Espejo Expedition.

POSSIBLE ADDITIONAL PUEBLOS

Pueblo	_Households_	Estimated Population
Pueblo Nuevo	20 or 25	100 or 125 persons
LA 284	41+	205 persons
LA 285	41±	205 "
Totals:	102 or 107	510 or 535 persons

+ Rough approximation based on average size of Piro pueblos.
Conservative Population Estimate: 1,960 persons.
High Population Estimate: 2,495 persons.

Table 7-4

Causes of population loss mentioned in the Spanish Colonial documents include warfare with Spaniards and Apacheans, famines, and epidemics; these and other possible factors will be discussed after delineation of the Piro and Tompiro populations.

Piro and Tompiro Populations: 1582–1682

No population figures for the Piros and Tompiros are available before the period of explorations in the early 1580s, the only information from the Vazquez de Coronado Expedition of 1540–1542 being brief mention of four Piro pueblos with no details as to size or population. (Pedro de Castaneda, in Hammond and Rey 1940: 245) The Piros and Tompiros are discussed separately below, except for the period after 1672 when some if not all of the Tompiros apparently moved into the Rio Grande Valley after abandoning their pueblos in the Salinas Province.

The Piros: to ca. 1672

1582: The Rodriguez-Chamuscado Expedition of 1581–1582 and the Espejo Expedition of 1582–1582 both recorded the sizes of individual Piro pueblos (see Table 7-3), but the Espejo party seems to have "rounded up" their household figures compared to those given by the earlier expedition, hence I am included to give more credence to the household numbers recorded by Hernan Gallegos in 1581. The Espejo party obviously used an average of eight persons per household to arrive at their numbers of persons (see Table 7-3), but this seems rather high and I will use a more conservative average of five persons per household[1] to calculate the population of the Piro pueblos. Before doing so, however, there is the problem that the Rodriguez-Chamuscado party failed to visit and record data for two pueblos (LA 283 and LA 31744): I am therefore supplying the missing figures by using the household numbers given by the Espejo party, less the average number of extra households (9 households) produced by their "rounding up" tendency. (See Table 7-4.)

The resulting conservative total for the Piro pueblos in 1582 is 1960 persons. However, there is the possibility that the site known as Pueblo Nuevo to the Rodriguez-Chamuscado party and as El Corvillo to the Espejo party (and possibly correlating with the San Juan Bautista of the Onate colony) is also a contemporary Piro pueblo, hence adding another 20 or 25 households (100 or 125 persons) to the total (the Gallegos and Pedrosa lists give differing numbers of households). Furthermore, it is possible that LA 284 and LA 285 near Magdalena were also occupied by Piros at this.[2] If the average numbers of households per pueblo (41 households, 205 persons) is added for each of these latter two sites, then a high estimate of from 2,470 to 2,495 persons is reached for the total Piro population in 1582.

In his relacion Hernan Gallegos of the Rodriguez-Chamuscado party claimed more than 12,000 persons for the Piro pueblos (Hammond and Rey 1966: 82), which is easily seen to be a fanciful figure perhaps obtained by arbitrarily assigning a population 1,000 persons to each pueblo. Antonio de Espejo also gave a figure of more than 12,000 persons (Hammond and Rey 1966: 219), which may have been copied from that of Gallegos.

Late 1620s: Benavides provides a total of 6,000 persons for the Piros in the 1630 edition of his book (see Table 7-2), which total is probably inflated by at least a factor of three and is essentially unusable for any serious population study.

ca. 1656: The missions census published by Scholes 1929: 50) lists "400 souls" for Socorro and its two visitas, Alamillo and Sevilleta. As I have discussed earlier in this chapter, I believe that a paragraph listing Senecu with a population of 210 persons was inadvertently omitted from this census. Thus, there was a total of 610 Piros remaining in 1656, a decrease of between 68.88% and 75.55% from 1582 (depending on which population estimate for 1582 one uses); the lower percentage decrease compares well with the overall Pueblo Indian population decrease of 67.82% from 1598. (Table 7-1)

ca. 1660: Some fragmentary information on Piro population is available from the governorship of Lopez de Mendizabal (1659–1661) in the form of unpaid labor claims against the governor made by some of the pueblos. (Scholes 1942: 47-49) Amongst these were fifty Indians from Senecu, thirsty-six from Socorro, and ten from Alamillo, and a number of pack mules and horses from each pueblo were employed for about two weeks transporting pinon to a warehouse in Senecu. (Scholes 1942: 48)

If it is assumed that these laborers were all men between the ages of 14 and 45 and that for each man in this age range there were four more persons in the pueblo (children, women, and viejos), then these figures can be multiplied by five[3] to obtain the following estimates: Senecu: 250 persons, Socorro: 180 persons, Alamillo: 50 persons. The total for Alamillo probably represents only a large fraction of the pueblo's population at the time; the Socorro total may approach that pueblo's population, but is probably below the true figure; whereas the Senecu total appears to be too high when compared with the 210 persons at Senecu in 1656. Lopez de Mendizabal protested that some of the claims made against him were exaggerated (Scholes 1942: 47-48), and the Senecu claim is probably one of these: if we assume that the whole male population of the pueblo in the stated age range was commandeered for the task, then at most 42 men would have been unavailable.

Another claim noted by Scholes (1942: 48) comprised "sixty-three Indians from Socorro worked for three days carrying salt from the east bank of the Rio Grande to the pueblo of Socorro." If these Indians were all men and the same multiplier was applied, a total 315 persons would result, which seems too high. Either the number of workers was exaggerated, or some women also participated in the task. Not much faith can be put in the above figures and estimations, but they do suggest that the scale of population among the Piros was indeed about what the 1656 census indicated.

After this time, there are no more individual figures for the Piros, as those given by Vetancurt (1697) appear to reflect the immigration of the Tompiros after 1672.

The Tompiros and Salinas Tiwas: 1582 to ca. 1672

1582: As with the Piros, both Spanish exploring expeditions of the early 1580s provide data on pueblo populations in the Salinal Province, but this information is less complete owing to lack of visits by either party to the Jumanes Mesa area or to the interior of the Chupadera Basin. Table 7-5 provides the household data recorded by the Rodriguez-Chamuscado Expedition in 1582 for Tiwas and the Tompiros of the Abo Pass. The Espejo Expedition also visited the two Tompiro pueblo in Abo Pass, but did not provide household counts, instead claiming that both had populations of 800 persons (Hammond and Rey 1966: 176), which is unlikely since the more reliable figures from the earlier expedition suggest only 800 persons total for the two pueblos. The Rodriguez-Chamuscado party reported from hearsay that "three very large pueblos" existed near the saline lakes (Hammond and Rey 1966: 107, 119), apparently reference to LA 120, LA 51 and LA 83. Espejo claimed 11 pueblos for the Salinas Province, which, when the Abo Pass pueblos, the Salinas Tiwa pueblos, and the Jumanes Mesa pueblos are eliminated, leaves three extra pueblos, perhaps reference to sites in the Chupadera Basin.

ca. 1600: The little data available for the period of the Onate Colonization are not very information. During Onate's visit to the Salinas Province in October 1598 the pueblos of Jumanes Mesa were described: "They comprise three pueblos, one large, like Zia, and two small one." (Hammond and Rey 1953: 393) Unfortunately, there is no statement in the Onate documents as to precisely how large Zia was in 1598, consequently extrapolation is not possible. In early 1601 occurred the "Jumano War" in which a force of Tompiros and Tiwas was besieged at Cuarac by the Spaniards: one source claimed that "more than 800 Indians" attacked the Spaniards there, and another claimed that the Spaniards killed "more than 900" persons. (Hammond and Rey 1953: 705, 615) If the figure of 800 Indians means 800 warriors, then a projected population of 4000 (using a multiplier of five) would be indicated for the Tompiro plus at least Cuarac among the Salinas Tiwas. Unfortunately, while it is possible, this figure cannot be confirmed from any other line of evidence. The figure of "900 killed" seems excessive to me: it derives from an anti-colony statement and is nowhere repeated or confirmed.

Late 1620s: Benavides claims 3,000 persons for the pueblo of Las Humanas (Hodge, Hammond and Rey 1945: 66) and more than 10,000 persons for the Tompiros (and Salinas Tiwas), which figures I consider to be literally incredible. (See Table 7-2.)

ca. 1656: The mission census published by Scholes (1929: 48) lists all of the Tompiros together under the missions at Abo (with Las Humanas and Tabira as visitas) for a total of 1,580 persons. The three Tiwa pueblos are listed individually: Chilili with 250 persons, Tajique with 484 persons, and Cuarac with 658 persons. Both Chilili and Tajique show decreases in population from 1582 of 60% and 51.6% respectively (compare with the 67.82% decrease in overall Pueblo Indian population: Table 7-1), but Cuarac shows a 46.2% increase over the 1582 figure! How can this increase be accounted for when the overall Pueblo Indian population was declining? One possible explanation is that the 658-person figure is an error, either of transcription in the document or in Scholes' translation, which possibility cannot be checked at this time. The second possible explanation is immigration into the Salinas Province by Tiwas from Tiguex (the area of Tiwa occupation between Bernalillo and Los Lunas along the Rio Grande), which possibility must await a comprehensive study of the Tiguex population before it can be evaluated.

1668: In the midst of several years of crop failures, 1668 was noted for widespread famine and Fray Juan Bernal reported that more than 450 Indians died of this cause at Las Humanas in that year. (Hackett 1937: 272)

Abandonment: 1672–1677: Sometime during this period all pueblos in the Salinas Province were abandoned as a consequence of Apache attacks. Population figures for the pueblos at the time of abandonment were given as: Cuarac = more than 200 families, Tajique (Las Salinas) = more than 300 family, Chilili = more than 100 families, Abo = more than 300 families, Las Humanas = more than 500 families. (Hackett 1937: 298; Maas 1929: 52) I am very doubtful about the term "families" which was applied to the figures by Fray Francisco de Ayeta. Since Ayeta was attempting to convince the viceroy of New Spain to supply special aid to New Mexico, I suspect that he inflated his figures for refugees by the substitution of the term "families" in place of "persons." Consequently, I accept the figures, per se, but only as referring to persons, not to families.

For the Salinas Tiwas I am replacing the fuzzy "more than" component of the abandonment figures with an arbitrary 5% of the basic figure, hence: Cuarac = 210 persons, Tajique = 315 persons, Chilili = 105 persons. The Salinas Tiwa population between 1582 and ca. 1672 is summarized in Figure 7-2 and Table 7-6. If the hypothesis that the rise in population at Cuarac was caused by immigration from Tiguex is true, then the sharp drop in Cuarac's population prior to abandonment might be explained by a counter-migration back to Tiguex during the years of drought and famine from 1666 through 1670.

Vetancurt (1697: 103) records the following populations for the Salinas Tiwas: Cuarac = more than 600 persons, Tajique = 300 persons, Chilili = more than 500 persons. These figures, which have no time specification, do not seem to fit or approximate the known figures as a set, hence I do not see any way of fitting them into the known scheme of population figures for the Salinas Tiwas.[4]

Returning now to the Tompiros, the data are so incomplete and compounded as to make very difficult the kind of tabular and graphic summaries presented for the Salinas Tiwas. I am attempting to render these data more amenable to such presentation through a limited series of manipulations and projections.

First of all, as discussed in Chapter 5, there is no evidence that the pueblo of Tabira survived until 1672, likely it was abandoned during the extreme famine year of 1668 and its population added to that of its nearest neighbor, Las Humanas. Therefore, the abandonment figure for Las Humanas should present all remaining Tompiros of the Jumanes Mesa area. Likewise, since Tenabo (LA 200) and probably been abandoned by 1650 and its population joined to that of Abo, the abandonment figure for Abo should represent all

Tompiros of the Abo Pass area. The Jumanes Mesa Tompiros therefore constituted 62.5% and the Abo Pass Tompiros 37.5% of the Tompiro population in ca. 1672.

If one assumes that both components of the Tompiro population, the Jumanes Mesa and Abo Pass groups were equally affected by the famines and other events between 1656 and 1672, then their relative proportions within the total Tompiro population should have been the same in 1656 as in 1672. Given this, the 1656 population can be divided as follows: 37.5% of 1,580 persons yielding 592 persons for Abo, and 62.5% yielding 988 persons for Las Humanas and Tabira together.

Subtracting a 1668 famine toll of 454 ("more than 450" being set at 450 plus 5%) from the 988 persons of 1656 leaves a total of 534 persons which can serve as a good approximation for the "more than 500" persons at Las Humanas at abandonment. Therefore, with 534 equivalent to 62.5% in 1672, the Abo figure can be fixed at approximately 320 persons at abandonment.

It would be a simple procedure at this point to use these same relative proportions between Abo Pass and Jumanes Mesa Tompiros to calculate the missing population figure for the Jumanes Mesa area in 1582, however there is a complication which militates against this. For 1582, the Tompiro population of the Chupadera Basin must also be brought into the calculations.

I suspect that after 1600 the Chupadera Basin Tompiro pueblos emptied through emigration to the other Tompiro areas, otherwise we should have further records of them beyond the names recorded by Onate in 1598. This suspicion is strengthened when it is noted that the decrease of population in the Abo Pass is only 26% between 1582 and 1656, a great contrast to the decrease of at least 68.88% among the Piros, the decrease of 60% at Chilili and 51.6% at Tajique, and the overall Pueblo Indian decrease of 67.82%. The simplest explanation for the blunting of the effects of depopulation of the Tompiros of the Abo Pass is an immigration from the Chupadera Basin pueblos.

This raises a further problem: did emigrants from the Chupadera Basin all go to Abo Pass, or did a significant or equal number go to the Jumanes Mesa area? On the basis of the glaze pottery situation at Las Humanas (LA 120), I suggest that only a few persons from the Chupadera Basin are likely to have immigrated to the Jumanes Mesa pueblos. My reasoning is as follows: glaze pottery sites in the Chupadera Basin show the same ceramic frequency pattern as in Abo Pass, a dearth of black-on-white decorated pottery amidst a preponderance of glaze-decorated pottery (i.e., glaze pottery was locally manufactured, but black-on-white pottery was not). This contrasts greatly with the Jumanes Mesa situation where black-on-white pottery continued to be made until the time of abandonment, and glaze pottery was mainly imported (as shown by the foreign temper types in the glaze pottery at Las Humanas, see Warren 1981: 67-68, 182). If a sizeable number of people from the Chupadera Basin had immigrated to Las Humanas in the early 1600s, then it is reasonable to expect that the potters among them would continue to make glaze pottery using the local tempering material, hence there should be an appreciable jump in the amount of locally tempered glaze pottery for Glaze E and F types at Las Humanas (a small percentage, less than 5%, of locally tempered glaze pottery was present for Glaze A types, probably due to inmarriage of potters from the other Tompiros). Such a jump does not occur according to percentages available in Warren's study (1981: 182), instead there continues to be only a small percentage of locally tempered glaze pottery, indicating no major influx of glaze potters.

If this reasoning is correct, then most Chupadera Basin Tompiros immigrated into Abo Pass, blunting the population decline there. To determine the proportion of the 1656 Abo population derived from Chupadera Basin, I assume that, if uninfluenced by immigration, the Abo Pass population would have taken the same trajectory as did the Piros of the Rio Grande Valley between 1582 and 1656, i.e., a 68.88% decrease.[5] Hence, in 1656 at Abo the population would have been composed of 249 persons of Abo Pass origin, leaving 343 persons representing the immigrants. This in turn implies a population of ca. 1,102 persons for the various sites in the Chupadera Basin in 1582.

Using the same percentage of decrease (68.88%), a projected population for Jumanes Mesa in 1582 would be 3,175 persons, divided among three sites (LA 120, LA 83, and LA 51). LA 120 (Cueloce, Las Humanas) could easily have accommodated 2,000 persons or more, leaving perhaps 500 persons for each of the other two pueblos. If lesser rates of decrease are assumed, then smaller 1582 populations would result. See Figure 7-3 and Table 7-7 for a summary of the Tompiro population.

As a final note on Tompiro population, Vetancurt's (1697: 103) figure of 800 persons for Abo appears to include all Tompiros for the time of abandonment, as it approaches the total of ca. 854.

Table 7-5: POPULATION ESTIMATE FOR TOMPIROS

AND SALINAS TIWAS (1582)

(Data from Hammond and Rey 1966: 107, 119)

Pueblos	Households	Estimated Populations
Tompiros:		
LA 97: La Joya	95	475 persons
LA 200: Franca Vila	65	325 "
totals:	160 households	800 persons
Salinas Tiwas:		
LA 847: Zacatula	125	625 persons
LA 381: Ruiseco	200	1,000 "
LA 95: La Mesa	90	450 "
totals:	415 households	2,075 persons

Table 7-5

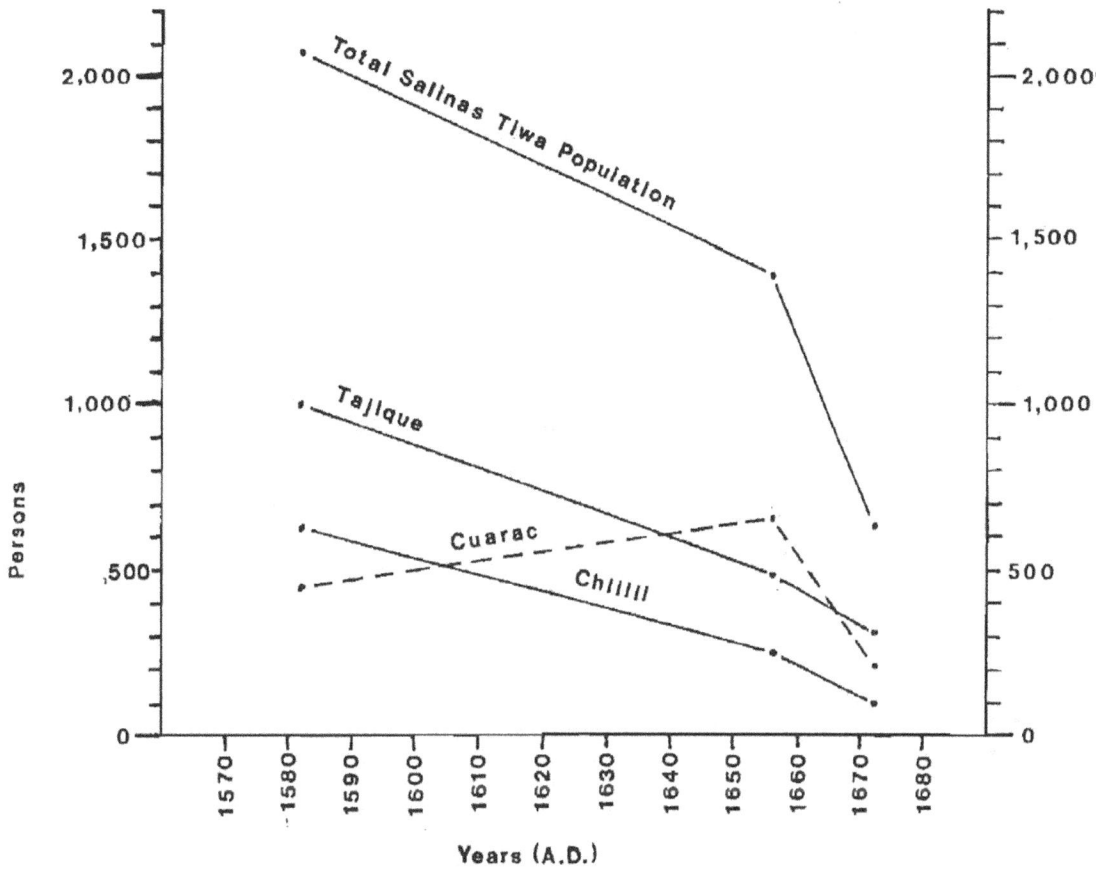

SALINAS TIWA POPULATION: 1582–1672

Figure 7-2

Figure 7-2

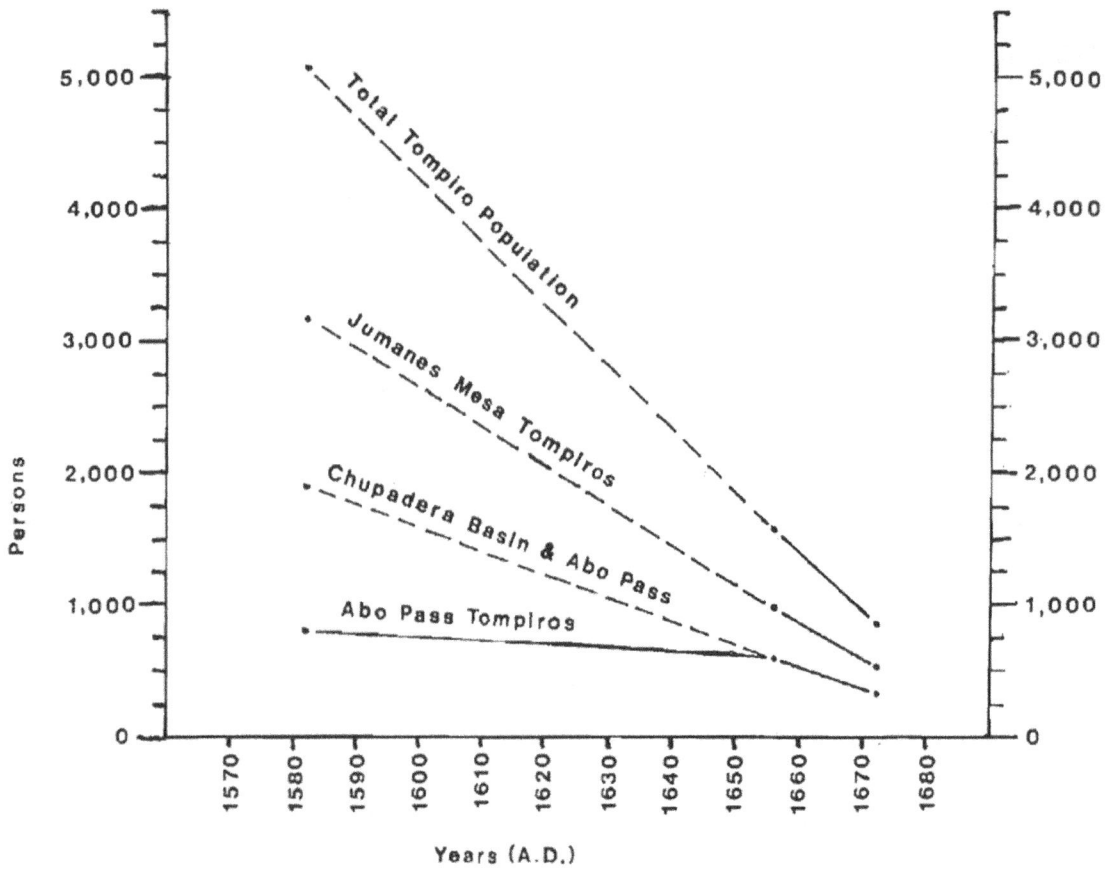

TOMPIRO POPULATION: 1582-1672

Figure

7 - 3

Figure 7-3

Table 7-7: TOMPIRO POPULATION (1582-1672)

(see also Figure 7-3)

Area/Year	Population	Change from Previous Pop.	Change from 1582 Pop.
Abo Pass:			
1582 Abo: 475 |			
| 800		- - -	- - -
Tenabo: 325 |			
ca. 1656:	ca. 592	-26%	-26%
ca. 1672:	ca. 320	-45.95%	-60%
Jumanes Mesa:			
1582:	ca. 3,175*	- - -	- - -
ca. 1656:	ca. 988	-68.88%+	-68.88%+
ca. 1672:	ca. 534	-45.98%	-83.18%
Chupadera Basin:			
1582:	ca. 1,102	- - -	- - -
Totals:			
1582:	ca. 5,075*	- - -	- - -
ca. 1656:	1,580	-68.88%+	-68.88%+
ca. 1672:	ca. 854	-45.95%	-83.18%

* projected figures.   + assumed rates.

Table 7-7

1680: How many Piros and Tompiros were living along the Rio Grande in the pueblos of Sevilleta, Alamillo, Socorro, and Senecu at the time of the Pueblo Revolt (1680) is not easily determined. Vetancurt (1697: 98) lists these figures as representing revolt year congregations:

Sevilleta = three families, Alamillo = 300 persons, Socorro = 600 persons; Vetancurt does not give a population figure for Senecu. Unfortunately, no other source gives population figures for these pueblos in 1680. I doubt Vetancurt's figure of three family (ca. 15 persons) for Sevilleta, it seems too low for practical defense of the pueblo given the concurrent dangers of Apache attack; my guess is that Vetancurt wrote trece (thirteen) in his manuscript, but that the typesetter misread it as tres (three). Thirteen families (ca. 65 persons) is a more realistic figure and compares well with figures of 14 households for some Piro pueblos in 1582.

Vetancurt's figures for Alamillo and Socorro clearly reflect the influx of Tompiros from the Salinas Province and I have no reason to doubt them, beyond the fact that they appear to be rounded figures. The lack of a population figure for Senecu may be overcome since Fray Francisco de Ayeta notes that Senecu, after being abandoned ca. 1676 or 1677 because of an Apache attack, was reoccupied ca. 1678 by "more than 100 families" (Hackett 1937: 297; Maas 1929: 51-52), where I again suspect the term "families" as being a propaganda substitute for "persons." In attempting to secure a more precise figure for Senecu, it should be noted that as many as ten families (up to 50 persons) were taken from Senecu in 1659 or 1660 to the mission of Guadalupe at El Paso to assist in the conversion of the Mansos (Hughes 1914: 308), which would lower the population from about 210 (the 1656 figure) to about 160 Piros. Then, if the general decline in Pueblo Indian population of 14.79% between 1656 and 1678 is applied to Senecu, this figure of 160 would shrink further to about 136 persons, which should be a good approximation for "more than 100" persons to repopulate Senecu in 1678.

I would estimate, then, that Senecu with ca. 136 persons and Sevilleta with ca. 65 persons remained Piro, while Alamillo and Socorro received most of the Tompiro influx, resulting in about 276 Piros and 624 Tompiros at the two pueblos.[6] Since about 854 Tompiros constituted the refugee population, around 200 persons or more are unaccounted for, but they may be individuals and family who for one reason or another dispersed to other pueblos. For example, some may have gone to El Paso to join relatives since Hughes (1914: 314) states that some person from Abo were recorded as living at the Guadalupe mission in 1670 and 1671.

Figure 7-4 summarizes the Piro and Tompiro populations from 1582 through 1680. Total populations for the Piro-speaking Pueblo Indians were (1) between 7,035 and 7,570 persons in 1582 (11.35 to 12.21% of the 1598 total Pueblo Indian population), (2) about 2,190 persons in 1656 (10.98% of the 1656 total Pueblo Indian population), and (3) about 1,151 to 1,351 persons in 1680 (6.98 to 8.19% of the 1680 total Pueblo Indian population). The great change in percentage of the total Pueblo Indian population between 1656 and 1680 appears to be a result of the heavy losses by the Tompiros in the family years of 1666–1670.

Removal and Dispersal (1680–1682): In August 1680 the Pueblo Revolt caused the flight to El Paso of those Spaniards not killed in the first few days of the conflict. With them, the Spaniards removed some Pueblo Indians, principally Piro-Tompiros and Tiwas. Most or all of the populations of Sevilleta, Alamillo, Socorro, and Senecu joined the retreat of the first group of Spanish refugees under the command of Maestro de Campo Alonso Garcia, which moved south from Socorro along the camino real to the camping spot of Fra Cristobal between August 26 and September 4, 1680. There the first party remained until joined by the second group of Spanish refugees under the command of Governor Otermin on September 13. However, it is clear that in the interval most of the Piros and Tompiros deserted the first refugee party and returned to their pueblos, since the combined number of Tiwas and Piro-Tompiros to reach El Paso along with the Spaniards on October 2, 1680 only number 317 persons (Hackett 1942: I: 159), about a third of which were Tiwas.[7] This would mean that about 900 Piro-Tompiros returned to take up residence in their four pueblos and only about 200 continued on to El Paso.

When Otermin passed through the Piro area on his way north in November and December 1681, he found the pueblos abandoned, but showing signs of residence and of having been attacked by Apaches. (Hackett 1942, II: 203-207) Some Piro-Tompiros were found at Isleta, but how many is uncertain although it was clearly not the whole surviving population as only a total of some 500 persons were found there, Tiwas and Piros combined. (Hackett 1942, II: 208) The Spaniards learned that some Piros were at 'Acoma. (Hackett 1942, II: 340, 362) Upon his retreat back to El Paso in early 1682, Otermin brought back 389 persons (Hackett 1942, II: 362), some of whom were Piros, but how many is unclear.

In 1692 Diego de Vargas records the presence of scattered Piro individuals at various pueblos: San Cristobal and Taos being specifically noted. (J.M. Espinosa 1940: 145,

156) And in 1696 Piros are noted as living with the Tanos of San Cristobal and San Lazaro. (J.M. Espinosa 1942: 234) It seems clear then, that those Piro-Tompiros who did not go to El Paso were scattered among other Pueblo Indian groups after 1681.

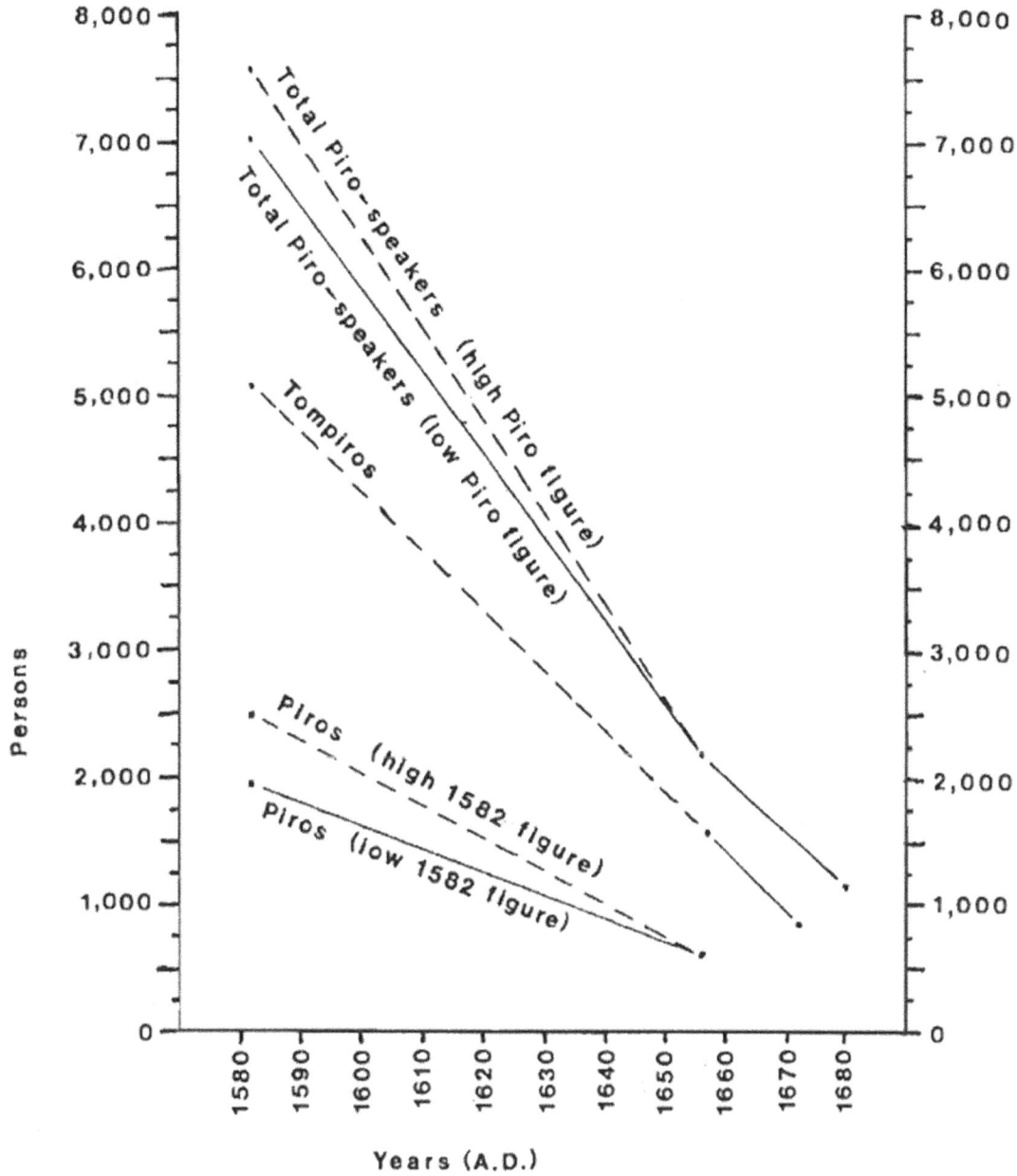

THE PIRO-SPEAKING POPULATION: 1582-1680

Figure 7-4

Causes of the Population Decline

Spanish colonial sources recognize several causes of population decline among the Pueblo Indians: famines, epidemics, and warfare. Other causes not generally acknowledged by the Spanish but still contributing to the overall decline are execution, enslavement, orphan seizure, and assimilation by non-Pueblo Indian groups (such as the Apacheans). These causes are documented and evaluated below.

Famine and its Causes

Recorded famines among the Pueblo Indians have usually been caused by climatic factors, principally drought and killing frosts, but crops were sometimes seized and/or destroyed in the course of warfare with Spaniards and Apacheans or reduced below critical levels through tribute levies by Spanish authorities.

Table 7-8 lists the famines known for the period 1598–1680 and their causes, and includes a correlation with the tree-ring growth record for the northern Rio Grande shown in Figure 7-5.[8] Of five famine periods, three correlate positively with drought periods shown in the tree-ring record (AD 1600–1601, 1624–1626, and 1668). The famines with poor or negative correlations (1658–1659 and 1670) may reflect factors other than annual moisture conditions. It must be remembered that the tree-ring growth record reflects tree growth responding to conditions in tree habitats, not agricultural crop responses in their own habitats. For example, lack of rain in the late summer could cause withering and failure to ripen in crops, but have little effect on tree-ring growth. (See the discussion of seasonality of pinon ring growth in Fritts 1976: 86–87.) Therefore, while a valuable record of moisture variations that effect tree growth, the tree-ring record cannot be relied upon absolutely as a record of agricultural growth conditions.

Given the year-to-year uncertainty in agricultural conditions, it is not surprising that the Pueblo Indians attempt to store any surplus of grain against possible crop failure in future years. The ideal in corn production is to end the growing season with sufficient supplies to last at least two years. (For the Hopis, see Titiev 1944: 181, footnote 7; for the Zunis, see Stevenson 1904: 353; for San Juan Pueblo, see Ford 1968: 162.) This is also noted for the Tewas in the early AD 1600s. (See testimony of Gines de Herrera Horta and Juan de Ortega in 1601: Hammond and Rey 1953: 653, 660.) Such storage of foodstuffs is a common anti-famine strategy among self-reliant societies. (Colson 1979: 21–22)

The tree-ring record (see Figure 7-5) suggests that both AD 1600 and 1601 were drought years in the northern Rio Grande. If 1599 was a normal year, as suggested by the tree-ring record, then the poor harvest of 1600 would be blunted by the stored crops, which would be redistributed during the winter and spring through a series of social mechanisms. (See extended discussion of food redistribution aspects of Pueblo Indian social relations in Ford 1972: 8–14.) However, for the Tewas at least, the system was short-circuited by the imposition of a food tribute by the as yet not self-sufficient Spanish colony. In a letter to the viceroy of New Spain, Captain Luis de Valasco describes the situation as of March 22, 1601: The system employed during this time (since arrival of the colony in 1598) to feed more than five hundred (Spanish) persons, men women, and children, has been to send people out every month in various directions to bring maize from the pueblos. The feelings of the natives against supplying it cannot be exaggerated, for I give your lordship my word that they weep and cry out as if they and all their descendants were being killed. But, in the end, necessity has compelled us to do this to keep from starving to death...I have even seen and observed that the natives pick up the individual kernels of maize that fall to the ground; the Indian women will follow behind the loads for two leagues for this purpose. If there were an abundance of maize, the Indians would not have been so miserly and saving. Aside from maize, there are no other provisions except beans and calabashes. During Lent we ate meat three days in the week for lack of anything else. Our supply of everything is decreasingly daily, to such a point that we fear we will soon be entirely wanting. (Hammond and Rey 1953: 609–610)

This is confirmed by testimony of Gines de Herrera Horta: Every month the solders go out by order of the governor (Onate) to all the pueblos to procure maize. The solders go in groups of two or three and come back with the maize for their own sustenance. The Indians part with it with much feeling and weeping and give it of necessity rather than of their own accord, as the soldiers themselves told this witness. If any kernels fall on the ground, the Indians follow and pick them up, one by one. This witness has seen this happen many times. (Hammond and Rey 1953: 653)

Table 7-8: KNOWN FAMINES IN NEW MEXICO (1598-1680)

YEARS	GROUPS EFFECTED	CAUSES/ASSOCIATED EVENTS	CORRELATION WITH TREE-RING RECORD	SOURCES
1600-1601	Pueblo Indians & Spaniards	Summer drought, early frost / Spanish tribute	Positive: 1600 & 1601 show much below normal growth.	Hammond & Rey 1953: 609-610, 653, 674, 679, 684, 687, 693, 696, 698.
1624-1626	Jémez pueblos	No cause stated / Návajo raids.	Positive: 1624 & 1625 show much below normal growth, 1626 shows slightly below normal growth.	Forrestal & Lynch 1954: 25-26; Scholes 1936: 145-146.
1658-1659	Pueblo Indians & Spaniards	No cause stated.	Poor: 1658 within normal range, 1659 shows only slightly below normal.	Hackett 1937: 187, 191.
1668	Pueblo Indians & Spaniards	No crops harvested in 1666, 1667 and 1668 / Apache attacks in 1668; locust plague in 1667.	Positive: 1664 and 1667 much below normal; 1666, 1668, 1669 show below normal growth.	Hackett 1937: 271-272; Hankins 1962: 15-17.
1670	Pueblo Indians & Spaniards	No cause stated / epidemic follows in 1671.	Negative: 1670 & 1671 within normal growth range.	Hackett 1937: 302; Maas 1929: 57.

Table 7-8

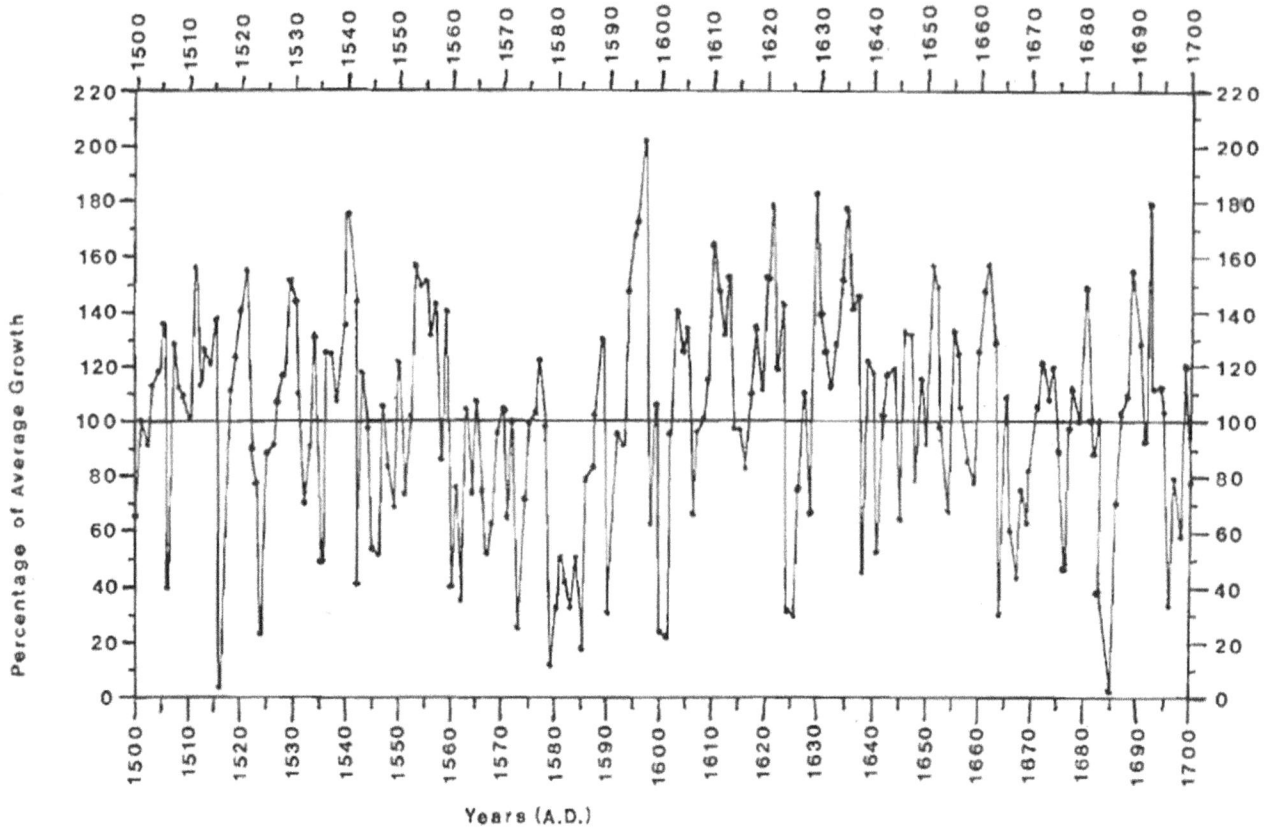

TREE-RING GROWTH RECORD: A.D. 1500–1700

(Data from Smiley, Stubbs and Bannister 1953:55)

Figure

7 – 5

Figure 7-5

By September of 1601, the situation had worsened, as can be seen from the testimony of Fray Francisco de San Miguel: The fact is that in order to induce the Indians to furnish corn for food, it has been necessary to torture the chieftains, even to hanging and killing them. We find ourselves in extreme need of food and see the natives starving to death, eating whatever filth there is in the fields, even the twigs from the trees, dirt, (char-)coal, and ashes. This witness knows that many of them have died of hunger. There has been and is hunger in the (Spanish) camp, and no possible way to relieve it, because there is no ripe corn anywhere in the land, and the cornfields are in the worst condition that they have ever been. (Hammond and Rey 1953: 674)

Confirmed by the testimony of Fray Lope de Izquierdo: This matter has come to such a point that it is well known to the friars and settlers, and especially to this witness, that many natives have starved and are starving to death, since there was absolutely no food in some pueblos. The country's only products are some fruits and roots, with which the people occasionally alleviate their hunger, and ground charcoal and ground cornstalks, which the people eat without even waiting for the ears to develop. (Hammond and Rey 1953: 679)

And by the testimony of Captain Bernabe de las Casas: In fact, this witness has seen many of them (Indians) on the banks of rivers and arroyos, making some holes shaped like cups and filling them with tomatoes[9] mixed with sand and dirt and using it for food as they had nothing else to live on because we had taken away from them by force and against their will what they had saved up for many years. (Hammond and Rey 1953: 687)

And by Fray Juan de Escalona in a letter to the viceroy: The governor (Onate) did not want to sow a community plot to feed his people, although we friars urged him to do so, and the Indians agreed to it so that they would not be deprived of their food. This effort was all to no avail, and now the Indians have to provide everything. As a result, all the corn they had saved for years past has been consumed, and not a kernel is left over for them. The whole land has thus been reduced to such need that the Indians drop dead from starvation wherever they live; and they eat dirt and charcoal ground up with some seeds and a little corn in order to sustain life. (Hammond and Rey 1953: 693)

Particularly interesting in the above graphic descriptions are the accounts of famine foods used by the Pueblo Indians. Such descriptions are found again in the records for the famine of 1958–1959, as described in a letter to the viceroy by Franciscan custos and definidores of New Mexico:

This poor kingdom...has just been through so serious a famine that the natives had to sustain themselves on the seeds of grasses, tierra blanca, and herbs of very injurious character; and most of the Spaniards on bran, quilites[10], green barley, and other herbs which they happily were able to find, after much search, and which they ate, it appears, in the whole villa of Santa Fe. (Hackett 1937: 187)

And again, in a description of the famine of 1670 by Fray Francisco de Ayeta: "...in the year 1670, there was a very great famine in those provinces (New Mexico), which compelled the Spanish inhabitants and Indians alike to eat the hides that they had and the straps of the carts, preparing them for food by soaking and washing them and toasting them in the fire with maize (sic, should be "like maize") and boiling them with herbs and roots." (Hackett 1937: 302)[11]

While it is clear that the Spanish food tribute was a major contributor to the famine conditions in the northern Rio Grande in 1600–1601, subsequent famines probably were not so greatly affected on the negative side by the Spanish presence. During the first famine, the Tewas, and to a lesser extent, the Eastern Queres, Tanos, and Northern Tiwas probably bore the major burden of supplying the early Spanish colony at its base at San Gabriel de Yunque (near present-day Espanola). However, once the colony's capital had been moved to the site of Santa Fe in 1609/1610, the encomiendas had been established, and the Spanish colonists had become at least partly self-sufficient through agriculture and stock-raising, the burden would be both lightened and more broadly dispersed.

The encomienda was a grant of "income" in the form of tribute in kind from a number of Indian households to a Spanish captain who would bear arms himself and arm additional men for the defense of the colony against internal revolt and external attack, such as raids by the Apacheans. Technically the tribute was the property of the Spanish King, hence the encomienda was a royal grant of the King's own "income" to the solder-captain in payment for his services. This encomienda tribute was collected twice a year, in May and October and consisted in May of a piece of woven cloth (manta) almost 1.5 square meters valued at six reales and in October after the harvest of a fanega of corn valued at four reales.[12] This tribute was levied by the household (casa) rather than by the individual. (See descriptions of the encomienda system in Hackett 1937: 109-110; Maas 1929: 23, 34; Scholes 1942: 130-131; Hodge, Hammond and Rey 1945: 169; also, the recent summary by H. A. Anderson 1985.)

Using the 1656 census as a basis for estimation, there were 18,751 missionized Indians (this does not include

1,200 Zunis who were not missionized at the time). Given an average of five persons per household (see chapter note 1), there were about 3,750 households. However, each Franciscan mission was granted ten households of Indians to labor for the missions and these households, termed casas reservadas, were exempt from encomienda tribute. (Scholes 1942: 25, 260-263)[13] Since there were 26 missions (counting in Senecu) in 1656, there were 160 casas reservadas, leaving a total of 3,490 tributary households. Since there were approximately 35 encomiendas (Scholes 1942: 130-131), the average number of tributary households per encomendero was 99.7 (essentially 100 households per encomendero).[14] Therefore, in 1656 an average encomendero could expect to receive 100 mantas and 100 fanegas of maize in tribute from "his" Indians.[15]

Based on the above, the total encomienda tributes in ca. 1656 would be 3,490 mantas and 3,490 fanegas of maize each year, spread out over about 42 pueblos. Contrast this to an annual tribute to support the new colony in 1600-1601 of five or six thousand fanegas of maize and beans, two thousand mantas and 500 dressed skins, probably drawn from only about 25 pueblos (estimate in testimony of Jusepe Brondate, in Hammond and Rey 1953: 630). Clearly then the tribute in 1600-1601 was a much heavier burden than the regularized encomienda tribute of later years.

Nevertheless, the fact remains that the encomienda tribute necessarily decreased the security of the Pueblo Indians by acting as a constant drain upon their agricultural supplies; and the encomendero would demand his tribute in bad agricultural years as well as good years. Furthermore, with the constant decrease in Pueblo Indian population, the number of tributary households would also decrease, hence an encomendero was tempted to "squeeze" his tributaries in various ways in order to maintain a higher tribute than that to which he was legally entitled. This was already becoming a problem in the late AD 1620s, as discussed by Fray Alonso de Benavides:

The encomenderos compel the Indians whose houses may have fallen down, or which they may have lost for other reasons, to pay tribute, even though they live in someone else's house. It is requested of your Majesty (the King) that the Indians of New Mexico do not pay tribute by the person, but by the house, as has always been done; that, as the encomendero is ready to receive the tribute of houses added to the pueblo, he should also be ready to lose and cease taking tribute from abandoned houses, even though the owners live in someone else's house. (Hodge, Hammond and Rey 1945L: 170)

As a partial counter-balance to the drains by the encomienda, the stock herds and grain raised by the Franciscan missions were distributed by the priests in time of famine. For example, the Franciscan custos and definidores of New Mexico described these relief efforts to the viceroy regarding the famine of 1658-1659:

"...it is well known throughout the kingdom that in the convents of Senecu, Socorro, La Isleta, Tajique, Cuarac, and others which had some wheat, corn, and cattle, during the entire time of famine rations were distributed to their parishioners, whenever requested, on Sundays for the entire week, lest they should run away...Furthermore, many of the religious, Sir, have succored the Spaniards; especially did the former father custodian do this, dividing among them over five hundred fanegas of wheat and corn which had been received in the tithe. In the more remote conversions the Minim fathers of Xongopavi and Oraibi distributed as many more fanegas, the entire pueblos being thus supported in time of famine." (Hackett 1937: 191)

However, another negative factor which must be considered was the destruction and carrying-off of grain supplies by Apacheans during raids on Pueblo Indians and Spaniards alike. For instance, it was reported that in 140 alone the Apaches burned 20,000 fanegas of maize during raids. (Scholes 1936: 324) Such raids could be expected during times of widespread famine since the Apacheans themselves would be suffering food shortfalls.[16] This is confirmed in Table 7-8 by the records of Navajo attacks during the 1624-1626 famine and Apache attacks during the 1668 famine.

Finally, it should be pointed out that population would decrease during famines not only from starvation deaths, but from the effects of malnutrition on the birth rate: lower fertility, hence lower rates of conception, and greater risk of miscarriage before a pregnancy could come to term.

Epidemic Disease

The role of epidemic disease has been given relatively little recognition in historical and anthropological studies of New Mexico, the sole specific study to date being Simmons (1966) on the smallpox epidemic of 1780-1781. Table 7-9 shows the recorded epidemics for the period AD 1598-1680 within New Mexico. This listing may be incomplete, particularly for the period AD 1635 to 1640.

Table 7-9: RECORDED EPIDEMICS IN NEW MEXICO, 1598-1680

Years	_Disease_	Deaths/Associated_Events/Sources
early-mid 1630s	smallpox, cocoliztli	Not recorded (Hackett 1937: 108; Maas 1929: 21).
1640	"a pest"	3,000 Pueblo Indians; Apache attacks; Scholæs (1936: 324).
1671	"a great pest"	Not recorded; follows a year of famine; Maas (1929: 57), Hackett (1937: 302).

Table 7-9

Table 7-10: POSSIBLE CORRELATIONS OF NEW MEXICO EPIDEMICS

New_Mexico	_Other_Locality_and_Source_
early-mid 1630s: smallpox, cocoliztli	Mesoamerica: 1629-1631: cocoliztli (Gibson 1964: 449); 1633-1634: cocoliztli and chichimecas (a cough) (Gibson 1964: 450).
1640: "a pest"	Mesoamerica: 1639: sarampion (measles) (Gibson 1964: 450).
1671: "a great pest"	Spanish Florida: 1672 or before: "epidemic" (Milner 1980: 44).

Table 7-10

The term *cocoliztli* is a Nahuatl word, defined by Molina (1571: 23) as "sickness or pestilence"[17], a general term, but by the late 16th century it may have come to mean a specific disease, which Ashburn suggests is typhus (1947: 94-95). In seeking to identify the diseases involved in the 1640 and 1671 epidemics, I have looked for possible correlations in other areas of North America, from which or to which the disease might have spread. (See Table 7-10.) The 1640 epidemic may be a continuation of the 1639 measles epidemic reported in Mesoamerica, and the 1671 epidemic might be related to an unidentified epidemic in Spanish Florida.

Thus, diseases specifically mentioned are smallpox, what is probably typhus, and what is likely to be measles. The unidentified disease might be one of these (although probably not smallpox), or it might be a form of influenza, which is highly infectious. It is of some importance to consider each of these diseases as to how they are spread and their symptoms.

Smallpox: Smallpox, Poxvirus variolae, is what is called a two-factor complex: the virus and the host, the latter being man. Spread of the virus is either through direct contact with an infected person, or indirectly through contact with contaminated objects such as bedclothes or by breathing in contaminated dust or water droplets in the air. The virus is extremely stable, thus it may be dried within organic particles, such as desiccated puss, and survive in such a state for over a year.

Entrance to the human body is through the respiratory system, and the virus multiplies first in the lymph nodes, then invades the blood and is spread to various internal organs. During this incubation period, which lasts from seven to sixteen days, but usually is twelve days long, the victim is not infectious and feels no symptoms of illness. At the end of the incubation period there occurs a new invasion of the blood stream by viruses (called "viremia") and viruses become lodged in the skin tissues. This viremia triggers the defensive mechanism of the human body and the first symptoms of illness appear: fever, headache, backache, pains in the limbs, and sometimes vomiting. In serious cases, hemorrhaging may occur in the skin and eye tissues, from the mouth, the nose, the vagina, and the bowels.

This phase lasts four to six days. On the third or fourth day, a skin rash appears and the victim is now contagious, i.e., viruses are present on his body surface and may be transmitted to others. At this point the fever abates and the victim feels much better. However, within about three days the rash had deepened in lesions which become filled with puss. During this period, the viruses are active within the body cells, hence are protected from the antibodies within the blood stream. Destruction of the cells by the viruses releases toxic waste products, hence the appearance of puss within the lesions is accompanies by recurrence of fever. Hemorrhaging may occur at this time.

Eight to nine days after the appearance of the skin rash, the lesions begin to dry up and crust over, and the fever abates. About three days later the crusting is completed. Subsequently, the skin heals and the scabs drop off at the end of the third week from the onset of the first fever. However, pock marks on the skin may be left as life-long reminders of the infection.

Death may occur before the appearance of the skin rash and any time thereafter until signs of crusting demonstrate the defeat of the disease by the body's defenses.

The mild form of smallpox, called variola minor, has a fatality rate under 1%; while the severe form, called variola major, has about a 30% fatality rate. While the disease can occur at any season, the colder months of winter and spring seem to favor it. In the majority of cases, survival of an attack of smallpox confers life-long immunity. This description is based on the discussions in Deutschmann (1961: 11-3, 7-8, 12) and Downie (1965: 932, 936, 938-940, 944, 946).

Measles: Also called rubeola, measles is also a two-factor complex as the virus has only one host: man. It is renown as the most readily communicated disease known to medicine. It is unknown how long the virus can survive outside the human body. Transmission appears to be from an infection victim via contaminated water droplets in the air to the respiratory tracts of new hosts.

For nine to eleven days after exposure the virus incubates within the respiratory tract. Then the first symptoms occur: fever, an irritating cough, inflammation nasal tissues accompanied by discharge of mucus, and inflammation of eye tissues. The victim is now infectious and the coughing associated with the onset of symptoms is probably the major source of infected water droplets. The fever frequently reaches 104-105 degrees F (40 degrees C) and shortness of breath and rapid breathing occur.

Three of four days after onset of the above symptoms the rash appears on the skin, accompanies by inflammation of the mouth and throat. The rash persists three of four days, then forms a small scab that is shed after another three days. There is no permanent disfigurement, such as occurs with smallpox. Survival of the infection results in life-long immunity in almost all cases. As with smallpox, the colder weather of winter and spring seems to favor the disease.

The most serious aspect of measles is its tendency

to temporarily weaken the resistance of its victim to other diseases. A large number of deaths attributed to measles are probably causes by these secondary infections. These include encephalitis (with a 30% mortality rate and an additional 30% incidence of residual motor, intellectual and emotional disorders), ear infections such as otitis and mastoiditis, other respiratory illnesses, and hemolytic streptococcus. The above description is based upon the discussions by May (1958: 264-266) and Katz and Enders (1965: 790-795).

Typhus: Typhus, Rickettsia prowazekii, should not be confused with typhoid fever, as they are distinct diseases. Typhus infects both man and the human louse, Pediculus humanus, which transmits the disease between human beings. The louse infests clothing which is not laundered, laying its eggs in the seams or other spaces in undergarments. Incubated by human body heat, the eggs hatch after eight days. The results nymphs develop into adults within two weeks. Lice remain on human beings and their clothes as they are dependent upon the human body for nourishment: human blood being their only food.

The louse becomes infected by typhus in the blood of the human host. In the course of the disease, the human host develops a fever which is uncomfortable to the louse, causing it to abandon the sick person in search of a human host with a normal temperature. Likewise, the louse will abandon the cooling corpse of a disease fatality. Lice do not jump or fly, but can crawl for several meters.

Once the infected louse has found a new host it will feed four to six times a day. The site of infection within the louse is in its intestines, hence its feces are contaminated with typhus. At the same time as it bites its human host, the louse defecates. The bite would be irritating to the human host, who will scratch or rub the area of the bite, thus spreading the infection louse feces into the wound. The human host is now infected. It is only cold comfort to know that the infected louse is itself always killed by the disease, usually seven to ten days after becoming infected.

The course of the disease within the human being is as follows: there is an incubation period of ten to fourteen days after infection, then there is a sudden onset of symptoms, headache, chills, weakness, general aches and pains, and a generalized feeling of being ill. During the first two or three days, the body temperature fluctuates between normal (98.6 degrees F or 37 degrees C) and 102 degrees F (39 degrees C), but then fever sets in which may reach 106 degrees F (41 degrees C), where it remains until recover or death of the victim. It is about this time that infected lice abandon the victim.

Shaking chills may occur during the first week of symptoms. Headache increases in severity and is a constant feature of illness. Dry cough is also characteristic of the first week. Vomiting and constipation may occur. A faint rash appears between the fourth and seventh day of symptoms but this is difficult to detect on dark skinned persons. Flushing of the face and mental dullness occur; rarely delirium. The rash deepens in the second week.

The second and third weeks are the critical period: the victim cannot eat or drink without assistance. The mental dullness may progress to a stupor or coma. Death comes between the ninth and eighteenth days. Unlike measles, there is little risk of secondary infection. However, typhus may recur years later in a milder form, known as Brill-Zinsser or Brill's disease. Epidemic, louse borne typhus is restricted to cold or temperate climates. In Mesoamerica, it is present in the Central Highlands, and from there north. The above description is based on the discussions in Snyder (1965: 1059–1081) and Fox, Hall and Elveback (1970: 51-77, 94, 212-213).

Influenza: "Influenza is an acute infectious respiratory disease of man, commonly encountered in epidemic form, caused by one of the influenza viruses." (Francis and Maasab 1965: 689) Epidemics are characterized by sudden appearance, rapid but uneven spread through a region, peaking in three weeks, and the epidemic completed in another three to four weeks.

Presumably air-borne from victim to victim in contaminated water droplets, the virus attacks the respiratory tract, particularly in the nose, but may extend to the trachea and the lungs. The incubation period is short: one or two days. Onset of symptoms is abrupt: sudden chills, headache, fatigue, and general pains. Within 24 hours the body temperature rises between 101 and 104 degrees F (38-40 degrees C). Headache and aching of the back and limbs are more characteristic of adults than children. Growing fatigue, sneezing and nasal discharge of mucus usually occur.

Three to four days after the onset of symptoms the fever declines quickly and the other symptoms subside. The shortness of the attack is characteristic of the disease. Unfortunately, the viruses are highly mutable and new forms of the disease may not be effected by the antibodies from previous attacks. In other words, no true immunity is obtained. This description is based on the discussion in Francis and Maasab (1965: 689-720).

Given the above noted characteristics of the diseases likely to be involved in the epidemics of 17th century New Mexico, certain observations can be made. First, three of the diseases (smallpox, measles and typhus) have incubation periods between seven and sixteen days between infection and the appearance of the first symptoms, therefore these diseases could be carried into New Mexico from localities as far away as 105 to 240 miles distant (assuming a travel rate of 15 miles per day) by superficially healthy individuals. Second, three diseases (smallpox, measles, and influenza) would need to be periodically reintroduced from outside New Mexico in order to recur, since each epidemic would leave behind a survivor population completely immune to the disease, or a particular variation in the case of influenza. (Black 1975: 517) The local population density in New Mexico was too low to possibly serve as a reservoir for such "crowd diseases" (Newman 1976: 668), leaving Mesoamerica as the most likely source of reinfection. Typhus, on the other hand, apparently can remain latent within a survivor for years, only to reappear in mild form as Brill's disease. However, lice feeding on victims of Brill's disease become infection with typhus and can start a new epidemic. Hence, survivors of typhus themselves act as a reservoir of the disease (Snyder 1965: 1081), and it need not (but can be) reintroduced from outside.

Once in New Mexico, certain cultural conditions would promote the spread of these diseases. Most basic was the lack of the germ theory of disease among both Spaniards and Indians. Ignorance of the cause and transmission of the diseases meant failure to quarantine or otherwise isolate sick individuals, and failure to sterilize contaminated objects. These provided perfect conditions for the spread of smallpox, measles and influenza. Conditions for the spread of typhus were also good, since there was no shortage of lice and other vermin, as witness an early complaint by the first Spanish settlers regarding the insect guests which came with the quarters they had appropriated from the Tewas at San Gabriel: "The country breeds an infinite number of mice, bedbugs, and other vermin" (Captain Luis de Velasco, in Hammond and Rey 1953: 610); "it is also a land where the bedbugs, during the four summer months are extremely numerous and irritating, and there are numerous field mice, which breed a species of lice[18] whose bites are very painful." (Captain Juan de Ortega, in Hammond and Rey 1953: 669)

The famines, discussed above, would debilitate the Indians through malnutrition, rendering them more susceptible to disease; it is thus no surprise that the epidemic of 1671 should follow a year of general famine.

Spanish methods of disease treatment included bleeding the patient, thus inducing anemia at a time when it was critical that the body have its full strength for resistance.

(Gibson 1964: 137) While most Indians would not be exposed to the dubious advantages of 17th century Spanish medicine, no doubt some were so-treated by well-meaning Franciscan missionaries.

In the cases of smallpox and measles, undoubtedly of Old World origin, and perhaps typhus, which may be an Old-World disease, there were no established native cures or treatments. (Newman 1976: 671) Influenza was probably native to the Americas (Newman 1976: 669), but Europeans no doubt introduced new strains from the Old World on a regular basis; indeed Mesoamerica could possibly be looked upon as a major disease crossroads of the 17th century, what with direct contact with east Asia via the Manila galleon, with Europe through the Spanish Flota, and with Africa through the continual importation of Negro slaves to the New World. (Mellafe 1973)

It is apparent that Old World "crowd diseases" such as smallpox and measles were particularly lethal at the time of their first contact with Indian populations. This is the "virgin soil" situation, where no individuals within the populations had previous contact with the disease, hence no one was immune and whole communities would become infected at the same time. This was a catastrophic situation: (1) with everyone sick, there is no one to act in the capacity of a nurse, hence some individuals who might otherwise have survived will die from simple neglect; (2) other necessary tasks, such as tending crops or guarding against enemies, will be left undone, possibly leading to a poor, failed or stolen harvest and to other problems for the survivors; (3) internal factionalism may be increased if the epidemic is blamed on internal practice of witchcraft; and (4) the psychological shock of an unknown disease, particularly a gruesome and disfiguring one such as smallpox, might lead to suicides or loss of the will to live among potential survivors. The higher rates of mortality among such "virgin soil" populations may thus be attributable to "practical" problems of survival created by the disease. (For further discussion with examples see Crosby 1976: 292-299.)

A graphic description of a virgin soil epidemic of smallpox is available for the AD 1520 epidemic in Tenochtitlan, in the Aztecs' own words: While the Spaniards were in Taxcala, a great plague broke out here in Tenochtitlan. It... lasted for seventy days, striking everywhere in the city and killing a vast number of our people. Sores erupted on our faces, our breasts, our bellies; we were covered with agonizing sores from head to foot.

The illness was so dreadful that no one could walk or move. The sick were so utterly helpless that they could only lie on their beds like corpses, unable to move their limbs or even their heads. They could not lie face down or roll from one side to the other. If they did move their bodies, they screamed with pain.

A great many died from this plague, and many others died of hunger. They could not get up to search for food, and everyone else was too sick to care for them, so they starved to death in their beds. Some people came down with a milder form of the disease; they suffered less than the others and made a good recovery. But they could not escape entirely. Their looks were ravaged, for wherever a sore broke out, it gouged an ugly pockmark in the skin. And a few of the survivors were left completely blind. (Leon-Portilla 1962: 92-93)

Unfortunately, we have so little information on the 17th century epidemics in New Mexico that we cannot know for sure whether or not any of them were virgin soil phenomena. The 1640 epidemic, probably measles, carried off 3,000 Pueblo Indians, or, in Scholes' estimation, more than 10% of the total Pueblo Indian population. (Scholes 1936: 324) It seems likely that the epidemics of smallpox and cocoliztli noted for the early AD 1630s were virgin soil events, since the Franciscans appear to blame them for most of the loss of more than 20,000 Indians since AD 1598. (Hackett 1937: 108; Maas 1929: 21) Certainly, the drop of over 36% in Pueblo Indian population between 1598 and ca. 1635 would favor such an interpretation. (See Table 7-1.) A further drop of almost 39% between 1635 and 1640 (Table 7-1) suggests that additional, unrecorded virgin soil epidemics may have occurred during that period. It would seem, then, that the decade of the AD 1630s was the period of major crisis with regard to disease for the Pueblo Indians.

Warfare

Warfare is considered here only as armed conflict between the Pueblo Indians and the Spaniards or the Apacheans. Table 7-11 lists the most notable of these events. This table is obviously incomplete, not only because of incompleteness and imperfection of the historical record, but also because limitations on my research time forced me to concentrate mainly upon those records directly relevant to the Piros and Tompiros. Hence, events involving Pueblo Indians other than the Piros and Tompiros are not fully represented. Also, the Pueblo Revolt of 1680 is not included since I am concerned only with population changes prior to that event.

Considering conflict with the Spaniards, the event most costly in terms of lives to the Pueblo Indians was probably the Battle of Acoma in 1599, where over 600 persons were killed out of a total population of ca. 2,500 (ca. 25% of the population).[19] Another ca. 580 persons were captured by the Spanish, the majority of whom were sentenced to servitude for 20 years (Hammond and Rey 1953: 477-478); however, almost all of these had escaped from Spanish hands by late AD 1601. (Hammond and Rey 1953: 706) It was claimed in an interview between Fray Juan de Escalona and the lawyer Gines de Herrera Horta in March 1601 that Acoma was being reestablished by runaways and that Onate was turning a blind eye to it. (Hammond and Rey 1953: 649-650) Later, in 1617, Onate claimed that the pueblo was fully reestablished with as large a population as before the battle. (Hammond and Rey 1953: 1129)[20]

The second Spanish/Indian clash, the "punishment" of Las Humanas, was only a minor incident in terms of lives lost. Its historic significance will be discussed in Chapter 5. Of considerably greater importance was the so-called "Jumano War" of early 1601, which will be discussed in detail in the next chapter. At this point I must say that I believe Luis de Velasco's figure of 900+ Indians killed to be a gross exaggeration. Later in 1601 Fray Juan de Escalona estimated that the Battle of Acoma and the Jumano War together resulted in only 800+ fatalities among the Indians (Hammond and Rey 1953: 693), which if we allow 600+ killed at Acoma, only indicates about 200 deaths resulting from the Jumano War. Likewise, Velasco's claim of 200+ enslaved prisoners is countered by considerable testimony indicating that of ca. 500 persons captured, only about 70 were enslaved (soon to escape) and the rest pardoned and set free.

While there were later Spanish/Pueblo Indian clashes, little is recorded other than that various Pueblo Indian groups would revolt and kill or expel the Franciscan missionaries. There is no information suggesting Spanish reprisals greater than a few executions. (These will be dealt with separately below.) The main loss of life through warfare after 1601 seems to be in raids by Apacheans on the pueblos, but the scale of these losses is impossible to judge given the vagueness of the records and the frequent co-occurrence of other causes of death such as famine and epidemics. However, the Apache attacks, at least, were severe enough to compel abandonment of individual pueblos, such as Sevilleta (early 1620s?), the Salinas pueblos (1672–1675), and Senecu (1675). For a general discussion of Apachean warfare against the Pueblo Indians and Spaniards in the 17th century see Worcester (1941).

Table 7-11: WARFARE: ATTACKS ON PUEBLO INDIANS

Years	Event	Associated Events	Pueblo Indian Deaths, etc.	Sources
1599: Jan. 21-23	Battle of 'Acoma: siege & capture by Vicente de Zaldívar	killing of some Spaniards at 'Acoma in early December 1598.	between 600 and 800 killed; ca. 580 captured & enslaved	Hammond & Rey 1953: 426-427, 460-463, 471, 473, 476, 477-478, 614-615, 648-650, 880, 888, 1127-1129; G. Espinosa 1933: 228-268.
1599: July or later	"Punishment" of Las Humanas.	refusal of tribute by Las Humanas.	5-6 killed, others wounded; 2 hanged.	Hammond & Rey 1953: 620, 650-651.
Feb. or early Mar. 1601: six day battle	"Jumano War": siege & capture of Cuarac by Vicente de Zaldívar.	killing of 2 Spaniards at Abó	Velasco: 900+ killed, 200+ prisoners; actually: ca. 200 killed, 70 enslaved.	Hammond & Rey 1953: 615, 704-705, 708, 710-711, 715, 719, 723, 787, 789, 791-792, 795-796, 798-799, 802-803, 805-807, 838.
early 1620s (?)	Dispersal of Sevilleta Pueblo by Apaches.	burning & abandonment of pueblo.	unrecorded: "many killed"	Ayer 1916: 17, 96; Hodge, Hammond & Rey 1945: 64.
1623	punitive expedition against Jémez pueblos by Spanish (failure)	Jémez pueblos revolt against Spanish.	Benavides: more than half of Jémez population dies - mainly from famine & Návajo raids.	Scholes 1938: 68-69; Scholes 1936: 145-146; Forrestal & Lynch 1954: 25-26.
1624-1626	Návajo raids.	Famine.		
1640	Apache raids	Epidemic.	unrecorded	Scholes 1936: 324.
ca. 1658	Apaches raid Salinas Province, Jémez, San Felipe, San Ildefonso.	Famine.	"some killed"	Hackett 1937: 187.
1668	Apache attacks general.	Famine.	unrecorded	Hackett 1937: 271-272.
1672	Apache attacks general.	Follows year of epidemic.	unrecorded	Hackett 1937: 302; Maas 1929: 57.
1672-1675	Apache attacks on Salinas Province.	Abandonment of Salinas Province.	unrecorded	Hackett 1937: 298; Maas 1929: 52.
1675	Senecu attacked by Apaches.	Priest killed by Apaches.	unrecorded	Maas 1929: 51-52; Hackett 1937: 297-298.

Table 7-11

Executions and Enslavement

Executions and enslavement of Pueblo Indians by the Spaniards were the results of failed revolts against Spanish authority. Generally, hanging was the execution method employed (gunpowder was not in plentiful supply), sometimes done summarily (as in the case of the "punishment" of Las Humanas in 1599), but frequently after a trial for treason. Table 7-12 gives a list of the cases known to me. The 29 Jemez Indians hung in ca. 1645 seems to be the largest number executed at any one time.

In addition, however, some would-be rebels were "sold as slaves," meaning that they were sent to work as slaves in the silver mines of the Parral district in Nueva Vizcaya (present-day Chihuahua). This is specifically noted in 1645, 1650 and 1666. (See Table 7-12.) For descriptions of the Parral district and its mines in the 17th century see Lister and Lister (1966: 33-34, 44-45) or West (1949). Since the period of enslavement in the Parral mines was for ten years, and conditions were harsh, it is unlikely that these Indians survived to the ends of their sentences.

Early enslavements, namely those following the Battle of Acoma and the "Jumano War," were of a different nature: being sentences of personal servitude where the sentenced Indian was "given" to a Spaniard as a personal servant. As already noted above, these personal servants escaped back to their home pueblos long before the sentences were completed.

Orphan Seizure

In effect, orphan seizure was another form of personal servitude in that an Indian orphan, seized from his/her pueblo by the civil authorities, was raised in a Spanish household as a life-long personal servant. Theoretically, this was supposed to "save the soul" of the orphan by guaranteeing a Christian upbringing, but such religious training was often slighted, and the emphasis placed on the servitude portion of the arrangement. (Scholes 1935: 83) Such children, if they did not succeed in escaping from their masters, were essentially as lot to their people as if they had died, especially the youngest children who over time would lose their knowledge of their parents' language and become assimilated into the lowest level of Spanish society in New Mexico.

Assimilation

This category concerns only assimilation of Pueblo Indians into other Indian groups. For the 17th century this appears to only occur to women and children captured during raids by the Apacheans. Fray Alonso de Posada, who served as a missionary in New Mexico from AD 1650 to 1665, considered this a regular feature of Apachean warfare: "They attack the Indian pueblos from previously prepared ambushes killing the men atrociously and carrying off the women and children as legitimate captives of war." (Tyler and Taylor 1958: 303) The only specific instance I have at hand is the raid on Las Humanas during the governorship of Juan de Samaniego y Xaca (1652–1656) in which the Apaches captured 27 women and children; a Spanish retaliatory expedition left the Apaches "well punished" but it is unclear whether or not the captives were recovered. (Scholes 1942: 17)[21]

Summary

Assessment of the relative importance of the several factors involved in the population decline is somewhat hindered by the lack of precise mortality figures for each factor. However, I would rank the factors from most to least important, as follows: 1) Most important: epidemic disease, 2) famine, 3) warfare deaths, and 4) least important: executions, enslavement, orphan seizure, and assimilation.

Of these, surely famine and warfare death were factors present prehistorically, as would be assimilation of captives into other Indian groups. Of the factors introduced by the Spaniards, only epidemic disease can be seen as a major cause of death. Epidemic disease is almost certainly the chief factor in the 17th century depopulation of the Pueblo Indians.

A Tentative Population Model for AD 1525–1598

This final section represents a very tentative model of Pueblo Indian population in the 16th century. It is very tentative for two reasons: (1) that historical sources of population data are even fewer and more limited in scope than for the 17th century, and (2) I am using the population of only a single pueblo as a model for the total Pueblo Indian population. I believe the whole exercise to be worthwhile, however, since it brings to light a significant phenomenon, a curiously low Pueblo Indian population of only 20,000 to 25,000 persons for the year AD 1540, and thus allows an exploration of what may have been the first European impact upon the Pueblo Indians: the suggested New World pandemic of smallpox in the early AD 1520s.

The model is based upon population figures for the pueblo of Acoma and is presented in Figure 7-6 and Table 7-13. Discussion will begin with the year AD 1598 and work backwards to AD 1525.

1598: On October 27, 1598, Onate visited the pueblo of Acoma and recorded its size as 500 houses. (Hammond and Rey 1953: 394) Using the figure of five persons per household (see chapter note 1) gives an estimate of 2,500 persons for the population of Acoma. This is 4.03% of the approximately 62,000 persons making up the total Pueblo Indian population at that time.

Bandelier (1890: 121, n.1) would not agree with this figure, as in his opinion "on the rock of Acoma there is, furthermore, not room for much over 1,000 people." However, it should be pointed out that in Onate's day there did not exist the large, space-wasting church-convento-camposanto complex which has dominated the mesa top since the mid-1600s. (Kulber 1940: 92-95) Furthermore, despite the fact that every family still maintains a dwelling on the mesa top (Eggan 1950: 223), and that the population had risen to 2,419 persons by the beginning of 1965 (A. Smith 1966: 92), there is still considerable unoccupied space on top of Acoma Mesa. I therefore see no reason to doubt Onate's figure of 500 houses.

1582: Accounts of the Rodriguez-Chamuscado Expedition give the size of Acoma as 500 houses. (Hammond and Rey 1966: 107, 120)[22] As this is the same as for 1598, there would appear to have been a population plateau in existence during the last two decades of the 16th century. The lack of population increase between 1582 and 1598 may be explicable by noting the period of much below normal tree-growth between 1579 and 1585 and again in 1590 and 1598. (See Figure 7-5.) These may indicate possible droughts and concomitant famines or periods of malnutrition which work against population growth.

1540: Pedro de Castaneda gives a count of 200 warriors for Acoma in 1540. (Winship 1896: 430) Multiplying this figure by a factor of five (see chapter note 3) gives a total Acoma population of ca. 1,000 persons. This is confirmed by the figure of 200 houses given in the Relacion Postrera de Sivola (Winship 1896: 566), which also yields a population of ca. 1,000 persons for Acoma.

If the Acoma population of 1540 held the same relative relationship to the total Pueblo Indian population as it did in 1598 (i.e., equaling 4.03% of the total population),

then the total Pueblo Indian population in 1540 was only about 24,814 persons. This is a surprisingly low figure, but finds some confirmation in Pedro de Castaneda's estimate of 20,000 Pueblo Indians (Winship 1896: 454), which probably does not include some peripheral groups (such as the Piros, Tompiros, and Salinas Tiwas).

If we are to believe either Castaneda's figure or my estimate, then there was a great rise in Pueblo Indian population between 1540 and 1580 on the order of 150%. The major question this raises is why was the Pueblo Indian population so low in 1540?

A possible answer is that the Southwest may have suffered an epidemic of European disease(s) prior to 1540. The most likely such epidemic would be the great smallpox epidemic which spread out from Mesoamerica in the early 1520s. (See Crosby 1967.) This likely would spread west from Central Mexico to the Tarascans, thence north along the relatively heavily settled zone in Nayarit, Sinaloa, and Sonora to Southern Arizona, and from there to the Pueblo Indians by about 1524 or 1525.

1524/1525: what then would be the population figures for immediately before and immediately after this postulated epidemic? First there must be taken into account about fifteen years' worth of population rebound between 1525 and 1540. To calculate this I would have used birth and mortality figures from San Juan Pueblo for the fifteen-year period following the smallpox epidemic of 1781 to obtain a rate of increase of 28.99% over the remnant population of 1781.[22] Applying this to Acoma and the total Pueblo Indian population of 1540 produces post-epidemic estimate for AD 1525 of 775 persons for Acoma and 19,231 persons for the total Pueblo Indian population.

The above gives us a basis for estimating the pre-epidemic populations. However, we must guess at the mortality rate: virgin-soil epidemics can vary greatly in mortality; from ca. 30% to 70% of the population depending upon secondary factors. I propose then to make three projections, utilizing three different assumed rates of mortality, as follow:

Scenario 1: An assumed rate of 33.98% mortality (which is the rate experienced at San Juan Pueblo in 1781), yielding pre-epidemic populations of 1,174 persons for Acoma and 29,131 persons for the total Pueblo Indian population.

Scenario 2: A higher rate of 55% mortality (that noted for the Pueblo Indian population in general in 1781, see Aberle, Watkins, and Pitney 1940: 167), yielding pre-epidemic populations of 1,722 persons for Acoma and 42,729 persons for the total Pueblo Indian population.

Scenario 3: Assuming the worst, a mortality rate of 70%, yielding pre-epidemic populations of 2,583 for Acoma and 64,094 persons for the total Pueblo Indian population.

Are there any reasons to favor one of these scenarios over the others? Examination of Figure 7-5 reveals much below normal tree-growth in 1524, a significantly below normal year in 1523, and below average growth years in 1522, 1525 and 1526. These records may indicate climatic conditions also unfavorable for agriculture raising the possibility of crop failures or shortfalls during these years. If, indeed, famine or poor nutrition coincided with the postulated epidemic, then conditions would much favor the higher mortality scenarios. My guess is that scenario 3 is the most likely, therefore I would expect the pre-epidemic Pueblo Indian population to have been in a range similar to that for the 1582–1598 period.

Tentatively, then, the picture of Pueblo Indian population in the 16th and 17th centuries is one of drastic fluctuations; a precipitous drop ca. 1524/1525 due to a virgin-soil epidemic of smallpox coupled with possible famine conditions, a population rebound to former heights by ca. 1580, a population plateau between 1582 and 1598, another drastic decline caused by epidemics in the 1630s, followed by a much more gradual decline with a tendency towards leveling off.[23]

Table 7-12: EXECUTIONS AND ENSLAVEMENTS

Year	Event	Indians Involved and Sources
1599: July or later	"Punishment" of Las Humanas	Two Tompiros hanged, also an Indian interpreter (Hammond and Rey 1953: 620, 650-651).
1600 or 1601	Refusal of tribute to Spaniards.	Unrecorded number of Pueblo Indian leaders "hanged and killed" (Hammond and Rey 1953: 674).
ca. 1645	Jemez Indians kill a Spaniard	29 Jemez Indians hanged, some whipped, and some enslaved (Scholes 1938: 95-96; Hackett 1942, II: 266, 299).
1650	Conspiracy to revolt at Jemez, Isleta, Alameda, Sandia, Cochiti and San Felipe.	Nine Indians hanged, "many others" sold as slaves for ten years (Scholes 1938: 96; Hackett 1942, II: 266, 299).
ca. 1668	Piros & Apaches ambush and kill alcalde mayor Valencia & four other Spaniards.	Six Piros hanged, some others burned (?), some enslaved (Hackett 1942, II: 266, 299).
ca. 1669	Discovery of Salinas Province revolt plans.	Don Esteban Clemente, Tompiro leader, hanged (Hackett 1942, II: 299-300).
ca. 1676	Witchcraft accusations.	47 Tewas arrested: four hanged, some whipped, others released (Hackett 1942, II: 300-301).

Table 7-12:

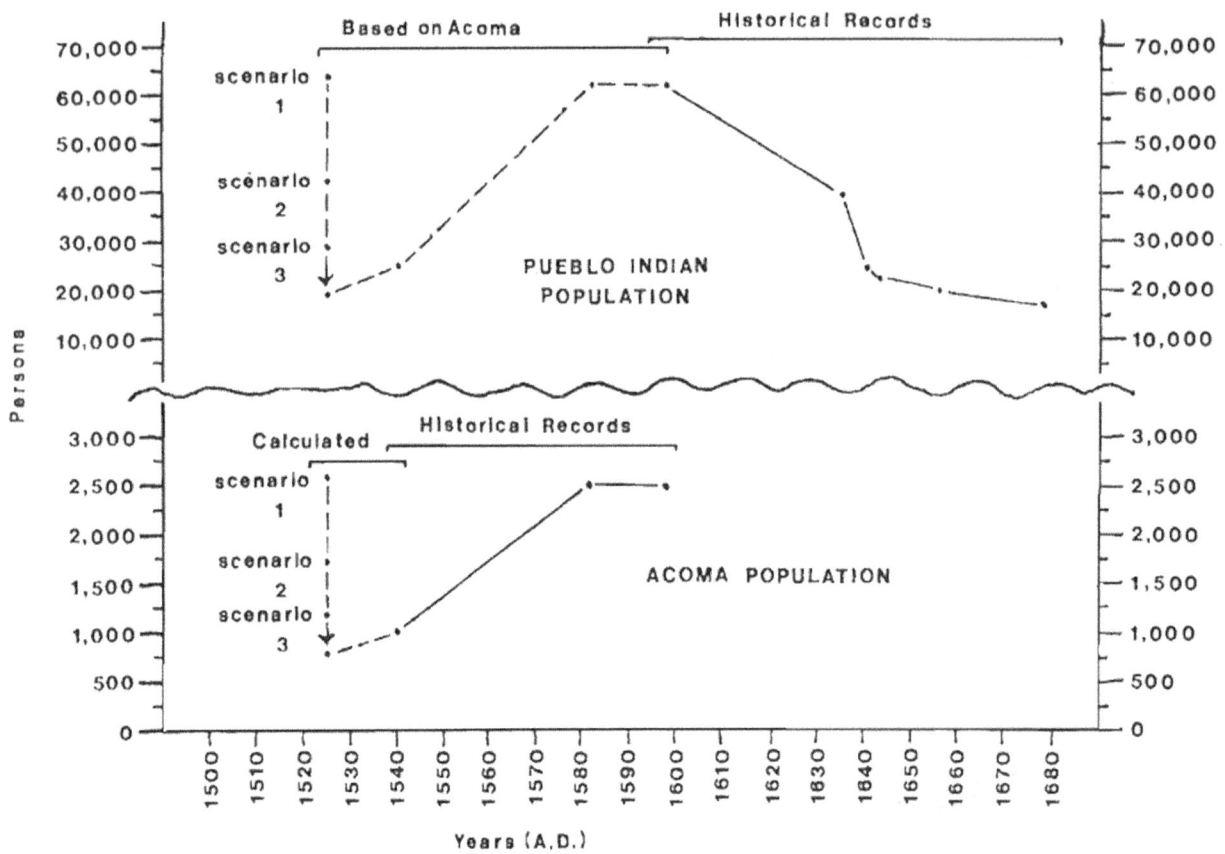

ACOMA AND PUEBLO INDIAN POPULATIONS: 16th CENTURY

Figure
7 - 6

Figure 7-6

Table 7-13: 16th CENTURY POPULATION OF 'ACOMA
AND THE DERIVED TOTAL PUEBLO INDIAN POPULATION

Year	Acoma Population	Change from Previous Population	Pueblo Indian Population
A.D. 1525 (pre-epidemic)			
	Scenario_1:	---	Scenario_1:
	1,174 persons		29,131 persons
	Scenario_2:	---	Scenario_2:
	1,722 persons		42,729 persons
	Scenario_3:	---	Scenario_3:
	2,583 persons		64,094 persons
1525 (post-epidemic)	775 persons	Scenario_1: -33.98%	ca. 19,231 persons
		Scenario_2: -55%	
		Scenario_3: -70%	
1540	1,000 persons	+28.99%	24,814 persons
1580	2,500 persons	+150%	62,000 persons
1598	2,500 persons	0%	62,000 persons

Table 7-13

Notes:

1. Five persons per household is the average obtained from population and household figures (ca. 40,000 persons and ca. 8,000 households) given for the Pueblo Indians for ca. 1635. (See Hackett 1937: 110; Maas 1929: 23.)

2. If, to the nine pueblos listed in Table 7-3 and 7-4, we add Pueblo Nuevo, LA 284 and LA 285 a total of 12 pueblos is reached, which would match the total of 12 Piro pueblos noted in Obregon's description of the Rodriguez-Chamuscado Expedition. (Hammond and Rey 1928: 290)

3. The age range of population percentage used in these calculations derive from figures for 1790 at San Juan Pueblo given in Aberle, Watkins and Pitney (1940: 155). The actual percentage of San Juan males between ages 14 and 45 is 19.12%, but I would expect that a few hearty viejos of 45 to 50 years in an effective pueblo workforce, thus swelling such a body to about 20% of total population.

4. It has previously been recognized that other portions of Vetancurt's information on the Salinas Tiwas are confused at best, consequently this lack of congruence between his population figures and those from other sources is not particularly surprising.

5. I do not use the Salinas Tiwa rates of decrease since they also may be showing the effects of immigration.

6. To arrive at these figures I took the 1656 population of 400 persons for Sevilleta, Alamillo, and Socorro, and (1) applied the 14.79% decrease to obtain a figure of 341 persons, (2) then deducted 65 persons for the Sevilleta population to obtain a figure of 276 Piros, and (3) deducted 276 from the total population 900 persons for Alamillo and Socorro to obtain the figure of 624 Tompiros.

7. I estimate this on the basis of the relative strength of the groups of warriors who marched north with Governor Otermin on his attempted reconquest in November 1681: 30 Tiwas and 54 Piro-Tompiros, making up 36% and 64% of the total of 84 respectively. (Hackett 1942, II: 200-201)

8. The growth indices are based on 37 specimens from the Galisteo and Tewa Basins. An index of 100 represents an average ring size and thus average growing conditions for pinon (Pinus edulis) and ponderosa (P. ponderosa). An index lower than 100 represents drier conditions, and one greater than 100 represents wetter conditions. "Normal" moisture conditions are represented by the zone between indices of 75 and 125; indices lower the 75 indicate drought conditions of varying intensities, while indices above 125 indicate wet years.

9. Probably one of two native New Mexican fruits now known as tomatillo: *Lycium pallidum* or *Solanum elaeagnifolium.* (Curtin 1965: 59-60, 188-189) *Lycium pallidum,* specifically, is known to the Tewa. (Robbins, Harrington and Freire-Marreco 1916: 47)

10. Should be quelites, the wild fresh greens of either the lamb's quarter, *Chenopodium album,* or the pigweed, *Amaranthus powellii,* usually eaten in the spring. (Curtin 1965: 168-169)

11. Where either Bandelier or Hackett reads "con maiz," Mass (1929: 57) reads "como maiz," which makes better sense in the context.

12. The manta or cotton cloth is described as being a vara and a half square (Hodge, Hammond and Rey 1945: 169; Maas 1929: 34), or six palmas square (Hackett 1937: 110; Maas 1929: 23), which are roughly equivalent if one assumes a palma of about eight inches and a vara of about 32 inches. According to former governor Francisco Martinez de Baeza, a bison hide, a buckskin, or a rawhide could be substituted for the cotton Manta. (Maas 1929: 34)

The exact size of this fanega is uncertain, but it lay somewhere in the range of 1.5 to 2.5 bushels. (Simmons 1968: 220) I will use a median figure of two bushels (70.4766 liters), or ca. 112 lbs. of grain.

13. Scholes (1942: 109) states that it was ten Indians who were granted tribute-free status; however, the document reinstating the original decree regarding them clearly refers to ten casas (households) per missions. (Scholes 1942: 260-263)

14. Obviously, some large pueblos were split into two or more encomiendas, and indeed Las Humanas is specifically known to have been so divided. (See Scholes 1942: 84.)

15. This is only a mathematical average; the real situation was quite variable, as witness the large number of tributary households held by Francisco Gomez Robledo ca. AD 1660. (Kessell 1979b: 186-188)

16. It is recognized that both the Navajo of northwestern New Mexico and the Apaches of northeastern New Mexico maintained a mixed subsistence of agriculture and hunting during the AD 1600s, hence drought effected these groups as well as the Pueblo Indians. (See Brugge 1983: 490-491; Gunnerson 1979: 167.)

17. In Spanish: "enfermedad o pestilencia."

18. These lice would not be the ones carrying typhus, but are probably the kind which in the present day carry bubonic plague.

19. I have calculated the population of Acoma in late 1598 as being 2,500 persons based on Onate's statement that Acoma had 500 houses (Hammond and Rey 1953: 394), which I then multiplied by a factor of five. (See chapter note 1.) Onate states a population of 3,000 Indians for Acoma (Hammond and Rey 1953: 485) and other Spaniards estimate either "more than 2,000" (Hammond and Rey 1953: 814, 821, 828) or "more than 1,500." (Hammond and Rey 1953: 880, 888)

20. Given a population of ca. 2,500 before the Battle of Acoma, then 600+ fatalities and ca. 580 prisoners would only equal about 1,200 persons, i.e., about 50% of the population. Presumably the remainder escaped, and formed the nucleus for the new Acoma. These, plus the escaped prisoners, would make for a population of ca. 1,800 persons or more in late 1601. Conceivably, then, Onate's claim in 1617 that the population was back up to its 1598 level might be true.

21. While assimilation of captives is not specifically mentioned in the 17th century, it was an Apache practice in later times (see Basso 1971: 285-286) and was common throughout North America.

22. The figure of more than 6,000 persons for Acoma given by Espejo (Hammond and Rey 1966: 224) is literally incredible.

23. The calculations are as follows: given a total population of 203 persons for San Juan in 1790, the following chart of births and deaths for five year periods can be constructed. (Aberle, Watkins, and Pitney 1940: 150, 160, 165):

To get the rebound rate following the 1781 smallpox epidemic for a fifteen-year period 1781–1795, it is necessary to eliminate the births and deaths for 1780, and the epidemic-related deaths of 1781. Aberle, Watkins, and Pitney (1940: 167) list 15 deaths for the year 1780, and on the basis of the birth figures from 1765–1779 I have calculated a birth rate of 11 persons per year, resulting in a net loss of 4 persons from the population in the year 1780 (260-4 = 256 beginning AD 1781). For 1781, the total number of burials was 95, of which 87 burials occurred during the six-week period of the epidemic and thus may be attributed to it (Aberle, Watkins and Pitney 1940: 167+168), thus leaving only eight deaths in 1781 which were not epidemic related.

It is also necessary to remove the effect of a minor epidemic in 1788–1789 which caused five deaths. (Aberle, Watkins and Pitney 1940: 169) For the year 1795, approximately 12 births and eight deaths can be calculated from the figures given in the above table. Thus, the adjusted 15-year period following the 1781 epidemic at San Juan looks like this:

San Juan Population at end of 1780 = 256 person.

Total epidemic victims in 1781 = 87 persons (33.98% of 1780 population.

Total Adjusted Population Change in post-epidemic period: post-epidemic population = 169 persons (the remnant population);

net gain in population by 1795 = 49 persons (28.99% increase over remnant population);

total calculated population by 1795 = 218 persons.

24. After this chapter had been completed two additional studies related to Pueblo Indian populated were published: Palkovich (1985) and Joham (1986). Palkovich provides an overview of Pueblo Indian population trends from AD 1540 to 1910, of which span I will comment only on her treatment of the 17th century. Palkovich's main conclusions regarding the Pueblo Indian population during that century are contained in her comments on the census information published in Scholes (1929), where she states: "This (census total) is approximately the same range for the total population size estimated over a hundred years earlier by Castaneda (in the 1540s), suggesting a relatively stable overall Eastern Pueblo population size for this period. It is also possible widespread epidemics had not yet devastated these populations." (Palkovich 1985: 409) Comparing this to the contradictory evidence on both points that I have cited above in this chapter, it is clear that Palkovich has been superficial in her use of the published historical evidence on population size and epidemics during the 17th century, with the result of completely erroneous conclusions.

Upham (1986) concentrates on a detailed study of smallpox epidemiology, with the general conclusion that conditions in the Southwest were favorable to the repeated incursion of the disease in epidemic form. He then states that there is a "lack of textual information pertaining to the occurrence of smallpox in the Southwest before 1780" (Upham 1986: 125), which is incorrect (see Table 7-9, above), and then goes on to speculate on possible smallpox epidemics in the Southwest prior to AD 1780. The intention of his article is to provide indirect support for his previous greatly inflated population estimates for proto-historical Western Pueblo groups. I say, "greatly inflated" on the basis of my examination of his argument in his published work (Upham 1982: 36-49) where he accords preferential treatment to the highest (and most unreliable) population figures provided by the Spaniards in the 16th and 17th centuries. Again, I say "preferential treatment" since only the "high" figures receive full attention and most lower figures are ignored altogether.

8

Piro-Tompiro Ethnohistory: Historical Narrative

Cuando tu olvides,
el poema Habra muerto.
  —Jose Hierro (Cohen 1960: 453)

This chapter presents a narrative history of the Piros and Tompiros in the 16th and 17th centuries. For the prehistory of the Piros reference should be made to Chapter 3 and to Marshall and Walt (1984). The prehistory of the Tompiros is covered in Part III in Volume II. No account has yet been written on the historical twilight of the Piro-speaking people in the El Paso area during the 18th, 19th and 20th centuries.

The Piros in the 16th Century

Locations of the Piro pueblos are discussed in Chapter 5 and descriptions of individual sites can be found in Marshall and Walt (1984: 135-234). It is uncertain at this point whether the two pueblos in the Magdalena area west of the Rio Grande (LA 284 and LA 285) are culturally more affiliated with the Piros of the Rio Grande Valley or with the Western Tompiros of Abo Pass and the Chupadera Basin. For simplicity's sake, I assume the former herein, but true determination of their affiliations can only be accomplished through future archaeological excavations.

As discussed in Chapter 3, I consider the great migrations of the AD 1100s and 1200s to have culminated in a Grand Synthesis ca. AD 1275 to 1350 from which a renewed and enriched cultural pattern emerged. The full flowering of this new cultural pattern occurred in the Pueblo Indian communities during the AD 1300s and 1400s. Hence, I perceive the Piros of the first quarter of the 16th century as being full participants in this rich and rewarding cultural tradition.

AD 1524/1525

This first event is at present a hypothetical one: the possible arrival in 1524 or 1525 of the first New World

Pandemic of smallpox. (See discussion in Chapter 7.) If smallpox did indeed hit the Pueblo Indians at this time there would have been a great mortality, probably at least 30%, and likely greater, as this would be a virgin soil epidemic. It can be expected that all age groups suffered greatly, but that young children who seem to have a greater natural resistance to the disease, should have had a higher survival rate than their elders. Thus, a great many orphans would be created by the epidemic, to be absorbed into the surviving family groups. There would also be many new widows and widowers, many with dependent children. A reasonable response in terms of Pueblo Indian culture would thus be a spate of new marriages in the wake of the epidemic and larger than normal households for a period of years thereafter.

Due to the horrible nature of this previously unknown disease, during the course of the epidemic there would probably have been a large number of witchcraft accusations, both within and between villages. (See Hawley 1950a, F. Ellis 1970.) Villages with pre-existing factionalism may have fissioned immediately, with one or more factions moving out possibly after a certain amount of inter-faction violence (i.e., attempts to assassinate specific persons accused of witchcraft). Factional rifts may have appeared within previously harmonious villages, or such villages may have united further through a process of blaming outsiders for the epidemic. The upshot of all this was probably the assassination or execution of a good number of innocent persons by hysterical fellow villagers and the creation of deep-seated suspicions between factions and between villages. These terrific strains on the social fabric must have taken years to heal.

Other serious social consequences may have been the loss of elders who possessed important ritual knowledge. Some villages may have completely lost important ceremonies in this way, which would further strain their cohesion since the community's capability to adequately meet its ritual obligations vis-à-vis the supernatural world, and thus to survive, would be thrown into questions.

External relations of trade and economic cooperation may have lapsed for a year or more as individual communities struggled for survival. Such an upset of commercial relations may explain the attack by the Teyas (Plains Jumanos) on Pecos Pueblo and the Tanos of the Galisteo Basin. In 1541, the Spaniards of the Vazquez de Coronado Expedition passed through the Galisteo Basin and noted evidence of recent destruction of a pueblo and partial destruction of another. Upon inquiring at Pecos Pueblo, they were told that, sixteen years before (ca. AD 1525), some people called Teyas had come to this country in great numbers and had destroyed these villages. They had besieged Cicuye (Pecos Pueblo) but had not been able to capture it, because it was strong, and when they left the region, they had made peace with the whole country. (Winship 1896: 453, 523-524)

My guess is that the Plains Jumanos (the Teyas) returned to the Pueblo Indian country from their autumn bison hunt to discover the Pueblo Indians in the immediate aftermath of the smallpox epidemic. Either the Teyas were refused their customary trade in corn (since there may have been a concurrent drought, see discussion in Chapter 7), or they saw the numerical weakness of their trading partners and decided to take advantage of it thus attacking with the intention of seizing the supplies normally obtained through trade. One way or the other, I very much suspect that the postulated epidemic and the Teya attack are linked events.

Thus, by AD 1525 the first dark cloud of European presence in the New World had passed over the Southwest in the form of disease, leaving behind it a shrunken population and a greater or lesser degree of social and economic dislocation. What is remarkable is the apparent rebound in both population and social spirit in succeeding years. The population appears to have recovered to former levels by ca. AD 1580, if not slightly earlier. (See Chapter 7.) And in 1539 through 1541 the various Pueblo Indian groups who faced and fought the Spanish invaders showed no especial timidity or lack of spirit.

On the other hand, it seems possible that the seeds of the ultra-conservatism of the eastern Pueblo Indians may have been sown in the interaction of the epidemic and Puebloan witchcraft beliefs. I have argued in Chapter 3 that the famous "Pueblo Conservatism" is probably a result of the culture shock created by the clash of Spanish and Puebloan cultures in the 17th and 18th centuries. But the latent potential suspicion of all outsiders, even one's cultural and linguistic compatriots, which resides within Puebloan witchcraft concepts, may have been exacerbated in the 16th century by this first smallpox epidemic to create a background of heightened suspicion to be further fed and intensified by Spanish conquest, reconquest, and colonial rule in the 17th century.

AD 1535

The passage of Cabeza de Vaca and his party through Texas, Chihuahua and Sonora had no direct impact on the Pueblo Indians, although the story of this group probably joined the other confused rumors of the Spaniards which had drifted up from the south since about 1520.

AD 1539–1542

The first appearance of the Spaniards and their agents within the area of the Pueblo Indians occurred with the entry of Fran Marcos de Niza and his forerunner, Estebanico, into the region of the Zunis. (See F. Bandelier 1905: 203-231; Bolton 1964: 23-39; Winship 1896: 353-373.) The story of the killing of Estebanico by the Zunis had no sooner circulated among the Pueblo Indians than more serious news came: a large Spanish force had appeared before the Zuni pueblo of Hawikuh and, after a skirmish and siege, had captured the town.

Like the other Pueblo Indians, the Piros must have waited with growing apprehension as successive runners and traders brought them tales of the activities of these strange bearded men and their incredible horses. The kinds of fantastic tales that were spread about can be judged by the stories reaching the Hopis that horses ate human beings. (Winship 1896: 428, 488) Such fantasy elements aside, the stories took an even more frightening turn with the news of the Spaniards' mistreatment, besieging, and killing of many people in the Tiguex area during the winter of 1540–1541. (Bolton 1964: 201-230; Winship 1896: 433-439, 494-501) While there was no love lost between the Piros and Southern Tiwas (rather the reverse, in fact), such reports could only alarm the Piros, who had no idea of Spanish goals or intentions.

During Vazquez de Coronado's absence on the plains during the summer of 1541 various explorations of the Pueblo Indian area were carried out by the Spaniards based in the Tiguex area. One of these headed south down the Rio Grande towards the Piros:

Another Captain went down the river in search of the

settlements which the people at Tutahaco (the Isleta area Tiwas) had said were several days distant from there. This captain went down 80 leagues and found four large villages which he left at peace. He proceeded until he found that the river sank into the earth.... (Winship 1896: 455, 511)

Eighty leagues (208 miles) south of Tiguex would be somewhere between Truth-or-Consequences, New Mexico and the southern end of the Caballo Mountains. Which side of the river was traveled is unknown, hence which four Piro pueblos are referred to is uncertain. There is no indication of face-to-face contact between Spaniards and Piros, much to the relief of the latter, no doubt. The Spanish party was probably shadowed by Indian scouts during its whole trip and upon its approach to a pueblo the alarm was doubles given, the ladders pulled up, and the population gathered on the rooftops ready to repel the feared assault. Alternately, as was done during several later Spanish visits, if time permitted a pueblo might be abandoned, the population crossing the river to hide in the brush of the far bank.

After his return from his fruitless journey to Quivira, Vazquez de Coronado and his expedition spent a second winter (1541–1542) as the unwanted guests of the Southern Tiwas, but on December 27, 1541 the leader was injured in a riding accident from which he never fully recovered, causing the expedition's departure back to New Spain in April 1542. (Bolton: 326-334)

The Pueblo Indians had not been left with a positive impression of the Spaniards. Subsequent Spanish expeditions were greeted with apprehension and distrust, if not outright hostility, wherever they went the bitter experiences of the Tiwas were not forgotten.

AD 1581–1583

A lapse of some 39 years occurred before the Pueblo Indians had the dubious pleasure of again meeting the Spaniards. The route of the Rodriguez-Chamuscado Expedition through the Piro area along the Rio Grande has been reviewed in detail in Chapter 5. Ascending the east bank of the Rio Grande they reached a ruinous pueblo of the Piros (LA 487), which they named San Felipe, on August 21, 1581. The next day they approached the first inhabited pueblo (LA 757), later to be known as San Pascual, only to find that the inhabitants had fled and were in hiding after being warned of the Spaniards' approach by hunters who had spotted the explorers on the previous day. (Hammond and Rey 1928: 288-289, 1966: 81-82)

By their own accord, the explorers conducted themselves well while they were along the Piros. In the case of the first pueblo, they entered it and examined its contents, but refrained from appropriating anything. Contact was made with the Piros at a camp set up by the explorers a league from the pueblo. Communication was only through gesture (apparently not sign language) as none of the Indians brought with the explorers could understand the Piros. They were presented with gifts of foodstuffs, cotton blankets, and "other things;" in return the Piros were "given the gifts possible." (Hammond and Rey 1928: 289-290, 1966: 82) The Piros were no doubt greatly relieved at the moderate behavior of the explorers, as well as the smallness of their numbers.

The explorers passed through the Piro area peacefully, going on north to the Southern Tiwas. They were informed by the Piros that the Tiwas "were their enemies and waged war on them." (Hammond and Rey 1928: 290-291, 1966: 82-83) It was probably the southern cluster of Tiwa pueblos, in the Los Lunas area, that was at active hostilities with the Piros at this time.

The Rodriguez-Chamuscado Expedition continued on to explore most of the Pueblo Indian area, but did not enjoy equally harmonious relationships with some of the inhabitants, coming to blows with the Tanos of the Galisteo Basin over the killing of some horses. (Hammond and Rey 1966: 97-99) Upon returning to New Spain the expedition left two priests at the Tiwa pueblo of Puaray, who were summarily killed by the Tiwas as soon as they thought it safe to do so. (Hammond and Rey 1928: 313, 1966: 108-109) The expedition again passed through Piro territory on its way south in February 1582, but without any reported incident.

A year later, the Espejo Expedition arrived in the Piro area from the south. Ostensibly to rescue the priests left at Puaray, it is generally suspected that its purpose was more on the other of exploration in hope of personal gain by the participants. Ascending the west bank of the Rio Grande, the expedition passed two ruined Piro pueblos (LA 597 and LA 244) on January 31 and February 1, 1583, arriving at the pueblo later known as Senecu on the latter day. (See chapter 5 for this expedition's full itinerary through the Piro area.)

Perhaps because of the good conduct of the preceding expedition, the Espejo party was received at Senecu without either hostility or the population taking flight. The expedition passed on through Piro territory with little incident, arriving at the pueblo later to be known as Sevilleta on February 8th. There they learned that the Tiwas had killed the two priests the year before and were now up in arms, ready to resist what they had every reason to believe was a punitive expedition against them. (Hammond and Rey 1928: 321,

1966: 174) Apparently, it was at this time, before proceeding north to the Tiwas, that Espejo and two companions made their side trip to visit the Tompiros of Abo Pass. (See below.)

Proceeding onwards up the Rio Grande, the Espejo Expedition found all of the Tiwa pueblos empty, their inhabitants "had fled to the sierra", the Manzano and Sandia ranges, out of fear of retribution for the killing of the priests. (Hammond and Rey 1966: 176-178) After visiting the Keres, and a trip to the Acoma, Zuni, and Hopi, the explorers returned to Tiguex, finding the pueblos there at least party reoccupied. They were received with hostility, and in retaliation captured and burned the pueblo of Puaray and executed 16 Indians (some others being burned to death in the pueblo). (Hammond and Rey 1966: 203-204) The news of this event spread quickly among the Pueblo Indians, with the result that the Keres and the Tanos of Galisteo were quick to supply the explorers when they passed through their areas. (Hammond and Rey 1966: 204-206) However, they were rebuffed from another large Tano pueblo, whose inhabitants claimed, "that there was a lack of rain, and they were uncertain they would gather any corn." The people of Pecos also attempted to refuse them supplies, for the same reason, but the Spaniards forced them to give up the supplies at point of arms. (Hammond and Rey 1966: 206) This violent and overbearing behavior by the Spaniards at Puaray and Pecos in 1583 no doubt confirmed the impressions held by the Pueblo Indians concerning the mercurial and dangerous character of the Spaniards.

As a sidelight, the mention of a lack of rain (in late June 1583) is an important confirmation of the drought conditions indicated by the tree-ring growth record for the years 1579 through 1585. (See Figure 7-5.) This drought would have less effect on groups like the Piros, who could and did irrigate their fields from the Rio Grande, but other groups such as the Tompiros and Tanos may have had to depend on trade with the river valley groups in order to obtain adequate corn and beans for subsistence.

AD 1590–1593

By ascending the valley of the Rio Pecos, the Castano de Sosa Expedition did not directly contact the Piros in 1590, although it is sure that word of its coming preceded it. On the other hand, Juan de Morlete, who was sent north to arrest Castano de Sosa, did pass through the Piro area in March 1591 (and on the return in April), but his account of the journey is partly lost, including his description (if any) of the Piros. (Hammond and Rey 1966: 303) From what is known it is clear that the Tiwas of Tiguex again fled their pueblos out of justifiable fear of the Spaniards.

It is likely that the Leyva and Humana party would have used the Rio Grande route through the Piro area in 1593, but again there is no surviving account of their experiences.

This closes my account of 16th century Piro history: only a few glimpses of the Indians themselves and their actions, mainly in direct response to intruding Spanish explorers. All of these events, even the epidemic of 1524/1525, were but a foretaste of life under Spanish rule, which is the story of the next century.

The Tompiros in the 16th Century

In Chapter 5, the locations and identifications of the Tompiro pueblos are discussed in detail, along with the pueblos of the Salinas Tiwas. Descriptions of the sites and basic archaeological data can be found in Mera (1940; Scholes and Mera), Vivian (1964), Hayes (Hayes 1981, Hayes, Young and Warren 1981), Toulouse and Stephenson (1960), Wilson (Wilson, Leslie and Warren 1983), Dutton (1981), and elsewhere in this study. For detailed discussion of Tompiro prehistory see Chapter 3 and the chapters in Part III.

At the beginning of the 16th century I visualize the Tompiros, like the Piros, as inheritors of the new cultural pattern produced by the Grand Synthesis of ca. AD 1275–1350, although with some significant differences which are discussed in Chapter 3. I see as a very strong factor in Tompiro life their position on the western edge of the Southern Plains, giving them some direct access to the resources of that region such as the bison but, more importantly, involving them in an east/west trade route of trans-continental status. The major partners of the Tompiros in this east/west trade were the Plains Jumanos to the east and the Zunis to the west. Of the Tompiro pueblos I would see Xenopue (Tabira, LA 51) and the Cueloce-Pataoce pair (LA 120 and LA 83) on Jumanes Mesa and the Abo-Abena community (LA 97 and LA 200, Tenabo) in Abo Pass as the main participants in this trade. Evidence for considering Abo and Tenabo a single community is reviewed in the section on the Tompiros in the 17th century.

AD 1524/1525

The postulated smallpox epidemic would also have struck the Tompiros and Salinas Tiwas with equal force as the other Pueblo Indians. It seems possible that the abandonment of several Tompiro pueblos including LA 476 (Pueblo Colorado) on Jumanes Mesa, and LA 1070, LA 1072 and LA 1073 in the Chupadera Basin may have been caused by the divisive effects of this epidemic.

Was the attack of the Plains Jumanos upon Pecos and the Tano pueblos repeated or duplicated in the case of the Salinas Province pueblos? I know of no evidence upon which to base either a negative or positive answer at present. However, I suspect that the answer was probably negative with regard to at least Cueloce (LA 120), which may have had the closest relations with the Plains Jumanos of any Pueblo Indian group.

AD 1535

Neither Cabeza de Vaca nor any of his group visited the Pueblo Indians, but it is very likely that the Plains Jumanos who had seen these wanderers visited Cueloce and imparted their stories.

AD 1539–1542

The Salinas Province appears to be the only sector of the Pueblo Indian area not to have received any visitation at all from the Vazquez de Coronado Expedition. No doubt, however, the Tompiros followed events from afar and even may have sent spies to watch the Spaniards' movements. It is also reasonably likely that some refugees from Tiguex may have joined the Salinas Tiwa pueblos in the winter of 1540–1541 in order to escape the Spaniards. These would have provided firsthand accounts of the more negative aspects of the Spanish visitation. It is also likely that the Plains Jumanos (Teyas) who guided the Spaniards to Quivira and then back to the Rio Pecos would have subsequently visited the Tompiros and described the Spaniards and their activities.

AD 1581–1583

In December 1581 and January 1582, the Rodriguez-Chamuscado Expedition entered the Salinas Province from Tiguex by way of Tijeras and Cedro canyons. (See discussion in Chapter 5.) The explorers visited five pueblos, which I identify as Chilili, Tajique, Cuarac, Abo, and Tenabo (see Chapter 5), and also visited the salt lakes. While there they were told through signs (probably not sign language) that three other large pueblos lay beyond probably the Eastern

Tompiro pueblos but they did not visit them due to bad weather with snow and lack of supplies. (Hammond and Rey 1966: 107, 119, 131-132, 137) No incidents with the Indians are recorded. No doubt the Indians received them cautiously and encouraged them to pass on as quickly as possible.

Hammond and Rey (1966: 55) have suggested that Fray Juan de Santa Maria, a priest who left the exploring party in September 1581 to return to New Spain, was killed by "eastern Tiguas," however, it is clear from Gallegos' statement that Tanos of the Galisteo Basin followed the priest and were responsible for his death. (Hammond and Rey 1966: 95-96)

The second encounter of Salinas Province Indians with the Spaniards came in February 1583 when three Spaniards of the Espejo Expedition made a side trip from Sevilleta into Abo Pass to visit Abo and Tenabo. (See discussion in Chapter 5.) Tenabo was the first pueblo visited, as described by Luxan: At sunset (we) reached the first pueblo of the province...Most of the people of that pueblo began to flee when they observed us, while other came to meet us peacefully. We at once reassured them, and that night all the people came and gave us turkeys and corn. That night we kept watch with much care. We erected a large cross in token of possession...(Hammond and Rey 1966: 175)

From comments in the description about the "warlike" nature of the people of Tenabo, and the passage quoted above regarding keeping a sharp watch at night, one can suppose that a certain amount of tension was present between Spaniards and Tompiros. Despite this, the Spaniards were apparently allowed into some of the houses as Luxan mentions the presence of household fetishes and Espejo notes the presence of "metals" in the houses. (Hammond and Rey 1966: 175, 222) The visit to Abo elicits little comment from the explorers and must have been brief.

AD 1590–1593

The various explorations by Castano de Sosa, Morlete, and the ill-fated Leyva and Humana party seem not to have touched upon the Salinas Province, but word of their passage was surely circulated. For example, the Eastern Tompiros no doubt received various accounts of the Castano de Sosa Expedition from Plains Jumanos who had encountered those Spaniards along the Rio Pecos. (See Chapter 6.)

It can be seen then that by AD 1598 the Piros of the Rio Grande Valley had had more direct contact and experience of the Spaniards than had their highland relatives, the Tompiros. Neither group had yet directly suffered at the hands of the Spaniards, but both were doubtless quite aware of the experiences of other Pueblo Indians, in particular the Southern Tiwas.

The Piros in the 17th Century

I am arbitrarily including the years 1598–1600 within the 17th century since AD 1598 marks the beginning of a continuous Spanish presence in New Mexico. That year also marks the beginning of Spanish colonial rule of the Pueblo Indians, some features of which have been described in Chapter 7 as part of the assessment of their impact upon the Pueblo Indian population. For major published descriptions of Spanish Colonial New Mexico in the 17th century see Kessell (1979b) and Scholes (1935, 1936, 1937, 1942).

AD 1598: The Onate Colony

On May 4, 1598, the royal colonizing venture headed by Don Juan de Onate forded the Rio Grande at the site of modern El Paso and headed north up the east bank of the river. The colony traveled slowly, sometimes as little as half a league per day, consequently, on May 12th Onate sent ahead a mounted exploring party headed by Captain Pablo de Aguilar. (Pacheco et alia 1871b: 243-246) According to Gaspar de Villagra:

His orders were to advance as secretly as possible, and, at the first sight of a town, to return immediately and report to the general...Aguilar marched forth, taking a direction along the course of the river, northward; we followed with the army...We went along the stream for quite a distance and were preparing to leave the Rio del Norte and go in an opposite direction, across the plain (the Jornada del Muerto), when we met Captain Aguilar and his party returning from their mission. Captain Aguilar informed the general that they had arrived at the first pueblo of the land and had entered it.

The general was very displeased that his commands had been so flagrantly disobeyed. Captain Aguilar came very near being executed then and there, and it was due solely to the entreaties of his men that this was not done. (G. Espinosa 1933: 138-139)

Captain Aguilar rejoined the main party on May 20th (Pacheco et alia 1871b: 247), thus probably reached the first Piro pueblo about May 16, 1598. This pueblo was probably LA 757, later to be known as San Pascual. There is no information regarding the reception of Aguilar's party

by the Piros. To continue with the narrative of Villagra:

Onate was very apprehensive that the natives of these pueblos, having been apprised of the coming of the Spaniards, would abandon their pueblos, taking with them all their supplies. Accordingly, he left the royal ensign in command of the main army, with order to follow, while he with thirty well-armed horsemen, accompanied by the commissary and Fray Cristobal, hastened ahead. He advanced by forced marches and soon came in sight of the first of the pueblos. (G. Espinosa 1933: 139-140)

Apparently, Onate broke the trail across the Jornada del Muerto that was followed by the main colonizing party. Onate's advance party were the first Spaniards to cross the Jornada del Muerto, all earlier parties having followed the river. The first pueblo was again LA 757 (San Pascual). According to Villagra:

As the party...approached the pueblo, the elements it seemed clashed in terrible conflict, for the sky became darkened with heavy black clouds and the entire earth shook and trembled as with the force of a mighty earthquake. A terrible tempest arose, with a veritable downpour of rain, accompanied by such mighty claps of thunder that we were terrified; the good priests prayed to heave to aid us in this extremity...God took compassion on us...for the skies cleared as suddenly as they had become clouded and the sun shone forth bright and clear. (G. Espinosa 1933: 140)

Making allowance for the somewhat purple prose, the above is a rather good description of a rip-roaring Southwestern gully-washer. Whether or not a storm actually occurred at this particular time or Villagra simply inserted it for dramatic effect, is another matter. Storm or not storm, the advance party would have been approaching San Pascual on about the 25th or 26th of May.

Again, according to Villagra: The inhabitants saw us approaching and all came forth and welcomed us in a most hospitable manner. They received us into their town and gave us quarters, acting most friendly toward us, and showing great reverence for the crucifix the priests had, which they approached and kissed. (G. Espinosa 1933: 140)

Meanwhile, the main party of colonists had been toiling across the parched Jornada del Muerto, finally reaching the Rio Grande again on May 25th at the camping spot later to be known as Fra Cristobal. (Pacheco et alia 1871b: 247-249) At this point, the carts lagged behind the rest of the party. This latter passed San Pascual on May 28th and reached the vicinity of Qualacu that same day. The Piros of Qualacu were disturbed by the appearance of such a large party of Spaniards, so to ease their minds the Spaniards distributed "trinkets", probably beads and such like, and made a point of camping down along the river instead of occupying the pueblo. (Pacheco et alia 1871b: 249-250) The fears of the Piros are quite understandable, since the only previous Spanish expedition comparable in size had been the Vazquez de Coronado Expedition that had treated the Tiwas so badly. Also, Onate had no sooner appeared at San Pascual than he began to collect levies of the Indians' supplies in order to feed his colonists. For subsistence agriculturalists, such unanticipated demands upon their food stocks were bound to be unpopular.

It is probably for the above reasons that the Spaniards found Piros waiting for them in only three pueblos: San Pascual (LA 757), Qualacu (LA 755-768-31798), and at Teipana (LA 283). This latter pueblo was called "Socorro" by the Spaniards because its "captain" (an outside chief?) named Letoc provided Onate with a great amount of corn, as well as accurate information about the country up-river. The main body of the colonial party remained encamped near Qualacu from May 28 until June 14, the cart train finally catching up to it on June 12, 1598. (Pacheco et alia 1871b: 250-251)

The whole colony recommenced its journey on June 14 and arrived at the temporarily abandoned pueblo of Nueva Sevilla (later to be known as Sevilleta) on June 16. The Spaniards occupied the pueblo until June 22, while awaiting the arrival of more grain supplies. It was also during this period that a side exploration was made into Abo Pass. (Pacheco et alia 1871b: 251-252)

On June 23rd the colony moved north another four leagues to a newly built pueblo that they named San Juan Bautista. This pueblo has not yet been correlated with a known ruin, but should have been in the vicinity of the confluence of Abo Arroyo with the Rio Grande. (See Chapter 5.) This may have been a Piro pueblo, but the inhabitants, like those of Sevilleta, had fled upon the approach of the Spaniards. The Spaniards remained there on June 24th to celebrate the feast day of Saint John the Baptist. These celebrations were attended by various curious Pueblo Indians, many of whom the Spaniards suspected of being spies sent to find out the Spaniards' intentions. Included among these was a party of three from the Keres pueblo of Santo Domingo, who caused a considerable stir, as described by Villagra:

When the celebrations were over the governor mingled with his men, talking with them, and while he was so occupied, three naked savages approached; one of them, drawing near to the general, said in a loud voice, "Thursday, Friday, Saturday, and Sunday."

We were astounded to hear these words from his lips...We urged the savage to speak more, but he would not utter another word. The general had all three arrested, when in fear the savage said, "Tomas, Cristobal," pointing to a direction and giving us to understand that the persons who bore these names were two journeys away. (G. Espinosa 1933: 141-142)

Tomas and Cristobal turned out to be two Mexican (Aztec) Indians of the Castano de Sosa Expedition who had remained at Santo Domingo since 1591, and were to be pressed into service as translators for Onate. (Pacheco et alia 1871b: 252-253; G. Espinosa 1933: 142-143) On June 25th the colony passed on northwards, leaving the Piro area behind.

Later, on September 8, 1598, in the proclamation of the Vassalage of San Juan Bautista (the Tewa pueblo, not the one mentioned above), the Piros were assigned to the mission province of Fray Juan de Claros. (Hammond and Rey 1953: 346) While it does appear that Fray Claros established himself at a Tiwa pueblo in the Los Lunas area (see Chapter 5), there is no evidence that he ever visited the Piros.

From this time on, however, Spaniards were to pass through the Piro area on journeys to and from New Spain. No specific events for the Piros are recorded for a considerable span of time (AD 1598 until 1626), although Fray Alonso de Benavides states: "they always assisted those (Spaniards) who arrived in their land, weary from the long journey (from New Spain)...." (Hodge, Hammond and Rey 1945: 62) Clearly the Piros preferred to keep a low profile and to watch from the sidelines such violent Spanish-Indian encounters as the Acoma War of 1599 and the Jumano War of 1601.

AD 1626–1629: Beginning of the Missions

The arrival of Fray Alonso de Benavides in New Mexico in 1626 marked the beginning of Franciscan missionary activity among the Piros. While Benavides was the custos of the New Mexico missions, and thus had a full share of administrative duties, he was nothing if not zealous for the conversion of the Indians, hence he made it his special duty to found missions among the Piros where no missions had been before. (Forrestal and Lynch 1954: 15; Ayer 1916: 17) The story of these years is thus that of individual pueblos and their missions.

Sevilleta: The Piro pueblo of Seelocu or Tzelaqui, called Nueva Sevilla by the Onate colonists but modified to Sevilleta sometime before 12, is readily identified with the ruin LA 774. It is situated on the east bank of the Rio Grande on a gravel terrace overlooking the river flats and the route of the camino real. (See Chapter 5 and Marshall and Walt 1984: 203-207.) Benavides provides the following information on the history of Sevilleta:

When I entered upon the conversation of this province (the Piros), the people of this pueblo of Seelocu, which the Spaniards named Sevilleta, had for several years been at war with some other Indians, their enemies, who had burned their pueblo and killed many of them. Those who had escaped were wandering about in the neighboring hills. I undertook to found their pueblo anew and to bring them back to live in it...Thus the pueblo is now (1634) settled, dedicated to San Luis Obispo of our holy order. (Hodge, Hammond and Rey 1945: 64)

Who the enemy Indians were is unstated, but I would favor the Apaches, since the Southern Tiwas, another unfriendly group, had previously been missionized (Sandia in 1610, Isleta in 1612: Scholes and Bloom 1944: 334) and the Spaniards would have suppressed internecine warfare among the Pueblo Indians. There is no record of a priest ever being assigned to the mission of San Luis Obispo de Sevilleta, consequently it may have been founded as a visita of Socorro. (See below.) There is surface evidence of a sizeable adobe church at Sevilleta, but no certain information on when it was built.

Socorro: As noted above, the name "Socorro" was applied by the Onate colonists to the Piro pueblo of Teipana (LA 283) because of the great amount of foodstuffs provided to them by the inhabitants. Benavides chose the nearby pueblo of Pilabo (LA 791) as a mission site, probably because it had a greater population than Teipana (see Chapter 5), but true to his nature as a propagandist of his faith Benavides could not let a good story go to waste, hence the name "Socorro" was applied to the Pilabo mission: Nuestra Senora del Socorro. (Forrestal and Lynch 1954: 15-16; Ayer 1916: 17)

Benavides claims that on his first missionary visit to the Piros he accomplished the deathbed conversion of "the principal chief of that place (Pilabo)" and of the chief's son, and that the chief "ordered that a house should be given to me in which to live." (Hodge, Hammond and Rey 1945: 63) Construction of a permanent church and convento were probably begun by Fray Martin de Arvide, the first known assigned priest to this mission, beginning in 1626. (See discussion on the founding of the Socorro mission in Scholes and Bloom 1945: 76-81.) Vetancurt's (1697: 98, 1698: 7) attribution of the "founding" of this mission to Fray Garcia de San Francisco is clearly mistaken, although this priest

may very well have overseen the completion of the church and convento buildings. It is likely that Sevilleta, Teipana, Qualacu, and other nearby Piro pueblos were served from Socorro as mission visitas.

Senecu: The Piro pueblo furthest south on the west bank of the Rio Grande was that of Tzenacu, Hispanized to "Senecu." (See Chapter 5.) As a Sevilleta, Benavides founded a formal mission there, probably in the late 1620s only amounting to a small convento of remodeled Indian rooms plus some sort of structure to serve as a chapel, with the name of San Antonio de Padua. (Forrestal and Lynch 1954: 15-16; Ayer 1916: 17) It is likely, again as in the case of Sevilleta, that Senecu was a visita of Socorro at this time since there is no record of a priest stationed there before 1630.

The Piros of Senecu apparently maintained trade relations at this time with both the Apaches de Xila and the Apaches del Perillo. However, it is clear that the latter were not completely trusted by the Piros, suggesting an ambivalent sometimes trade/sometimes raid relationship similar to that known to exist between the Vaquero Apaches and the other Pueblo Indians. (Hodge, Hammond and Rey 1945: 82, 84-85)

Exactly what the Piros thought of missions and missionaries is unknown, but Benavides' claim that they lived "in a state of great perfection and Christianity" may be reasonably doubted. Any clear understanding of Christianity by the Piros probably had to wait until the 1630s, when missionaries such as Fray Garcia de San Francisco became conversant in the Piro language.

AD 1630s: The Decade of Epidemics

It was during the 1630s that the great drop in Pueblo Indian population occurred. (See Chapter 7.) The Piros appear to have suffered just as heavily as the other Pueblo Indians, but we have no specific accounts of epidemics within the Piro area. However, it is likely that the abandonment of most Piro pueblos happened during this decade, namely: LA 31717, Teipana (LA 283), LA 28, Qualacu (LA 755-768-31798), LA 31744, and possibly San Pascual (LA 757). (See chapter 5 for maps showing the locations of these sites.) It is also possible that a new pueblo name Alamillo was founded at this time on the east bank of the Rio Grande between Sevilleta and Socorro in order to congregate survivors from some of the other pueblos. (Conversely, there may have already been a pueblo named Teyaxa at the location of Alamillo at the time of the Onate colony: see Chapter 5). At any rate, four Piro pueblos emerge as permanent settlements from the demographic upsets of the decade: Sevilleta, Alamillo, Socorro, and Senecu.

Alamillo: The pueblo and mission of Alamillo were established at least by the year 1638 when there is mention of Fray Diego Lopez as the guardian of the Convento del Santo Angel de la Guarda del Alamillo. (Scholes and Bloom 1945: 81) Sevilleta was probably a visita of Alamillo during much of this decade.

Socorro: A priest, Fray Juan Juarez, is known for this mission only in the years 1638–1640; earlier it may have been a visita of Senecu. Vetancurt (1697: 7) attributes to Fray Garcia de San Francisco, who was a lay brother assisting Fray Antonio de Arteaga at Senecu, the elaboration of the mission:

He adorned the temple (church) and sacristy with ecclesiastic zeal (with) rich ornaments, an organ, and music (a chair?), and a vineyard from which was obtained wine for this mission and many others (in New Mexico).

Of course, some of this work may have been accomplished during the 1640s and 1650s since Fray Garcia was to be a long-term missionary among the Piros.

Senecu: While both Fray Antonio de Arteaga and his assistant, lay brother Fray Garcia de San Francisco, were stationed at Senecu from 1629 to 1638. Vetancurt (1697: 98) again attributes to the latter the physical improvements to the missions: "he adorned it with an organ and rich ornaments, and a vineyard from whose grapes wine was made, which was sent to the other conventos (of New Mexico)..."

Spanish Settlement and Activities: Little is known concerning Spanish activities among the Piros. It is possible that encomiendas were established at the same time or even before the beginning of the missions, but there is no sure information. An Onate colonist, Geronimo Marquez, is noted as occupying an estancia at Acomilla in 1631. (Chavez 1954: 69) This estancia may be the archaeological site LA 236 just north of present-day San Acacia. (See Marshall and Walt 1984: 199-201.) One of his sons, Francisco Marquez, was married to a Maria Nunez, said to be from "Socorro de los Piros." (Chavez 1954: 69) However, this woman does not appear to have been an Indian as she is supposed to be a daughter of Juan Rodriguez Bellido (Chavez 1954: 95), consequently it may simply be that her family maintained an estancia near Socorro.

Juan Garcia Holgado may have been the owner of the "place of Juan Garcia" on the east bank of the Rio Grande roughly opposite the pueblo of Senecu. (See Chapter 5.) If so, he may have been in residence between ca. 1638 and 1667.

(Chavez 1954: 32-33) Nothing is known of other Spaniards being resident in the area during the 1630s.

Generally speaking, the 1630s were a period of worsening relations between the church and the governors of New Mexico. Apparently taking advantage of the Indian orphans created by the epidemics, Governor Francisco de la Mora Ceballos (1632–1634) had them seized as laborers for his own properties and for distribution as servants to other Spaniards, a move opposed by the missionaries. (See letters by Fray Esteban de Perea in Hackett 1937: 129-131.) He also forced goods on the missionaries which they were supposed to sell to the Indians in exchange for antelope hides, and conducted himself in other objectionable ways that are delineated in the letters cited above. His successor, Governor Francisco Martinez de Baeza (1634–1637), was no improvement in that he forced the Indians to weave large numbers of mantas and collected pinon nuts and antelope hides for sale in New Spain. (Rea 1947: 25-26, 29-30) He is also remembered for failing to adequately protect the missionized Indians and the Spanish colonists from increasing Apache attacks. (Scholes 1936: 301)

AD 1637–1641: Governorship of Luis de Rosas

Under this governor, the sorry story continued in all its negative elements: epidemics, extortion of goods by the governor, Apache attacks, and continued church-state conflict within the Spanish colony. (See description in Kessell 1979b: 156-165.) Governor Rosas was in open conflict with the Franciscan missionaries, and his supporters invaded the confines of several conventos: "At Socorro the sacristy was violated, and Capt. Sebastian Gonzalez out on the habit of a Franciscan and summoned the Indians to kiss his hand." (Scholes 1936: 324)

However, as can be seen in Chapter 7, the population decline among the Pueblo Indians leveled out during the decade of the 1640s. There is no apparent improvement in overall conditions of life during this period, consequently the leveling off must be a biological function: namely that the surviving Pueblo Indian population now had an acquired immunity to the major killing diseases, smallpox and measles, at least.

AD 1649–1653: Governorship of Ugarte y la Concha

An administrative change was implemented in New Mexico during or before this governorship: the division of the "kingdom" into jurisdictions, each one under the control of an alcade mayor appointed by the governor. (See Scholes 1935: 91-93.)[1] The Piro area was included with the Tiwa pueblo of Isleta in a *jurisdiccion* known as "Isleta y Los Piros."

In 1650, a conspiracy to rebel against Spanish authority was discovered and destroyed, as described in the words of Sargento Major Diego Lopez Sambrano.

In the year '50, during the government of General Concha, he discovered another plot to rebel which the sorcerers and chief men of the pueblos had arranged with the enemy Apaches, and for that purpose the Christians (the Pueblo Indians), under the pretext that the enemy was doing it, turned over to them in the pastures the droves of mares and horses belonging to the Spaniards, which are the principal nerve of warfare. They had already agreed with the said apostates to attack in all the districts on the night of Holy Thursday, because the Spaniards would then be assembled (for worship). The said rebellion was discovered because of Captain Alonso Vaca and other solders having followed a drove of mares which the Indians were driving off, and the aggressors being overtaken, they declared that the Christians of the pueblo of Alameda and Sandia had turned them over to them, and that they were all plotting and conspiring with all the said Apaches to rebel and destroy the whole kingdom, and to be left in freedom as in ancient times, living like their ancestors...(thus) the treason was uncovered, and many Indians were arrested from most of the pueblos of this kingdom. As a result, nine leaders were hanged and many others sold as slaves for ten years. (Hackett 1942, II: 299)[2]

Juan Dominguez de Mendoza adds a few more details:

In the time of Senor General Hernando de Ugarte y la Concha there were hanged as traitors and confederates of the apaches some Tiguas Indians of La Isleta and of the pueblos of La Alameda, San Felipe, Cochiti, and Jemez, nine from the said pueblos being hanged. (Hackett 1942, II: 266)

This conspiracy is very significant in that previous revolts against Spanish rule in New Mexico had been limited in scope, involving a single pueblo (such as Acoma in 1599 or Taos in 1639) or a small group of pueblos bound together by a common language (such as the Tompiros in 1601, the Zunis in 1632, or the Jemez in 1623). This conspiracy is the first to involve several of the main Pueblo Indian groups (Tiwas, Keres, and Jemez in 1623). This conspiracy is the first to involve several of the main Pueblo Indian groups

(Tiwas, Keres, and Jemez) working together with the free Apaches toward a coordinated rebellion. It thus foreshadows the successful Pueblo Revolt of 1680 in its strategy of uniting disparate traditional enemies against the European invader. The tactic of choosing a Spanish religious day for the coordinated attack also anticipates the planning of 1680. It is clear that the Pueblo Indians had begun to understand the Spaniards, and to use that knowledge against them.

AD 1656–1661: Governors Manso and Lopez de Mendizabal

In 1656 an unusual event occurred: a new governor arrived by the tri-annual supply caravan from Mexico City who was a man friendly to the church: Juan Manso de Contreras, a brother of the Franciscan Fray Tomas Manso who had been operating the caravan since the early 1630s.[3] The supply caravan probably arrived in the spring of 1656 and, in anticipation of its return to Mexico City in the autumn, the missionaries in New Mexico compiled one of the rare censes of the Pueblo Indians as part of a summary description of the mission establishments (for the document and its date of composition see Scholes 1929 and 1944, and Baldwin 1984c). In this document Alamillo and Sevilleta are mentioned as being visitas of Socorro, but Senecu is not mentioned. (See, however, discussion in Chapter 7.)

Due to the unusual amity between secular and religious elements of the Spanish colony, the governor approved the removal of the Piros of Sevilleta and their congregation with the population of Alamillo in 1656. (Hackett 1937: 189) The reason given for this action was that the Piros of Sevilleta, not having a resident priest, were holding "very serious idolatries", meaning kachina dances and other ceremonies, away from their pueblo, reportedly on the lower reaches of the Rio Puerco which has its confluence with the Rio Grande only a short distance north of Sevilleta. It may have been at this time that the mission at Alamillo was renamed in honor of Santa Ana.[4] Relevant to this last point is the statement by the next governor, Lopez de Mendizabal, that when he was at Alamillo in 1659 a new church was under construction using Indian labor. (Hackett 1937: 213)

It was during this time that Fray Garcia de San Francisco of Senecu began mission work among the Mansos of the El Paso area. To aid in this he took down to El Paso some Piro families from Senecu, who taught the Mansos agriculture, the construction of irrigation ditches, and the use of adobe for construction. This mission became known as Nuestra Senora de Guadalupe de El Paso. (Hackett 1937: 189-190)

The rapprochement of church and state was rudely

terminated in 1659 with the appearance of a new governor, Bernardo Lopez de Mendizabal. Indeed, the rupture began even before the governor reached New Mexico as he is stated to have quarreled violently with Fray Juan Ramirez, the new custos for New Mexico, on the trip up from Mexico City. (Kessell 1979b: 174)

When the caravan reached the new mission at El Paso the governor is alleged to have interfered with an attempt by the Manso converts to honor the custos. (Hackett 1937: 189-190) The governor is further accused of creating a "triumphal entry" for himself by having ordered that all the settlers for fifty leagues roundabout should come down to the pueblo of Senecu...they were to go thither for the purpose of accompanying him to the villa of Santa Fe. Some two hundred persons were entertained in the convents, it being necessary to entertain them and the accused (the governor) without remuneration in these convents, because the natives of those parts (the Picos) have nothing wherewith to entertain guests. Hence the vanity of the accused (the governor) exhausted the convents through no fault but his own, for they were ruined by such great expense. (Hackett 1937: 203)

After his grand party at Senecu, at the Franciscans' expense, the governor continued northward: When the said governor entered the kingdom, this religious (Fray Benito de la Natividad) went out to receive him, dressed in his surplice, to the gate of the cemetery of the convent of Socorro. He received the governor with pealing of bells and other musical instruments which the churches in that custodia have, and with a large cross. But the governor began to have words with Father Fray Benito de la Natividad because he had not gone out two leagues from the convent to receive him... (Hackett 1937: 147)

Thus, it was clear from the beginning that an arrogant and self-seeking man was to be head of the government for the next three years, and Lopez de Mendizabal quickly gathered around him a fine assortment of scoundrels and rogues, prominent among whom were Nicolas de Aguilar and Diego de Guadalajara.

During the summer of 1659 Lopez de Mendizabal made a tour of New Mexico, probably to size up the potential for personal gain within the "kingdom." In the course of it, he seems to have actively sought to humiliate the priests before the Indians and otherwise aggravate the church authorities. Typical of these acts was what occurred at the pueblo of Alamillo:

When he was engaged in the visitation of the pueblo of Alamillo, he established himself publicly in the plaza with a table before him, and, in the presence of the entire pueblo

and of some solders, insisted to the Indians that they make charges...against their minister, who was a certain religious ninety-year-old. An Indian woman stood up saying that this religious had outraged her, and the accused (the governor) settled the case verbally, and ordered that the religious should pay the woman a piece of cloth worth one peso. (Hackett 1937: 200)[5]

The accusation against this priest seems improbably, especially when one closely studies the account given by Lopez de Mendizabal himself of this incident: "...According to custom, which is for the governors to seat themselves in the plaza or other public place to perform the visitation of pueblos, first convoking (the inhabitants) and asking them through an interpreter to tell him the things for which he came, he took his lodging in the convent of the pueblo of Alamillo, and then seated himself in the plaza. Among the Indian men and women who came forward to tell him their troubles and molestations, or to make whatever complaint they had against any person, was an old Indian woman...Immediately another Indian woman, a young one, arose, and gave her story to the interpreter, who was a servant of the doctrinero. When the accused (the governor) questioned her, she said that she was complaining against the old man who had outraged her...and the interpreter said: She is not speaking of this old man, Sir, but of the father, my master." (Hackett 1937: 215-216)

It is interesting that the accusation appears not to have come from the woman herself but from the interpreter! Did the interpreter have some grudge against the priest? We will never know the full truth of the matter, but it is clear that the governor was willing to give credence to any accusation against the churchmen. According to the articles of accusation against the governor the Indians of Alamillo were quite amused by the governor's judgment against the priest. (Hackett 1937: 200)

In his trial before the Inquisition in Mexico City, Lopez de Mendizabal accused the priest of Socorro, Fray Benito de la Natividad, of violating the secrecy of the confessional by divulging the sins of various of the Piros to the governor. (Hackett 1937: 196) In his turn, he was accused of extorting three hundred fleeces of wool from the guardian of Socorro so that the priest might retain two Indian helpers, then of distributing these same fleeces among the Piros of Socorro with orders for them to make wool stockings for him. (Hackett 1937: 153, 205) In his residencia Lopez de Mendizabal was charged with not paying the Indians for their labor in making these stockings: he owed the Piros of Socorro for 30 pairs, those of Senecu for

100 pairs, and those of Alamillo for 46 pairs. (Scholes 1942: 48-49)

He also reversed the previous governor's decision, and had the Piros of Sevilleta taken out of Alamillo and returned to the abandoned site of Sevilleta. He did this in connivance with Diego de Guadalajara, who possessed a hacienda a league north of Sevilleta (later to be known as the "hacienda de Felipe Romero," who was the son-in-law of Diego de Guadalajara), and wanted to use the Piros as *cargadores* to haul salt from the Salinas Province to the Rio Grande. Lopez de Mendizabal also engaged in procuring this salt, which was in wagons down the camino real to the silver mines at Parral. (See Hackett 1937: 188-189 , 206.) Of course, Lopez de Mendizabal told a different story. (Hackett 1937: 220)

More serious for New Mexico as a whole was the massive slave-catching expedition against the Apaches that the governor sent off "inland" in September 1659. The expedition results in some 70 captives, men and women, who were sold into slavery in the silver mines, thus further exacerbating Apachean bitterness against Spaniards and Pueblo Indians alike. (Hackett 1937: 186-187) This, and the various individual clashes between governor and church-men, resulted in the composition on November 11, 1659 of a letter of denunciation of the governor by the custos and other churchmen (Hackett 1937: 186-193), only the first of many to bombard the viceroy of New Spain.

The priests may have felt themselves grievously injured, but from their point of view much worse was yet to come. The Pueblo Indians had learned from previous church-state conflicts in New Mexico that governors would sometimes rule in their favor. Now, with the anti-clericalism of Lopez de Mendizabal clearly established for all to see, the Pueblo Indians obtained a reversal of the ban on kachina dances, apparently in October 1660. (Hackett 1937: 158)[6]

As he (the governor) has said, the Indians of the pueblo of Tesuque came to the villa of Santa Fe and, as he remembers, with them came their encomendero, Francisco Gomez, and Juan Griego as interpreter. Among the other things, they asked permission to dance the catzinas. The accused (the governor) asked what dance this was. The encomendero having replied, as he recalls, as well as the interpreter and others present, concerning the nature of the dance...the accused (the governor) wanted to see it... (and he) told them (the Indians) to dance. They did so...To the accused it seemed mere foolishness on the part of the Indians... (Hackett 1937: 223-224)

During this hearing before the Inquisition, Lopez de Mendizabal repeatedly states that he saw nothing bad in the kachina dances, which opinion seems to have been shared by at least some other secular Spaniards. (See, for example, the apparent lack of concern on the part of Juan de Mondragon, encomendero of Senecu, in Hackett 1937: 158.) The religious authorities, however, took a very narrow-minded view, denouncing kachina dances as "devil worship," and had forbidden them from the very beginning of missionization. (Hackett 1937: 207-208)

Apparently relishing the consternation of the priests over his permission to the Tesuques and other Tewas to conduct their kachina dances, the governor extended his original decree by commanding that all Pueblo Indians "dance the catzinas" and live as they had before the establishment of the missions. (Hackett 1937: 164) Indians throughout New Mexico reacted by openly resuming kachina dances and other previously suppressed ceremonies, to which the priests reacted by confiscating kachina masks and other paraphernalia.[7] It is specifically noted that Fray Francisco de Azebedo confiscated masks at the pueblo of Alamillo. (Hackett 1937: 186)

I would not label Governor Lopez de Mendizabal a champion of the Indians: he was merely using them to goad the priests, even as he used those of Sevilleta and the Salinas Province as beasts of burden in order to enrich himself. There is, of course, always the problem of whom to believe in the welter of charges and counter-charges between the secular and religious authorities. The best one can do is to weigh the various statements against each other, and against any independent evidence that may exist. For example, the priests' characterizations of the kachina dances as "devil" worship" are patently ridiculous from a modern perspective, although I am sure that the priests were sincere in their self-deception. On the other hand, it is clear that Lopez de Mendizabal had a coarse and abusive character, and would go out of his way to antagonize the clergy.

The whole farce came to an end in late 1661 with the appearance of a new governor, upon which Lopez de Mendizabal was arrested by the Inquisition and shipped off to Mexico City for trial. There, he died in prison before sentence could be passed.

Spaniards noted as living in the Piro area at this time include Diego de Guadalajara, owner of the estancia of San Antonio a league north of Sevilleta, which was soon to pass to Felipe Romero, the husband of Diego's daughter, Jacinta de Guadalajara y Quiros. (Chavez 1954: 42-43, 97; Hackett 1937: 189) The young Felipe Romero, 22 years old at the time, was accused in 1661 of killing cattle belonging to the pueblo of Alamillo; also accused of the same act was another young Spaniard, Bartolome Gomez Robledo, 21 or 22 years old at the time. (Chavez 1954: 36, 97)

Alonso Perez Granillo, who was alcalde mayor of the jurisdiccion of Isleta y Los Piros in 1660, held an estancia two leagues from the pueblo of Socorro. (Chavez 1954: 88; Hackett 1937: 148) This estancia may be the place called "El Nogal," north of Socorro on the west bank of the Rio Grande, that is noted during Otermin's return journey in 1682. (Hackett 1942, II: 363) Lopez de Mendizabal refers to the Granillo family and a "Juan Garcia," whom he calls a mulatto (presumably Juan Garcia Holgado, a resident of the Piro area), as his enemies. (Hackett 1937: 213)

Juan Alonso Mondragon is stated to be encomendero of Senecu in 1660 (Hackett 1937: 158); he was probably over 60 years old at the time. (Chavez 1954: 75) A younger man, Felix de Carvajal, is noted to have held "part" of the encomienda of Senecu in the early 1660s. (Chavez 1954: 15)

AD 1665–1673: Unrest Among the Piros

After the ministry of Fray Francisco de Azebedo, the mission at Alamillo lapsed back into being a visita of Socorro, taking Sevilleta with it, as listed in 1667. (Scholes 1929: 55) Two estancias are also listed as being served by the priest at Socorro, presumably those named El Nogal and San Antonio. However, in 1672 Alamillo was again given a resident priest. (Bloom and Mitchell 1938: 115) Also in that year, extensive lists of the church ornaments and vestments were made for the churches and sacristies of Senecu and Socorro. (Scholes and Adams 1952: 31-34, 37-38) On January 22, 1673 Fray Garcia de San Francisco died of old age in the convento of Senecu and was buried there. (Vetancurt 1698: 7-8)

Luis Lopez was known to be the alcalde mayor of the jurisdiction of Isleta y Los Piros in 1665. (Scholes 1942: 7) He owned an estancia on the east bank of the Rio Grande south of the abandoned pueblo of Qualacu. (See Chapter 5.) He was probably appointed to office by Governor Juan Duran de Miranda in 1664, or possibly earlier by Diego de Penalosa, the successor of Lopez de Mendizabal.

At any rate, it would seem that a new alcalde mayor was appointed in 1665 or 1666 by the new governor, Fernando de Villanueva (1665–1668), as Francisco de Valencia held that office in June 1668 and cited Villanueva as the governor appointing him to it. (Hackett 1937: 276) In 1668 Francisco de Valencia was 61 years old and owned an estancia south of Isleta Pueblo in the vicinity of the present-day town of Valencia. (Chavez 1954: 109) Apparently, he died sometime after June 11, 1668 but in the same year since his wife is referred to as his "widow" before the year was out. (Chavez 1954: 109) Thus, it is my suspicion that Francisco de Valencia is the alcalde mayor reported as killed along with four other Spaniards as part of the El Tanbulita conspiracy. (Hackett 1942, II: 299)

El Tanbulita was a Piro who, along with others, had apparently been conspiring with the Apaches against the Spaniards. He, along with some Piros and Apaches, ambushed a Spanish party in the "Sierra de la Magdalena" (now known as the Magdalena Mountains) west of the Rio Grande. El Tanbulita was said to have himself killed the alcalde mayor. The details of this fracas are not given, but El Tanbulita was captured and tried along with five other Piros for treason, and then hanged. Other Piros were convicted of "sorcery," and "burned", apparently, this means an auto da fe, burning at the stake reserved for those convicted of heresy. These hangings and "burnings" were done at the pueblo of Senecu, probably to serve as warnings to the other Piros. (Hackett 1942, II: 266, 299) Despite a long history of "docility," now even the Piros were becoming impatient with Spanish rule.

The next major event in Piro history was the influx of their cousins the Tompiros as refugees from the Apaches sometime between 1672 and 1675. Consequently, this and subsequent events are treated after the narrative of 17th century Tompiro history.

The Tompiros in the 17th Century

AD 1598: Arrival of the Spanish Colony

The Onate colony spent about five days (June 17-22, 1598) at the Piro pueblo of Sevilleta awaiting the arrival of supplies. During this period Onate's two nephews, the maese de campo Juan de Zaldivar and his brother sargento mayor Vicente de Zaldivar, made a side trip into Abo Pass for "the discovery of the pueblos of Abo." (Pacheco et alia 1971b: 252) This is the only information available on this visitation, which must have been to both Abo and Tenabo.

At this point I will review the historical evidence that suggests the Abo and Tenabo were a single community. The first is that cited immediately above, where the phrase "Los pueblos de Abo" clearly indicates that the community of Abo was considered to include more than one site. The second evidence is the reference to a "second pueblo of Abo" in the document describing Onate's visit to the Salinas

Province in the autumn of 1598. (See detailed discussion of this visitation in Chapter 5.) Finally, there is mention in a letter by Fran Alonso de Peinado, dated October 4, 1622, of "los del pueblo de Guerra de Abo y Penabo" (Scholes and Bloom 1945: 68), which translates as "those (people) of the warlike pueblo of Abo and Penabo (Tenabo)." This last clearly shows that the inhabitants of the two sites were considered to be one people. This may in part explain why there are so few references to Tenabo in the Spanish colonial documents, a reference to "Abo" being a reference to the two sites together as a united community. A similar situation may have obtained between Cueloce (LA 120) and Pataoce (LA 83, Pueblo Pardo) among the Eastern Tompiros, and between Yunque-Yunque and San Juan among the Tewas.

In the Vassalage of San Juan, dated September 9, 1598, the Salinas Province was given into the charge of the missionary Fran Francisco de San Miguel, along with the pueblo of Pecos, the pueblos of the Galisteo Basin, and the Vaquero Apaches, but there is no evidence that this priest ever visited any of the pueblos of the Salinas Province. (Hammond and Rey 1953: 345)

In October of 1598, Onate made a visit to the Salinas Province. (See Chapter 5 for a discussion of his route and identification of the pueblos visited.) At the pueblo of Acolocu (Cuarac) on October 12, 1598 a formal "Act of Obedience and Vassalage" was drawn up and assented to by the "chieftains": "Xay, captain of the pueblo of Paaco (La 24, near Tijeras); Acilici, said to be chieftain of the pueblo of Cuzaya (Chilili); Tegualpa, captain of the pueblo of Junetre (Taxique); (and) Ayquian and Aguin, chieftains of the pueblo of Acolocu (Cuarac)..." (Hammond and Rey 1953: 348) Again, on October 17, 1598, another "Act of Obedience and Vassalage" was drawn up at Cueloce (Gran Quivira) and assented to by "Yolha, chief of the pueblo and people of Cueloce; Pocataqui, chief of the pueblo of Xenopue (Pueblo Blanco, LA 51); Haye, chief of the pueblo of Patasci (Pueblo Pardo, LA 83); and Chili, chief of the pueblo of Abo. (Hammond and Rey 1953: 351)

These fantastic documents proclaimed to the Indians that the Spaniards had come to save their souls and protect them from their enemies, discussed the spiritual and temporal authorities of the Pope and the King of Spain, proclaimed the father commissary (Fray Alonso Martinez) as the representative of God and the Pope and the governor (Onate) as the representative of the King, and said that "they (the Indians) should submit to our king entirely of their own accord, as they were free and not subject to any other ruler... Therefore, they should consider whether they wished to render obedience." (Hammond and Rey 1953: 351-351)

The documents then continue: The chieftains, having listened to the above, discussed it among themselves, and having understood the meaning of it all, replied with signs of contentment, in spontaneous accord and agreement, that they desired to become vassals of our king and lord... (Hammond and Rey 1953: 352)

I seriously doubt that the Indians "understood the meaning of it all." I have already discussed the translation problem in Chapter 5, and, to compound it, there were a number of European concepts and institutions mentioned in the documents that had no Pueblo Indian counterparts, and it is even questionable whether the interpreter, Don Tomas, a Mexican (Aztec) Indian living at Santo Domingo since 1591, clearly understood these concepts himself. What probably got through to the "chieftains" was that the Spaniards wanted to be friends, would help them against their enemies, and wanted to perform a ceremony sealing the bargain. If this is so, then it is little wonder that an offer of friendship and alliance (as the Indians understood it) would be perfectly acceptable to them, as would be the performance of a ceremony to conclude the deal. This ceremony is described as follows: The governor (Onate) told them (the chieftains) that since they were going to do so (render obedience and vassalage), they should rise, as a sign that they did, for during all this time they had remained seated, kiss the hand of the father commissary (Fray Martinez) and his lordship (Onate), and embrace them. The chiefs did as they had been told... (Hammond and Rey 1953: 352-353)

On the basis of these farcical performances, the Spaniards could later claim that any resistance to their demands on the part of the Indians was an act of rebellion against the King of Spain.

AD 1599: "Rebellion" at Cueloce

Sometime in mid-1599, Vicente de Zaldivar passed through the Salinas Province on his way to "the South Sea" (the Pacific Ocean). On reaching a Tompiro pueblo, referred to as the pueblo of Los Jumanos and probably to be identified with Cueloce (Gran Quivira), he asked for supplies, and was refused them. As his force was small, apparently only four solders accompanied him, he did not attempt to enforce his will, but notified Onate, who responded with a punitive expedition against the pueblo (testimony of Captain Juan de Ortega, July 31, 1601 and Onate's report of March 22, 1601 in Hammond and Rey 1953: 620, 665).

The most detailed account of this incident is given by

Gines de Herrera Horta, July 30, 1601: A short time ago the governor (Onate) set out with a large force to collect what they call in that land the "tribute of the blankets." His aim also was to visit a pueblo of the Jumanes, which means striped Indians, those who have a striped painted across the nose. The governor said that he wanted to punish their insolence toward the sargento mayor, his nephew (Vicente de Zaldivar). The latter said that when he came by that pueblo with some solders and asked the inhabitants for provisions and tortillas, as his men were hungry and exhausted, the Indians refused to furnish any. On the contrary, this witness (Herrera Horta) was told that they offered them stones to eat.

When the governor arrived at this pueblo of the Jumanes, he asked them for blankets. The natives gathered about twelve or fourteen and gave them to him, explaining that they had no more which they could give. With this the governor withdrew to a watering place half a league away. On the following day, he returned to the pueblo, taking along an Indian interpreter who knew the language of the Jumanes. Through him he told them that he was going to punish them because they had refused to furnish the sargento mayor with provisions, and that those who submitted peacefully he would treat kindly. After this the governor at once ordered his men to set fire to certain groups of houses of the Indians, whereupon they took to their houses and terraces. Then the governor ordered that they be showered with a volley of harquebus shots. Five or six Indians were killed in this manner, not to mention those who must have been wounded. Two whom the governor considered very warlike he ordered hanged, and so they were. He asked the interpreter to tell the Indians something which this witness does not remember. A solder thought that what the interpreter was saying to them was against the interests of the Spaniards. He told the governor so, and the latter had the interpreter hanged. (Hammond and Rey 1953: 650-651)

The identity of the interpreter is unknown. This attack on the pueblo presumably occurred in the late summer or autumn of 1599. The Tompiros thus got their first taste of Spanish steel , but it apparently did not intimidate them, to judge by the subsequent events of the "Jumano War" in 1601.

AD 1601: "The Jumano War"[8]

Sometime between mid-April and mid-May of 1601 five Spanish soldiers attempted to desert the new colony. Their rout led them through the Salinas Province and to the pueblo of Abo, where they were attacked by the Tompiros. Two of their number, Juan de Castaneda and Bernabe de Santillan, were killed, along with more than twenty horses, apparently remounts for the long journey to New Spain. The other Spaniards escaped and returned to San Gabriel to warn of the "uprising." (Hammond and Rey 1953: 704, 789, 7895)

The news of this was probably very unwelcome to Onate as he was then making preparations for his journey out onto the southern Plains in search of the now-legendary land of Quivira. However, it appears that the killing of the two Spaniards caused a stir among the other Pueblo Indians, who had just spent three drought- and famine-ridden years supporting the Spanish colony through forced tribute. (See discussion in Chapter 7.) These signs of restlessness were viewed with considerable alarm by the colonists and the missionaries, who petitioned Onate not to leave on his expedition without first suppressing the threatened revolt.. (Hammond and Rey 1953: 704, 789, 791, 795, 798-799, 802, 805-805)

In response to the petition, Onate called a conference of the Spanish captains and solders, which agreed that the Tompiros should be punished without further delay. (Hammond and Rey 1953: 704, 802, 806) Vicente de Zaldivar, who had defeated the Acomas in 1599, was placed in charge of the punitive expedition. Most of our information regarding the events of the expedition derives from documents concerned with Zaldivar's services to the Spanish colony, hence his role and activities are well known, but the overall sequence of events is unevenly reported.

It is not certain how many Spaniards took part in the punitive expedition, but "more than thirty" are mentioned as being wounded during the siege of Acolocu, so perhaps about seventy men, the size of the Spanish force that attacked Acoma, may have been present. (Hammond and Rey 1953: 799)[9] Apparently this force approached the Salinas Province from the north by way of the Galisteo Basin and "as they were on their way to that pueblo (Abo), the Indians heard of it and appealed for help to their neighbors and surrounding pueblos and assembled their warriors at the pueblo of Agualagu (Acolocu, that is: Cuarac)." (Hammond and Rey 1953: 705)

As the Spanish force advanced towards Acolocu (Cuarac) its vanguard was attacked by a large force of warriors, said to number more than 800, and "a serious and dangerous clash took place since we (the Spaniards) were unprepared." (Hammond and Rey 1953: 7065, 795, 799, 802, 806) However, Vicente de Zaldivar arrived with the main Spanish force and drove the Indians into the pueblo, where they fortified themselves. The date on which this occurred is not specified, but we know it was on a Monday, probably around the end of May 1601.

As Cuarac itself probably only had a population of about 450 persons at the time. (See Chapter 7), this pueblo could only field about 90 warriors. Therefore, if the 800+ warrior figure is to be believed, there was a major concentration of warriors from the Tompiro pueblos. Abo and Tenabo together could probably field about 160 warriors, consequently the majority, some 550 warriors, must have come from Cueloce, Xenopue, and the Chupadera Basin pueblos. If my population calculations in Chapter 7 are correct for the AD 1580–1600 period, then the Jumanes Mesa and Chupadera Basin pueblos could have fielded up to 855 warriors. Clearly then, there was sufficient manpower among the Tompiros to provide the more than 800 warriors claimed by the Spaniards to have opposed them at Acolocu. There is no indication that Tajique or Chilili contributed any warriors to this battle.

After driving the warriors back into Acolocu, Zaldivar rode around the pueblo with an interpreter and a group of ten Spaniards: "he summoned them to peace and promised them justice, repeating this offer at various places in the pueblo, but the Indians refused to accept and attacked with arrows and stones." (Hammond and Rey 1953: 806) The Spaniards made camp and held a meeting at which it was decided to besiege the pueblo. Another offer of peace was made to the Indians, but was answered with another shower of stones and arrows: the Tompiros wanted to fight. (Hammond and Rey 1953: 705, 795, 802-803, 806)

It is stated that the siege of Acolocu began on a Monday and lasted until the following Saturday, a total of six days and nights. (Hammond and Rey 1953: 705, 799) Apparently, the Spaniards encircled the pueblo with foot soldiers and reserved the horsemen for support to those sections coming under attack from the Indians. The full sequence of events is not known, but on one of the first two evenings of the siege there was "a great onrush of more than two hundred Indians" in the face of which the Spaniards wavered : "the solders wanted to withdraw and abandon the siege," states Captain Juan de Vitoria Carbajal but, as the "Indians attacked through a street,...the maese de campo (Zaldivar), who happened to be close by, fought them all alone with his horse and arms with such determination that he forced them to fall back and take refuge." (Hammond and Rey 1953: 792) Zaldivar was badly wounded in this engagement. (Hammond and Rey 1953: 792, 806)

The Spanish witnesses agree that the Spaniards were so hard pressed to keep the Indians bottled up in Acolocu that they had no time to eat or sleep. More than one Spaniard was impressed by the Indians' bravery, stating "the Indians defended themselves very well." (Hammond and Rey 1953: 792, 799)

By Wednesday evening it was apparent to the Tompiros that the Spaniards were not going to give up the siege. As a result, a group of over 300 broke out at dawn on Thursday and, after a clash with Zaldivar, Pero Gomez Duran, and Captain Gaspar Lopez de Tavora, who had pursued them on horseback, managed to escape. (Hammond and Rey 1953: 795-796, 799)

By noon Friday, Zaldivar was so tired from his exertions and weakened by his wounds that he had to be helped onto his horse in order to repel another escape attempt by the besieged Indians. (Hammond and Rey 1953: 792, 796, 803, 806-807) It appears, however, that at least some made good their escape.

Finally, on Saturday Acolocu surrendered. Of those Indians taken prisoner all of the women, old men, and young men of less than 25 years of age were set free with a warning against further rebellious activity. These numbered about 400 persons. The men over 25 years old were distributed as slaved to the Spanish solders who had taken part in the siege; it was later reported that within about six months most of these slaves had escaped. (Hammond and Rey 1953: 792, 796) What is interesting is that the total captured Indians was probably no more than about 500 persons, which is close to my 450-person population estimate for Cuarac. It would appear, then, that most of the Tompiro warriors managed to escape at various times during the siege, and that the persons captured by the Spaniards were mainly the native Tiwas of Cuarac. There is no count of the number of warriors killed, but I doubt that it exceeded 100 men.

With the capture of Acolocu (Cuarac), the punitive expedition returned to San Gabriel, and many of its members then participated in the expedition onto the Southern Plains. The Jumano War had thus come to a conclusion with a decisive victory for the Spaniards...or had it?

Let us briefly review the major points of this conflict: (1) the people of the Abo-Tenabo community killed two Spaniards and a number of horses; (2) this event provoked unrest among the other Pueblo Indians, which forced Onate to delay his Quivira expedition in order to punish the people of Abo; (3) upon being advised of the approach of the Spanish punitive expedition the people of Abo had marshaled a large force of 700+ warriors drawn not just from their own community, but also from other Tompiro communities;

(4) this Indian force did not wait for a Spanish attack upon Abo, but met the Spaniards at Cuarac and used Cuarac as a fortress against the Spaniards; (5) the Spanish siege of Cuarac took six days to force a surrender from the pueblo; (6) most of the Tompiros slipped away from Cuarac during the siege, leaving the native Tiwas of Cuarac to surrender to the Spaniards; (7) most of the Tiwas were pardoned by Zaldivar, but their warriors, together with those Tompiros who had not escaped, were temporarily enslaved; (8) the Spanish force withdrew without directly attacking Abo or its allied pueblos.

I suggest that the Tompiros showed an excellent grasp of strategy by their selection of a field of battle far removed from their own villages, where they could fight the Spaniards without endangering their own families or homes. Clearly, the Tiwas of Cuarac were the big losers: confronted by a force of over 700 Tompiro warriors they had no choice but to allow their village to be commandeered by the Tompiros as a staging point and fortress.

Zaldivar, when he arrived with his force at Cuarac, could not afford to by-pass the pueblo and continue on to Abo for fear of attack from the rear by the Indians concentrated at Cuarac. Thus, the Tompiros forced Zaldivar to commit himself to a siege at Cuarac. This siege exhausted and damaged the Spanish force so severely that for it to march on to Abo or any of the other Tompiro pueblos would have been to risk a disastrous defeat. In contrast, despite their losses in killed and wounded, the Tompiros still greatly outnumbered the Spaniards, were on their own home ground and thus had access to supplies, and had several pueblos of greater defensibility than Cuarac into which they could retreat.

I would guess that Zaldivar realized that he had won a hollow victory, and that this was a major factor behind his leniency towards the Tiwas of Cuarac. Being a good military man, Zaldivar also would realize that pursuit of the enemy was dangerous in the extreme. His best choice was that which he took: proclaim a factory and then withdraw in all due haste to San Gabriel. Thus, I would judge that while the siege was won by the Spaniards, the strategic victory belonged to the Tompiros, and the real victims of the whole affair were the Tiwas of Cuarac.

It is notable that the Spanish civil authorities did not bother the Tompiros for many years after the "Jumano War." That military encounter demonstrates the truth of the Tompiros' reputation for being "warlike," as noted by the Espejo Expedition in 1583 (Hammond and Rey 1966: 175) and by Fray Alonso de Peinado in 1622. (Scholes and Bloom 1945: 68)

This reputation as being "rough customers" apparently restrained the Spanish authorities from extending their control over the Tompiros until about AD 1630, preceded by a 15-year period of missionary penetration, and even then, there are hints that it was only after the great population decline that such authority was exerted to any great extent. A parallel situation seems to have existed among the Zunis, who revolted against Spanish authority in AD 1632 and apparently were not brought under control again until ca. 1659–1660, when they voluntarily accepted missionaries. (See Hodge 1937: 91-97; Baldwin 1984c.) This casts a slightly different light on Spanish-Pueblo Indians relations during the 17th century: it is now clear that some peripheral groups such as the Zunis and Tompiros existed for periods of some years completely outside of Spanish control, a geo-political situation previously only recognized for the Hopis during the 18th and early 19th centuries. (Dozier 1970: 86-88)

AD 1614–1629: Beginning of Missionization

Fray Alonso de Peinado arrived in New Mexico in 1610 as commissary (leader) of the missions in New Mexico.[10] He was soon replaced in that capacity by Fray Isidro Ordonez, who became embroiled in a dispute with Governor Pedro de Peralta, whereas Peinado was critical of Ordonez' conduct.

The relations between Ordonez and his predecessor (Peinado) became so strained that Peinado decided to "banish himself" and undertake the conversion of the pueblo of Chilili...His work there started not later than 1614, and possibly as early as 1613. In 1616 Fray Augustin de Burgos went to Chilili to assist him in the baptism of his neophytes. (Scholes and Bloom 1944: 335)

This founding of a mission among the Salinas Tiwas came only shortly after the founding of missions among the Southern Tiwas of the Rio Grande Valley at Sandia in 1610 by Fray Esteban de Perea and at Isleta in 1612 by Fray Juan de Salas, both of whom were later to come to the Salinas Province. (Scholes and Bloom 1944: 334) While Peinado's mission of La Natividad de Nuestra Senora was centered at Chilili, he undoubtedly made visitations to Taxique and Cuarac. By 1622 he, or perhaps his assistant Fray Burgos, had been received peacefully by the Abo-Tenabo community. (Scholes and Bloom 1945: 68) While Fray Peinado piously claimed that the Tompiros of Abo and Tenabo had been "reduced" to Christianity, it is more likely that the missionaries had simply been received with tolerance and allowed to preach and to perform some poorly-understood baptisms.[11] Peinado's missionary activity was terminated by his death on

November 26 of either 1622 or 1623 and he was buried at Chilili. (Vetancurt 1697: 103; Scholes and Bloom 1944: 335)

Another guardian is not known for Chilili until the 1630s, but Abo is recorded to have Fray Francisco Fonte in 162 and the mission at Cuarac[12] was founded at least by 1628 by Fray Juan Gutierrez de la Chica. (Scholes and Bloom 1945: 68, 73) It also appears that Fray Juan de Salas, the guardian of Isleta, was making trips into the Salinas Province in the mid- and late 1620s to administer to the Salinas Tiwas probably using the Hell's Canyon-Gotera Canyon route to pass through the Manzano Mountains. His activity is mentioned by Fray Alonso de Benavides in connection with the requests by the Plains Jumanos for priests to come visit them in their home territories; in Benavides' own words:

> Years ago, while a friar named Fray Juan de Salas was going about engaged in the conversion of the Tompiro and Salinero Indians, the largest salt deposits in the world are in their territory, which on that side (i.e., east of the Manzano foothills) borders the Xumanas, a war was being waged between them. When Father Fray Juan de Salas returned in quest of the Salineros, the Xumanas said that those who came back in search of the poor were good people. Therefore, they took a liking to the priest and begged him to go live among them, and every year they came to seek him. (Forrestal and Lynch 1954: 57; Spanish test in Anonymous 1962: 57-58)[13]

Benavides' ambiguous phraseology makes it unclear which of the three groups mentioned (Tompiros, Salineros, and Plains Jumanos) were at war, but in the second edition (1634) of his book he states:

> Several years earlier, messengers came from this nation (the Plains Jumanos) every summer to beg Father Fray Juan de Salas, in particular, that he go to baptize them, as they wanted to become Christians. They had become attached to him on seeing him come to the rescue of some unfortunate people that they were ill-treating. (Hodge, Hammond and Rey 1945: 92)

Since it appears that Fray Salas' main concern was with the Salinas Tiwas (the Salineros), and since it is doubtful the Tompiros would have put up with any mistreatment from the Plains Jumanos, it would appear that the "war" was between the Salinas Tiwas and the Plains Jumanos. It is likely that Fray Salas was present on an occasion when the Tiwas were attacked by the Plains Jumanos and had intervened between the combatants, achieving a promise of peace between the two hostile groups. I suspect that the Plains Jumanos characterization of the Tiwas was "poor people" was an expression of contempt for the Tiwas, rather than the charitable expression Benavides makes it out to be. (Benavides always did see the world through rose-tinted glasses.)

In 1627 Benavides made a tour of the Salinas Province in his capacity of custos, during which he visited Las Humanas (LA 120, Gran Quivira) and had an encounter with an "Indian sorcerer": "The sorcerer became greatly enraged, and shouted in a loud voice: "Because you Spaniards and Christians are crazy and live as crazy people, you wish to teach us to be crazy. I asked him in what respect we were crazy. He must have seen a Holy Week procession of flagellants in some Christian pueblo, for he answered: "You Christians are so crazy that you all go along the streets together scourging yourselves like crazy people and shedding your blood. Thus, you must be trying to make this pueblo crazy, too." With this, he left the pueblo, loudly crying and enraged, saying that he did not want to be crazy. All laughed at this, and I more than the others, for I realized and felt certain that it was the demon who was fleeing, confounded by the power of the divine word." (Forrestal and Lynch 19554: 21-22)

The extravagant behavior of this "sorcerer" suggests that he may have actually been a Pueblo Indian clown who was mocking Benavides, hence the laughter of the other Indians. After all, the Pueblo Indians themselves use flagellation with yucca whips for initiations into religious societies and in coming-of-age ceremonies!

AD 1630s–1950s: Assertion of Spanish Control

The records for this 30-year period are very scant, hence it is mainly through comparing the situations at the beginning and end of the period that we may chart what must have been the significant developments. As already noted for the Piros and in Chapter 7, the 1630s was the decade of drastic population decline among the Pueblo Indians, yet for the Salinas Province there is no surviving mention of the epidemics and their consequences. It may very well be, however, that the weakening of Tompiro numerical strength was the factor that encouraged Spanish settlement in the Manzano foothills near the pueblos of the Salinas Tiwas, especially near Taxique. In 1629, there was not a single

Spaniard in the Salinas Province other than missionaries, but in 1659 around two dozen families of Spaniards were present.[14] There is no record of Spanish settlement near Tompiro pueblos, hence they may still have been feared (or perhaps the Tompiros made it clear they would not tolerate any encroachment on their farmlands). Some of the Spanish families had sufficiently close relationships with the Indians that family members later acted as translators, e.g., Jose de (Gonzalez) Apodaca and Jose de Leyva (Nevares) as Tiwa interpreters for Governor Otermin in 1682 (Hackett 1942, II: 359) and Hernan Martin Serrano as interpreter of the Plains Jumano language in 1684. (Chavez 1954: 72)

With the arrival of additional missionaries in 1629, missionization of the Tompiros began in earnest. Fray Francisco Letrado was assigned to Las Humanas in 1629 and constructed (with Indian labor) the sizeable church of San Isidro. He also had a temporary convento built onto the southwestern corner of an Indian room block (Mount 7) that included several remodeled Indian rooms. Both the church and convento have been excavated. (See Vivian 1964: 60-83; Hayes 1968; Hayes, Young and Warren 1981: 31-36.) However, by 1632 Letrado had been reassigned to the Zunis and the mission lapsed into the status of a visits of Abo until 1659. It thus seems unlikely that Christianity had any great impact upon the Tompiros of Las Humanas during this period. A chapel was also constructed at Tabira, attributed to Fray Francisco de Azebedo, and has also been excavated. (Vetancurt 1698: 81-82; Stubbs 1959)

While the Tompiros of Jumanes Mesa remained on the mission frontier, Abo became a major mission center. Construction of the church and convento of San Gregorio de Abo was probably begun early in the 1630s. A tree-ring cutting date of AD 1649r from the west bell-tower of the church is a probably indicator of the completion date for the church. (Robinson, Hannah, and Harrill 1972: 83), and, after sufficient funds had been obtained by collecting pinon nuts and sending them for sale in Mexico City, an organ was purchased for the church and transported to New Mexico, probably in 1656. (See Baldwin 1984c.) The excavation of the church and convento is reported in Toulouse (1949). It is said that a chapel was constructed at Tenabo by Fray Francisco de Azebedo (Vetancurt 1698: 81-82), but it has not yet been located archaeologically. No historical events involving the church or pueblo at Abo are known for the period 1629–1659, other than what has been mentioned above.

I believe that Tenabo was abandoned before 1659 since the major documentation of the years 1659–1662 does not once mention it. The people of Tenabo were probably resettled within Abo. It is possible, however, that Tenabo might have been occupied seasonally until abandonment of the Salinas Province in 1672–1675 since it is situated near some of the best agricultural land in Abo Pass. The Chupadera Basin pueblos were probably abandoned during the great depopulation of the 1630s, with the survivors moving into the Abo-Tenabo community. (See discussion in Chapter 7.)

The three Salinas Tiwa missions seem to have had priests throughout this period. Few events are known, but in 1640 supporters of anti-clerical Governor Rosas (1637–1641) raided the convento of Cuarac: "At Cuarac the room that served as headquarters for the business of the Holy Office (the Inquisition) was desecrated..." (Scholes 1936: 323-324), possibly with intent to destroy documents dangerous to the governor. This raid may be that later recounted second hand by Governor Diego de Penalosa during his own hearing before the Inquisition:

When the defendant (Penalosa) was in New Mexico on his way to visit the province of Las Salinas, certain persons who were with him...told him that Don Diego de Guadalajara...and a son of his, named Don Francisco de Guadalajara..., went to the pueblo of Cuarac in Las Salinas with a judicial order... and climbed into the convent of the pueblo, sacked the pantries and other offices, and even ate from the chests in the sacristy (i.e., ate the consecrated bread and drank the consecrated wine of the Host), from which they took also some ornaments, or vestments and chasubles, which were (afterward) recognized upon Don Diego and don Francisco de Guadalajara. When the defendant was dining in the convent (of Cuarac) this matter came up in the conversation, and Father Fray Francisco de Salazar, guardian of the convent, said: "It happened in this very house." He was corroborated by Fray Juan de la Ascencion, Fray Fernando de Velasco, and Fray Nicolas de Fleitas (sic, Freitas), who were all at the table eating. (Hackett 1937: 259)

It was also during these decades of church-state infighting that Apache attacks became a major menace to both the Spanish colony and the Pueblo Indians. We have little specific information, but it is unlikely that the Salinas Province profited very much from the supposed protection provided by the armed encomenderos. Scholes (1942: 17) states:

During the administration of Governor Samaniego (1652–1656) the Apaches raided the Jumano pueblo east of Abo, profaned the church and carried off twenty-seven women and children captives. An expedition led by Juan Dominguez de Mendoza was sent against them and left them "well punished."

It is unclear which of the Eastern Tompiro pueblos was involved in the above event, but Tabira being the smaller in population, and thus the less formidable is a good possibility.

These three decades come to an end with the famine years of 1658 and 1659, when it is recorded that the conventos of Taxique and Cuarac were among those that distributed supplies to their parishioners in the form of "wheat, corn, and cattle." (Hackett 1937: 191) It is clear from this, as well as from the records of the early 1660s, that the missions maintained agricultural fields and herds of domestic animals for three reasons: (1) to feed the priests, (2) to provide income to the Franciscan order through sales of the products to the Spanish colonists, and (3) to provide emergency food stocks during famine periods. Indians herders and agriculturalists were employed by the missions to maintain these herds and fields. These individuals and their families were among those included in the ten casas reservadas, the households exempted from the encomienda in order that they might support the mission and its priest. (Scholes 1942: 109, 260-263)

AD 1659–1661: Nicolas de Aguilar vs the Priests

This period is that of the self-serving and anti-clerical Governor Lopez de Mendizabal, whose chief minion in the Salinas Province was a ruffian named Nicolas de Aguilar. As part of the changes made in New Mexico by the new governor the previous alcalde mayor of the jurisdiccion of Las Salinas, Captain Pedro de Leyva, was dismissed and replaced with Aguilar "because he (Lopez de Mendizabal) knew that Leyba was partial to the affairs of the Church." (Hackett 1937: 181, 205) This change in the office of alcalde mayor seems to have occurred in the autumn of 1659-1660.

However, even before Aguilar's appointment, the governor had made his present felt. During his visitation of the Salinas Province, probably in the summer of 1659, the governor commanded the Indians to carry salt from the salt lakes down to the Rio Grande:

For the purpose of loading the mine wagons (that had been constructed by the governor's order), he (the governor) obliged the Indians of the six pueblos of Las Salinas to carry the salt on their shoulders and on their own animals as far as the hacienda of Captain Don Diego de Guadalajara, which

is distant from the said pueblos twenty-four, twenty-eight, and thirty leagues, one way only, without giving any pay, either to the carpenters (who constructed the wagons) or to those who carried the salt. He oppressively and violently commanded them to do it, and did not even furnish them with food. (Hackett 1937: 188)

Furthermore: Taking out the salt...has occasioned among the native serious illnesses and convulsions, some of them being permanently incapacitated, as was found to be the case in the pueblo of Cuarac, both on account of the haste and the misfortunes attending their departure, and because of the long distance which they carried the salt. (Hackett 1937: 189)

This salt was loaded on the wagons and went for sale to the Parral mining district in Nueva Vizcaya, and it was claimed that the governor had the alcaldes mayores seize all sorts of hides, buckskins, and even the sleeping mats of the Indians for use as coverings for the wagons. (Hackett 1937: 188) It was also to facilitate this salt trade that the governor had the Indians of Sevilleta re-installed at their old pueblo, as has already been described above. This salt export was to become a continuing feature of the governor's relationship with the Salinas Province, as salt storage for the governor is noted at the pueblo of Abo in 1660 when Nicolas de Aguilar removed some Indians from Mass on Sunday to work for the governor (Hackett 1837: 155; Kessell n.d.: 360, and in 1661 the governor had 87 fanegas of salt stored at Abo which were seized by the new governor, Diego de Penalosa. (Hackett 1937: 254)

In addition to the salt, the governor also forced the Indians to transport large quantities of pinon nuts: "sixty laborers from Cuarac were forced to go to the pueblo of the Jumanos (Las Humanas) and from there to the Rio Grande with loads of pinon, and were engaged in this labor for seventeen days." (Scholes 1942: 48)

Shortly after installment of Nicolas de Aguilar as alcalde mayor of Las Salinas the priests came under attack from the civil government. The first incident was an accusation against Fray Diego de Parraga, guardian of the missions at Taxique, leveled by an Indian of Taxique named Francisco Muza or Mussa[15], either a cantor or sacristan in the church, who claimed that Fray Parraga had cohabited with Muza's wife for three years, the relationship producing a daughter. The governor sent Aguilar to Taxique in order to bring the woman to Santa Fe, and Aguilar claimed that at the pueblo Fray Parraga admitted his paternity of the little girl to Aguilar. During the subsequent investigation of the charges by Fray Garcia de San Francisco, who was acting as vice-custodian at the time, a jurisdictional clash occurred between Aguilar and the vice-custodian that resulted in the excommunication of Aguilar in May 1660. According to Fray Nicolas de Freitas, Fray Parraga was found to be innocent by the church authorities. (Hackett 1937: 134-135, 167, 169-171, 202, 214-215; Kessell n.d.: 51-54, 176-177, 208-211)

This excommunication did not slow down Aguilar: he made himself so generally obnoxious to the priests that Gray Nicolas de Freitas resigned in protest from his mission post at Cuarac in June 1660 and it was not long before most of the other mission priests of the Salinas Province also resigned their posts and joined Fray Freitas at the convento of Senecu, which was the headquarters of the vice-custodian. The various acts by Aguilar prompting these resignations were his forbidding any Indians to serve the priests as cooks, herdsmen, interpreters, or in other capacities needed to keep the missions functioning; his forbidding of the punishment of miscreant Indians by the priests or the Indian authorities; his forbidding the Indians of Cuarac to attend church services; and his punishment of Indian cantores of Cuarac who had gone to Las Humanas in June 1660 to help celebrate the fiesta of San Buenaventura. (Hackett 1937: 135-156, 150-151, 159-160; Kessell n.d.: 24-27, 54-60) Most of these priests subsequently returned to their posts.

However, in October of 1660 Aguilar caused new consternation among the churchmen by his active support of the governor's decree that the Indians were free to "dance the catzinas." This appears to have been taken up with enthusiasm by the Salinas Tiwas of Cuarac and Taxique: a kachina dance being held in public at Cuarac where Fray Diego de Parraga chided the Indians for performing it, and two dances are reported at Taxique one on the "day of San Miguel" (October 16)[16] and a second a few days later when the kachinas danced on the roof of the church itself. (Hackett 1937: 131-132, 137, 142, 172, 177, 178-179; Kessell n.d.: 3, 9, 85-86, 220) Fray Fernando de Velasco later collected all the masks at Taxique. (Hackett 1937: 145; Kessell n.d.: 243-244) There is no mention of public kachina danced at any of the Tompiro pueblos. This brief period of religious freedom for the Pueblo Indians in 1660 and 1661 came to an end with the arrival of a new governor in late 1661.

In 1659, a priest was again assigned to Las Humanas. Fray Diego de Santander served both as missionary to Las Humanas and as secretary to the vice-custodian, which latter duty must have kept him absent from his mission for considerable periods of time. Nonetheless, he accomplished at least the beginning of construction of the massive church and convento of San Buenaventura, both of which have been excavated. (See Vivian 1964: 84-93.)

The Apaches de los Siete Rios, who had replaced the Plains Juanos along the Rio Pecos, were noted as coming to trade with the Eastern Tompiros at Las Humanas and Tabira, but were on hostile terms with the Salinas Tiwas due, at least in party, to the killing of some Apaches by the inhabitants of Cuarac. (Hackett 1937: 143, 144; Kessell n.d.: 225-226, 232-233)

AD 1666–1671: Troublous Times in the Salinas Province.

The year AD 1666 marked the beginning of the end for the Salinas Province: in that year began a series of crop failures within the whole of New Mexico that led to a famine in 1668 which resulted in the deaths of more than 450 persons at Las Humanas alone. (Hackett 1937: 272) These crop failures correlate with years of below normal tree-ring growth (Table 7-8), suggesting drought conditions, and a report of a "plague of locusts" in 1667. (Hankins 1962: 15) And these hardships were exacerbated by raids from Apacheans. (Hackett 1937: 271-272)

Apparently, there was some relief in 1669, but in 1670 famine again occurred throughout New Mexico, to be followed in 1671 by an epidemic. (Hackett 1937: 302; Maas 1929: 57)

During this period of misfortune unrest with Spanish rule apparently grew up among the Tompiros, as it did among their relatives, the Piros of the Rio Grande Valley. Sometime after the suppression of El Tanbulita's Piro conspiracy in 1668, another anti-Spanish conspiracy was exposed among the Indians of the Salinas Province. This was headed by Don Esteban Clemente, a native of Abo who was well educated in Spanish culture and who had supported the church authorities against Governor Lopez de Mendizabal and the alcalde mayor Nicolas de Aguilar in 1660. (Kessell 1980) Perhaps Don Esteban was reacting to the misfortunes of his people, as suggested by Kessell (1980: 16); certainly, he embraced the traditional Pueblo Indian religion as the Spanish "found in his house a large number of idols and entire kettles full of idolatrous powdered herbs, feathers, and other trifles." (Hackett 1942, II: 300) Don Esteban was hanged for his role as leader of the conspiracy.

Also, as I have suggested in Chapter 5, it appears that Tabira was abandoned sometime during this period. It seems likely that the population losses sustained by the Tompiros and Salinas Tiwas during the famines and epidemic were a major factor in weakening their hold on the Salinas Province, eventually leading to its abandonment.

AD 1672–1677: Abandonment of the Salinas Province

On August 13, 1672, in convocation at the mission of San Diego de Jemez, the Franciscan missionaries in New Mexico officially installed the missionaries who were to serve for the next three years. (Bloom and Mitchell 1938) For the Salinas Province, these were Fray Diego de Parraga at Cuarac, Fray Sebastian de Aliri at Tajique and Chilili, and Fray Gil de Avila at Abo and Las Humanas. A week later, on August 20, 1672, the missionary for the prior triennium at Tajique and Chilili, Fray Francisco Gomez de la Cadena, prepared an inventory of the two missions. (Scholes and Adams 1952: 29-31) This latter is the last firm date we have for the Spanish-Pueblo Indian occupation of the Salinas Province.

The actual events of the abandonment of the Salinas Province are poorly known. Only two contemporary accounts are available: (1) a petition for aid, dated 1676, to the Viceroy of New Spain by Fray Francisco de Ayeta, accompanied by several documents composed by the local authorities in New Mexico; and (2) a further petition for aid by Ayeta, dated 1679.

Fran Francisco de Ayeta, the newly appointed procurador in charge of the triennial supply caravan from New Spain, arrived in New Mexico for the first time in the spring of 1675. (Hankins 1962: 26) Upon his return to Mexico City in 1676, Ayeta presented the first petition noted above and its accompanying documents. In these it is stated that the Apacheans had "destroyed five villages, setting fire to the churches, carrying off the sacred vessels, (and) profaning the holy images." (Hankins 1962: 28) These attacks had occurred between the departure of the supply caravan for Mexico City in 1672 and its return to New Mexico in the spring of 1675. It should be noted that the five villages were neither named nor attributed to the Salinas Province, and that Apache attacks on two named Pueblo Indians villages were noted: that upon Hawikuh in October 1672 and that upon Senecu in January 1675. (Hankins 1962: 18, 28)

Ayeta left New Mexico with the supply caravan, probably in the autumn of 1675, carrying with him the documents upon which the above petition was based, and probably arrived back in Mexico City in the spring of 1676. (Hankins 962: 26) Ayeta and the next supply caravan set out

for New Mexico in February 1677 and arrived in November 1677. (Hankins 1962: 30, 32) During Ayeta's absence from New Mexico, further conflicts with the Apacheans had occurred, including the depopulation of the Piro pueblo of Senecu.

Ayeta carried the news of these developments back to Mexico City, where they were presented in his second petition, which contains the following statements:

> It is public knowledge that from the year 1672 until your Excellency (the Viceroy) adopted measures for aiding that kingdom (of New Mexico), six pueblos were depopulated namely, that of Cuarac, with more than two hundred families, that of Las Humanas with more than five hundred, that of Abo with more than three hundred (in this latter they (the Apaches) burned the convent after having sacked it an murdered the missionary, who was Father Fray Pedro de Ayala, a native of Campeche, stripping him of his clothing, putting a rope around his neck, flogging him most cruelly, and finally killing him with the blows of the macana; after he was dead they surrounded the body with dead white lambs, and covered the privy parts, leaving him in this way, a thing t hat caused astonishment to the inhabitants of the said provinces when they went to see him...; His Divine Majesty knows the secret of this), that of Chilili with more than one hundred, Las Salinas (Tajique) with more than three hundred restored, as has been said, and Senecu. (Hackett 1937: 298; Spanish text in Maas 1929: 52)

This statement would seem to identify the five destroyed villages noted in Ayeta's first petition with the five Salinas pueblos that had survived until 1672. It is on this basis, plus the statement by Fray Silvestre Velez de Escalante in 1778[17], that modern writers had accepted an abandonment of the Salinas Province between 1672 and 1675. (e.g., A. Bandelier 1892: 256-257; Scholes in Scholes and Mera 1940: 283; Toulose 1949: 4; Vivian 1964: 30; Hayes in Hayes, Young and Warren 1981: 8).

However, there is another relevant statement within Ayeta's second petition: The carts in my (Ayeta's) charge in which the reinforcements were transported arrived in the said provinces (New Mexico) nine months after the 27th of February 1677, on which they left this City of Mexico. They immediately reinforced the frontiers with men and arms, and an effort was made to settle, as was done, those of Las Salinas (Tajique) and Senecu, which are the principal frontiers of the said provinces, and which, with Cuarac and Chilili, had been depopulated in the brief time between the departure of the petitioner from those provinces to ask for succor and his arrival with it (because) the barbarous Apaches compelled them by constant attacks to abandon (those places)... (Hackett 1937: 297; Spanish text in Maas 1929: 51)

This clearly places the abandonment of the Salinas Tiwa pueblos as being between the autumn of 1675 and November 1677, and suggests that Abo and Las Humanas may have been abandoned significantly earlier.

Further. There are curious distortions of the truth in Fray Ayeta's 1679 petition: (1) where he substitutes the term "families" for "persons" when describing the population sizes of the pueblos, as has been discussed in Chapter 7; and 92) in his colorful description of the fate of the priest at Abo, which is a direct steal, priest's name and all, from the events of the Apachean attack on Hawikuh in October 1672. (See Hodge 1937: 99.) These departures from the truth appear to be exercises in propaganda designed to favorably influence the authorities in Mexico City towards the grant of aid to the New Mexico colony. Unfortunately, from the historical point of view, such detected departures open up the remainder of Fray Ayeta's assertions to skepticism.

For example, Wilson (1985: 114-115) has challenged the generally accepted view that Apachean attacks were the primary cause of Salinas abandonment by pointing out that the Apacheans may have been used as convenient scapegoats to explain away current misfortunes.

Fray Ayeta's 1676 petition asserts direct Apachean assaults on the five unnamed villages, accompanied by looting, vandalism and burning of the churches. At Abo, Bandelier noted some evidence that may support a violent end to the occupation:

They (the Hispanic residents of Abo in the 1880s) tell me here that in the small rooms which still were found intact, when they first unearthed them, entire skeletons were found intact, not buried, but lying on the (?) floor. Also, that there were many signs of combustion, even in the church itself. I noticed that on some of the few beams still at the latter edifice, there are marks of burning, so that it looks as if the people had been slaughtered and the place burnt. (Lange and Riley 1966: 390)

Bandelier's report is partially confirmed by the results of Toulouse's excavation of the church and convento at Abo wherein "those (roof materials) recovered from the excavations were charred, presumably by a fire after the building was abandoned." (Toulouse 1949: 6) Further, a burned bench was found on the east porch of the convento. (Toulouse 1949: Plate 38)

Similarly, at Cuarac excavations of the church revealed evidence of burning: "charred and burned material from the roof, (and) charred and burned material from the choir loft in the area directly below its location" (Senter 1934: 173); and "charred rafters, fallen from the roof." (Ely 1935: 1353) Unfortunately, "very little information has been preserved on the excavation of the large church of San Buenaventura and its attached convento (at Las Humanas)" (Vivian n1964: 86), consequently it is unknown if similar evidences of burning were present there.

However, the above evidences of burning in the churches of Abo and Cuarac do not unequivocally favor Ayeta's attack-burn-and-plunder scenario of Salinas abandonment. It is possible that the pueblos were abandoned for other reasons, and the churches burned at a later date when parties of Apacheans or some other group investigated the empty villages. There was actually some archaeological evidence of this in the church of Cuarac where "blown drift and other debris" overlay the stone flagged floor and made a distinct layer between that floor and the fallen roof materials. (Senter 1934: 173)

In summary, contemporary documentation suggests an abandonment of Abo and Las Humanas between late 1672 and early 1675, and of the Salinas Tiwa pueblos between late 1675 and late 1677. There is some non-contemporary testimony dating to 1759, that Cuarac was abandoned before Tajique. (See Kessell 1979a.)

There is no clear statement as to where the Tompiro population of Abo and Las Humanas went after the abandonment of the Salinas Province, but on the basis of the population figures discussed in Chapter 7 it appears that the Tompiros joined their linguistic relatives, the Piros, in the Rio Grande Valley.

Bandelier (1892: 234, 257) states that after abandonment, the Salinas Tiwas joined the Southern Tiwas along the Rio Grande, basin this opinion on claims by the Tiwas of Ysleta del Sur to be descended from those of Cuarac.

Spanish residents of the Salinas Province dispersed to various locations in New Mexico: some to the Rio Grande Valley in the vicinity of the Piros and Southern Tiwas and come to the Galisteo Basin.[18] There is documentation that part of the aid given to refugees from the Salinas Province was deposited at the convento of Galisteo pueblo. (Hackett 1937: 288; Spanish text in Maas 1929: 48)

The Piros and Tompiros Together

AD 1674–1680: Before the Revolt

It seems probable that the influx of Tompiro refugees to the Rio Grande Valley pueblos of the Piros occurred before the end of 1674. The priest assigned to Abo in 1672, Fray Alonso Gil de Avila, apparently accompanied them, as he is noted as being in charge of the mission at Senecu during the winter of 1674–1675, where he was killed during an Apache attack. (Hackett 1937: 297; Maas 1929: 51) Due to the great decrease in population that had occurred prior to the influx of refugees, there was probably no difficulty in finding suitable arable lands along the Rio Grande for the agricultural support of the increase population. On the basis of population figures (see Chapter 7) I suggest that Socorro and Alamillo absorbed most or all of the Tompiro influx.

Apache attacks, however, continued to menace the mixed Piro-Tompiro population as during the summer of 1676 when Apaches operating from the Ladron and Magdalena Mountains raided the herds of sheep, cattle and horses at Socorro and Senecu. (Hankins 1962: 33) These attacks appear to have resulted in the abandonment of Senecu pueblo sometime between July 1676 and November 1677, as noted in Ayeta's petition of 1679. (Hackett 1937: 297; Maas 1929: 51)

Fray Ayeta used some of the men, arms and supplies brought by the caravan to New Mexico in 1677 to reestablish Senecu, repopulating it "with more than one hundred families of Christian Indians". (See my discussion of this in Chapter 7.)

AD 1680 and After: The Pueblo Revolt and its Aftermath

I will not rehash the main events of the famous Pueblo Revolt of 1680, as they have been adequately covered elsewhere. (e.g., Hackett 1942, Kessell 1979b, Chavez 1967) For the Piros and Tompiros, the most significant fact was that they were excluded from what was otherwise a universal plot against the Spaniards, according to the testimony of a Tewa Indian from Tesuque. (Hackett 1942, II: 234) Certainly, they did not rise in revolt on August 10 and 11, 1680.

In the northern half of the colony, the Spanish inhabitants of Santa Fe, together with refugees from La Canada and Los Cerrillos, were placed under siege by a large army of Pueblo Indians and Apacheans, and effectively lost contact with the rest of the colony. Most other Spaniards were killed almost immediately, except for a group of refugees who came under the command of Maestre de Campo Alonso Garcia in the Tiguex area, and who retreated south to the Piro pueblos under the mistaken belief that the governor and other Spaniards at Santa Fe were dead.

The presence of Alonso Garcia and a party of armed Spaniards at Isleta pueblo had prevented the outbreak of the revolt there. The Spanish refugees left Isleta for the south on August 14 and arrived at Socorro on August 24. They passed through Sevilleta on August 21 or 22, and its inhabitants joined in their retreat southward. (Hackett 1942, I: 70) While this party must have passed the pueblo of Alamillo, no mention was made of it.

Meanwhile, an "ambassador" of the revolting Indians had entered Socorro and been hidden there for three days until discovered by a Spaniard. (Hackett 1942, I: 74) Presumably, the Piros and Tompiros were being belatedly urged to join in the revolt. The presence of this emissary was one factor of many persuading the Spanish refugees to abandon Socorro on August 26 in order to continue their retreat southward along the camino real. (Hackett 1942, I: 72-83)

The retreating refugees had almost reached the camping spot of Fra Cristobal south of Senecu when they were overtaken by messengers from Governor Otermin on September 4, 1680. The refugees pitched camp at Fra Cristobal while Alonso Garcia and a group of Spaniards returned up the Camino Real to meet the governor's party. (Hackett 1942, I; 58-59)

Documents referring to the retreat from New Mexico indicate that Piros (and Tompiros) from all four Piro pueblos accompanied the Spaniards to the El Paso area. (Hackett 1942, I: 159, 204-205) The removal of the Indians from Alamillo and Senecu was not specifically noted during the retreat, while the removal of the Sevilleta Piros as far as Socorro is specifically noted, as is the expressed wish of the population of Socorro to leave with the Spaniards for fear of attack from the rebel Pueblo Indians. (Hackett 1942, I: 70-71)

At any rate, only 317 Piros and Tiwas (from Isleta) arrived at El Paso. As discussed in Chapter 7, this leaves about 900 Piros and Tompiros unaccounted for. Apparently, some Piros and Tompiros deserted the retreating Spaniards during the period of encampment at Fra Cristobal, according to the testimony of Lucas, a Piro from Socorro. (Hackett 1942, II: 243) Others may have slipped away at other times during the retreat, or even before the Spaniards left Socorro.

Essentially, then, only about 200 Piros-Tompiros reached El Paso, whereas some 900 persons returned to their pueblos to pick up the threads of their disrupted lives. This would have been during September 1680, in time to harvest the crops that had been left standing in the fields.

While Otermin's attempted reconquest of 1681–1682 is well documented (Hackett 1942), there appears to have been an earlier Spanish penetration at least as far north as Senecu, probably during the summer of 1681:

The governor (Otermin) decided that the father missionaries, with some solders, should enter the kingdom (New Mexico), and they traveled some seventy leagues to the north to the pueblo of Zenecu, where crops had been planted. When the fathers sought the Indians, they fled to the high sierra and refused to come down at their call, being suspicious, perhaps, that it might be their purpose to punish them for the outrage of the preceding year of 1680, and up to the present (1744) they have not come back to settle. (Hackett 19137: 398)

Lucas, the Piro of Socorro questioned by Otermin in December 1681, stated that he came in company with others of his nation from the place which they call Fray Cristobal to the pueblo of El Socorro, where they stayed for some time, during which the Apaches twice ambushed the, and later the Tiguas Indians came down for them by order of a captain, he does not know who he is, to bring them to the pueblo of La Isleta, where he has been most of the time. (Hackett 1942, II: 243)

Otermin, on his journey of attempted reconquest in November and December 1681, observed evidences confirming Lucas' account of Apache attacks on and abandonments of the Piro pueblos. Approaching the pueblo of Senecu, the Spaniards recognized many signs of the apache enemies on horseback and on foot, and going to the said pueblo to see what people there were, and what might be done, they found the said pueblo deserted and depopulated, the holy temple and the convent burned, only the walls having remained, and these badly demolished in parts. In the Towers of the church they found two bells, and another fallen in the cemetery...(and) a small piece of bronze ordinance... They saw many signs of the apostates having deserted the place from fear, being oppressed by the heathen Apaches... the houses of the pueblo...were standing and without a sign of being burning... (Hackett 1942, II: 203-204)

At the pueblo of Socorro it was found deserted and without people, the church and all the convent burned...and in the cloister, were the skeletons of two dead persons...the main plaza of the pueblo...was found enclosed and fortified with a low entrenchment made of adobes...On skirting its circumference there were found in a maize field the bones and skulls of two other dead persons...The whole circuit of the plaza was full of ears of maize by which it was known that the place had been sacked... (Hackett 1942, II: 205)

At the pueblo of Alamillo, the Spaniards "found it entirely deserted, and the church, convent, and crosses burned...There were only some ruined and burned houses..." (Hackett 1942, II: 206)

And finally, at the pueblo of Sevilleta they found it depopulated, and that the apostates had left it for fear of the Apaches and had gone to join the rebels in the interior. Here the hermitage...was found entirely demolished, and the wood from it made into an underground estufa of idolatry. Some of the houses of the pueblo were burned, and a short distance away from it were found some deep subterranean chambers, in four parts, full of maize, most of it spoiled in earthen jars, calabashes, and some pots. (Hackett 1942, II: 207)

It is specifically noted that Otermin had the surviving houses of Senecu, Socorro and Alamillo burned on his way north. Upon reaching Isleta, the Spaniards found it occupied by Tiwas, and by Piros from Socorro, Alamillo, and Sevilleta. (Hackett 1942, II: 208) As only about 500 persons were found at Isleta, and more than half of the population were probably Tiwas, the majority of Piros-Tompiros must have been dispersed elsewhere among the Pueblo Indian towns. Some are known to have been at Acoma. (Hackett 1942, II: 340, 362)

When Diego de Vargas reconquered New Mexico in 1692, he found Piro-Tompiros scattered among various pueblos, such as Taos and the Tano pueblo of San Cristobal, and in 1696 Piros were noted as living at San Cristobal and San Lazaro. (J.M. Espinosa 1940: 145, 156, 234). It seems clear, then, that the Piro-Tompiros were scattered throughout the other Pueblo Indians after removal from their own pueblos in 1681.

Those Piro-Tompiros remaining in the northern Rio Grande area may have formed an element in the polyglot population said to have been settled at Laguna after the reconquest of New Mexico. (Adams and Chavez 1956: 183; F. Ellis 1959: 325-327)

Some of the Tompiros may have accompanied refugees from the Southern Tiwa pueblos who went to live among the Hopis after Otermin burned their pueblos of Isleta, Alameda, Puaray and Sandia in the winter of 1681–1682. The Tiwa refugees are known to have settled at Payupki (NA 1040) on Second Mesa. (See Fewkes 1898: 583-584, Fewkes 1902b: 25, Twitchell 1914: 220, Velez de Escalante 1876: 194.)

During the 1984 Pecos Conference at the Museum of Northern Arizona, I and Pat Medlin took the opportunity to examine the MNA's surface collection from Payupki. Amongst the potsherds from that site were observed a polished-red carinated bowl form that closely resembles Salinas Red, and mineral-painted B/W sherds with a grey paste and Tabira-like designs that strongly suggest Tabira B/W. Are these evidences of a Tompiro element in the refugee population at Payupki?

Meanwhile, during the early 1680s, two Piro-Tompiro pueblos, Socorro and Senecu, and a Tiwa pueblo, Ysleta del Sur, were established under Spanish control in the El Paso area. The populations of Socorro and Senecu were composed of Piros and Tompiros brought south during the 1680 retreat from New Mexico, plus those brought back from Isleta by Otermin in 1682. A few more Piro individuals were added in 1692 when Diego de Vargas returned from his reconquest of New Mexico. A complete history of these new pueblos is not yet available, but portions may be found in various sources. (Houser 1970, Eckhart 1967, Hughes 1914, J.M. Espinosa 1941, Bronitsky 1987, Timmons 1977, Fewkes 1902a)

Notes:

1. H. A. Anderson (19785: 367) places the beginning of the jurisdicciones and alcaldes mayores as the year 1659, but I find mention of an alcalde mayor for the Sandia jurisdiccion in 1650. (Hackett 1942, II: 299)
2. The Holy Thursday mentioned is probably Ascension Day, which is the fortieth day after Easter, which should place the planned date of the uprising as sometime in May 1650.
3. For information on this Spanish supply system see Scholes (1930).
4. However, the first mention of the name "Santa Ana" in connection with Alamillo comes in 1672. (Bloom and Mitchell 1938: 115)
5. This minister was Fray Francisco de Azevedo, who had been guardian at Abo in the 1630s and 1640s, and probably in the 1650s. He was actually 89 years old in 1659 and his ministry at Alamillo in 1659 and 1660 may have been his last active assignment as a missionary. On the basis of his age alone, this tale of the molestation of an Indian woman at Alamillo seems rather improbably.
6. October marks the beginning of the important winter ceremonial season for the Pueblo Indians.
7. Pueblos noted to have done so include Tesuque, San Ildefonso, Pojoaque, Jemez, Isleta, Sandia, Alameda, Tajique, Cuarac, San Marcos, and Galisteo.
8. Throughout the documents relating to this event the Tompiros are referred to as "Jumanos."
9. Besides Vicente de Zaldivar and one or more interpreters, seven Spaniards are specifically names as being present on the expedition: Cristobal Baca, Gonzalo Hernandez, Juan de Vitoriz Carbajal, Pero Gomez Duran, Gaspar Lopez de Tavora, Francisco de Rascon, and Isidro Xuarez Figueroa.
10. The frontier mission province of New Mexico was not raised to the status of custodia until ca. AD 1616. (Scholes 1932: 61)
11. A list of mission priests distributed by Salinas National monument claims the founding of a "convent" at Abo in 1622, but I know of no documentary evidence to support this claim, and certainly the source cited by the flyer. (Scholes and Bloom 1945: 689) contains no mention of any convento or other mission building.
12. The Cuarac mission was known as either Nuestra Senora de la Concepcion or Nuestra Senora de la Inmaculada Concepcion in the 17th century documents, therefore, Wilson's (1973) use of the name La Purisima Concepcion appears to be historically inaccurate.
13. This is the first historical use of the term "Salinero" to refer to the Salinas Tiwas.
14. Family names noted in the Salinas Province include the following: Gonzalez de Apadoca, de 'Avalos ('Abalos), de Ledesma, de Leyva, Martin Barba, Martin Serrano, de Mestas, Montano, Nieto, and Ruiz Caceres. (See Chavez 1954.)
15. Hackett (1937: 169) gives the name as Mutra, but this is a misreading of Mussa.
16. The feast day of San Miguel (St. Michael) is on September 29, which is too early in the autumn to be the day referred to since the governor did not approved kachina dances until sometime in October 1660. Consequently, the occasion must be October 16, the day of the "apparition of Saint Michael on his mountain." (Holweck 1924: 711)
17. Velez de Escalante's statement reads as follows: Pocos anos antes de la sublevacion (de 1680), destruyeron los enemigos apaches con casi continuas invasiones, siete pueblos de los cuarenta y seis dichos: uno en la princia de Zuni, que fue Jahuicu, y sieta (seis) en el valle de las Salinas, que fueron Chilili, Tagique (Tajique) y Quarac, de indios tehuas. Abo, Jumancas y Tabira, de tumpiros, todos los cuales estaban en las falda oriental de la sierra de Sandia, menos dos que estaban distantes de dicha sierra hacia las Salinas. (Anonymous 1962: 307)
18. Among these are Hernan Martin Serrano and his family and Pedro de Layva and his family. (Chavez 1954: 53, 72)

References

(Facsimiles from
Original Document)

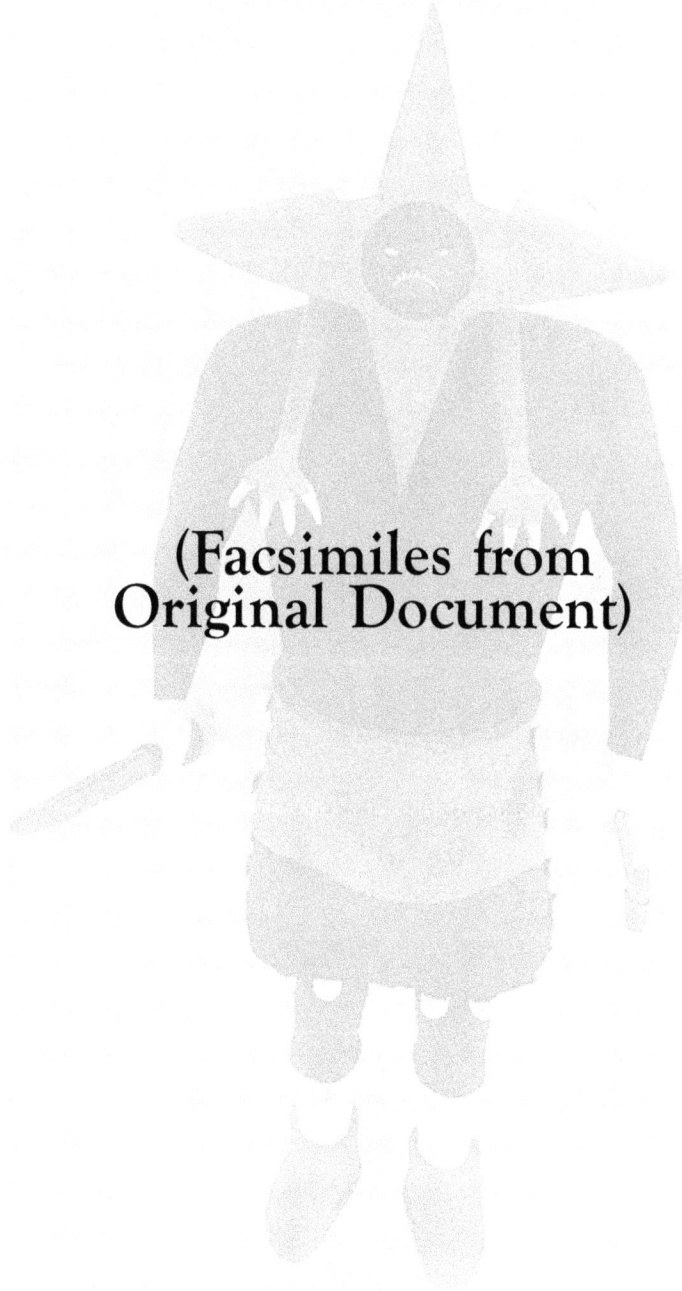

REFERENCES CITED

Abbey, Edward
  1975   The Monkey Wrench Gang. Avon Books, New York.

  1979   Abbey's Road. E.P. Dutton, New York.

Abel, Leland J.
  1955   Pottery Types of the Southwest: Wares 5A, 10A,
          10B, 12A: San Juan Red Ware, Mesa Verde Gray, and
          White Ware, San Juan White Ware . Ceramic Series
          No. 3-B, Museum of Northern Arizona, Flagstaff.

Aberle, David F.
  1987   What Kind of Science Is Anthropology? American
          Anthropologist 89 (3): 551-566.

Aberle, S.D., and J.H. Watkins and E.H. Pitney
  1940   The Vital History of San Juan Pueblo. Human
          Biology 12 (2): 141-187.

Abert, J.W.
  1848   Report of Lieut. J.W. Abert of His Examination of
          New Mexico in the Years 1846-'47. In W.L. Marcy,
          Report of the Secretary of War; 30th Congress, 1st
          Session, Senate Executive Document No. 23; Washington,
          D.C. Pp. 3-132.

Adams, Eleanor B., and Angelico Chavez
  1956   The Missions of New Mexico, 1776. University of
          New Mexico Press, Albuquerque.

Agogino, George, and Frank C. Hibben
  1958   Central New Mexico Paleo-Indian Cultures. American
          Antiquity 23 (4): 422-425.

Alexander, Hubert G., and Paul Reiter
  1935   Report on the Excavation of Jemez Cave, New Mexico.
          Monograph No.4, School of American Research, Santa Fe.

American Geological Institute
  1962   Dictionary of Geological Terms. Dolphin Books,
          Garden City.

Anderson, Eugene Carter
  1957   The Metal Resources of New Mexico and Their
          Economic Features through 1954. Bulletin 39, New

Mexico State Bureau of Mines and Mineral Resources,
Socorro.

Anderson, Frank G.
  1955   The Pueblo Kachina Cult: A Historical
          Reconstruction. Southwestern Journal of Anthropology
          11 (4): 404-419.

Anderson, H. Allen
  1985   The Encomienda in New Mexico, 1598-1600. New
          Mexico Historical Review 60 (4): 353-377.

Anonymous
  1925   Gran Quivira and Mimbres. El Palacio 19 (6):   141.

  1926   Work at Gran Quivira. El Palacio 21 (7-8):
          217-218.

  1962   Documentos para Servir a la Historia del Nuevo
          Mexico, 1538-1778. Coleccion Chimalistac No. 13,
          Ediciones Jose Porrua Turanzas, Madrid.

  1965   Acoma-Zuni Pottery Types. Seventh Southwestern
          Ceramic Seminar, Museum of Northern Arizona,
          Flagstaff.

Antevs, Ernst
  1952   Arroyo-Cutting and Filling. Journal of Geology 60
          (4): 375-385.

  1962   Late Quaternary Climates in Arizona. American
          Antiquity 28 (2): 193-198.

Anyon, Roger, and Steven A. LeBlanc
  1984   The Galaz Ruin. Maxwell Museum of Anthropology and
          University of New Mexico Press, Albuquerque.

Ashburn, P.M.
  1947   The Ranks of Death: A Medical History of the
          Conquest of America. Coward-McCann., New York.

Ayer, Mrs. Edward E. (trans.)
  1916   The Memorial of Fray Alonso de Benavides, 1630.
          Privately printed, Chicago.

Bachhuber, Frederick W.
  1971   Paleolimnology of Lake Estancia and the Quaternary
          History of the Estancia Valley, Central New Mexico.
          Ph.D dissertation, Department of Geology, University
          of New Mexico, Albuquerque.

Bailey, Jessie Bromilow
1940   Diego de Vargas and the Reconquest of New Mexico.
        University of New Mexico Press, Albuquerque.

Bailey, Reed W.
1935   Epicycles of Erosion in the Valleys of the Colorado
        Plateau Province. Journal of Geology 43 (4):
        337-355.

Bailey, Vernon
1931   Mammals of New Mexico. North American Fauna No.
        53, U.S. Department of Agriculture, Washington, D.C.

Bain, James G.
1976   Art on the Rocks. El Palacio 82 (2): 9-11.

Baker, Ele M.
1936   Report of Stratification Tests at Quarai. Ms.:
        typescript copy on file at Salinas National Monument,
        Mountainair.

Baldwin, Stuart J.
1976   Archaeological Salt at Mesa Verde and Trade with
        Areas to the North and West. The Kiva 42
        (2): 177-191.

1981   A Brief report on the Piro-Tompiro Archaeology and
        Ethnohistory Project, 1981 Field Season. Ms.

1983a   A Tentative Occupation Sequence for Abo Pass,
        Central New Mexico. COAS 1 (2): 12-28.

1983b   Preliminary Report on 1982 Excavations at the
        Pueblo of Abo, Salinas National Monument. Ms.

1983c   Tenabo Survey -- 1982. Typescript notes
        accompanying site forms submitted to the Laboratory of
        Anthropology, Santa Fe.

1984a   An Initial Study of Roomsize Patterns in Mesa
        Verdean and Chacoan Sites. Ms.: typescript copy at
        Department of Archaeology, University of Calgary,
        Calgary.

1984b   Hendron's Stratigraphic Test at Alameda Pueblo and
        Its Implications for the Rio Grande Glaze Sequence.
        Pottery Southwest 11 (2): 3-6.

1984c   A Reconsideration of the Dating of a
        Seventeenth-Century New Mexican Document.   New Mexico
        Historical Review 59 (4):   410-413.

1986   The Mountain Lion in Tompiro Stone Art.   In Anne V.
        Poore (ed.), By Hands Unknown:_ Papers on Rock Art and
        Archaeology in Honor of James G._ Bain.   Papers
        No. 12, Archaeological Society of New Mexico,
        Albuquerque.   Pp. 8-17.

n.d.   A Review of the Rio Grande Glaze Problem.   Ms in
        progress.

Baldwin, Stuart J., and K.P. Medlin and Kenneth M. Hewett
    1984   Analyses of the Ceramics from LA 45885 and the Fite
        Ranch Site (LA 45884).   Ms. report to the Museum of
        New Mexico, Santa Fe.

Bandelier, A.F.
    1890   Final Report of Investigations Among the Indians of
        the Southwestern United States, Carried on Mainly in
        the Years from 1880 to 1885, Part I.   American Series
        Papers Vol. 3, Archaeological Institute of America,
        Cambridge.

    1892   Final Report of Investigations Among the Indians of
        the Southwestern United States, Carried on Mainly in
        the Years from 1880 to 1885, Part II.   American Series
        Papers Vol. 4, Archaeological Institute of America,
        Cambridge.

Bandelier, Fanny (trans.)
    1905   The Journey of Alvar Nuñez Cabeza de Vaca.   A.S.
        Barnes and Company, New York.

Barnett, Franklin
    1969   Tonque Pueblo.   Albuquerque Archaeological Society,
        Albuquerque.

    1973   Dictionary of Prehistoric Indian Artifacts of the
        American Southwest.   Northland Press, Flagstaff.

Bartlett, John Russell
    1854   Personal Narrative of Explorations and Incidents in
        Texas, New Mexico, California, Sonora, and Chihuahua,
        Connected with the Unites States and Mexican Boundary
        Commission, During the Years 1850, '51, '52, and '53:
        Vol._ 1. D. Appleton and Co., New York.

1909   The Language of the Piro.   American Anthropologist
        11 (3):   426-433.

Basso, Keith H. (ed.)
    1971   Western Apache Raiding and Warfare.   University of
        Arizona Press, Tucson.

Bates, Robert L., and Ralph H. Wilpolt, Archie J. MacAlpin
and Georges Vorbe
    1947   Geology of the Gran Quivira Quadrangle, New Mexico.
        Bulletin 26, New Mexico Bureau of Mines and Mineral
        Resources, Socorro.

Beals, Ralph L.
    1932   The Comparative Ethnology of Northern Mexico Before
        1750.   Ibero-Americana No. 2, University of
        California, Berkeley.

Beckett, Patrick H.
    1981a   An Archaeological Survey and Assessment of Gran
        Quivira National Monument, New Mexico.   Cultural
        Resources Management Division, Department of Sociology
        and Anthropology, New Mexico State University, Las
        Cruces.

    1981b   An Alternate Hypothesis to the Mystery Disks of the
        Tompiro.   The Artifact 19 (3-4):   179-202.

    1985   Distribution of Chupadero Black-on-white: Or, The
        Black and White of Jug Use.   In Charles H. Lange
        (ed.), Southwestern Culture History: Collected Papers
        in Honor of Albert H. Schroeder.   Papers No. 10,
        Archaeological Society of New Mexico, Albuquerque.
        Pp. 27-30.

Bell, Willis H., and Edward F. Castetter
    1937   Ethnobiological Studies in the American Southwest,
        V: The Utilization of Mesquite and Screwbean by the
        Aborigines in the American Southwest.   Biological
        Series Bulletin Vol. 5, no. 2, University of New
        Mexico, Albuquerque.

    1941   Ethnobiological Studies in the American Southwest,
        VII: The Utilization of Yucca, Sotol, and Beargrass
        by the Aborigines in the American Southwest.
        Biological Series Bulletin Vol. 5, no. 5, University
        of New Mexico, Albuquerque.

Benedict, Ruth
  1930   Eight Stories from Acoma. Journal of American
          Folk-Lore 43 (167): 59-87.

Binford, Lewis R.
  1962   Archaeology as Anthropology. American Antiquity 28
          (2): 217-225.

  1965   Archaeological Systematics and the Study of Culture
          Process. American Antiquity 31: 203-210.

  1968   Archeological Perspectives. In New Perspectives in
          Archeology, Sally R. Binford and Lewis R. Binford
          (eds.); Aldine Publishing Co., Chicago. Pp. 5-32.

Binford, Lewis R., and Jeremy A. Sabloff
  1982   Paradigms, Systematics, and Archaeology.
          Journal of Anthropological Research 38
          (2): 137-153.

Black, Francis L.
  1975   Infectious Diseases in Primitive Societies.
          Science 187 (4176): 515-518.

Bloom, Lansing B.
  1934   The "Penalosa" Map. New Mexico Historical Review 9
          (2): 228-229.

  1936   The Sanson Map. New Mexico Historical Review 11
          (2): 210 and frontispiece.

  1945   A Du Val Map of 1670. New Mexico Historical Review
          20 (3): 276-278 and frontispiece.

Bloom, Lansing B., and Lynn B. Mitchell
  1938   The Chapter Elections in 1672. New Mexico
          Historical Review 13 (1): 85-119.

Bolton, Herbert E.
  1911   The Jumano Indians in Texas, 1650-1771. Texas
          Historical Association Quarterly 15: 66-84.

  1964   Coronado: Knight of Pueblos and Plains.
          University of New Mexico Press, Albuquerque.

Bourke, John G.
  1884   The Snake-Dance of the Moquis of Arizona. Charles
          Scribner's Sons, New York.

Bourlier, Bob G., and R.E. Neher, D.B. Crezee, K.J. Bowman
and D.W. Meister
   1969   Soil Survey of Torrance Area, New Mexico.
          U.S. Government Printing Office, Washington, D.C.

Bradfield, Maitland
   1971   Rodents of the Hopi Region, in Relation to Hopi
          Farming. Plateau 44 (2): 75-77.

Brandt, John C., and Ray A. Williamson
   1977   Rock Art Representations of the A.D. 1054
          Supernova: A Progress Report. In Anthony F. Aveni
          (ed.), Native American Astronomy. University of Texas
          Press, Austin. Pp. 171-177.

   1979   The 1054 Supernova and Native American Rock Art.
          Archaeoastronomy 1: 1-38.

Bray, Alicia
   1982   Mimbres Black-on-White: Melamine or Wedgewood? A
          Ceramic Use-wear Analysis. The Kiva 47 (3): 133-149.

Breternitz, David A.
   1966   An Appraisal of Tree-ring Dated Pottery in the
          Southwest. Anthropological Papers No. 10, University
          of Arizona, Tucson.

Breternitz, David A., and Arthur H. Rohn, jr. and Elizabeth
A. Morris
   1974   Prehistoric Ceramics of the Mesa Verde Region.
          Ceramic Series No. 5, Museum of Northern Arizona,
          Flagstaff.

Brody, J.J.
   1977   Mimbres Painted Pottery. School of American
          Research, Santa Fe and University of New Mexico Press,
          Albuquerque.

Brody, J.J., and Catherine J. Scott and Steven A. LeBlanc
   1983   Mimbres Pottery. Hudson Hills Press, New York.

Bronitsky, Gordon
   1987   Indian Assimilation in the El Paso Area. New
          Mexico Historical Review 62 (2): 151-168.

Brown, Donald Nelson
   1967   The Distribution of Sound Instruments in the
          Prehistoric Southwestern United States.
          Ethnomusicology 11 (1): 71-90.

1971   Ethnomusicology and the Prehistoric Southwest.
        Ethnomusicology 15 (3): 363-378.

Brugge, David M.
  1981   Comments on Athabaskans and Sumas. In David
          R. Wilcox and W. Bruce Masse (eds.), The Protohistoric
          Period in the North American Southwest,
          A.D. 1450-1700. Anthropological Research Papers No.
          24, Arizona State University, Tempe. Pp. 282-290.

  1982   Apache and Navajo Ceramics. Southwestern Ceramics:
          A Comparative Review, Albert H. Schroeder (ed.). The
          Arizona Archaeologist 15: 279-295.

  1983   Navajo Prehistory and History to 1850. In Alfonso
          Ortiz and William C. Sturtevant (eds.), Handbook of
          North American Indians, Volume 10:_ Southwest.
          Smithsonian Institution, Washington, D.C.
          Pp. 489-501.

Bryan, Kirk
  1925   Date of Channel Trenching (Arroyo Cutting) in the
          Arid Southwest. Science 62 (1607): 338-344.

  1928a   Historic Evidence on Changes in the Channel of Rio
          Puerco, A Tributary of the Rio Grande in New Mexico.
          Journal of Geology 36 (3): 265-282.

  1928b   Change in Plant Associations by Change in Ground
          Water Level. Ecology 9 (4): 474-478.

  1929   Flood-water Farming. The Geographical Review 19
          (3): 444-456.

  1941   Pre-Columbian Agriculture in the Southwest, as
          Conditioned by Periods of Alluviation. Annals of the
          Association of American Geographers 31 (4): 219-242.

Bryan, Kirk, and Joseph H. Toulouse, jr.
  1943   The San Jose Non-ceramic Culture and Its Relation
          to a Puebloan Culture in New Mexico. American
          Antiquity 8 (3): 269-280.

Bunzel, Ruth L.
  1932   Zuñi Katcinas. 47th Annual Report of the Bureau of
          American Ethnology...1929-1930. U.S. Government
          Printing Office, Washington, D.C. Pp. 837-1086.

Bussey, Stanley D., and Richard Kelly and Judith Southward
  1976   LA 4921, Three Rivers, Otero County, New Mexico.

Report No. 69, Cultural Resources Management Division,
Department of Sociology and Anthropology, New Mexico
State University, Las Cruces.

Campbell, John Martin, and Florence Hawley Ellis
  1952   The Atrisco Sites: Cochise Manifestations in the
         Middle Rio Grande Valley. American Antiquity 17 (3):
         211-221.

Caperton, Thomas J.
  1981   An Archaeological Reconnaissance. In Alden
         C. Hayes (ed.), Contributions to Gran Quivira
         Archaeology. Publications in Archaeology No. 17,
         U.S. National Park Service, Washington, D.C. Pp. XII,
         3-14, 160-163.

Carleton, James Henry
  1855   Diary of an Excursion to the Ruins of Abo, Quarra,
         and Gran Quivira, in NEM, under the Command of Major
         James Henry Carleton, U.S.A. 9th Annual Report of the
         Smithsonian Institution, Washington, D.C.
         Pp. 296-316.

Carlson, Roy L.
  1970   White Mountain Redware. Anthropological Paper
         No. 19, University of Arizona, Tucson.

  1982   The Mimbres Kachina Cult. In Patrick H. Beckett
         and Kira Silverbird (eds.), Mogollon Archaeology:
         Proceedings of the 1980 Mogollon Conference. Acoma
         Books, Ramona. Pp. 147-155.

Carmack, Robert M.
  1972   Ethnohistory: A Review of Its Development,
         Definitions, Methods, and Aims. In Annual Review of
         Anthropology 1: 227-246.

Chamberlin, T.C.
  1931   The Method of Multiple Working Hypotheses.
         Journal of Geology 39: 155-165.

Chapman, Kenneth M.
  1936   The Pottery of Santo Domingo Pueblo. Memoirs Vol.
         I, Laboratory of Anthropology, Santa Fe.

Chavez, Angelico
  1954   Origins of New Mexico Families in the Spanish
         Colonial Period. Historical Society of New Mexico,
         Santa Fe.

1967   Pohe-yemo's Representative and the Pueblo Revolt of
        1680. New Mexico Historical Review 42 (2): 85-126.

de Cobarruvias Orozco, Sebastian
  1979   Tesoro de la Lengua Castellana o Española.
          Ediciones Turner, Madrid.

Cohen, J.M.
  1960   The Penguin Book of Spanish Verse. Revised
          edition. Penguin Books, Harmondsworth.

Cole, Sally J.
  1984   The Abo Painted Rocks Documentation and Analysis.
          Ms.: copy at Salinas National Monument, Mountainair.

Colson, Elizabeth
  1979   In Good Years and in Bad: Food Strategies of
          Self-Reliant Societies. Journal of Anthropological
          Research 35 (1): 18-29.

Colton, Harold S.
  1959   Hopi Kachina Dolls. 2nd edition. University of
          New Mexico Press, Albuquerque.

Condie, Carol J.
  1981   Cultural Resources Inventory on the Chilili Land
          Grant, Bernalillo County, New Mexico. Publication 32,
          Quivira Research Center, Albuquerque.

Coon, Carleton Stevens
  1931   Tribes of the Rif. Harvard African Studies Vol. 9,
          Peabody Museum of Harvard University, Cambridge.

Cordell, Linda S.
  1979   A Cultural Resources Overview of the Middle Rio
          Grande Valley, New Mexico. U.S. Forest Service and
          Bureau of Land Management, Albuquerque and Santa Fe.

Corominas, J.
  1954   Diccionario Critico Etimologico de la Lengua
          Castellana. A. Francke, A.G., Berne. Four volumes
          separately paginated.

Cosgrove, H.S., and C.B. Cosgrove
  1932   The Swarts Ruin. Papers Vol. 15, no. 1, Peabody
          Museum of American Archaeology and Ethnology, Harvard
          University, Cambridge.

Crosby, Alfred W.
  1967   Conquistador y Pestilencia: The First New World

Pandemic and the Fall of the Great Indian Empires. _Hispanic American Review_ 47 (3): 321-337.

 1976   Virgin Soil Epidemics as a Factor in the Aboriginal
         Depopulation in America. _The William and Mary
         Quarterly_ 33 (2), (3rd series): 289-299.

Culin, Stewart
   1907   Games of the North American Indians. 24th Annual
         Report of the Bureau of American Ethnology...1902-03.
         U.S. Government Printing Office, Washington, D.C.
         Pp. 1-846.

Curtin, L.S.M.
   1965   _Healing Herbs of the Upper Rio Grande_. Southwest
         Museum, Los Angeles.

Cushing, Frank Hamilton
   1883   Zuñi Fetiches. _2nd Annual Report of the Bureau of
         Ethnology...1880-'81_. U.S. Government Printing
         Office, Washington, D.C. Pp. 3-45.

 1920   _Zuñi Breadstuff_. Indian Notes and Monographs
         Vol. 8, Museum of the American Indian-Heye Foundation,
         New York.

Daggett, Pierre M., and Dale R. Henning
   1974   The Jaguar in North America. _American Antiquity_ 39
         (3): 465-469.

Dart, Allen (ed.)
   1980   _Archeological Investigations at San Antonio de
         Padua, LA 24, Bernalillo County, New Mexico_. Lab Note
         No. 167, Laboratory of Anthropology, Santa Fe.

Davis, Irvine
   1959   Linguistic Clues to Northern Rio Grande Prehistory.
         El Palacio 66 (3): 73-84.

Densmore, Frances
   1938   _Music of Santo Domingo Pueblo, New Mexico_. Papers
         No. 12, Southwest Museum, Los Angeles.

Denton, George H., and Wibjorn Karlen
   1973   Holocene Climatic Variations -- Their Pattern and
         Possible Cause. _Quaternary Research_ 3 (2): 155-205.

Deutschmann, Z.
   1961   The Ecology of Smallpox. In Jacques M. May (ed.),
         Studies in Disease Ecology. Studies in Medical

Geography Vol. 2, The American Geographical Society, New York. Pp. 1-13.

Dick, Herbert W.
1965b Picuris Pueblo Excavations. Typescript report on file at Southwest Region, U.S. National Park Service, Santa Fe.

DiPeso, Charles C., and John B. Rinaldo and Gloria J. Fenner
1974 Casas Grandes:_ A Fallen Trading Center of the Gran Chichimeca. Eight Volumes. Amerind Foundation, Dragoon.

Dittert, Alfred E., jr.
1959 Culture Change in the Cebolleta Mesa Region, Central Western New Mexico. Ph.D dissertation, Department of Anthropology, University of Arizona, Tucson.

Dobyns, Henry F.
1966 Estmating Aboriginal American Population: An Appraisal of Techniques, with a New Hemispheric Estimate. Current Anthropology 7 (4): 395-416, 425-449.

Dodge, Natt N.
1967 100 Roadside Wildflowers of Southwestern Uplands in Natural Color. Southwestern Monuments Association, Globe.

Dodge, Natt N., and Jeanne R. Janish
1954 Flowers of the Southwest Deserts. Popular Series No. 4, Southwestern Monuments Association, Globe.

Dodge, William A.
1980 Prehistory of the Sacramento Mountains. In Bruce G. Harrill (ed.), A Cultural Resource Management Plan for Timber Sale and Forest Development Areas on the Mescalero Apache Indian Reservation, Volume 1. Forestry Archeological Program, Bureau of Indian Affairs, Albuquerque. Pp. 48-52.

Dorroh, J.H., jr.
1946 Certain Hydrologic and Climatic Characteristics of the Southwest. Publications in Engineering No. 1, University of New Mexico, Albuquerque.

Downie, Allan W.
1965 Poxvirus Group. In Frank L. Horsfall, jr. and Igor Tamm (eds.), Viral and Rickettsial Infections of Man

4th edition. J.B. Lippincott Company, Toronto.
Pp. 932-964.

Dozier, Edward P.
  1955   Kinship and Linguistic Change Among the Arizona
          Tewa. International Journal of American Linguistics
          21 (3): 242-257.

  1965   Southwestern Social Units and Archaeology.
          American Antiquity 31 (1): 38-47.

  1970   The Pueblo Indians of North America. Holt,
          Rinehart and Winston, Toronto.

Driver, Harold E., and William C. Massey
  1957   Comparative Studies of North American Indians.
          Transactions, new series, Vol. 47, part 2, American
          Philosophical Society, Philadelphia.

Dunnell, Robert C.
  1978   Style and Function: A Fundamental Dichotomy.
          American Antiquity 43 (2): 192-202.

  1980   Evolutionary Theory and Archaeology. In Advances
          in Archaeological Method and Theory, Volume 3, Michael
          B. Schiffer (ed.); Academic Press Inc., Toronto.
          Pp. 35-99.

  1982   Science, Social Science, and Common Sense: The
          Agonizing Dilemma of Modern Archaeology. Journal of
          Anthropological Research 38 (1): 1-25.

Dutton, Bertha P.
  1963   Sun Father's Way: The Kiva Murals of Kuaua.
          University of New Mexico Press, Albuquerque.

  1981   Excavation Tests at the Pueblo Ruins of Abo. In
          Albert H. Schroeder (ed.), Collected Papers in Honor
          of Erik Kellerman Reed. Papers No. 6, Archaeological
          Society of New Mexico, Albuquerque. Pp. 177-195.

  1985   Excavation Tests at the Pueblo Ruins of Abo, Part
          II. In Nancy Fox (ed.), Prehistory and History in the
          Southwest: Collected Papers in Honor of Alden
          C. Hayes. Papers No. 11, Archaeological Society of
          New Mexico, Albuquerque. Pp. 91-104.

Earle, W. Hubert
  1963   Cacti of the Southwest. Science Bulletin No. 4,
          Desert Botnical Garden of Arizona, Phoenix.

Ebinger, Michael H.
  1980   New Information on Pottery Smudging. Pottery
      Southwest 7 (4): 1-2.

Eckhart, George B.
  1967   Spanish Missions of Texas, 1680-1800. The Kiva 32
      (3): 73-95.

Eggan, Fred
  1950   Social Organization of the Western Pueblos.
      University of Chicago Press, Chicago.

Elliott, J.H.
  1966   Imperial Spain, 1469-1716. Mentor Books, New York.

Ellis, Bruce T.
  1957   Crossbow Boltheads from Historic Pueblo Sites. El
      Palacio 64 (7-8): 209-214.

Ellis, Florence Hawley
  1959   An Outline of Laguna Pueblo History and Social
      Organization. Southwestern Journal of Anthropology 15
      (4): 325-347.

  1964   Archaeological History of Nambe Pueblo, 14th
      Century to the Present. American Antiquity 30
      (1): 34-42.

  1966   The Immediate History of Zia Pueblo as Derived from
      Excavation in Refuse Deposits. American Antiquity 31
      (6): 806-811.

  1967   Where Did the Pueblo People Come From?   El
      Palacio 74 (3): 35-43.

  1970   Pueblo Witchcraft and Medicine. In Deward
      E. Walker (ed.), Systems of North American Witchcraft
      and Sorcery. University of Idaho, Moscow. Pp. 37-72.

  1976   Datable Ritual Components Proclaiming Mexican
      Influence in the Upper Rio Grande in New Mexico. In
      Albert H. Schroeder (ed.), Collected Papers in Honor
      of Marjorie Ferguson Lambert. Papers No. 3,
      Archaeological Society of New Mexico, Albuquerque.
      Pp. 85-108.

Ellis, Florence Hawley, and J.J. Brody
  1964   Ceramic Stratigraphy and Tribal History at Taos
      Pueblo. American Antiquity 29 (3): 316-327.

Ellis, Florence Hawley, and Laurens Hammack
  1968   The Inner Sanctum of Feather Cave, A Mogollon Sun
        and Earth Shrine Linking Mexico and the Southwest.
        American Antiquity 33 (1): 25-44.

Ely, Albert Grim
  1935   The Excavation and Repair of Quarai Mission. El
        Palacio 39 (25-26): 133-144.

Emslie, Steven D.
  1981   Prehistoric Agricultural Ecosystems: Avifauna from
        Pottery Mound, New Mexico.   American Antiquity 45
        (4): 853-861.

Enciclopedia Universal Ilustrada
  1928a Durango. In Tomo 18 (Segunda Parte).
        Espasa-Calpe, S.A., Madrid. Pp. 2580-2590.

  1928b Tavira. In Tomo 59. Espasa-Calpe, S.A., Madrid.
        Pp. 952-953.

Espinosa, Gilberto (trans.)
  1933   History of New Mexico by Gaspar Perez de Villagra,
        Alcala, 1610. Publications Vol. 4, The Quivira
        Society, Los Angeles.

Espinosa, J. Manuel
  1940   First Expedition of Vargas into New Mexico, 1692.
        Coronado Quarto Centennial Publications Vol. 10,
        University of New Mexico Press, Albuquerque.

  1941   Population of the El Paso District in 1692.
        Mid-America 23 (1): 61-84.

  1942   Crusaders of the Rio Grande: The Story of Don
        Diego de Vargas and the Reconquest of New Mexico.
        Institute of Jesuit History, Chicago.

Ewers, John C.
  1980   Climate, Acculturation, and Costume: A History of
        Women's Clothing Among the Indians of the Southern
        Plains. Plains Anthropologist 25 (87): 63-82.

Farwell, Robin E.
  1981   Pot Lids, Plates and Pukis. Pottery Southwest 8
        (3): 1-4.

Fenenga, Franklin
  1956   Excavations at Site LA 2579, A Mogollon Village
        near Gran Quivira, New Mexico. In Fred Wendorf, Nancy

Fox and Orin L. Lewis (eds.), Pipeline Archaeology.
Laboratory of Anthropology, Santa Fe and Museum of
Northern Arizona, Flagstaff. Pp. 226-233.

Fenenga, Franklin, and Thomas S. Cummings
   1956   Archaeological Survey of the Permian-San Juan
          Pipeline Right-of-Way between Plains, Texas, and
          Correo, New Mexico. In Fred Wendorf, Nancy Fox and
          Orin L. Lewis (eds.), Pipeline Archaeology.
          Laboratory of Anthropology, Santa Fe and Museum of
          Northern Arizona, Flagstaff. Pp. 215-226.

Ferdon, Edwin N., jr.
   1955   A Trial Survey of Mexican-Southwestern
          Architectural Parallels. Monograph No. 21, School of
          American Research, Santa Fe.

Ferg, Alan
   1983   LA 25860, The Sheep Chute Site. In Nancy
          S. Hammack, Alan Ferg and Bruce Bradley, Excavations
          at Three Developmental Period Sites Near Zia and Santa
          Ana Pueblos, New Mexico. CASA Papers No. 2, Complete
          Archaeological Service Associates, Cortez. Pp. 7-89.

Fewkes, Jesse Walter
   1898   Archeological Expedition to Arizona in 1895. 17th
          Annual Report of the Bureau of American
          Ethnology...1895-96, Part 2, U.S. Government Printing
          Office, Washington, D.C. Pp. 519-744.

   1899   The Alosaka Cult of the Hopi Indians. American
          Anthropologist 1 (3): 522-544.

   1902a The Pueblo Settlements Near El Paso, Texas.
          American Anthropologist 4 (1): 57-75.

   1902b Sky-God Personations in Hopi Worship. Journal of
          American Folk-Lore 15 (56): 14-32.

   1903   Hopi Katcinas Drawn by Native Artists. 21st Annual
          Report of the Bureau of American
          Ethnology...1899-1900. U.S. Government Printing
          Office, Washington, D.C.. Pp. 13-190.

   1909   Antiquities of the Mesa Verde National Park:
          Spruce-tree House. Bulletin 41, Bureau of American
          Ethnology, Washington, D.C.

   1924   The Use of Idols in Hopi Worship. Annual
          Report...of the Smithsonian Institution...1922.

U.S. Government Printing Office, Washington, D.C.,
Pp. 377-397.

Forbes, Jack D.
1959a Unknown Athapaskans: The Identification of the
Jano, Jocome, Manso, Suma, and Other Indian Tribes of
the Southwest. Ethnohistory 6 (2): 97-159.

1959b The Appearance of the Mounted Indian in Northern
Mexico and the Southwest, to 1680. Southwestern
Journal of Anthropology 15 (2): 189-212.

Ford, Richard Irving
1968   An Ecological Analysis Involving the Population of
San Juan Pueblo, New Mexico. Ph.D dissertation,
University of Michigan, Ann Arbor.

1972   An Ecological Perspective on the Eastern Pueblos.
In Alfonso Ortiz (ed.), New Perspectives on the
Pueblos. University of New Mexico Press, Albuquerque.
Pp. 1-17.

Ford, Richard I., and Albert H. Schroeder and Stewart
L. Peckham
1972   Three Perspectives on Puebloan Prehistory. In New
Perspectives on the Pueblos, Alfonso Ortiz (ed.);
University of New Mexico Press, Albuquerque.
Pp. 19-39.

Forrestal, Peter P., and Cyprian J. Lynch (eds.)
1954   Benavides' Memorial of 1630. Academy of American
Franciscan History, Washington, D.C.

Fowler, Catherine S., and Don D. Fowler
1981   The Southern Paiute: A.D. 1400-1776. In David
R. Wilcox and W. Bruce Masse (eds.), The Protohistoric
Period in the North American Southwest,
A.D. 1450-1700. Anthropological Research Papers
No. 24, Arizona State University, Tempe. Pp. 129-162.

Fox, John P., and Carrie E. Hall and Lila R. Elveback
1970   Epidemiology: Man and Disease. Collier-MacMillan
Ltd., London.

Francis, Thomas, jr., and Hunein F. Maassab
1965   Influenza Viruses. In Frank L. Horsfall, jr. and
Igor Tamm (eds.), Viral and Rickettsial Infections of
Man. 4th edition. J.B. Lippincott Company, Toronto.
Pp. 689-740.

Frank, Larry, and Francis H. Harlow
   1974   Historic Pottery of the Pueblo Indians, 1600-1880.
   New York Graphic Society, Ltd., Boston.

Fritts, Harold C.
   1965   Tree-ring Evidence for Climatic Changes in Western
   North America. Monthly Weather Review 93
   (7): 421-443.

   1976   Tree-rings and Climate. Academic Press, New York.

Frizell, Jon
   1982   Lithic Analysis of LA-677. In Michael P. Marshall,
   Excavations at Nuestra Señora de Dolores Pueblo
   (LA677). Office of Contract Archaeology, University
   of New Mexico, Albuquerque. Pp. 85-102.

Gebhard, David
   1966   The Shield Motif in Plains Rock Art. American
   Antiquity 31 (5): 721-732.

Gerlach, Arch C. (ed.)
   1970   The National Atlas of the United States of America.
   U.S. Geological Survey, Washington, D.C.

Gibson, Charles
   1964   The Aztecs Under Spanish Rule. Stanford University
   Press, Stanford.

Gifford, D.S., and E.W. Gifford
   1949   The Cochise Culture Olivella. American Antiquity
   15 (2):   163.

Gifford, E.W.
   1940   Culture Element Distributions: XII, Apache-Pueblo.
   Anthropological Records Vol. 4, no. 1, University of
   California, Berkeley.

   1947   Californian Shell Artifacts. Anthropological
   Records Vol. 9, no. 1, University of California,
   Berkeley.

Goggin, John M.
   1968   Spanish Maiolica in the New World. Publications in
   Anthropology No. 72, Yale University, New Haven.

Gould, James L., and Peter Marler
   1987   Learning by Instinct.   Scientific American 256
   (1): 74-85.

Grande Enciclopedia Portuguesa e Brasileira
   n.d.   Tavira.   In Volume 30.   Editorial Enciclopedia,
      Limitada, Lisboa e Rio de Janeiro.   Pp. 832-841.

Green, Earl
   1955   Excavations near Gran Quivira, New Mexico.
      Bulletin of the Texas Archeological Society
      26: 182-185.

Greer, John W.
   1977   Some Simple Methods for Computing Vessel Diameters
      from Sherds.   Pottery Southwest 4 (1): 6-9.

Gregg, Josiah
   1954   Commerce of the Prairies.   Edited by Max
      L. Moorhead.   University of Oklahoma Press, Norman.

Griffen, William B.
   1969   Culture Change and Shifting Populations in Central
      Northern Mexico.   Anthropological Papers No. 13,
      University of Arizona, Tucson.

   1979   Indian Assimilation in the Franciscan Area of Nueva
      Vizcaya.   Anthropological Papers No. 33, University of
      Arizona, Tucson.

   1983   Southern Periphery: East.   In Alfonso Ortiz and
      William C. Sturtevant (eds.), Handbook of North
      American Indians, Volume 10: Southwest.   Smithsonian
      Institution, Washington, D.C.   Pp. 329-342.

Guernsey, Samuel James
   1931   Explorations in Northeastern Arizona.   Papers
      Vol. 12, no. 1, Peabody Museum of American Archaeology
      and Ethnology, Harvard University, Cambridge.

Gunnerson, James H.
   1979   Southern Athapaskan Archeology.   In Alfonso Ortiz
      and William C. Sturtevant (eds.), Handbook of North
      American Indians, Volume 9: Southwest.   Smithsonian
      Institution, Washington, D.C.   Pp. 162-169.

Gustafson, Ralph (ed.)
   1958   The Penguin Book of Canadian Verse.   Penguin Books,
      London.

Hack, John T.
   1942   The Changing Physical Environment of the Hopi
      Indians of Arizona.   Papers Vol. 35, no. 1, Peabody

Museum of American Archaeology and Ethnology, Harvard University, Cambridge.

Hackett, Charles Wilson (trans.)
  1937   _Historical Documents Relating to New Mexico, Nueva Vizcaya, and Approaches Thereto, to 1773: Volume 3._ Publication No. 330, Carnegie Institution, Washington, D.C.

  1942   _Revolt of the Pueblo Indians of New Mexico and Otermin's Attempted Reconquest, 1680-1682, Volumes I and II._ Coronado Cuarto Centennial Publications Vols. 8 and 9, University of New Mexico Press, Albuquerque.

Halfpenny, James
  1986   _A Field Guide to Mammal Tracking in North America._ Johnson Books, Boulder.

Hall, E. Raymond, and Keith R. Kelson
  1959   _The Mammals of North America._ 2 volumes. Ronald Press Co., New York.

Hall, Edward Twitchell, jr.
  1944   Recent Clues to Athapascan Prehistory in the Southwest. _American Anthropologist_ 46 (1): 98-105.

Hall, H.U.
  1926   Some Shields of the Plains and Southwest. _The Museum Journal_ 17: 36-61.

Hall, Stephen A.
  1977   Late Quaternary Sedimentation and Paleoecologic History of Chaco Canyon, New Mexico. _Geological Society of America Bulletin_ 88: 1593-1618.

Halseth, Odd S.
  1926   Fieldwork at Gran Quivira, 1926. _El Palacio_ 21 (9): 223-226.

Hamilton, T.M.
  1982   _Native American Bows._ 2nd edition. Special Publications No. 5, Missouri Archaeological Society, Columbia.

Hammack, Laurens C.
  1966   _The Tunnard Site._ Research Records No. 3, Museum of New Mexico, Santa Fe.

Hammond, George P., and Agapito Rey
  1928   Obregon's History of 16th Century Explorations in
          Western America. Wetzel Publishing Company, Los
          Angeles.

  1940   Narratives of the Coronado Expedition, 1540-1542.
          Coronado Cuarto Centennial Publications Vol. 2,
          University of New Mexico Press, Albuquerque.

  1953   Don Juan de Oñate, Colonizer of New Mexico,
          1595-1628. Coronado Cuarto Centennial Publications
          Vols. 5 and 6, University of New Mexico Press,
          Albuquerque.

  1966   The Rediscovery of New Mexico, 1580-1594. Coronado
          Cuarto Centennial Publications Vol. 3, University of
          New Mexico Press, Albuquerque.

Hankins, Russell L.
  1962   Fray Francisco de Ayeta in the Service of New
          Mexico, 1673-1683. M.A. thesis, Department of
          History, University of New Mexico, Albuquerque.

Hanson, Jeffrey R.
  1979   Ethnohistoric Problems in the Crow-Hidatsa
          Separation. Archaeology in Montana 20 (3): 73-85.

Hargrave, Lyndon L.
  1970   Mexican Macaws. Anthropological Papers No. 20,
          University of Arizona, Tucson.

Harlow, Francis H.
  1973   Matte-paint Pottery of the Tewa, Keres and Zuni
          Pueblos. Museum of New Mexico, Santa Fe.

Harrington, John Peabody
  1909   Notes on the Piro Language. American
          Anthropologist 11 (4): 563-594.

  1916   The Ethnogeography of the Tewa Indians. 29th
          Annual Report of the Bureau of American
          Ethnology...1907-1908. U.S. Government Printing
          Office, Washington, D.C. Pp. 29-636.

  1939   Kiowa Memories of the Northland. In Donald
          D. Brand and Fred E. Harvey (eds.), So Live the Works
          of Men. University of New Mexico Press, Albuquerque.
          Pp. 162-176.

1940   Southern Peripheral Athapaskawan Origins,
        Divisions, and Migrations. In _Essays in Historical_
        Anthropology of North America. Smithsonian
        Miscellaneous Collections Vol. 100, Smithsonian
        Institution, Washington, D.C. Pp. 503-532.

Harris, Arthur H., and James S. Findley
  1964   Pleistocene-Recent Fauna of the Isleta Caves,
        Bernalillo County, New Mexico. _American Journal of_
        Science 262 (1): 114-120.

Haury, Emil W.
  1932   _Roosevelt:9:6, A Hohokam Site of the Colonial_
        Period. Medallion Paper No. 11, Gila Pueblo, Globe.

  1936   _The Mogollon Culture of Southwestern New Mexico._
        Medallion Paper No. 20, Gila Pueblo, Globe.

  1950   _The Stratigraphy and Archaeology of Ventana Cave._
        University of Arizona Press, Tucson.

  1976   _The Hohokam._ University of Arizona Press, Tucson.

Hawley, Florence M.
  1936   _Field Manual of Prehistoric Southwestern Pottery_
        Types. Anthropological Series Bulletin Vol. 1, no. 4;
        University of New Mexico, Albuquerque.

  1937   Kokopelli, of the Prehistoric Southwestern Pueblo
        Pantheon. _American Anthropologist_ 39 (4): 644-646.

  1938   _Classification of Black Pottery Pigments and Paint_
        Areas. Anthropological Series Bulletin Vol. 2, no. 4,
        University of New Mexico, Albuquerque.

  1940   Squash-blossom Headdress in Basket Maker III.
        American Antiquity 6 (2): 166-167.

  1950a   The Mechanics of Perpetuation in Pueblo Witchcraft.
        In Erik K. Reed and Dale S. King (eds.), _For the Dean:_
        Essays in Anthropology in Honor of Byron Cummings.
        Hohokam Museums Association, Tucson and Southwestern
        Monuments Association, Santa Fe. Pp. 143-158.

  1950b   Keresan Patterns of Kinship and Social
        Organization. _American Anthropologist_ 52
        (4): 499-512.

Hayes, Alden C.
   1968   The Missing Convento of San Isidro. El Palacio 75
         (4): 35-40.

   1981   Contributions to Gran Quivira Archeology, Gran
         Quivira National Monument, New Mexico. Editor.
         Publications in Archeology No. 17, U.S. National Park
         Service, Washington, D.C.

Hayes, Alden C., and Jon Nathan Young and A.H. Warren
   1981   Excavation of Mound 7, Gran Quivira National
         Monument, New Mexico. Publications in Archeology
         No. 16, U.S. National Park Service, Washington, D.C.

Haynes, C.V., jr.
   1955   Evidence of Early Man in Torrance County, New
         Mexico. Bulletin of the Texas Archeological Society
         26: 144-164.

Hedrick, John A.
   1971   Investigations of Tigua Potters and Pottery at
         Ysleta del Sur, Texas. The Artifact 9 (2): 1-17.

Heidenreich, C. Adrian
   1979   The Bearing of Ethnohistoric Data on the
         Crow-Hidatsa Separation(s). Archaeology in Montana 20
         (3): 87-111.

Hendron, J.W.
   1935   A Stratigraphic Study of the Pottery of Alameda
         Pueblo. M.A. thesis, Department of Anthropology,
         University of New Mexico, Albuquerque.

   1940   Prehistory of Rito de los Frijoles, Bandelier
         National Monument. Technical Series No. 1,
         Southwestern Monuments Association, Coolidge.

Hewett, Edgar Lee
   1909   The Excavations at Tyuonyi, New Mexico, in 1908.
         American Anthropologist 11 (3): 434-455.

   1923   Verbal Report by Director Edgar L. Hewett on
         Season's Work. El Palacio 15 (5): 78-82.

   1924   Excavations During 1924. El Palacio 27
         (11): 270-271.

   1938   Pajarito Plateau and Its Ancient People.
         University of New Mexico Press, Albuquerque.

Hibben, Frank C.
   1975   Kiva Art of the Anasazi at Pottery Mound. KC
          Publications, Las Vegas.

Hill, W.W.
   1982   An Ethnography of Santa Clara Pueblo, New Mexico.
          Edited by Charles H. Lange, University of New Mexico
          Press, Albuquerque.

Hodder, Ian
   1985   Postprocessual Archaeology. In Advances in
          Archaeological Method and Theory, Volume 8, Michael B.
          Schiffer (ed.); Academic Press, Inc., Toronto.
          Pp. 1-26.

Hodge, Frederick Webb
   1911   The Jumano Indians. Proceedings of the American
          Antiquarian Society 20: 249-268.

   1937   History of Hawikuh, New Mexico. The Frederick Webb
          Hodge Anniversary Publication Fund Publication Vol. 1,
          Southwest Museum, Los Angeles.

   1953   Pueblo Names in the Oñate Documents. In George
          P. Hammond and Agapito Rey, Don Juan de Oñate,
          Colonizer of New Mexico, 1595-1628. Coronado Cuarto
          Centennial Publications Vol. 5, University of New
          Mexico Press, Albuquerque. Pp. 363-374.

Hodge, Frederick Webb, and George P. Hammond and Agapito Rey
(trans.)
   1945   Fray Alonso de Benavides' Revised Memorial of 1634.
          Coronado Cuarto Centennial Publications Vol. 4,
          University of New Mexico Press, Albuquerque.

Holweck, Rt. Rev. F.G.
   1924   A Biographical Dictionary of the Saints. B. Herder
          Book Co., London.

Honea, Kenneth H.
   1966   Eighth Southwestern Ceramic Seminar, Santa Fe.
          Typescript (compiler).

   1968   Material Culture: Ceramics. The Cochiti Dam
          Archaeological Salvage Project, Part 1: Report on the
          1963 Season, Charles H. Lange (ed.). Research Records
          No. 6, Museum of New Mexico, Santa Fe. Pp. 111-169.

Houser, Nicholas P.
  1970   The Tigua Settlement of Ysleta del Sur. The Kiva
          36 (2): 23-39.

Howard, James H.
  1976   Yanktonai Ethnohistory and the John K. Bear Winter
          Count. Plains Anthropologist Memoir 11, Lincoln.

Howard, Richard M.
  1959   Comments on the Indians' Water Supply at Gran
          Quivira National Monument. El Palacio 66 (3): 85-91.

  1960   Tabira -- Identification and Historical Sketch. El
          Palacio 67 (2): 68-71.

Hubbard, John P.
  1978   Revised Check-list of the Birds of New Mexico.
          Publication No. 6, New Mexico Ornithological Society,
          Albuquerque.

Hughes, Anne E.
  1914   The Beginnings of Spanish Settlement in the El Paso
          District. Publications in History Vol. 1, no. 3,
          University of California.

Hurt, Wesley R.
  1942   Folsom and Yuma Points from the Estancia Valley,
          New Mexico. American Antiquity 4 (4): 400-402.

  1986   The 1939-1940 Excavation Project at Quarai Pueblo
          and Mission Buildings. Ms.: Salinas National
          Monument, Mountainair.

Irwin-Williams, Cynthia
  1973   The Oshara Tradition: Origins of Anasazi Culture.
          Contributions to Anthropology Vol. 5, no. 1, Eastern
          New Mexico University, Portales.

Jelinek, Arthur J.
  1967   A Prehistoric Sequence in the Middle Pecos Valley,
          New Mexico. Anthropological Papers No. 31, Museum of
          Anthropology, University of Michigan, Ann Arbor.

Jernigan, E. Wesley
  1978   Jewelry of the Prehistoric Southwest. School of
          American Research, Santa Fe and University of New
          Mexico Press, Albuquerque.

John, Elizabeth A.H.
  1985   An Earlier Chapter in Kiowa History. New Mexico
          Historical Review 60 (4): 379-397.

Johnson, Ross B., and Charles B. Read (eds.)
  1952   Guidebook of the Rio Grande Country, Central New
          Mexico. 3rd Field Conference, New Mexico Geological
          Society, Socorro.

Judge, W. James
  1973   The Paleo-Indian Occupation of the Central Rio
          Grande Valley, New Mexico. University of New Mexico
          Press, Albuquerque.

Katz, Samuel L., and John F. Enders
  1965   Measles Virus. In Frank L. Horsfall, jr. and Igor
          Tamm (eds.), Viral and Rickettsial Infections of Man.
          4th edition. J.B. Lippincott Company, Toronto.
          Pp. 784-801.

Kehoe, Alice B.
  1981   Revisionist Anthropology: Aboriginal North America.
          Current Anthropology 22 (5): 503-517.

Kelley, J. Charles
  1952a   Factors Involved in the Abandonment of Certain
          Peripheral Southwestern Settlements. American
          Anthropologist 54 (3): 356-387.

  1952b   The Historic Indian Pueblos of La Junta de los Rios
          (part 1). New Mexico Historical Review 27
          (4): 257-295.

  1953   The Historic Indian Pueblos of La Junta de los Rios
          (part 2). New Mexico Historical Review 28 (1): 21-51.

  1955   Juan Sabeata and Diffusion in Aboriginal Texas.
          American Anthropologist 57 (5): 981-995.

  1986   Jumano and Patarabueye: Relations at La Junta de
          los Rios. Anthropological Papers No. 77, Museum of
          Anthropology, University of Michigan, Ann Arbor.

Kelley, Jane Holden
  1984   The Archaeology of the Sierra Blanca Region of
          Southeastern New Mexico. Anthropological Papers
          No. 74, Museum of Anthropology, University of
          Michigan, Ann Arbor.

Kelley, Vincent C.
 1952   Tectonics of the Rio Grande Depression of Central
        New Mexico. In Ross B. Johnson and Charles B. Read
        (eds.), Guidebook of the Rio Grande Country, Central
        New Mexico 3rd Field Conference, New Mexico Geological
        Society, Socorro. Pp. 92-105.

Kent, Kate Peck
 1983   Prehistoric Textiles of the Southwest. School of
        American Research, Santa Fe and University of New
        Mexico Press, Albuquerque.

Kessell, John L.
 n.d.   El Señor Fiscal de este Santo Oficio contra El
        Capitan Nicolas de Aguilar por Proposiciones.
        Compiler. Typescript of Inquisicion, Tomo 512,
        Expediente 1 from the Archivo General y Publico,
        Mexico.

 1979a A tale of Two Pueblos. El Palacio 85 (3): 2-5.

 1979b Kiva, Cross, and Crown: The Pecos Indians and New
        Mexico, 1540-1840. U.S. National Park Service,
        Washington, D.C.

 1980   Esteban Clemente: Precursor of the Pueblo Revolt.
        El Palacio 86 (4): 16-17.

Keyser, James D.
 1975   A Shoshonean Origin for the Plains Shield Bearing
        Warrior Motif. Plains Anthropologist 20
        (69): 207-215.

Kidder, Alfred Vincent
 1927   Southwestern Archaeological Conference.   El
        Palacio 23 (22): 554-561.

 1932   The Artifacts of Pecos. Papers of the Southwestern
        Expedition No. 6, Robert S. Peabody Foundation for
        Archaeology, Phillips Academy, Andover.

 1958   Pecos, New Mexico: Archaeological Notes. Papers
        Vol. 5, Robert S. Peabody Foundation for Archaeology,
        Phillips Academy, Andover.

 1962   An Introduction to the Study of Southwestern
        Archaeology. Revised edition. Yale University Press,
        New Haven.

Kidder, Alfred Vincent, and Charles Avery Amsden
  1931   The Pottery of Pecos, Volume I.   Papers of the
         Southwestern Expedition No. 5; Department of
         Archaeology, Phillips Academy, Andover.

Kidder, Alfred Vincent, and Samuel J. Guernsey
  1919   Archeological Explorations in Northeastern Arizona.
         Bulletin 65, Bureau of American Ethnology, Washington,
         D.C.

Kidder, Alfred Vincent, and Anna O. Shepard
  1936   The Pottery of Pecos, Volume II.   Papers of the
         Southwestern Expedition No. 7; Department of
         Archaeology, Phillips Academy, Andover.

Kintigh, Keith W.
  1985   Settlement, Subsistence and Society in Late Zuñi
         Prehistory.   Anthropological Papers No. 44, University
         of Arizona, Tucson.

Knight, Terry
  1980   Ceramic Analysis of Surface Samples from Sites in
         the Bajadan Community, WSNM.   In Archaeological
         Reconnaissance in White Sands National Monument, Peter
         L. Eidenbach and Mark Wimberly.   Human Systems
         Research, Inc., Tularosa.   Pp. 47-70.

Koster, William J.
  1957   Guide to the Fishes of New Mexico.   University of
         New Mexico Press, Albuquerque.

Kroeber, A.L.
  1934a Native American Population.   American
         Anthropologist 36 (1): 1-25.

  1934b Uto-Aztecan Languages of Mexico.   Ibero-Americana
         No. 8, University of California Press, Berkeley.

Kubler, George
  1939   Gran Quivira -- Humanas.   New Mexico Historical
         Review 14 (4): 418-421.

  1940   The Religious Architecture of New Mexico.   Taylor
         Museum, Colorado Springs.

Kuellmer, Frederick J.
  1963   Guidebook of the Socorro Region, New Mexico.   14th
         Field Conference, New Mexico Geological Society,
         Socorro.

Kurath, Gertrude P.
   1959   Cochiti Choreographies and Songs.   In Charles H.
      Lange, Cochiti.   University of Texas Press, Austin.

Kurath, Gertrude Prokosch, and Antonio Garcia
   1970   Music and Dance of the Tewa Pueblos.   Research
      Records No. 8, Museum of New Mexico, Santa Fe.

Lambert, Marjorie F.
   1954   Paa-ko, Archaeological Chronicle of an Indian
      Village in North Central New Mexico.   Monograph 19,
      School of American Research, Santa Fe.

Lange, Charles H.
   1950   Notes on the Use of Turkeys by Pueblo Indians.
      El Palacio 57 (7): 204-209.

   1959   Cochiti: A New Mexico Pueblo, Past and Present.
      University of Texas Press, Austin.

   1968   The Cochiti Dam Archaeological Salvage Project.
      Editor.   Research Records No. 6, Museum of New Mexico,
      Santa Fe.

Lange, Charles H., and Carroll L. Riley (eds.)
   1966   The Southwestern Journals of Adolph F. Bandelier,
      1880-1882.   University of New Mexico Press,
      Albuquerque and Museum of New Mexico Press, Santa Fe.

   1970   The Southwestern Journals of Adolph F. Bandelier,
      1883-1884.   University of New Mexico Press,
      Albuquerque.

Lawrence, Barbara
   1951   Post-cranial Skeletal Characteristics of Deer,
      Pronghorn, and Sheep-Goat, with Notes on Bos and
      Bison.   Papers Vol. 35, no. 3, part II, Peabody Museum
      of American Archaeology and Ethnology, Harvard
      University, Cambridge.

Leap, William L.
   1971   Who Were the Piro? Anthropological Linguistics 13
      (7): 321-330.

LeGuin, Ursula K.
   1986   Always Coming Home.   Bantam Books, Toronto.

Lehmer, Donald J.
   1948   The Jornada Branch of the Mogollon.   Social Science
      Bulletin No. 17, University of Arizona, Tucson.

Lekson, Stephen H.
  1982   Labor Investment in Chacoan Building.   New
      Mexico Archeological Council Newsletter 4
      (5-6): 21-22.

Leon-Portilla, Miguel (ed.)
  1962   The Broken Spears: The Aztec Account of the
      Conquest of Mexico. Beacon Press, Boston.

Leonard, Irving Albert (ed.)
  1932   The Mercurio Volante of Don Carlos de Siguenza y
      Gongora: An Account of the First Expedition of Don
      Diego de Vargas into New Mexico in 1692. Publications
      Vol. 3, Quivira Society, Los Angeles.

Leopold, Luna B.
  1951   Vegetation of Southwestern Watersheds in the
      Nineteenth Century. The Geographical Review 41
      (2): 295-316.

Lintz, Christopher
  1986   The Historical Development of a Culture Complex:
      The Basis for Understanding Architectural
      Misconceptions of the Antelope Creek Focus. In
      Current Trends in Southern Plains Archaeology, Timothy
      G. Baugh (ed.); Memoir 21, Plains Anthropologist,
      Lincoln. Pp. 111-128.

Lister, Florence C., and Robert H. Lister
  1966   Chihuahua: Storehouse of Storms. University of
      New Mexico Press, Albuquerque.

  1976   Distribution of Mexican Maiolica Along the Northern
      Borderlands. In Albert H. Schroeder (ed.), Collected
      Papers in Honor of Marjorie Ferguson Lambert. Papers
      No. 3, Archaeological Society of New Mexico,
      Albuquerque. Pp. 113-140.

Lister, Robert H., and Florence C. Lister
  1969   The Earl H. Morris Memorial Pottery Collection.
      Series in Anthropology No. 16, University of Colorado
      Studies, Boulder.

Little, Elbert L., jr.
  1950   Southwestern Trees. Agriculture Handbook No. 9,
      U.S. Department of Agriculture, Washington, D.C.

Lyons, Thomas R.
  1969   A Study of Paleo-Indian and Desert Culture
      Complexes of the Estancia Valley Area, New Mexico.

Ph.D dissertation, Department of Anthropology,
University of New Mexico, Albuquerque.

Lyons, Thomas R., and Ronald R. Switzer
  1975   Archaeological Excavations at Tillery Springs,
          Estancia, New Mexico. In Theodore R. Frisbie (ed.),
          Collected Papers in Honor of Florence Hawley Ellis.
          Papers No. 2, Archaeological Society of New Mexico,
          Santa Fe. Pp. 312-337.

Maas, Otto
  1929   Misiones de Nuevo Mexico: Documentos del Archivo
          General de Indias (Sevilla) Publicados por Primera Vez
          y Anotados. Imprenta Hijos de T. Minuesa de los Rios,
          Madrid.

McCluney, Eugene B.
  1962   A New Name and Revised Description for a Mogollon
          Pottery Type from Southern New Mexico. Southwestern
          Lore 27 (4): 49-55.

McGregor, John C.
  1945   Nose Plugs from Northern Arizona. American
          Antiquity 10 (3): 303-307, plate XXV.

McKechnie, Jean L. (ed.)
  1977   Webster's New Twentieth Century Dictionary of the
          English Language, Unabridged, 2nd Edition.
          Collins-World.

McKern, W.C.
  1939   The Midwestern Taxonomic Method as an Aid to
          Archaeological Culture Study.   American Antiquity 4
          (4): 301-313.

Mackey, James
  1977   A Multivariate, Osteological Approach to Towa
          Culture History.   American Journal of Physical
          Anthropology 46 (3): 477-482.

McKusick, Charmion R.
  1981   The Faunal Remains of Las Humanas. In Alden
          C. Hayes (ed.), Contributions to Gran Quivira
          Archeology. Publications in Archeology No. 17,
          U.S. National Park Service, Washington, D.C.
          Pp. 39-65, 177-181.

Mallery, Garrick
  1881   Sign Language Among North American Indians. 1st
          Annual Report of the Bureau of Ethnology, 1879-'80.

U.S. Government Printing Office, Washington, D.C.
Pp. 263-552.

Mallory, William Wyman (editor-in-chief)
1972   *Geologic Atlas of the Rocky Mountain Region.* Rocky
Mountain Association of Geologists, Denver.

Marshall, Michael P., and Bill Gossett, Cye Gossett and
Henry Walt
1981   *Piro Project: Archeological Investigations in the
Rio Abajo.* Advance Notes No. 1, New Mexico Historic
Preservation Division, Santa Fe.

Marshall, Michael P., and John R. Stein, Richard W. Loose
and Judith E. Novotny
1979   *Anasazi Communities of the San Juan Basin.* Public
Service Company of New Mexico and New Mexico State
Historic Preservation Bureau.

Marshall, Michael P., and Henry J. Walt
1984   *Rio Abajo: Prehistory and History of a Rio Grande
Province.* New Mexico Historic Preservation Division,
Santa Fe.

Marshall, Susan, and Stuart J. Baldwin
1982   Inventory Data and Analytical Notes on Petroglyph
Sites near Tenabo. Data file in possession of
S.J. Baldwin.

Martin, Paul S. [Schultz]
1963   *The Last 10,000 Years.* University of Arizona
Press, Tucson.

Martin, Paul S. [Sidney], and John B. Rinaldo
1950a   *Turkey Foot Ridge Site.* Fieldiana:Anthropology
Vol. 38, no. 2, Chicago Natural History Museum,
Chicago.

1950b   *Sites of the Reserve Phase, Pine Lawn Valley,
Western New Mexico.* Fieldiana:Anthropology Vol. 38,
no. 3, Chicago Natural History Museum, Chicago.

1960   *Table Rock Pueblo, Arizona.* Fieldiana:Anthropology
Vol. 51, no. 2, Chicago Natural History Museum,
Chicago.

Martin, Paul S. [Sidney], and John B. Rinaldo and Elaine
Bluhm
1954   *Caves of the Reserve Area.* Fieldiana:Anthropology
Vol. 42, Chicago Natural History Museum, Chicago.

Martin, Paul S. [Sidney], and John B. Rinaldo, Elaine Blumm,
Hugh C. Cutler and Roger Grange, jr.
    1952   Mogollon Cultural Continuity and Change: The
        Stratigraphic Analysis of Tularosa and Cordova Caves.
        Fieldiana:Anthropology Vol. 40, Chicago Natural
        History Museum, Chicago.

Matthews, G.H.
    1979   Glottochronology and the Separation of the Crow and
        Hidatsa. Archaeology in Montana 20 (3): 113-125.

May, Jacques M.
    1958   The Ecology of Human Disease. Studies in Medical
        Geography Vol. 1, American Geographical Society, New
        York.

Mecham, J. Lloyd
    1926   The Second Spanish Expedition to New Mexico. New
        Mexico Historical Review 1 (3): 265-291.

Medlin, K.P.
    1983   Plains-Pueblo Relationships: The Archaeological
        Potential of the Salinas Province. COAS 1 (1): 27-40.

Mehringer, Peter J.
    1967   Pollen Analysis and the Alluvial Chronology. The
        Kiva 32 (3): 96-101.

Mellafe, Rolando
    1973   Breve Historia de la Esclavitud Negra en America
        Latina. SepSetentas 115, Secretaria de Educacion
        Publica, Mexico, D.F.

Mera, H.P.
    1931   Chupadero Black on White. Technical Series
        Bulletin No. 1, Laboratory of Anthropology, Santa Fe.

    1933   A Proposed Revision of the Rio Grande Glaze Paint
        Sequence. Technical Series Bulletin No. 5, Laboratory
        of Anthropology, Santa Fe.

    1935   Ceramic Clues to the Prehistory of North Central
        New Mexico. Technical Series Bulletin No. 8,
        Laboratory of Anthropology, Santa Fe.

    1940   Population Changes in the Rio Grande Glaze-Paint
        Area. Technical Series Bulletin No. 9, Laboratory of
        Anthropology, Santa Fe.

1943   An Outline of Ceramic Developments in Southern and
        Southeastern New Mexico. Technical Series Bulletin
        No. 11, Laboratory of Anthropology, Santa Fe.

Miller, Jay
   1975   Kokopelli. In Theodore R. Frisbie (ed.), Collected
           Papers in Honor of Florence Hawley Ellis. Papers
           No. 2, Archaeological Society of New Mexico, Santa Fe.
           Pp. 371-380.

Miller, John P., and Fred Wendorf
   1958   Alluvial Chronology of the Tesuque Valley, New
           Mexico. Journal of Geology 66 (2): 177-194.

Miller, Merton Leland
   1898   A Preliminary Study of the Pueblo of Taos, New
           Mexico. University of Chicago Press, Chicago.

Miller, Wick R.
   1983   A Note on Extinct Languages of Northwest Mexico of
           Supposed Uto-Aztecan Affiliation. International
           Journal of American Linguistics 49 (3): 328-334.

Milner, George R.
   1980   Epidemic Disease in the Postcontact Southeast: A
           Reappraisal. Midcontinental Journal of Archaeology 5
           (1): 39-56.

Mindeleff, Victor
   1891   A Study of Pueblo Architecture, Tusayan and Cibola.
           8th Annual Report of the Bureau of American
           Ethnology...1886-'87. U.S. Government Printing
           Office, Washington, D.C. Pp. 3-228.

de Molina, Alonso
   1571   Vocabulario en Lengua Castellana y Mexicana.
           Antonio de Spinola, Mexico. [1944 facsimile edition:
           Ediciones Cultura Hispanica, Madrid].

Montgomery, Arthur
   1963   The Source of Fibrolite Axes. El Palacio 70
           (1-2): 34-48.

Mooney, James
   1928   The Aboriginal Population of America North of
           Mexico. Edited by John R. Swanton. Smithsonian
           Miscellaneous Collections Vol. 80, no. 7, Smithsonian
           Institution, Washington, D.C.

Morris, Earl H.
   1924   Burials in the Aztec Ruin. Anthropological Papers
          Vol. 26, part 3, American Museum of Natural History,
          New York.

   1927   The Beginnings of Pottery Making in the San Juan
          Area. Anthropological Papers Vol. 28, part 2,
          American Museum of Natural History, New York.

   1939   Archaeological Studies in the La Plata District.
          Publication No. 519, Carnegie Institution of
          Washington, Washington, D.C.

Morris, Earl H., and Robert F. Burgh
   1941   Anasazi Basketry: Basket Maker II Through Pueblo
          III. Publication 533, Carnegie Institution of
          Washington, Washington, D.C.

Morris, Elizabeth Ann
   1980   Basketmaker Caves in the Prayer Rock District,
          Northeastern Arizona. Anthropological Papers No. 35,
          University of Arizona, Tucson.

Mulloy, William
   1942   The Hagen Site. Publications in the Social
          Sciences No. 1, University of Montana, Missoula.

Murphy, Robert F.
   1971   The Dialectics of Social Life: Alarms and
          Excursions in Anthropological Theory. Basic Books,
          Inc., New York.

Myers, Donald A.
   1977   Geologic Map of the Scholle Quadrangle, Socorro,
          Valencia, and Torrance Counties, New Mexico.
          U.S. Geological Survey, Washington, D.C.

Naylor, Thomas H.
   1981   Athapaskans They Weren't: The Suma Rebels Executed
          at Casas Grandes in 1685. In David R. Wilcox and
          W. Bruce Masse (eds.), The Protohistoric Period in the
          North American Southwest, A.D. 1450-1700.
          Anthropological Research Papers No. 24, Arizona State
          University, Tempe.

Needham, C.E., and Robert L. Bates
   1943   Permian Type Sections in Central New Mexico.
          Bulletin of the Geological Society of America
          54: 1653-1667.

Newcomb, W.W., jr.
  1961   The Indians of Texas. University of Texas Press,
      Austin.

Newcomb, W.W., and W.T. Field
  1974   An Ethnohistoric Investigation of the Wichita
      Indians in the Southern Plains. In Robert E. Bell,
      Edward B. Jelks and W.W. Newcomb (eds.), Wichita
      Indian Archaeology and Ethnology: A Pilot Study.
      Garland Publishing Inc., New York. Pp. 271-434.

Newman, Marshall T.
  1976   Aboriginal New World Epidemiology and Medical Care,
      and the Impact of Old World Disease Imports. American
      Journal of Physical Anthropology 45 (3): 667-672.

Nordby, Larry V., and Joseph James Trott
  1982   Results of June 11-12, 1981 Visit to Abo State
      Monument Portion of the Abo Unit -- Salinas National
      Monument. Ms.: Salinas National Monument,
      Mountainair.

Northrop, Stuart A.
  1975   Turquois and Spanish Mines in New Mexico.
      University of New Mexico Press, Albuquerque.

Nuttall, Zelia
  1892   On Ancient Mexican Shields. Internationales Archiv
      fur Ethnographie 5: 34-53, 89.

Oakes, Yvonne Roye
  1979   Excavations at Deadman's Curve, Tijeras Canyon,
      Bernalillo County, New Mexico. Lab Note No. 137,
      Laboratory of Anthropology, Santa Fe.

  1986 The Fite Ranch Project. Laboratory of Anthropology
      Note 432, Museum of New Mexico, Santa Fe.

Olsen, Stanley J.
  1960   Post-cranial Skeletal Characteristics of Bison and
      Bos. Papers Vol. 35, no. 4, Peabody Museum of
      Archaeology and Ethnology, Harvard University,
      Cambridge.

  1964   Mammal Remains from Archaeological Sites, Part
      1: Southeastern and Southwestern United States.
      Papers Vol. 56, no. 1, Peabody Museum of American
      Archaeology and Ethnology, Harvard University,
      Cambridge.

1968a   _Fish, Amphibian and Reptile Remains from_
        Archaeological Sites, Part 1: Southeastern and
        Southwestern United States. Papers Vol. 56, no. 2,
        Peabody Museum of American Archaeology and Ethnology,
        Harvard University, Cambridge.

1968b   The Osteology of the Wild Turkey. In Olsen, _Fish,_
        Amphibian and Reptile Remains from Archaeological
        Sites, Part 1: Southeastern and Southwestern United
        States. Papers Vol. 56, no. 2, Peabody Museum of
        American Archaeology and Ethnology, Harvard
        University, Cambridge. Pp. 107-137.

1972   _Osteology for the Archaeologist, No. 4: North_
        American Birds. Papers Vol. 56, no. 4, Peabody Museum
        of American Archaeology and Ethnology, Harvard
        University, Cambridge.

Opler, Morris E.
  1983   The Apachean Culture Pattern and Its Origins. In
         Alfonso Ortiz and William C. Sturtevant (eds.),
         Handbook of North American Indians, Volume 10:
         Southwest. Smithsonian Institution, Washington, D.C.
         Pp. 368-392.

Oppelt, Norman T.
  1984   Worked Potsherds of the Prehistoric Southwest:
         Their Forms and Distribution. _Pottery Southwest_ 11
         (1): 1-6.

Ortiz, Alfonso
  1969   _The Tewa World._ University of Chicago Press,
         Chicago.

Pacheco, Joaquin F., y Francisco de Cardenas y Luis Torres
de Mendoza
  1865   _Coleccion de Documentos Ineditos Relativos al_
         Descubrimiento, Conquista y Organizacion de las
         Antiguas Posesiones Españolas en America y Oceania,
         Tomo IV. Imprenta de Frias y Compañia, Madrid.

  1870a _Coleccion de Documentos Ineditos Relativos al_
         Descubrimiento, Conquista y Organizacion de las
         Antiguas Posesiones Españolas en America y Oceania,
         Tomo XIII. Imprenta de Jose Maria Perez, Madrid.

  1870b _Coleccion de Documentos Ineditos Relativos al_
         Descubrimiento, Conquista y Organizacion de las
         Antiguas Posesiones Españolas de America y Oceania,
         Tomo XIV. Imprenta de Jose Maria Perez, Madrid.

1871a Coleccion de Documentos Ineditos Relativos al
       Descubrimiento, Conquista y Organizacion de las
       Antiguas Posesiones Españolas de America y Oceania,
       Tomo XV. Imprenta de Jose Maria Perez, Madrid.

1871b Coleccion de Documentos Ineditos Relativos al
       Descubrimiento, Conquista y Organizacion de las
       Antiguas Posesiones Españolas de America y Oceania,
       Tomo XVI. Imprenta del Hospicio, Madrid.

Palkovich, Ann M.
  1985 Historic Populations of the Eastern Pueblos:
        1540-1910. Journal of Anthropological Research 41
        (4): 401-426.

Parsons, Elsie Clews
  1925 The Pueblo of Jemez. Papers of the Southwestern
        Expedition No. 3, Phillips Academy, Andover.

  1926 Tewa Tales. Memoirs Vol. 19, American Folk-Lore
        Society, New York.

  1929 The Social Organization of the Tewa of New Mexico.
        Memoirs Vol. 36, American Anthropological Association,
        Menasha.

  1932 Isleta, New Mexico. 47th Annual Report of the
        Bureau of American Ethnology...1929-1930, Washington,
        D.C. Pp. 193-446.

  1936 Hopi Journal of Alexander M. Stephen. 2 volumes.
        Columbia University Press, New York.

  1938 The Humpbacked Flute Player of the Southwest.
        American Anthropologist 40 (2): 337-338.

  1939 Pueblo Indian Religion. 2 volumes. University of
        Chicago Press, Chicago.

  1970 Isleta Paintings. 2nd edition; edited by Esther
        S. Goldfrank. Smithsonian Institution Press,
        Washington, D.C.

Patraw, Pauline M., and Jeanne R. Janish
  1953 Flowers of the Southwest Mesas. Popular Series
        No. 5, Southwestern Monuments Association, Globe.

Pease, Douglas S.
  1975 Soil Survey of Valencia County, New Mexico, Eastern
        Part. Soil Conservation Service, U.S. Department of

Agriculture and Bureau of Indian Affairs,
U.S. Department of the Interior.

Peckham, Stewart
  1976   Taylor Draw: A Mogollon-Anasazi Hybrid? In Albert
          H. Schroeder (ed.), Collected Papers in Honor of
          Marjorie Ferguson Lambert. Papers No. 3,
          Archaeological Society of New Mexico, Albuquerque.
          Pp. 37-72.

  1979   When Is a Rio Grande Kiva? In Collected Papers in
          Honor of Bertha Pauline Dutton, Albert H. Schroeder
          (ed.); Papers No. 4, Archaeological Society of New
          Mexico, Albuquerque. Pp. 55-86.

Pimentel, Francisco
  1865   Cuadro Descriptivo y Comparativo de las Lenguas
          Indigenas de Mexico. Tomo 2. Imprenta de Andrade y
          Escalante, Mexico.

Pogue, Joseph E.
  1915   The Turquois. Memoirs Volume 12, 3rd Memoir,
          National Academy of Sciences, Washington, D.C.

Rea, Vargas (ed.)
  1947   Autos Sobre Quejas de los Religiosos Franciscanos
          del Nuevo Mexico, 1636. Biblioteca Aportacion
          Historica, Mexico.

Real Academia Española
  1956   Diccionario de la Lengua Española, 18a Edicion.
          Madrid.

Reed, Erik K.
  1949   Sources of Upper Rio Grande Pueblo Culture and
          Population. El Palacio 56 (6): 163-184.

  1950   Eastern-central Arizona Archaeology in Relation to
          the Western Pueblos. Southwestern Journal of
          Anthropology 6 (2): 120-138.

  1951   Turkeys in Southwestern Archaeology. El Palacio 58
          (7): 195-205.

Reher, Charles A. (ed.)
  1977   Settlement and Subsistence Along the Lower Chaco
          River: The CGP Survey. University of New Mexico
          Press, Albuquerque.

Reiter, Paul
1938   The Jemez Pueblo of Unshagi, New Mexico. Monograph
        Series Vol. 1, no. 5, University of New Mexico and
        School of American Research, Albuquerque.

Renaud, Etienne B.
1948   Kokopelli: A Study in Pueblo Mythology.
        Southwestern Lore 14 (1-2): 25-40.

Riley, Carroll L.
1982   The Frontier People:_ The Greater Southwest in the
        Protohistoric Period. Occasional Paper No. 1, Center
        for Archaeological Investigations, Southern Illinois
        University at Carbondale, Carbondale.

Rinaldo, John B., and Elaine Bluhm
1956   Late Mogollon Pottery Types of the Reserve Area.
        Fieldiana:Anthropology 36 (7), Chicago Natural History
        Museum, Chicago.

Robbins, Wilfred William, and John Peabody Harrington and
Barbara Freire-Marreco
1916   Ethnobotany of the Tewa Indians. Bulletin 55,
        Bureau of American Ethnology, Washington, D.C.

Robinson, T.W.
1965   Introduction, Spread and Areal Extent of Saltcedar
        (Tamarix) in the Western States. Professional Paper
        491-A, U.S. Geological Survey, Washington, D.C..

Robinson, William J., and John W. Hannah and Bruce
G. Harrill
1972   Tree-Ring Dates from New Mexico I, O, U:_ Central
        Rio Grande Area. Laboratory of Tree-ring Research,
        Tucson.

Robinson, William J., and Bruce G. Harrill and Richard
L. Warren
1974   Tree-Ring Dates from New Mexico B:
        Chaco-Gobernador Area. Laboratory of Tree-ring
        Research, Tucson.

Roe, Frank Gilbert
1970   The North American Buffalo:_ A Critical Study of
        the Species in Its Wild State. 2nd edition.
        University of Toronto Press, Toronto.

Roemer, Erwin, jr., and Paul R. Katz
1977   Ceramics. In Thomas R. Hester (ed.), An
        Archaeological Survey of the Radium Springs Area,

Southern New Mexico. Archaeological Survey Report
No. 26, Center for Archaeological Research, University
of Texas at San Antonio, San Antonio. Pp. 79-111.

Rogers, R.N.
    1980   The Chemistry of Pottery Smudging. Pottery
        Southwest 7 (2): 2-4.

Rohn, Arthur H.
    1971   Mug House, Mesa Verde National Park, Colorado.
        Archeological Research Series No. 7-D, U.S. National
        Park Service, Washington, D.C.

    1977   Cultural Change and Continuity on Chapin Mesa. The
        Regents Press of Kansas, Lawrence.

Roosa, William B.
    1956   The Lucy Site in Central New Mexico. American
        Antiquity 21 (3): 310.

Ruppe, Reynold J.
    1966   The Archaeological Survey: A Defense. American
        Antiquity 31 (3): 313-333.

Salas, Alberto Mario
    1950   Las Armas de la Conquista. Emece Editores, S.A.,
        Buenos Aires.

Salmon, Merrilee H.
    1976   "Deductive" Versus "Inductive" Archaeology.
        American Antiquity 41 (3): 376-381.

    1978   What Can Systems Theory Do for Archaeology?
        American Antiquity 43 (2): 174-183.

    1980   Reply to Lowe and Barthe.   American Antiquity 45
        (3): 575-579.

Scarbrough, Lorna Lee, and Arthur H. Harris
    1985   Archaeological Excavations: A Plea for a More
        Refined Technique. In Michael S. Foster and Thomas
        C. O'Laughlin (eds.), Proceedings of the Third
        Jornada-Mogollon Conference. In The Artifact 23
        (1-2): 179-185.

Schaafsma, Curtis F.
    1981   Early Apacheans in the Southwest: A Review. In
        David R. Wilcox and W. Bruce Masse (eds.), The
        Protohistoric Period in the North American Southwest,

_A.D._ _1450-1700._ Anthropological Research Papers
No. 24, Arizona State University, Tempe. Pp. 291-320.

Schaafsma, Polly
  1968   The Los Lunas Petroglyphs. _El Palacio_ 75 (2):
         13-24.

  1972   _Rock Art in New Mexico._ University of New Mexico
         Press, Albuquerque.

  1975   _Rock Art in the Cochiti Reservoir District._ Papers
         in Anthropology No. 16, Museum of New Mexico, Santa
         Fe.

  1980   _Indian Rock Art of the Southwest._ School of
         American Research, Santa Fe and University of New
         Mexico Press, Albuquerque.

Schaafsma, Polly, and Curtis Schaafsma
  1974   Evidence for the Origins of the Pueblo Katchina
         Cult as Suggested by Southwestern Rock Art. _American_
         Antiquity 39 (4): 535-545.

Schoenwetter, James
  1966   A Re-evaluation of the Navajo Reservoir Pollen
         Chronology. _El Palacio_ 73 (1): 19-26.

Schoenwetter, James, and Alfred E. Dittert
  1968   An Ecological Interpretation of Anasazi Settlement
         Patterns. In Betty J. Meggers (ed.), _Anthropological_
         Archaeology in the Americas. Anthropological Society
         of Washington, Washington, D.C. Pp. 41-66.

Scholes, France V.
  1929   Documents for the History of the New Mexican
         Missions in the Seventeenth Century. _New Mexico_
         Historical Review 4 (1-2): 45-58, 195-201.

  1930   The Supply Service of the New Mexican Missions in
         the Seventeenth Century. _New Mexico Historical Review_
         5(1, 2 and 4): 93-115, 186-210, 386-404.

  1932   Problems in the Early Ecclesiastical History of New
         Mexico. _New Mexico Historical Review_ 7 (1): 32-74.

  1935   Civil Government and Society in New Mexico in the
         Seventeenth Century. _New Mexico Historical Review_ 10
         (2): 71-111.

1936   Church and State in New Mexico, 1610-1650. New Mexico Historical Review 11 (1-4): 9-76, 145-178, 283-294, 297-349.

1937   Church and State in New Mexico, 1610-1650. New Mexico Historical Review 12 (1): 78-106.

1938   Notes on the Jemez Missions in the Seventeenth Century. El Palacio 44 (7-9, 13-15): 61-71, 93-102.

1942   Troublous Times in New Mexico, 1659-1670. Publications in History Vol. 11, Historical Society of New Mexico, Albuquerque.

1944   Correction. New Mexico Historical Review 19 (3): 243-246.

Scholes, France V., and Eleanor B. Adams
1952   Inventories of Church Furnishings in Some of the New Mexico Missions, 1672. In William M. Dabney and Josiah C. Russell (eds.), Dargan Historical Essays. Publications in History No. 4, University of New Mexico, Albuquerque. Pp. 27-38.

Scholes, France V., and Lansing B. Bloom
1944   Friar Personnel and Mission Chronology: 1598-1629. New Mexico Historical Review 19 (4): 319-336.

1945   Friar Personnel and Mission Chronology: 1598-1629. New Mexico Historical Review 20 (1): 58-82.

Scholes, France V., and H.P. Mera
1940   Some Aspects of the Jumano Problem. Contributions to American Anthropology and History No. 34, Carnegie Institution of Washington, Washington, D.C.

Schroeder, Albert H.
1962   A Re-analysis of the Routes of Coronado and Oñate into the Plains in 1541 and 1601. Plains Anthropologist 7 (15): 2-23.

1964   The Language of the Saline Pueblos: Piro or Tiwa? New Mexico Historical Review 39 (3): 235-249.

1968   Birds and Feathers in Documents Relating to Indians of the Southwest. Collected Papers in Honor of Lyndon Lane Hargrave, Schroeder (ed.); Papers No. 1, Archaeological Society of New Mexico, Santa Fe. Pp. 95-114.

1979   Pueblos Abandoned in Historic Times. In Alfonso
        Ortiz and William C. Sturtevant (eds.), Handbook of
        North American Indians, Volume 9: Southwest.
        Smithsonian Institution, Washington, D.C.
        Pp. 236-254.

Schroeder, Albert H., and Dan S. Matson
    1965   A Colony on the Move: Gaspar Castaño de Sosa's
            Journal, 1590-1591. School of American Research,
            Santa Fe.

Schuetz, Mardith K.
    1980   The Archaeology of Mission Socorro. The Artifact
            18 (2): 1-34.

Scott, Tom (ed.)
    1970   The Penguin Book of Scottish Verse. Penguin Books
            Ltd., Harmondsworth.

Senter, Donovan
    1934   The Work on the Old Quarai Mission, 1934. El
            Palacio 37 (21-23): 169-174.

Shaul, David Leedom
    1984   (Tom)Piro as a Tanoan Language. Ms.

Shepard, Anna O.
    1942   Rio Grande Glaze Paint Ware. Contributions to
            American Anthropology and History No. 39, Carnegie
            Institution of Washington, Washington, D.C.

Simmons, Marc
    1966   New Mexico's Smallpox Epidemic of 1780-1781. New
            Mexico Historical Review 41 (4): 319-326.

    1968   Spanish Government in New Mexico. University of
            New Mexico Press, Albuquerque.

    1979   History of Pueblo-Spanish Relations to 1821. In
            Alfonso Ortiz and William C. Sturtevant (eds.),
            Handbook of North American Indians, Volume 9:
            Southwest. Smithsonian Institution, Washington, D.C.
            Pp. 178-193.

Sims, Agnes C.
    1948   An Artist Analyzes New Mexico's Petroglyphs. El
            Palacio 55 (10): 302-309.

    1950   San Cristobal Petroglyphs. Southwest Editions,
            Santa Fe.

Skinner, S. Alan, and Chester Shaw, Carol Carter, Maynard
Cliff and Carol Heathington
  1980   Archaeological Investigations at Nambe Falls.
          Research Report 121, Archaeology Research Program,
          Southern Methodist University.

Smiley, Terah L., and Stanley A. Stubbs and Bryant Bannister
  1953   A Foundation for the Dating of Some Late
          Archaeological Sites in the Rio Grande Area, New
          Mexico. Bulletin No. 6, Laboratory of Tree-ring
          Research, Tucson.

Smith, Anne M.
  1966   New Mexico Indians: Economic, Educational and
          Social Problems. Research Records No. 1, Museum of
          New Mexico, Santa Fe.

Smith, Marvin T., and Mary Elizabeth Good
  1982   Early Sixteenth Century Glass Beads in the Spanish
          Colonial Trade. Cottonlandia Museum Publications,
          Greenwood.

Smith, Watson
  1952   Kiva Murals at Awatovi and Kawaika-a. Papers
          Vol. 37, Peabody Museum of American Archaeology and
          Ethnology, Harvard University, Cambridge.

Smith, Watson, and Richard B. Woodbury and Nathalie
F.S. Woodbury
  1966   The Excavation of Hawikuh by Frederick Webb Hodge.
          Contributions Vol. 20, Museum of the American Indian -
          Heye Foundation, New York.

Snow, David H.
  1973   Prehistoric Southwestern Turquoise Industry. El
          Palacio 79 (1): 33-51.

  1982   The Rio Grande Glaze, Matte-Paint, and Plainware
          Tradition. Southwestern Ceramics: A Comparative
          Review, Albert H. Schroeder (ed.). The Arizona
          Archaeologist No. 15: 235-278.

Snyder, John C.
  1965   Typhus Fever Rickettsiae. In Frank L. Horsfall and
          Igor Tamm (eds.), Viral and Rickettsial Infections of
          Man. 4th edition. J.B. Lippincott Company, Toronto.
          Pp. 1059-1094.

1205

Spicer, Edward H.
1962   *Cycles of Conquest*. University of Arizona Press,
       Tucson.

Spiegel, Zane
1955   *Geology and Ground-Water Resources of Northeastern
       Socorro County, New Mexico*. Ground-Water Report 4,
       State Bureau of Mines and Mineral Resources, Socorro.

Stallings, W.S., jr.
1937   Southwestern Dated Ruins: I. *Tree-ring Bulletin* 4
       (2): 3-5.

Stanislawski, Michael B.
1969   What Good Is a Broken Pot? An Experiment in
       Hopi-Tewa Ethno-Archaeology. *Southwestern Lore* 35
       (1): 11-18.

Stark, J.T.
1956   *Geology of the South Manzano Mountains, New Mexico*.
       Bulletin 34, State Bureau of Mines and Mineral
       Resources, Socorro.

Stark, J.T., and E.C. Dapples
1946   Geology of the Los Pinos Mountains, New Mexico.
       Bulletin of the Geological Society of America 57:
       1121-1172.

Stebbins, Robert C.
1954   *Amphibians and Reptiles of Western North America*.
       McGraw-Hill Book Co., New York.

Steed, Paul P., jr.
1980   Rock Art in Chaco Canyon. *The Artifact* 18 (3):
       I-VI, 1-146.

Steen, Charlie R.
1980   LA 10607: The Manzanares Site. In Albert
       H. Schroeder (ed.), *Collected Papers in Honor of Helen
       Greene Blumenschein*. Papers No. 5, Archaeological
       Society of New Mexico, Albuquerque. Pp. 129-139.

1982   *Pajarito Plateau Archaeological Surveys and
       Excavations, II*. Los Alamos National Laboratory, Los
       Alamos.

Stevenson, Matilda Coxe
1904   The Zuñi Indians. *23rd Annual Report of the Bureau
       of American Ethnology...1901-1902*. U.S. Government
       Printing Office, Washington, D.C. Pp. 3-634.

Steward, Julian H.
   1942   The Direct Historical Approach to Archaeology.
           American Antiquity 7 (4): 337-343.

Stewart, Guy R.
   1940   Conservation in Pueblo Agriculture, II.   Scientific
           Monthly 51 (3):   329-340.

Stewart, Guy R., and Maurice Donnelly
   1943   Soil and Water Economy in the Pueblo Southwest,
           Part II.   Scientific Monthly 56 (2):   134-144.

Stirling, Matthew W.
   1942   Origin Myth of Acoma and Other Records.   Bulletin
           135, Bureau of American Ethnology, Washington, D.C.

Stokes, William Lee
   1969   Scenes of the Plateau Lands and How They Came To
           Be.   Publishers Press, Salt Lake City.

Stone, George Cameron
   1934   A Glossary of the Construction, Decoration and Use
           of Arms and Armor in All Countries and in All Times.
           Southworth Press.

Stuart, David E., and Robin E. Farwell
   1983   Out of Phase: Late Pithouse Occupations in the
           Highlands of New Mexico.   In Joseph C. Winter (ed.),
           High Altitude Adaptations in the Southwest.   Cultural
           Resources Management Report No. 2, U.S. Forest
           Service.   Pp. 115-158.

Stuart, David E., and Rory P. Gauthier
   1981   Prehistoric New Mexico: Background for Survey.
           Historic Preservation Bureau, Santa Fe.

Stubbs, Stanley A.
   1950   Bird's-Eye View of the Pueblos.   University of
           Oklahoma Press, Norman.

   1959   "New" Old Churches Found at Quarai and Tabira
           (Pueblo Blanco).   El Palacio 66 (5):   162-169.

Stubbs, Stanley A., and W.S. Stallings, jr.
   1953   The Excavation of Pindi Pueblo, New Mexico.
           Monograph No. 18, School of American Research and
           Laboratory of Anthropology, Santa Fe.

Suhm, Dee Ann, and Edward B. Jelks (eds.)
   1962   Handbook of Texas Archeology: Type Descriptions.

Texas Archeological Society and Texas Memorial Museum, Austin.

Suhm, Dee Ann, and Alex D. Krieger and Edward B. Jelks
1954   An Introductory Handbook of Texas Archeology. In Bulletin of the Texas Archeological Society 25.

Sullivan, Alan P.
1978   Inference and Evidence in Archaeology: A Discussion of the Conceptual Problems. In Advances in Method and Theory in Archaeology, Volume 1, Michael B. Schiffer (ed.); Academic Press, New York. Pp. 183-222.

Sundt, Willaim M.
1973   Progress Report on AS-5: The Excavation of a Primitive Indian Lead Mine. Awanyu 1 (4): 22-26.

1979   Socorro Black-on-White. Pottery Southwest 6 (3): 4-6.

Switzer, Ronald R.
n.d.   The Origin and Significance of Snake-Lightning Cults in the Pueblo Southwest. Special Report No. 11, El Paso Archaeological Society, El Paso.

1969   Tobacco, Pipes, and Cigarettes of the Prehistoric Southwest. Special Report No. 8, El Paso Archaeological Society, El Paso.

Tainter, Joseph A.
1979   The Mountainair Lithic Scatters: Settlement Patterns and Significance Evaluation of Low Density Surface Sites. Journal of Field Archaeology 6 (4): 463-469.

1985   Perspectives on the Abandonment of the Northern Tularosa Basin. In Colleen M. Beck (ed.), Views of the Jornada Mogollon. Contributions in Anthropology Vol. 12, Eastern New Mexico University, Portales. Pp. 143-147.

Tainter, Joseph A., and Frances Levine
1987   Cultural Resources Overview: Central New Mexico. U.S. Forest Service and U.S. Bureau of Land Management, Albuquerque and Santa Fe.

Tamaron y Romeral, Pedro
1937   Demostracion del Vastisimo Obispado de La Nueva Vizcaya - 1765: Durango, Sonora, Arizona, Nuevo

Mexico, Chihuahua y Porciones de Texas, Coahuila y Zacatecas. Anotated by Vito Alessio Robles. Biblioteca Historica Mexicana de Obras Ineditas No. 7, Antigua Libreria Robredo de Jose Porrua e Hijos, Mexico.

Taylor, John F.
  1979   Tenting on the Plains: Archaeological Inferences About the Awatixa Hidatsa - Mountain Crow Schism from the Missouri River Trench. _Archaeology in Montana_ 20 (3): 31-41.

Taylor, Walter W.
  1967   _A Study of Archeology._ 2nd edition; Southern Illinois University Press, Carbondale.

Tedlock, Dennis
  1972   _Finding the Center._ Dial Press, New York.

Thomas, Alfred Barnaby (ed.)
  1932   _Forgotten Frontiers: A Study of the Spanish Indian Policy of Don Juan Bautista de Anza, Governor of New Mexico, 1777-1787._ University of Oklahoma Press, Norman.

Thomas, David Hurst
  1971   On Distinguishing Natural from Cultural Bone in Archaeological Sites.   _American Antiquity_ 36 (3): 366-371.

  1978   The Awful Truth About Statistics in Archaeology. _American Antiquity_ 43 (2): 231-244.

Thomas, H.E., _et alia_
  1963   _Drought in the Southwest, 1942-56._ Professional Paper 372, U.S. Geological Survey, Washington, D.C.

Tichy, Marjorie Ferguson
  1939   The Archaeology of Puaray. _El Palacio_ 46 (7): 145-163.

Timmons, W.H.
  1977   The Population of the El Paso Area -- A Census of 1784. _New Mexico Historical Review_ 52 (4): 311-316.

Titiev, Mischa
  1939   The Story of Kokopele. _American Anthropologist_ 41 (1): 91-98.

1944   Old Oraibi. Papers Vol. 22, no. 1, Peabody Museum
        of American Archaeology and Ethnology, Harvard
        University, Cambridge.

Titus, Frank B.
  1969   Late Tertiary and Quaternary Hydrogeology of
          Estancia Basin, Central New Mexico. Ph.D
          dissertation, Department of Geology, University of New
          Mexico, Albuquerque.

Tolstoy, Leo
  1968   War and Peace. The New American Library, New York.

Toulouse, Joseph H., jr.
  1949   The Mission of San Gregorio de Abo. Monographs
          No. 13, School of American Research, Santa Fe.

Toulouse, Joseph H., jr., and Robert L. Stephenson
  1960   Excavations at Pueblo Pardo. Papers in
          Anthropology No. 2, Museum of New Mexico, Santa Fe.

Trager, George L.
  1942   The Historical Phonology of the Tiwa Languages.
          Studies in Linguistics 1 (5): 1-10.

  1943   The Kinship and Status Terms of the Tiwa Languages.
          American Anthropologist 45 (4): 557-571.

  1967   The Tanoan Settlement of the Rio Grande Area: A
          Possible Chronology. In Dell H. Hymes (ed.), Studies
          in Southwestern Ethnolinguistics. Studies in General
          Anthropology III. Pp. 335-350.

Turner, Christy G., II
  1963   Petrographs of the Glen Canyon Region. Bulletin
          38, Museum of Northern Arizona, Flagstaff.

Twitchell, Ralph Emerson
  1914   The Spanish Archives of New Mexico, Volume 2. The
          Torch Press, Cedar Rapids.

Tyler, S. Lyman, and H. Darrel Taylor
  1958   The Report of Fray Alonso de Posada in Relation to
          Quivira and Teguayo. New Mexico Historical Review 33
          (4): 285-314.

Ubelaker, Douglas H.
  1976   Prehistoric New World Population Size: Historical
          Review and Current Appraisal of North American

Estimates. *American Journal of Physical Anthropology*
45 (3): 661-665.

Underhill, Ruth
  1944 *Pueblo Crafts.* U.S. Bureau of Indian Affairs,
    Washington, D.C.

Updike, John
  1969 The Dance of the Solids. *Scientific American* 220
    (1): 130-131.

Upham, Steadman
  1982 *Politics and Power: An Economic and Political
    History of the Western Pueblo.* Academic Press,
    Toronto.

  1986 Smallpox and Climate in the American Southwest.
    American Anthropologist 88 (1): 115-128.

Van Valkenburgh, Sallie P.
  1964 Other Artifacts. In Gordon Vivian, *Excavations in
    a 17th-Century Jumano Pueblo, Gran Quivira.*
    Archeological Research Series No. 8, U.S. National
    Park Service, Washington, D.C. Pp. 122-139.

Velez de Escalante, Silvestre
  1856 Carta del Padre Fray Silvestre Velez de Escalante,
    escrita en 2 Abril de 1778 Años. *Documentos Para la
    Historia de Mexico, Serie III (Tomo I);* Imprenta de
    Vicente Garcia Torres, Mexico. Pp. 113-208.

de Vetancurt, Augustin
  1697 *Teatro Mexicano, Quarta Parte: Chronica de la
    Provincia del Santo Evangelio de Mexico.* Mexico.
    [Facsimile reprint 1971, Editorial Porrua, S.A.,
    Mexico, D.F.]

  1698 *Menologio Franciscano de los Varones mas Señalados.*
    Mexico. [Facsimile reprint 1971, bound with Vetancurt
    1697, Editorial Porrua, S.A., Mexico, D.F.]

Vivian, Gordon
  1932 A Restudy of the Province of Tiguex. M.A. thesis,
    University of New Mexico, Albuquerque.

  1964 *Excavations in a 17th-Century Jumano Pueblo, Gran
    Quivira.* Archeological Research Series No. 8,
    U.S. National Park Service, Washington, D.C.

Vivian, Gordon, and Paul Reiter
  1960   The Great Kivas of Chaco Canyon and Their
          Relationships. Monograph No. 22, School of American
          Research, Santa Fe.

Voll, Charles B.
  1961   The Glaze Paint Ceramics of Pottery Mound, New
          Mexico. M.A. thesis, Department of Anthropology,
          University of New Mexico, Albuquerque.

Warren, A. Helene
  1970   Notes on Manufacture and Trade of Rio Grande
          Glazes. The Artifact 8 (4): 1-7.

  1980   Prehistoric Pottery of Tijeras Canyon. In Linda
          S. Cordell (ed.), Tijeras Canyon: Analyses of the
          Past. University of New Mexico Press, Albuquerque.
          Pp. 149-168.

  1981   A Petrographic Study of the Pottery. In Alden
          C. Hayes (ed.), Contributions to Gran Quivira
          Archeology. Publications in Archeology No. 17,
          U.S. National Park Service, Washington, D.C.
          Pp. 67-73, 182-183.

  1982   Prehistoric Mineral Resources of the Lower Rio
          Puerco. In Peter L. Eidenbach (ed.), Inventory Survey
          of the Lower Hidden Mountain Floodpool, Lower Rio
          Puerco Drainage, Central New Mexico. Human Systems
          Research, Inc., Tularosa. Pp. 66-75.

Warren, A. Helene, and Frances Joan Mathien
  1985   Prehistoric and Historic Turquoise Mining in the
          Cerrillos District: Time and Place. In Charles
          H. Lange (ed.), Southwestern Culture History:
          Collected Papers in Honor of Albert H. Schroeder.
          Papers No. 10, Archaeological Society of New Mexico,
          Santa Fe. Pp. 93-127.

Watson, Patty Jo, and Steven A. LeBlanc and Charles
L. Redman
  1971   Explanation in Archeology. Columbia University
          Press, New York.

Weber, Robert H.
  1963   Cenozoic Volcanic Rocks of Socorro County. In
          Frederick J. Kuellmer (ed.), Guidebook of the Socorro
          Region, New Mexico. 14th Field Conference, New Mexico
          Geological Society, Socorro. Pp. 132-143.

Wedel, Waldo R.
   1970   Coronado's Route to Quivira, 1541.   Plains
           Anthropologist 15 (49): 161-168.

Wellmann, Klaus F.
   1970   Kokopelli of Indian Paleology. Journal of the
           American Medical Association 212 (10): 1678-1682.

   1972   New Mexico's Mutilated Hand. Journal of the
           American Medical Association 219 (12): 1609-1610.

   1979   A Survey of North American Indian Rock Art.
           Akademische Druck-und Verlagsanstalt, Graz.

Wendorf, Fred
   1953   Excavations at Te'ewi. In Wendorf (ed.), Salvage
           Archaeology in the Chama Valley, New Mexico.
           Monograph No. 17, School of American Research, Santa
           Fe. Pp. 34-93.

   1954   A Reconstruction of Northern Rio Grande Prehistory.
           American Anthropologist 56 (2): 200-227.

Wendorf, Fred, and Erik K. Reed
   1955   An Alternative Reconstruction of Northern Rio
           Grande Prehistory.   El Palacio 62 (5-6): 131-173.

Whalen, Michael E.
   1981   Origin and Evolution of Ceramics in Western Texas.
           Bulletin of the Texas Archeological Society 52:
           215-229.

White, Leslie A.
   1932   The Acoma Indians. 47th Annual Report of the
           Bureau of American Ethnology...1929-1930.
           U.S. Government Printing Office, Washington, D.C.
           Pp. 17-192.

   1935   The Pueblo of Santo Domingo, New Mexico. Memoirs
           No. 43, American Anthropological Association, Menasha.

   1942   The Pueblo of Santa Ana, New Mexico. Memoirs
           No. 60, American Anthropological Association.

   1962   The Pueblo of Sia, New Mexico. Bulletin 184,
           Bureau of American Ethnology, Washington, D.C.

Wilcox, David R.
   1981   The Entry of Athapaskans into the American
           Southwest: The Problem Today. In Wilcox and W. Bruce

Masse (eds.), The Protohistoric Period in the North American Southwest, A.D. 1450-1700. Anthropological Research Papers No. 24, Arizona State University, Tempe. Pp. 213-256.

Willey, Gordon R., and Philip Phillips
1958   Method and Theory in American Archaeology. University of Chicago Press, Chicago.

Willey, Gordon R., and Jeremy A. Sabloff
1974   A History of American Archaeology. W.H. Freeman and Company, San Francisco.

Wilpolt, R.H., and A.J. MacAlpin, R.L. Bates and Georges Vorbe
1946   Geologic Map and Stratigraphic Sections of Paleozoic Rocks of Joyita Hills, Los Pinos Mountains, and Northern Chupadera Mesa, Valencia, Torrance, and Socorro Counties, New Mexico. Oil and Gas Inventory Preliminary Map 61, U.S. Geological Survey, Denver.

Wilson, John P.
1973   Quarai: Living Mission to Monument. El Palacio 78 (4): 14-28.

1985   Before the Pueblo Revolt: Population Trends, Apache Relations and Pueblo Abandonments in Seventeenth Century New Mexico. In Nancy Fox (ed.), Prehistory and History in the Southwest: Collected Papers in Honor of Alden C. Hayes, Papers No. 11, Archaeological Society of New Mexico, Albuquerquee. Pp. 113-120.

Wilson, John P., and Robert H. Leslie and A.H. Warren
1983   Tabira: Outpost on the East. In Nancy L. Fox (ed.), Collected Papers in Honor of Charlie R. Steen, Jr., Papers No. 8, Archaeological Society of New Mexico, Albuquerque. Pp. 87-158.

Winship, George Parker
1896   The Coronado Expedition, 1540-1542. 14th Annual Report of the Bureau of American Ethnology, 1892-93. U.S. Government Printing Office, Washington, D.C. Pp. 329-613.

Wiseman, Regge N.
1970   Hypothesis for Variation Observed in Late Pueblo Manos and Metates. Southwestern Lore 36 (3): 46-53.

1976   Multidisciplinary Investigations at the Smokey Bear
        Ruin (LA 2112), Lincoln County, New Mexico. Monograph
        No. 4, COAS Publishing and Research, Las Cruces.

1981   Further Investigations at the King Ranch Site,
        Chaves County, New Mexico. The Artifact 19 (3-4):
        169-198.

1982   The Intervening Years - New Information on
        Chupadero Black-on-White and Corona Corrugated.
        Pottery Southwest 9 (4): 5-7.

1983   Archaeological Taxonomy and Confusion -- Welcome to
        the Jornada!   COAS 1 (1): 17-26.

1984   Chupadero and Tabira Black-on-white: Continuum or
        Dichotomy? The Kiva 50 (1): 41-54.

1985   Bison, Fish and Sedentary Occupations: Startling
        Data from Rocky Arroyo (LA 25277), Chaves County, New
        Mexico. In Colleen M. Beck (ed.), Views of the
        Jornada Mogollon. Contributions in Anthropology
        Vol. 12, Eastern New Mexico University, Portales.
        Pp. 30-32.

1986   An Initial Study of the Origins of Chupadero
        Black-on-white. Technical Note No. 2, Albuquerque
        Archaeological Society, Albuquerque.

Wood, W. Raymond, and Alan S. Downer
  1977   Notes on the Crow-Hidatsa Schism. In Wood (ed.),
        Trends in Middle Missouri Prehistory: A Festschrift
        Honoring the Contributions of Donald J. Lehmer.
        Memoir 13, Plains Anthropologist, Lincoln.
        Pp. 83-100.

Woodbury, Richard B.
  1954   Prehistoric Stone Implements of Northeastern
        Arizona. Papers Vol. 34, Peabody Museum of American
        Archaeology and Ethnology, Harvard University,
        Cambridge.

Woodbury, Richard B., and Nathalie F.S. Woodbury
  1966   Decorated Pottery of the Zuni Area. In Smith,
        Woodbury and Woodbury (1966): 302-336.

Worcester, Donald E.
  1941   The Beginnings of the Apache Menace of the
        Southwest. New Mexico Historical Review 16 (1):
        1-14.

Wright, Barton
  1976   _Pueblo Shields from the Fred Harvey Fine Arts Collection_. Northland Press, Flagstaff.

Yeoman, R.S.
  1970   _A Catalog of Modern World Coins_. 9th edition. Western Publishing Company, Racine.

Young, Jon Nathan
  1981   Stone Artifacts of Mound 7. In Alden C. Hayes, Jon Nathan Young and A.H. Warren, _Excavation of Mound 7, Gran Quivira National Monument, New Mexico_. Publications in Archeology No. 16, U.S. National Park Service, Washington, D.C. Pp. 104-139.

Young, Robert W.
  1983   Apachean Languages. In Alfonso Ortiz and William C. Sturtevant (eds.), _Handbook of North American Indians, Volume 10: Southwest_. Smithsonian Institution, Washington, D.C. Pp. 393-400.

Zubrow, Ezra B.W.
  1974   _Population, Contact and Climate in the New Mexican Pueblos_. Anthropological Paper No. 24, University of Arizona, Tucson.

  1975   _Prehistoric Carrying Capacity: A Model_. Cummings Publishing Co., Menlo Park.

www.ingramcontent.com/pod-product-compliance
Lightning Source LLC
Chambersburg PA
CBHW080643270326

41928CB00017B/3180